The publisher and the University of California Press Foundation gratefully acknowledge the generous support of the Roth Family Foundation Imprint in Music, established by a major gift from Sukey and Gil Garcetti and Michael P. Roth.

The publisher also gratefully acknowledges the generous support of the General Fund of the American Musicological Society, supported in part by the National Endowment for the Humanities and the Andrew W. Mellon Foundation, in making this book possible.

Hearing Luxe Pop

Hearing Luxe Pop

GLORIFICATION, GLAMOUR,
AND THE MIDDLEBROW IN
AMERICAN POPULAR MUSIC

John Howland

UNIVERSITY OF CALIFORNIA PRESS

University of California Press
Oakland, California

© 2021 by John Howland

Library of Congress Cataloging-in-Publication Data

Names: Howland, John, 1964– author.
Title: Hearing Luxe Pop : glorification, glamour, and the middlebrow in
  American popular music / John Howland.
Other titles: California studies in music, sound, and media ; 2.
Description: Oakland, California : University of California Press, [2021] |
  Series: California studies in music, sound, and media ; 2 | Includes
  bibliographical references and index.
Identifiers: LCCN 2020044267 (print) | LCCN 2020044268 (ebook) |
  ISBN 9780520300101 (cloth) | ISBN 9780520300118 (paperback) |
  ISBN 9780520971646 (epub)
Subjects: LCSH: Popular music—United States—History and criticism. |
  Popular music—Production and direction—United States—History—
  20th century. | Popular music—United States—20th century—Philosophy
  and aesthetics. | Instrumentation and orchestration—United States—
  History—20th century. | Arrangement (Music)—United States—
  History—20th century.
Classification: LCC ML3477 .H68 2021 (print) | LCC ML3477 (ebook) |
  DDC 781.6409730904—dc23
LC record available at https://lccn.loc.gov/2020044267
LC ebook record available at https://lccn.loc.gov/2020044268

Manufactured in the United States of America

29 28 27 26 25 24 23 22 21
10 9 8 7 6 5 4 3 2 1

*To my father, Louis Philip Howland (1929–2019),
who through his everyday passions for music taught me
the invaluable lesson of listening widely and with curiosity.
I might not have known it in my youth, but your record
collection was a bedrock foundation that ultimately
led me to write this monograph.*

CONTENTS

ACKNOWLEDGMENTS

The work on this book, most of which was accomplished over the last decade, involved assistance and input from many friends, colleagues, librarians and archivists, willing contributors, and institutions. My gratitude is deep to all. My archival research includes studies of materials from collections held at the Institute of Jazz Studies (special thanks to Dan Morgenstern, Annie Kuebler, Tad Hershorn, and Vincent Pelote), the Smithsonian Institution, the Library of Congress, the British Library, the New York Public Library, many university archives (including USC, UCLA, Yale, the University of North Texas, Brigham Young University, and Columbia University), the riches of various family archives, Universal Records, the Sigma Sound Studios archive of Drexell University (special thanks to Toby Seay), the Rock & Roll Hall of Fame, the Country Music Hall of Fame, the Schubert Archive, and numerous other sites. At these institutions and more, many individuals have graciously helped in a multitude of ways, large and small. While these contributions are too many to mention, I want to express my sincere appreciation to the invaluable input of this volume's editors, as well as the generosity of Jack Nitzsche Jr., Kristian St. Clair, Daniel Henderson, Rosie Danvers, Keith Pawlak, Harry Weinger, Lance Bowling, Buddy Robbins, the American Society of Music Arrangers and Composers, and numerous others who made available invaluable source materials for this research. I also have a significant indebtedness to the many collectors, fans, and eBay sellers who publicly disseminated invaluable materials and information via the internet. I have further benefitted immensely from dialogues, formal and informal, with many scholarly colleagues, friends, and students. I offer my sincere gratefulness to Phil Ford, Andrew Flory, Albin Zak, James Buhler, Lewis Porter, Henry Martin, Howard Pollack, Robert Fink, Zachary Wallmark, Melinda Latour, Kate

Guthrie, Christopher Chowrimootoo, Faye Hammill, David Ake, Daniel Goldmark, Olle Edström, Mary Francis, Robynn Stilwell, Stephen Hinton, Thomas Grey, Fabian Holt, Mischa van Kan, John Wriggle, and my graduate jazz history students from Rutgers University (apologies to many others I have left out). I also truly appreciate the interviews I was granted with a range of indie-rock musicians, Nico Muhly, and contacts at the Brooklyn Philharmonic, all of whom provided discussions and research material that did not make it into the final form of this book but which nonetheless shaped this work in important ways. Over the last decade-plus, I have presented many guest lectures and conference papers on this work. My thanks to both my hosts and audiences for those opportunities and insightful dialogue. My work has been supported with stipends and research time made by Rutgers University–Newark, NTNU, Lund University, the Rock Hall of Fame, and Case Western University. Earlier versions on some material has been previously published in the *Routledge Companion to New Jazz Studies*, ed. Tony Whyton, Nicholas Gebhardt, and Nichole T. Rustin (New York: Routledge, 2018), *The Relentless Pursuit of Tone: Timbre and Popular Music*, ed. Robert Fink, Zachary Wallmark, and Melinda Latour (Oxford: Oxford University Press, 2018), *Jazz/Not Jazz: The Music and Its Boundaries*, ed. David Ake, Charles Garrett, and Daniel Goldmark (Berkeley: University of California Press, 2012), and the *Journal of the American Musicological Society* (2020).

Introduction

FROM PAUL WHITEMAN, TO BARRY WHITE, MAN

THIS MONOGRAPH EXPLORES a long-standing tradition of merging popular music idioms with lush string orchestrations, big-band instrumentation, traditional symphonic instruments, and other markers of musical sophistication, glamour, spectacle, theatricality, and epic or "cinematic" qualities. I call such deluxe—or "luxe"—pop arrangements and performance events "conspicuous symphonization." This phrasing underscores entertainment parallels to Thorstein Veblen's notion of "conspicuous consumption," wherein luxury goods and services are employed for displays of social status, wealth, or cultural sophistication. A colloquialism with a similar social meaning is "bling," a hip-hop slang term referring to displays of an ostentatious lifestyle of lavish and excessive spending. Conspicuous consumption and bling display are both tied to the purpose of inspiring envy. However, with bling, there is an aversion to melting-pot uniformity in that bling displays involve ironic stylistic tensions through juxtapositions of "low" vernacular/pop culture and the high-status symbols of social power, whether real or perceived. Similar qualities permeate the US "luxe pop" repertories and events explored in this book. This music further reflects important changes in the character and aesthetic discourses of American culture and entertainment.

Across the twentieth century, the United States experienced unprecedented economic prosperity, resulting in middle-class expansion, particularly following World War II. American popular media thrived and became a world-dominant force, frequently celebrating the American Dream. The latter is founded on aspirations and ideals of upward economic and social mobility, with the potential of prosperity and success "for all" in the freedom to engage in the "pursuit of happiness." American advertising and entertainment media have routinely depicted the look, mannerisms, values, life experiences, homes, fashions, and consumption habits of glamorous and successful individuals—often celebrities—leading the "good life" or, rather, comparatively cosmopolitan, modern, sophisticated lives. These media and goods were positioned as self-reflections of—and a tool for influencing and defining—middle-class experience, ideals, and social and economic aspirations. Popular music was central to these narratives, both personal and collective, and it accompanied images of elevated glamour, sophistication, prosperity, and social mobility.

The social hierarchies associated with music are central to the study in this book, with traditional "high" art music understood to lie at one end, and "low" popular culture at the other. There is, however, much activity that existed between these two poles. Especially through the mid-twentieth century, consumers widely understood many genres, styles, and idioms along the class-hierarchy continuum of the brows, high to low. The latter meant various things at different times, but lowbrow was commonly associated with popular music of the most democratic, commercial, and accessible sorts. While popular-music studies have long illustrated the complexity of "simple" lowbrow pop, class-hierarchy discourse on music typically overlooked the wealth of trends that resided in the broad "middle" between these poles. Within the past decade, however, scholars have started to explore this culturally middleish territory under middlebrow and middlebrow-music studies.[1]

Genres, styles, idioms, and instrumental textures can evoke loose associations tied to cultural and social class, with some musical textures being seen as more culturally elevated than others. In musicology, such evocative textures are termed "musical topics." Film music is one of the most obvious media practices that relies upon evocative music to convey cultural associations in the service of narrative and contextual understanding. Popular music routinely engages in such topical practices via textures that implicate the associations of genre and style as well as narrative and expressive qualities, registers, and modes. Certain practices of popular music reflect class discourse to audiences via instrumental timbre and texture, musical gestures, qualities of record production, and modes of presentation and promotion. This is the territory of luxe pop.

Hearing Luxe Pop concerns how a family of orchestral pop music intersects with historical aspirational notions tied to ideals of glamour, sophistication, cosmopolitanism, and otherwise "classy" lifestyles. This study's central questions are: how are the modes and class registers of glamour, sophistication, and cosmopolitanism expressed in these deluxe production trends, and how do these traits relate to the aspirational ideals of contemporaneous society and its reflection in entertainment?

The book centrally considers the era from the 1920s through early 1970s, though it also includes an introductory chapter that explores how select music from the early 2000s can be heard through the long legacy of this tradition. This monograph is further a musicological contribution to sound studies. Like other contributions to the "California Studies in Music, Sound, and Media" series, *Hearing Luxe Pop* builds its research around a complex web of interconnected cross-media history and audio culture. This recording-industry study further includes considerations of radio, film, stage, print, and technologies and platforms of the internet era, as well as the practices of production and promotion, and the phenomenologies and histories of listening, particularly in the associative and metaphorical senses. "Hearing" in the book means inserting the reader into cultural discourses of a given moment so that they can hear the music discussed with ears that are more finely attuned to period associative reception. This work closely considers the intellectual and social history of the associations tied to specific tone and timbre combinations in popular-music production and performance practice, and how pop has built up accretions of cultural and aural associations through networks of historically accumulated meaning, through the stylistic legacies of influential music, and through the rhetorical sense of sounds as they have grown over time.

Hearing Luxe Pop is also a study of record production. In its balance of thematic and subject-area concerns, there is indebtedness to the scholarship of both Albin Zak and Simon Zagorski-Thomas.[2] Particularly useful are Zagorski-Thomas's proposed eight categories for the study of recorded popular music, which build off of Zak. These areas include:

- record production as an expanded mode of creative composition that needs to be understood via the characteristics and metaphorical meanings of recorded sound, and how technology mediates the recording process ("sonic cartoons");
- the sonic space and stagings imparted by production that suggest particular interpretations of performances;
- the relations of recordings to the development of technology;
- how developments in technology affect production trends and sound;
- the creative roles of producers and engineers, as well as their historically situated practices;

- the studio as a performance environment; how perceived artistic authenticity relates to audience influence, production practice, and areas of production economics;
- how the production of recordings is impacted by music-industry business practices;
- and the role of consumer influence on aesthetics and creativity.[3]

While this list offers "a way to elucidate many of the complexities of the subject," this field of perspectives also reveals that "there are no fixed genres and there are no fixed rules" when attempting to "identify and quantify different musical communities through genre, historical period, geographical area or some other criteria."[4] Indeed, Zagorski-Thomas concedes that "there is a complex mass of individuals and there is no 'system'—just an unholy mess."[5] *Hearing Luxe Pop* resonates with this sentiment, and some of the "messiness" of the project is tied to its breadth; the multifarious associative connections simultaneously pointing in past, present, and future directions; and the intermedia connections that are articulated.

The case studies that form the chapters of this book follow no fixed rules and instead bring to the fore the most illuminating sides of the potential subfields that Zagorski-Thomas outlines. This list, however, is misleadingly imbalanced, as he advocates a "reception/production dichotomy" as the framework for "a way of explaining and interpreting musical activity rather than simply characterising it." Even more central here is "how the listener interprets a musical event or experience, how it was produced and how . . . technology, history, geography and sociology . . . have influenced both its creation and interpretation."[6] *Hearing Luxe Pop* aims for similar interpretive goals.

In this book's agenda of understanding and interpreting both the music itself and its cultural, historical, and multifarious individual contexts, my primary sources have involved a wide range of media and document types, including: manuscript and published arrangement scores and arrangement sketches, manuscript notebooks, copyright scores, and personally transcribed materials; artist diaries and career-clippings scrapbooks; correspondence; recordings, both commercial and unreleased studio outtakes and multitrack masters; pirate recordings—video or audio—from live performances; orchestration and instrumentation method books; commercial and private films; newspaper and magazine clippings; media kits and promotional materials; audiovisual and text-based advertising, marketing, and recording packaging; and concert programs, program notes, and album-liner notes. Beyond these media and writings, I have also included interviews of musicians; composers; arrangers; producers and engineers; critics; and concert-, record-, promotional-, and publishing-industry figures. Work with this panoply of sources embodies what Jann Pasler has called "postmodern positivism."[7] By this, Pasler means a mutually enriched and historically informed balance between (a) pre-1980 musicology's concerns for the primacy of historical source materials in guiding the interpretation of history, and (b) the interdisciplinary agenda of post-1985 "new musicology," which has placed primacy on deep engagement with critical theory for interpreting cultural meaning, particularly with relation to the politics and discourses of identity via class, gender, race, and so on. *Hearing Luxe Pop* is thus fundamentally a work of historical musicology, but cultural and sociological theory—when historically grounded and relevant to interpreting source-based evidence—firmly informs this book's methodological and interpretive practice.

While American-based sociological discourse on class hierarchy plays an important role across this book, this is not a sociological study. This work engages—*must* engage—areas of more recent class and taste-culture theory from central figures like Pierre Bourdieu and Richard Peterson, among others. Quite relevant, of course, is Bourdieu's conception of habitus, meaning socially reinforced communal beliefs, dispositions, knowledge, and perspectives that are so deeply embodied that they seem natural. Bourdieu articulates the relationship "established between the pertinent characteristics of economic and social condition" that shape an individual's habitus, on the one hand, and the "distinctive features associated with the corresponding position in the universe of life-styles," on the other hand. He argues that this relationship "only becomes intelligible" when habitus is understood to be "the generative formula which makes it possible to account both for the classifiable practices and products and for the [taste] judgements, themselves classified, which make these practices and works into a system of distinctive signs."[8] This system of signs and habitus determine the parameters and distinctions of taste cultures in the social world and lifestyles, and these are the central fields of inquiry under which luxe-pop music and culture must be examined.

Although luxe pop and its middlebrow-adjacent, classy- and glamour-based discourses are inherently linked to the habitus practices and conditions that intersect in American lower middlebrow culture (see chapters 4 and 5), following Bourdieu, the class, educational, and taste subculture trajectories do, in fact, change over time. Such changes are central to the narratives of *Hearing Luxe Pop*. Nonetheless, despite the immense value and influence of Bourdieu, for the purposes of this American-centric work, I have found greater critical value in culture-specific sociological studies relating to historical moments and contexts relevant to the present work. These materials are valuable tools— when employed critically with present-day insight—for guiding historically informed interpretations. For example, sociologist Herbert Gans's 1974 *Popular Culture and High Culture: An Analysis and Evaluations of Taste*, offers vital, research-based, period reading and explications of American taste cultures. This is nearly contemporaneous to Bourdieu's 1979 *Distinction*, and a 1999 edition does briefly place his work in relation to Bourdieu. Nonetheless, Gans focuses his taste-subculture study specifically on an American rather than French cultural/sociological demographic.[9] While archival interview materials do reveal private elements of the habitus of individual subjects, the present study documents habitus through historical primary sources and through widely circulated public discourse as present in the press, in the commentary of artists, and in the promotional material of recording companies, among other related sources, rather than fieldwork data.

The first chapter offers a broad overview of luxe-pop via considerations of recent hip-hop events involving full orchestral backing. With an eye toward low-high cultural tensions between, on the one hand, street-level hip-hop lyrics, thematic content, and cultural posturing and, on the other, artist adoptions and displays of aural and fashion luxury and status, the chapter examines Jay-Z's celebrated return from retirement in a lavish 2006 concert at New York's Radio City Music Hall with the so-called Hustler's Symphony Orchestra. The chapter sketches the relation of this event—historically and sonically—to the 1920s–1970s luxe-pop history and cultural discourses that are explored in depth across chapters 2 through 8. There are clear entertainment connections between this bestringed, spectacle-oriented hip-hop event and the image constructions, performance practices, and musical-style and genre-based sound worlds of earlier orchestral pop trends, even as far back as 1920s symphonic jazz, a cornerstone genre of orchestral pop, but an idiom that period "highbrow" critics disparaged as "the very essence of musical vulgarity" in its "perfect fusion of the pretentious and commonplace" (see chapter 2).

The book traces the development of luxe pop through four distinct eras. Chapters 2 and 3 examine an era of "glorified jazz," from the 1920s up through the 1940s. The pre-1960 subjects of chapters 2 and 3 include 1920s symphonic jazz dance bands, movie palace prologue revues, interwar radio orchestras, production numbers of stage and film musicals in the late 1920s and 1930s, areas of Hollywood film scoring, and ultimately the 1940s jazz-with-strings vogue—from early 1940s "symphonic swing" orchestras to the many jazz-soloist-plus-strings instrumental albums of the late 1940s and 1950s.

Chapters 4 through 8 follow both the further development of these initial jazz-related idioms across the postwar years and the transformation of luxe-pop arranging in the new popular music idioms up to through the 1970s. These chapters are structured around case studies that each illustrate an emergent moment for both luxe-pop subgenres and central associative qualities in post-1950 luxe pop. Each chapter further involves some attention to articulating broader historical developments, chains of influence, and the porous connections between distinct eras, artists, and international creative communities.

The second major era spans the 1950s and early 1960s. The pre-rock territory of this period helped to canonize what came to be called the "Great American Songbook," an idiom that the Recording Academy and the Grammys now refer to as "traditional pop." Chapter 4 considers areas of 1950s Capitol Records recordings, with emphasis on Nat "King" Cole and Frank Sinatra, but connecting the big-band-plus-strings swing of these artists to "classy" cocktail lounges, Hollywood "crime jazz" underscoring, mood music and exotica album trends, middle-of-the-road pop, and easy listening. This model informed trends in the pop music of the subsequent rock 'n' roll era, most notably in Brill Building pop (Burt Bacharach, et al.), Motown, and— chapter 5's main focus—the celebrated "Wall of Sound" ideals of producer Phil Spector's early 1960s hits with the Ronettes and the Crystals. The study explores the aspirational discourse of Spector and his arranger Jack Nitzsche, and situates their "teenage symphonies" in relation to lower-middlebrow aesthetics, string-laden instrumental surf rock, Tom Wolfe's interpretations of celebrity culture (the "statusphere"), and the glamorous image of the Ronettes.

Thomas Hine coined the term populuxe to describe prominent American consumer trends of the mid-1950s to mid-1960s (chapter 4).[10] This word's connections to notions of "popular luxury," and marketing of "luxury for all," make it an ideal term for the deluxe pop arranging traditions of this second era. By uncoupling and inverting the roots of this term to luxe pop, a term that I use to cover all the musical trends discussed in this book, I mean to carry many of the qualities of "populuxe" over to a general-purpose description of the broader aesthetic that defines the rich history of orchestral pop from the 1920s forward. (While the term orchestral pop is somewhat suitable, it does not convey the same mixed qualities of popular luxury, class-based consumer marketing, unnecessary embellishment, or glorified/ artful entertainment.)

Much of this music is undeniably tied to mid-century middlebrow or middlebrow-adjacent aesthetics. While often intended as an insult, middlebrow is not necessarily a pejorative, since this idea captures key historical notions of social aspiration and cultural power and invokes associative markers of self-conscious sophistication, glamour, and class (social class). I invoke this discourse not to denigrate the music, but to provide period-informed perspectives on American entertainment modes of high-low image construction. The case studies in this book, however, emphasize classy, glamorous entertainment as opposed to art-aspirational middlebrowism. This shift in focus to middlebrow adjacency argues for less-essentialized readings of brow discourse—that is, that American middlebrow-related culture was not exclusively engaged simply in aspirations toward high culture.

Chapters 6 through 8 examine the late 1960s into the early 1970s and explore this golden era of luxe pop via case studies concerning white soft rock, Black symphonic soul, and the emergence of disco. Each considers the multitude of ways that midcentury middlebrow-adjacent cultural discourse around glamour and classy showbiz practice shaped the entertainment excess and glitz of the 1970s.

As rock 'n' roll turned to "rock" in the late 1960s, populuxe gave way to new types of both white and Black orchestral pop. From the mid-1960s, there was a solidification of rock culture as cross-Atlantic, via the axes of the United States and Great Britain. While areas of luxe-pop discourse overlapped between the two nations, there were notable distinctions and differences between their various taste and entertainment cultures. While US music remains the central focus, chapters 6 through 8 further consider facets of this expanded, Anglo-American rock-pop culture.

Chapter 6 examines how the subgenres of 1960s Los Angeles "baroque pop" and "sunshine pop," combined with the era's rock-pop explosion of sound exploration and studio innovation, were central to the subsequent emergence of soft rock in the summer-1970 hits of the Carpenters and Bread. Central here is the milieu of Los Angeles studio pop and its relation to AM Gold, a later designation of middle-of-the-road ("MOR"), chart-topping pop. These intersecting trends led to prominent crossover connections between the *Billboard* Hot 100 and Easy Listening charts.

In companion chapters 7 and 8, through studies of musical and production practices, critical and audience reception, and artist images of Isaac

Hayes and Barry White, I outline the ways in which the traditions and topical associations of musical glamour, the middlebrow impulse, and American entertainment were manifest in the disco era. Through pivotal albums from Hayes, chapter 7 explores the messy late 1960s connections between symphonic soul, sophistisoul, progressive soul, psychedelia, funk, jazz traditions in flux, and Hollywood depictions of Black American culture. The chapter further builds on arguments from earlier chapters concerning jazz-related orchestral textures taking on luxe associative qualities in the postwar era. Chapter 8 explores how these same developments veered away from progressive tendencies toward the MOR mainstream, with specific attention being paid to orchestral spectacle in the music and performances of Barry White and his Love Unlimited Orchestra. White is positioned as a culmination of the entertainment aesthetics that are traced across this book. He was somewhat of a nexus of the classy entertainment discourses that ultimately epitomize much of mainstream disco, and this golden moment of luxe pop was manifest across large swaths of North American and European popular culture in the mid- to late 1970s.

Despite the demise of mainstream disco and orchestral pop in general (at least temporarily) by the early 1980s, the legacy of luxe pop has continued to have important musical and cultural resonances with post-1980 popular music. The book's afterword articulates important facets of this legacy and its relation to more recently theorized models of taste subcultures.

In the end, *Hearing Luxe Pop* aims to articulate the regular reinvention and persistence of an essential but critically overlooked musical aesthetic that defines fundamental class, taste, race, and economic tensions in American popular music from the 1920s to the present. By shifting back and forth between interrelated close considerations of musical texts and a myriad of cultural contexts, the innovative interdisciplinary studies of this book examine the rich cross-class and cross-genre interconnections among popular music, jazz, the culture of concert music, and discourses on race, commerce, media, technology, class-status, gender, and pop culture.

ONE

Hearing Luxe Pop

JAY-Z, ISAAC HAYES, AND THE
SIX DEGREES OF SYMPHONIC SOUL

THE MUSIC OF JAY-Z, the celebrated rapper, entrepreneur, and producer, has embodied dominant discourses in hip-hop culture from the mid-1990s forward. But Jay-Z's entertainment career has been celebrated on a number of auspicious occasions through a remarkably conventional sign for musical achievement—that is, his appearance with tuxedo-clad orchestras in celebrated New York concert halls, notably at Radio City Music Hall and Carnegie Hall in 2006 and 2012. In this chapter, I explore a central premise of this book, which is the value of attempting to hear the historical, cultural, and sociological signifiers embedded in popular music production and performance. This first chapter illustrates this premise by sketching out the cumulative musico-cultural associations of production textures and performance practice embedded in a single case study, Jay-Z's June 25, 2006, Radio City Music Hall concert, which commemorated the ten-year anniversary of his debut album, *Reasonable Doubt*. This event occurred at a moment when such hip-hop-meets-orchestra spectacles were something of a mini-vogue. As Jay-Z was then president of Def Jam Records, in terms of cultural power and geography, the event was at the very epicenter of period hip-hop. The totemic iconography of New York is of course spread across Jay-Z's entire recording output, up to and beyond his bid to out-Sinatra Frank Sinatra with a new theme song for the city, 2009's "Empire State of Mind" ("I'm the new Sinatra, . . . I made it here, I can make it anywhere"). And like his everyday concerts, these bestringed showcases celebrated both what critic Jon Parales characterized as Jay-Z's "often-told crack-to-riches story" and "old-fashioned showbiz."[1] This chapter aims to explore the cross-generational entertainment connection between modern hip-hop and traditional "showbiz" entertainment through an examination of the multilayered semiotic associations of certain evocative, historically informed, orchestral textures employed in popular music since the turn of the twenty-first century.

Jay-Z's aspirational career mythology is built on the bootstrap tale of a one-time drug dealer from the housing projects of Brooklyn mixing company with and being a financial equal of New York high society, a noted philanthropist, part-owner of the Brooklyn Nets, record label president, and husband to a glamorous pop diva. And yet Carnegie Hall still beckoned as the ultimate "high-class" venue. Carnegie Hall mixes with hip-hop culture quite easily, if one views the events hosted there through the legacy of old-fashioned pop entertainment. The lush orchestrations of these Jay-Z events are tied to the deep pop-culture well of symphonic soul, an early 1970s soul, funk, R&B, and proto-disco Black-pop production sound that emerged roughly in tandem with Isaac Hayes's album *Hot Buttered Soul* (1969). Though the use of orchestral instruments in soul and R&B recordings predates this moment, the idiom epitomized by Hayes's landmark release was in short order heard in blaxploitation and cop-show funk film and TV soundtracks, the lush soul of artists ranging from Marvin Gaye to Barry White, and Philly soul.[2] The modern-day cultural associations of symphonic soul derive from much earlier sonic roots than the 1970s, from both orchestral music in general ("art" music, film and radio orchestra music, concert pops repertory, Broadway show tunes, etc.) and orchestral pop in specific, as well as from the pop-culture reworkings of these sounds long after their heyday. Such high-low/Black-white musical tensions impart an *aura* of glamour, class, and sophistication via instrumental tonal juxtapositions, a hybrid orchestral-type sound (and live-performance model), *not* the affectation of actual classical music.

The idea that historical pop sounds, tones, and genre markers carry meaningful accretions of cultural and aural associations is central to what Simon Reynolds has termed "retromania." Reynolds's 2011 book of the same name primarily concerns pop music of the 2000s, a decade where he sees "a recombinant approach to music-making that typically leads to a meticulously organized constellation of reference points and allusions, sonic lattices . . . that span . . . decades."[3] While he notes that "retromania" is not at all new to pop, Reynolds takes keen interest in recent "music whose primary emotion is towards *other* music, *earlier* music."[4] Such music communicates through what musicologists call "musical topics," meaning textures of music that trigger clear style and culture associations.[5] Such "recombinant" music communicates through referential musical topics and evocative textures and rhythms, among other stylistic markers, that point "towards *other* music, *earlier* music." Referential music of this sort employs the semiotic power of what Philip Tagg calls musical synecdoche, wherein timbre "relates *indexically* to a musical style and genre, producing connotations of a particular culture or environment."[6] I use the words *timbre, tone,* and *texture* in this book to refer to similar musically referential qualities and sounds. For example, beyond the tone color qualities of a detail, moment, or passage of music, I also employ *tonal* as an analog to this word's use in linguistics to describe the semantic differences that result from varied intonations of words or syllables with similar sounds. In music, the tonal shadings of *how* distinct musical elements are performed in specific contexts can similarly convey musical meaning and associations toward other, earlier music.

The music I discuss in this chapter is part of a long tradition of merging Afro-diasporic music idioms with luxe orchestration textures, both orchestral and big band. It should come as no surprise, then, that hip-hop acts have participated in this trend, including Jay-Z, Kanye West, Diddy, Talib Kweli, Mos Def, Erykah Badu, and the Roots, among others. By extension, large ensembles like as the daKAH Hip Hop Orchestra and the Wired Strings have also contributed to this trend.[7] Through the conceit of the notion of "six degrees of separation," I will sketch a twentieth-century history of American luxe pop. This sonic history—the accretive associations of referential pop production and tonal topics—is ever present, even if not recognized, whenever audiences hear such stylistic recombinations. This luxe-pop outline both illuminates a genealogy and semiotic accretions and suggests the considerable value of closely studying often overlooked ways in which certain practices and aesthetics with broad, lasting appeal can cross genres; generations; communities; cultural, social, and racial distinctions; and eras. The wide-ranging scope of this book—and, in turn, this first chapter—seeks to demonstrate the historiographic rewards and critical insights of considering certain entertainment practices and aesthetics—in this case, American entertainment modes of glamour, glitz, sophistication, and class—*across* the commonly perpetuated divisions imposed by genre-based studies of popular music from both the jazz and rock-pop eras. The question of *how* such "constellation[s] of reference points" are produced closely correlates with *why* these recombinant textures are employed, and that "why" is related to artists and producers as creative consumers of historical popular culture. Jay-Z's 2006 Radio City concert frames my discussion of this aesthetic, with particular attention to the polysemous textures of the song "Can I Live," Jay-Z's invocations of symphonic soul, and specifically the luxe role of strings in such polystylistic productions.

The relevance of the term *luxe pop* to describe such intersections of lush symphonic soul and hip-hop culture is adumbrated in a 2007 *Harper's Bazaar* interview where Kanye West—Jay-Z's producer and close associate in the 2000s—was asked to describe his lavish lifestyle. He replied: "It's like . . . pop luxe. . . . Everything about me is pop and luxury."[8] The key elements of a "luxe-pop" aesthetic can be seen and heard in West's 2005 "Late Orchestration" concert at London's Abbey Road Studios with the all-female Wired Strings Orchestra. Though likely not intentional, the project resembles Barry White's lavishly produced 1976 Valentine's Day appearance at Radio City with a sixty-two-woman orchestra.[9] A second, more likely precedent was the less-opulent 2001 "Jay-Z Unplugged" performance for MTV (see the afterword).[10] West's 2005 concert, though, was the first full-scale event of this sort, and thus a precedent to Jay-Z's 2006 show.

"Late Orchestration" was designed to maintain West's career momentum after his multiple Grammy awards in 2005, when he appeared on the broadcast in an old-fashioned showbiz production number built on his hit, "Jesus Walks." The auratic aspirations of the Abbey Road concert are evidenced in the show's DVD commentary, which crows that "this was no ordinary concert. Just as . . . Kanye West is no ordinary superstar." The promotional copy remarks that the event was performed at "one of the most famous music venues in the world. . . . [with a] beautiful . . . all-girl string ensemble in black evening gowns and eye masks of deep red. One DJ. And King Kanye . . . looking extra fly . . . putting diamonds in the sky." West is further said to have "single-handedly propelled hip-hop to a whole new place, musically, stylistically and politically."[11] This is characteristic West braggadocio, but it captures core elements of the show. An ideal example is the concert opener, "Diamonds from Sierra Leone," also the lead single from West's 2005 album, *Late Registration*.[12] This release was produced and arranged by Los Angeles–based pop multi-instrumentalist and film composer Jon Brion. West was attracted to Brion's film-score work on *Eternal Sunshine of the Spotless Mind* (Focus Features, 2004) and Brion's orchestrations and production work for Fiona Apple (*Extraordinary Machine*, 2005). Brion's eclectic productions are often informed by "baroque pop" of the 1960s and 1970s. West also wanted *Late Registration* to have the dark "cinematic" sound of 1990s trip-hop by Massive Attack and Portishead.[13] He had been a fan of the latter group since its 1994 debut, *Dummy*, with its string-laden, moody mix of textures from downtempo soul, jazz, 1960s spy-film soundtracks, and hip-hop beats, scratching, and sampling. *Late Registration* was further inspired by the orchestrations and cover image of Portishead's 1998 live album, *PNYC*, which featured "a sea of string players."[14]

The lyric to "Diamonds from Sierra Leone" connects the music industry and Africa's economic-political crises through the image of "conflict diamonds" (stones mined in African war zones to fund violence). In lines such as "Throw your diamonds in the sky," "diamonds" is also reference to Roc-A-Fella Records, which is associated with Jay-Z's "diamond" hand sign (by connecting thumbs and index fingers). *Rock* is further a slang term for a diamond, an image in the logo for Roc Nation, Jay-Z's entertainment company. Both versions of "Diamonds"—the original track and a remix featuring Jay-Z—rely on samples from the theme song of the James Bond film, *Diamonds Are Forever* (United Artists, 1971), by John Barry and sung by Shirley Bassey. The main borrowing uses thirty-four seconds from the song's introduction. The sound of the repeating eighth-note figure beneath the melody of the intro—an unidentifiable "diamondlike" timbre that seemingly blends harp, harpsichord, and celeste—was unique to a specific electronic organ used in the soundtrack recording.[15] Starting with a quintessential Bond-film, upper-middle-register brass stinger chord, Barry surrounded the eighth-note figure with swelling lower-register string pads, rising harp runs, and discreet guitar wah-wah pedal sighs. As Bassey enters, woodwind responses are heard, while low brass creeps in before an accentuated cadence with Barry's tightly voiced big-band brass chords. Brion's production mixes hip-hop synth tones, sampled orchestral hits, textural samples, and drum-machine beats with live drums, harpsichord, piano, and guitars. The live performance added textures of live harp, a sixteen-member string ensemble, and female conductor (Rosie Danvers), along with tympani and brass samples, likely performed by a sampler onstage.

In homage to the main title sequence of *Diamonds Are Forever*, the concert DVD opens with video of falling lustrous diamonds on a black background. Then curtains rise, as a spotlight scans the masked female orchestra in a blue-lit hall. The original sample is replaced by live strings and a harp (though Bassey is heard). Dressed in white tuxedo pants and a black tuxedo jacket with red kerchief and boutonnière, West appears amid sweeping spotlights and the "diamond"-sparkle of disco-ball reflections. Commenting on the DVD, West gushed that when "we did 'Diamonds,' . . . people . . . were so taken aback by the lights and the strings—just how dashingly handsome

I was—that . . . they were in awe, like 'Oh my god, he looks so good' . . . I was like . . . 'okay, can you please get over it? . . . Can we clap now?'" On the greater show, he recalled

> Performing . . . a hip hop show in front of an orchestra . . . was so cutting edge. . . . And to . . . spit true, heartfelt rap lyrics, . . . [with] profanity . . . in front of an orchestra was just like juxtaposing these two . . . totally different forms of music. If you picture someone who listens to classical music . . . you would think they would hate rap music. And with someone who likes rap music, you would think they would hate strings. But it shows you how . . . hip hop brings everything together.[16]

West does not mention Portishead here, nor does he acknowledge the ubiquity of string textures in recorded hip-hop (whether generated by sampling or software), but he was right that a "hip-hop show in front of an orchestra" was cutting-edge. These cultural and musical juxtapositions are likewise at the heart of Jay-Z's Radio City concert.

THE LINEAGE OF "CAN I LIVE"

At Radio City, Jay-Z was backed by both the Roots and the "Hustler Symphony Orchestra," a reconfiguration of the Wired Strings. Both the concert and the original 1996 album epitomize Reynolds's notion of "pop culture's addiction to its own past."[17] The webs of associative retromania that can be drawn from "Can I Live" begin with its samples from Isaac Hayes's 1970 cover of Burt Bacharach's "The Look of Love," a song originally written as a sultry lounge track for Dusty Springfield and used in the James Bond espionage comedy, *Casino Royale* (Columbia, 1967).

Shawn Carter, a.k.a. Jay-Z, was born in 1969. According to biographer Mark Beaumont, Jay-Z's parents were "avid . . . collectors of music, stockpiling . . . crates full of . . . every great soul, Motown, R&B and jazz record."[18] Beaumont specifically calls out "soul grooves from Marvin Gaye, Donny Hathaway, . . . [and] The Soul City Symphony." He notes that "young Shawn" likewise "listen[ed] to the sweet, soulful sounds of The Jackson Five, Love Unlimited Orchestra, [and] The Commodores . . . [and] felt this music seep deep into his core."[19] Lush symphonic soul is prominent here, and this repertory was central to sampling choices on *Reasonable Doubt*. Jay-Z's producers "were encouraged to delve into Seventies soul for samples and inspiration, a rich source of . . . meaning for Jay; old tracks by Isaac Hayes, The Stylistics and The Four Tops had a . . . magic for him, and he . . . [felt] he was continuing the lineage of those immortal acts . . . , paying them the honor of re-imagining."[20] As DJ Irv Gotti—the producer for "Can I Live"—noted, this aural "re-imagining" of Hayes's sound was central to this track's aspirational narrative of transcending life in the projects.[21]

The album's black-and-white cover image shows Jay-Z—with obscured face—attired in a Sinatra-meets-*Goodfellas* ensemble of black suit, shirt, and fedora, contrasting white silk scarf, tie, and hat ribbon, and props of a fat cigar and mafioso ring bling. Similarly, the video for "Can't Knock the Hustle" mashes up borrowings from the 1970s gangster films of Francis Ford Coppola and Martin Scorsese. Shot in "artistic" black and white, the video places Jay-Z (of the album cover) in a Black Brooklyn hustle narrative that mixes *Godfather* iconography (referencing "I got the Godfather flow") with neo-blaxploitation hustlers, the champagne-soaked high-life of a luxury nightclub (evoking the Vegas glamor of Frank Sinatra's Rat Pack), and a cigar-chomping meeting of mob bosses.

In a documentary on the album, Jay-Z characterizes "Can I Live" as describing the life of a hustler.[22] He locates the core meaning in the lyric "I'd rather die enormous than live dormant." As he explains, these lines are "a take on the 'Live Free or Die Trying,' 'Liberty or Death' spirit . . . [of] be[ing] an American" and "about great ambition."[23] Gotti describes this as the "*Scarface* mentality," in reference to the 1983 Brian De Palma film with Al Pacino. Nevertheless, Jay-Z claims that *Reasonable Doubt* was misunderstood as merely another gangsta-rap record at the time. About this "mis-interpretation," the film's director, Barry Michael Cooper, argues that the album's samples (like those from Hayes) were "sweeping, jazzy, broad, colorful, lush. . . . He gave a very colorful, lurid depiction [of] . . . the street," and "was the voice of the crack generation . . . [and] like what Scorsese did with both *Mean Streets* and *Goodfellas*, *Scarface* . . . it became very cinematic.[24] In the discourse around the album, artistic meaning is consistently tied to the intertextual references of its lyrical, musical, and associated visual content. In the documentary, intertextual interest is generated through juxtapositions of the glamour of the Radio City show against slow-motion, nighttime drive-by shots of what seem to be the Marcy housing projects, the dangerous Brooklyn low-income complex where Jay-Z grew up and worked as a dealer. Both album and the Radio City performances underscore the story of *Reasonable Doubt* alongside grainy footage (again in slow-motion) from the 1970s Black street life in New York. The 1970s cinematic nostalgia is foregrounded, with blaxploitation evocations binding Jay-Z's mythic hustler story with vintage and new film stock.

Jay-Z, "Can I Live" (1996)

The beats on "Can I Live" were built on a mid-1990s Akai MPC3000 sampler. The production manipulates three borrowings from Hayes's "The Look of Love" and adds synthesized hip-hop drums. The three samples embody the symphonic-soul sound in this track, which derives from the Stax soul of the Bar-Kays rhythm section, with the Memphis horns and members of the Memphis Symphony. Jay-Z remembers, "I didn't know I was going to say 'Can I Live?' That [came from] listening to the strings . . . [which] brought out that . . . mentality . . . [It] was just mind-blowing . . . [It] wasn't done [in hip hop]."[25] (This book's afterword briefly discusses several earlier hip-hop uses of sampled string textures.)

The opening of "Can I Live" (0:00–0:38) is built from a two-part sample from the introduction to "The Look of Love" (0:05–0:11 and 0:11–0:18 on the album version of "Look").[26] This first borrowed passage is constructed around a descending, D minor jazz-flute riff (akin to early-1970s Herbie Mann) backed by wah-wah rhythm guitar, drums, acoustic piano, and possibly bass, all performing in a grooving, accentuated tempo. In "Can I Live," there is drum-machine enhancement, but the original feel and drum fills remain. The second borrowing (0:11–0:18 in "Look") is a varied repeat that concludes with blaring, open-brass chord stabs that, as in "Diamonds Are Forever," evoke jazzy period big-band crime-drama stingers. The main section of "Can I Live" kicks in at 0:38 ("Every nigga watching me closely"), with the "Look" drum groove greatly enhanced via hip-hop drum-machine overlay. The primary sample for the verses is based on 0:45–0:56 from "Look," which involves a two-bar melodic trumpet riff that rises and falls over a five-note D minor scale. The trumpet tone here recalls the subdued, staccato, easy-listening trumpet work of 1960s Burt Bacharach recordings. Under the trumpet is a heavy, drum-based groove with low-tom fills, funky wah-wah guitar, and electric-piano comping. The verses also use 0:57–1:09 of "Look," where the previous sampled section repeats with a lush, rising violin-section figure in a higher register (also a five-note D minor scale). Across 0:38–2:20 of "Can I Live," this sample appears twice. The third key sample from "Look" underscores the title lines, "can I live? can I live?" (at 2:20 and 3:24). This is heard after the protagonist dreams about a Rat Pack–like, high-rolling lifestyle ("Viva, Las Vegas," etc.). This Vegas-luxe sample is from 1:21–1:35 in "Look," and features lush big-band brass hits in a falling-then-rising series of chords with tom-drum accentuation and a wah-wah guitar countermelody. In "Can I Live," the hip-hop drum machine groove pulls back to a spare ride cymbal, exposing the Stax soul-drum fills.

Beyond the *Reasonable Doubt* documentary and amateur YouTube videos, the Radio City concert can also be seen in a promotional video produced by Coca-Cola, and there has been at least one set of decently mixed audio tracks, including "Can I Live," circulating on the internet.[27] These sources reveal that the show's arrangements—by the Wired Strings, Jay-Z, and Questlove—are close orchestral "re-imaginings" of the album's sample-based backings. The charts were developed by the Wired Strings director, Rosie Danvers, along with her husband, TommyD, and Sam Frank. Examples 1.1 and 1.3 show the concert realizations of the first part of the Sample 1 (jazz flute) and Sample 3

EX. 1.1. Excerpt 1 from Jay-Z's "Can I Live" at his 2006 Radio City Music Hall concert. Based on a sample from Isaac Hayes's "The Look of Love."

EX. 1.2. Excerpt 2 from Jay-Z's "Can I Live."

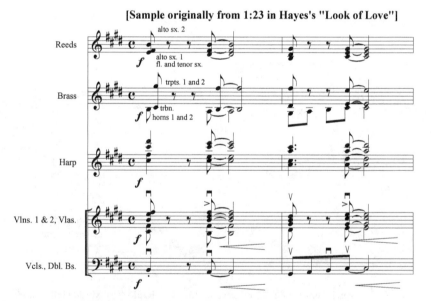

EX. 1.3. Excerpt 3 from Jay-Z's "Can I Live."

(Vegas luxe) Hayes borrowings, while Example 1.2 presents a later variation of the Sample 2 (trumpet riff) borrowing.

. . .

The Radio City concert began with portentous string music filling a hall bathed in red light, while a deep film-style narrator's voice extolled the significance of the event. Jay-Z shouts, "What's up?" as the velvet curtains lifts above blue-lit risers, tall side panels awash in blue-greens, a black backdrop, and art deco chandeliers, all framing an orchestra in black tuxedos and evening dress, a shapely, grooving female conductor (Danvers) in black cocktail dress with rhinestones, the Roots, and a DJ. Jay-Z dominates the event in his white tux and black silk scarf, the photographic "negative" of his album image. On the show's conception, Jay-Z remarked:

> That I drove a 1996 [status-symbol] Lexus on Radio City stage . . . [is] just gangster, right? . . . [And] I'm performing *Reasonable Doubt* to the most beautiful strings. . . . I'm saying *the* craziest [hustler] lyrics. The juxtaposition of these two things was . . . crazy. . . . That's just my type of humor. . . . That's just the sarcasm . . . I get off on. . . . Everything in there was beyond anything that I imagined where my career could go. . . . When you go to Radio City and have an event like that, people start looking at hip hop different. Hip hop being performed with a [live] band? . . . Hip hop being performed with a fifty-piece orchestra and these beautiful strings? . . . It brings it to . . . a whole 'nother level of respect.[28]

Since "Can I Live" was built on samples of orchestral pop, the concert arrangement easily translated the track's original structure and sound. The live performance here evokes the "polystylism" and "recombinant style topics" that Rebecca Leydon identifies in hip-hop sampling and sample-informed performance practice. She argues that such recombinant tendencies were "already present in certain musics of the past," but the digital revolution allowed "a detailed collective knowledge of popular music *history* among . . . fans and practitioners" and "a heightened self-consciousness of pop genealogies."[29] For a number of reasons that will be explored here, contemporary orchestral pop arrangements function in a similar manner: the stylistic markers of luxe pop can trigger a dense fabric of associations across music genres, meanings, media, cultural identities, and places.

The luxe sound of "Can I Live" functions as a musical synecdoche through recombinative invocations of textures that reference several generations of musical media. In part, this process involves a historically middlebrow, "glorified" entertainment aesthetic that, as when the art deco glitz of Radio City is crosscut with footage of the Marcy projects, deliberately juxtaposes status markers of high and low with emphases on visual, performative, and aural cues of spectacle, glamour, and sophistication. In recorded and live performances, "Can I Live" invokes a constellation of musical media from Rat Pack–era Sinatra to *Shaft*-era symphonic soul by way of mid-1990s hip-hop production and Jay-Z's fascination with cinematic "American gangster" pop mythology (to invoke his 2007 film-related album). To paraphrase Albin Zak, the production of "Can I Live" is deeply entwined with "a universe of other records."[30]

One "six-degrees" map (Figure 1.1) from this event back to the "symphonic" jazz of the 1920s can be sketched as follows. Jay-Z's evocation of Hayes's symphonic soul in "Can I Live" offers a virtual first degree of separation by way of sampling; a direct line can be drawn from there to Hayes by way of the Wired Strings, who worked with soul singer Barry White, who collaborated with Hayes on the 1991 ballad "Dark and Lovely (You Over There)." The second degree connects Hayes and crooner Billy Eckstine, with whom Hayes produced the 1970 album, *Stormy*. The third degree links Eckstine (whom *Time* magazine once dubbed the "Sepia Sinatra") to Frank Sinatra's arranger Nelson Riddle, who worked for Eckstine in the early 1950s, just before Riddle began his long-running association with Sinatra, a fourth degree of separation. Riddle's 1953 arrangement of "Young at Heart" became the title tune for a 1954 film. The musical director for the film *Young at Heart* was Ray Heindorf, a film conductor and arranger who helped disseminate the symphonic jazz sound in 1930s Hollywood. Heindorf was a protégé of Arthur Lange, a 1920s dance-band arranger who literally wrote the book on symphonic jazz arranging.[31] Heindorf and Lange form the fifth and sixth degrees of separation. An additional shortcut can be traced between Riddle and his former employer, bandleader Tommy Dorsey, who worked in 1927 for Paul Whiteman, a bandleader synonymous with symphonic jazz. This map suggests important craft and style connections across generations of entertainment. To echo Beaumont, Jay-Z found "rich meaning" in "re-imagining" 1970s soul classics, but those sources were themselves in a similarly reimagined "lineage" of earlier music. This book traces much of that lineage up to the mid-1970s, and many of the topics of the remaining chapters adhere to the outlines of this six-degrees chart. This lineage falls into four distinct eras: (1) the 1920s to the 1940s, an era defined by the big-band-plus-strings sound of "symphonic

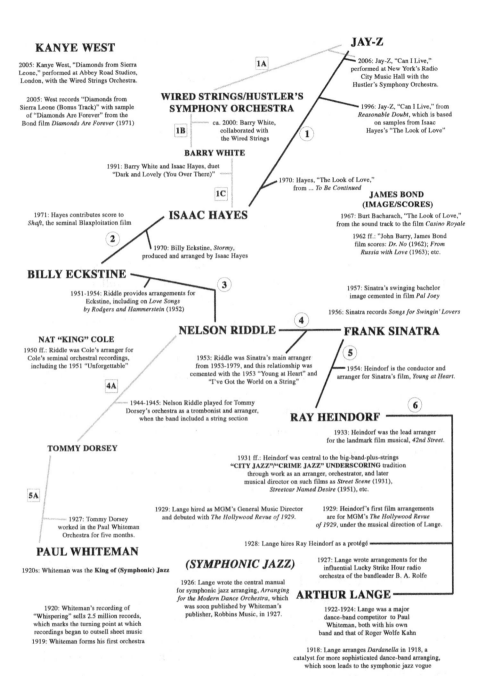

KANYE WEST

2005: Kanye West, "Diamonds from Sierra Leone," performed at Abbey Road Studios, London, with the Wired Strings Orchestra.

2005: West records "Diamonds from Sierra Leone (Bonus Track)" with sample of "Diamonds Are Forever" from the Bond film *Diamonds Are Forever* (1971)

1A

WIRED STRINGS/HUSTLER'S SYMPHONY ORCHESTRA

1B   ca. 2000: Barry White, collaborated with the Wired Strings

BARRY WHITE

1991: Barry White and Isaac Hayes, duet "Dark and Lovely (You Over There)"

1C

1971: Hayes contributes score to *Shaft*, the seminal Blaxploitation film

ISAAC HAYES

2

1970: Billy Eckstine, *Stormy*, produced and arranged by Isaac Hayes

BILLY ECKSTINE

1951-1954: Riddle provides arrangements for Eckstine, including on *Love Songs by Rodgers and Hammerstein* (1952)

3

NAT "KING" COLE

1950 ff.: Riddle was Cole's arranger for Cole's seminal orchestral recordings, including the 1951 "Unforgettable"

NELSON RIDDLE

4

1953: Riddle was Sinatra's main arranger from 1953-1979, and this relationship was cemented with the 1953 "Young at Heart" and "I've Got the World on a String"

4A

1944-1945: Nelson Riddle played for Tommy Dorsey's orchestra as a trombonist and arranger, when the band included a string section

TOMMY DORSEY

5A

1927: Tommy Dorsey worked in the Paul Whiteman Orchestra for five months.

1929: Lange hired as MGM's General Music Director and debuted with *The Hollywood Revue of 1929.*

PAUL WHITEMAN

1920s: Whiteman was the **King of (Symphonic) Jazz**

(SYMPHONIC JAZZ)

1926: Lange wrote the central manual for symphonic jazz arranging, *Arranging for the Modern Dance Orchestra*, which was soon published by Whiteman's publisher, Robbins Music, in 1927.

1920: Whiteman's recording of "Whispering" sells 2.5 million records, which marks the turning point at which recordings began to outsell sheet music
1919: Whiteman forms his first orchestra

JAY-Z

2006: Jay-Z, "Can I Live," performed at New York's Radio City Music Hall with the Hustler's Symphony Orchestra.

1996: Jay-Z, "Can I Live," from *Reasonable Doubt*, which is based on samples from Isaac Hayes's "The Look of Love"

1

1970: Hayes, "The Look of Love," from *... To Be Continued*

JAMES BOND (IMAGE/SCORES)

1967: Burt Bacharach, "The Look of Love," from the sound track to the film *Casino Royale*

1962 ff.: "John Barry, James Bond film scores: *Dr. No* (1962); *From Russia with Love* (1963); etc.

1957: Sinatra's swinging bachelor image cemented in film *Pal Joey*

1956: Sinatra records *Songs for Swingin' Lovers*

FRANK SINATRA

5

1954: Heindorf is the conductor and arranger for Sinatra's film, *Young at Heart.*

6

RAY HEINDORF

1933: Heindorf was the lead arranger for the landmark film musical, *42nd Street.*

1931 ff.: Heindorf was central to the big-band-plus-strings **"CITY JAZZ"/"CRIME JAZZ" UNDERSCORING** tradition through work as an arranger, orchestrator, and later musical director on such films as *Street Scene* (1931), *Streetcar Named Desire* (1951), etc.

1929: Heindorf's first film arrangements are for MGM's *The Hollywood Revue of 1929*, under the musical direction of Lange.

1928: Lange hires Ray Heindorf as a protégé

1927: Lange wrote arrangements for the influential Lucky Strike Hour radio orchestra of the bandleader B. A. Rolfe

ARTHUR LANGE

1922-1924: Lange was a major dance-band competitor to Paul Whiteman, both with his own band and that of Roger Wolfe Kahn

1918: Lange arranges *Dardanella* in 1918, a catalyst for more sophisticated dance-band arranging, which soon leads to the symphonic jazz vogue

FIG. 1.1. Map of the potential "six degrees of separation" between Jay-Z and the Hustler Symphony Orchestra and 1920s symphonic jazz.

jazz"; (2) the "populuxe" era of the 1950s and early 1960s; (3) the genre explosion of the late 1960s and 1970s, which gave rise to chamber pop, symphonic soul, disco, and mainstream AM Gold and MOR (middle of the road); and (4) after 1980, bestringed mainstream pop, retromania luxe (including hip-hop), and orchestral indie-rock trends. I pay particular attention here to the period between the early 1960s, when R&B first expanded its orchestrational palette, and early 1970s Hayes, and examine how the craft has been reimagined and subsumed into "Can I Live."

FROM R&B POPULUXE TO LUXE SOUL

In the populuxe era of the 1950s and early 1960s, the conspicuous symphonization of pop took a variety of forms, as country, rock and roll, R&B, and early soul music all embraced bestringed productions. The last development led to Hayes's symphonic soul. The migration of the arranging craft found in the lush, adult-marketed "traditional pop" of the early rock and roll era to a youth-oriented music market first involved pairings of white producers and arrangers with Black R&B talent. This development wed the supposedly rebellious, streetwise new styles of teenage pop to established adult-pop production markers for class, sophistication, and urbanity. The most influential models for early symphonic soul and R&B emerged in the productions of the Philles and Motown record labels across 1963–64, but producers Phil Spector and Berry Gordy (respectively) were in their turn influenced by the 1959–60 Atlantic Records orchestral R&B productions of Jerry Leiber and Mike Stoller for the Drifters and Ben E. King.

The Lieber-Stoller opulent R&B production aesthetic, as arranged by Stan Applebaum, first emerged in their initial session with the Ben E. King–led version of the Drifters for Atlantic on the 1959 single, "There Goes My Baby." This was backed with "Oh My Love," which includes an even slightly more active part for the string section. *Billboard*'s reviewers awarded the 45 only two stars ("moderate sales potential") and simply observed that the A side was a "good reading of a ballad with strings filling out the background, while the boys moan along behind" (on the B side, "the Drifters sell a ballad nicely, again helped out by a stringed background").[32] Apparently, the magazine saw nothing too unusual in the production in relation to other music on the charts, including mainstream pop, rock and roll, and other R&B. By contrast, Atlantic's Jerry Wexler disliked "There Goes My Baby" enough to reportedly call it and "overpriced production that sounds like a radio caught between two stations." But, as Stoller notes, the track nonetheless became a "hit #1, sold over a million copies," and Lieber and Stoller's "credentials as producers shot through the roof."[33] In support of *Billboard*'s humdrum review, among its various genre cliches, the number is rather routine in its use of a standard I-vi-IV-V doo-wop chord progression. What seems to have helped it stand out with the public, however—the track was repeatedly present on *Billboard*'s "Hot R&B Sides" list for weeks on end—was its over-the-top, maximalist production. Stoller credits the success of the production to the countermelody line he came up with that led to the addition of four violins and a cello to a basic R&B rhythm section. This was set in combination with "the Drifters' soaring vocals, Applebaum's soaring orchestration, . . . the studio's heavy echo, [and] . . . an awful lot going on," including a tympani part, and a Brazilian-inspired "baion beat," as Stoller calls it.[34] This "awful mess," as Wexler characterized it, was remixed for final release by the famed engineer, Tommy Dowd. Jack Nitzsche, Spector's primary arranger at Philles Records, recalled, "Applebaum . . . was the first arranger I really became aware of, [and] Lieber and Stoller, I think, were probably the first producers that used big choral groups and strings and horns on rock and roll records, the Drifters' early records. So Stan Applebaum was my hero . . . [and] the greatest arranger alive."[35] Spector's early career as a producer was in part boosted through a period under which he worked under the aegis of Lieber and Stoller and benefitted from their New York professional networks. The October 1960 Ben E. King "Spanish Harlem" best epitomizes the parallels and differences between Leiber and Stoller's productions and Spector and Nitzsche's "Wall of Sound" production aesthetic that took shape over 1962–63.[36] On "Spanish Harlem," Spector set the guitar part and the melody. Lieber provided the lyric, and the Spanish Harlem and Brazilian rhythm inspirations. As Stoller notes, "at the end of the fifties and start of the sixties, Jerry and I started introducing new elements into our records. . . . We loved using different percussion instruments. Latin grooves, for example, . . . [and] congas . . . , bongos . . . , and timbales, guiros, and cowbells."[37] On the track, Stoller added the marimba figure and other production details, including the varied percussion, and likewise worked "closely with Applebaum on the orchestration . . . , laying out the marimba and curved soprano sax sections in the instrumental breaks," and "fabulous string parts."[38]

Applebaum's pre–Leiber and Stoller arranging and orchestral pop work directly connects to the 1950s and early 1960s adult pop market, with such releases as his cowritten 1957 song, "Passing Strangers" (which was recorded as a single that year in a lush Applebaum arrangement with a duet by Sarah Vaughan and Billy Eckstine), or the big-band-plus-strings Applebaum arrangements of the 1958 *Swing Along with Al Martino*, both of which demonstrate a deep immersion in the adult-oriented populuxe idiom best epitomized in the 1950s and 1960s work of Sinatra and Riddle. The arrangements for these tracks are lush and sophisticated—in the traditional jazz-pop manner (which inherently involved plush jazz-derived harmonies, harmonic progressions, and scoring textures)—in comparison to the pared-back, bestringed ensemble work that Leiber and Stoller produced, though in their contextual genre framing, the latter were decidedly maximalist productions.

The attempted crossovers of former teen-pop artists into the mainstream adult market forms a notable trend in rock and roll's transitional years of the late 1950s and early 1960s. Neil Sedaka, then famous for teen-focused hits like the 1959 "Stupid Cupid" and "Oh Carol!," for example, released the 1961 Applebaum-arranged "All the Way," a lushly-scored jazz-pop standard ballad first recorded by Sinatra.[39] The goal here, of course, was to reach the broadest possible audience market, thereby bridging the generation gap. The Lieber and Stoller efforts opened up the R&B market to a variety of production efforts that tested this potentially lucrative cross-market territory, and the artists themselves seem to have found a range of positive career possibilities in this trend—ways of transitioning out of the limitations of the teen-oriented market (for some artists who were themselves becoming young adults), markers for musical and cultural maturity, and possibilities for escaping from the narrow race-focused confines of the R&B market, among other benefits. The 1960–61 period witnessed diverse R&B productions that embraced such expanded textural productions following the orchestral-pop models of the Leiber/Stoller/Applebaum hits for the Drifters and Ben E. King.

Sam Cooke is particularly notable in this area, and his entry into the mainstream marketplace illustrates important facets of these trends. Cooke's first single to add strings is the July 1960 hit, "Chain Gang," produced by Hugo and Luigi (Luigi Creatore and Hugo Peretti), a Brill Building production team. In near 1960 parallel, Hugo and Luigi were producing the first of their string of middle-of-the-road (MOR) adult-pop albums for the white crooner Perry Como, *For the Young at Heart* (the album was based around the song "Young at Heart," made famous by the 1953 Sinatra-Riddle hit recording). In contrast to both the Lieber and Stoller productions and the Como album, the "Chain Gang" strings are a minimal addition. These are employed as a single-line, high-register violin-section countermelody against vocal both on a late entry verse (at 1:06–1:28), and on the outro/pre-chorus return (repeating the same countermelody over 2:11–2:40). A similar minimal string-countermelody approach is heard on Cooke's 1960 single, "Sad Mood," but not on the 1961 single "That's It, I Quit." Nonetheless, with the next hit single of "Cupid," released May 1961, rising to number 17 on the charts (and produced by Luigi Creatore), there is obvious Applebaum influence in the track's opening French horn, Latin rhythms with some Latin percussion, fuller homophonic string section (shifting between single lines, and dyadic and triadic writing), and use of two or three guitars (electric, steel string, and possibly Spanish). Because of the prominence of Cooke singles from this era—from the 1960 "Chain Gang" (1960) to the 1964 "A Change Is Gonna Come"—Cooke is often positioned in a "Man Who Invented Soul" narrative in subsequent critical accounts concerning the emergence of soul.[40] That said, Cooke's lesser-known, pre-"Chain Gang" MOR album efforts have typically been dismissively framed as problematic in this same discourse.

Mark Burford's work on Sam Cooke's "crossover" from his gospel roots into the mainstream, a journey that involved "tapping the purchasing power of white middle-class consumers," focuses on Cooke's first three albums, each on Keen Records, and each squarely marketed at the adult pop market, 1957–60. The lessons from Burford's study are relevant to other period populuxe-soul releases and their hybrid, cross-market production textures, including both the early Motown and Philles releases. Each of Cooke's late-1950s albums involves varied strategies for this broader market, but the 1959 *Tribute to the Lady* (a Billy Holiday tribute album) notably encroaches upon the 1950s big-band-backed, jazz-pop-with-swingin'-vocals vogue—albeit without strings, in this case—in a way not seen on the other Cooke releases. This 1950s and early 1960s idiom was entwined with a postwar glamorization of "high-class" nightclubs and cocktail lounges, from the Copa Room at the Sands Hotel in Las Vegas to the Copacabana nightclub in New York, venues that were among the top career aspirations of many young artists Black and white, from Marvin Gaye and Sam Cooke to the Ronettes. Cooke would indeed later achieve this career marker, as heard on the 1964 live album, *Sam Cooke at the Copa*, which once more returned Cooke to a swinging, big-band, jazz-pop backing (again without strings).

As Burford observes, this pop era is defined in the American market by a singles-versus-albums (i.e., teens-versus-adults) industry and a marketing mindset defined by the generation gap.[41] In contrast to Cooke's singles for the teen-pop and R&B markets, these three MOR-focused albums have been routinely ignored or dismissed in soul history narratives. As Burford and Keir Keightley outline, in this period, the "age-stratified" broad MOR territory was "a nexus of considerations that included repertory (familiar hits of today and yesteryear), accompaniment (big band, jazz combo, or string backing), stylistic stability (not too explicitly country, rhythm and blues, modern jazz, or classical), class and generational appeal (marketed to middle-class adults), formatting (appropriate for long-playing albums), and temporality of market logic (slower but more continuous sales over a prolonged commercial life cycle)."[42] This same territory is indicative of much of this early 1960s orchestral soul. In the rock criticism tradition of the late 1960s to the present, such MOR traits have typically been seen as overtly commercial tendencies worthy of denigration.[43] Burford aptly quotes from critic Robert Palmer and other writers to illustrate a range of discourse themes typically aimed at this MOR side of Cooke's output, where the music of these MOR albums has been characterized as "filler" "Broadway-style tunes and standards," as showcases of "'pop' production treatment[s]" with "overdone orchestrations," as "syrupy," "pop schlock," and "middle-of-the-road confections" with "hovering strings and whitebread backup vocals," and as productions "laden with banal rococo effects of the sort thought to certify 'good music.'"[44] While there were certainly some who received this music in a similar manner circa 1960, this commentary is decidedly part of a later discourse that was not built on the predominant industry, press, and audience reception of Cooke from that day. As Burford reminds us, "though . . . 1950s adult pop continues to summon suffocating white, middle-class sensibilities, to many African American vocalists, postwar pop performances, particularly when circulated on LP, laid claim to easily granted forms of status, pleasure, social belonging, modern subjectivity, and modes of behavior with both symbolic and concrete economic value."[45] It is from this culturally and historically specific standpoint, from Ben E. King to Jay-Z on the stage of Radio City, that one needs to view how such luxe-production values take this Black music to "a whole 'nother level of respect," to quote Jay-Z. This territory involves a rich combination of cross-cultural, lower-middle- and middle-class negotiations of the class, taste, and social mechanisms of habitus, and these efforts are particularly relevant to Berry Gordy's Motown sound for sweet soul.

Leiber plausibly claims his Atlantic hit recordings were influential in the development of the orchestral soul of Motown's founding producer,

Berry Gordy.[46] Leiber recalls that at their first meeting, around 1959, Gordy "wanted to make R&B more appealing to whites by softening the sound." In his discussion of 1970s "soft soul," Mitchell Morris emphasizes that the pioneering sound of Tamla/Motown Records was "upwardly mobile and mainstreaming in practice, with Berry Gordy's ambitions pushing . . . its artists ever closer to a Hollywood–Las Vegas aesthetic . . . [through] elaborate, increasingly orchestral productions" that merged "soul with various breeds of more 'classical' music.'"[47] While I might disagree with the notion that Motown's strings sound "classical" (I will return later to Morris's use of this characterization), a brief consideration of a landmark 1960s record like "I Heard It Through the Grapevine" helps to illustrate Motown connections to Hayes's symphonic soul.

While Tamla's recordings included occasional strings as early as 1961, the label's iconic orchestral R&B sound emerged after "Be My Baby." Andrew Flory notes that "the earliest string parts on Motown songs were recorded in Chicago. . . . Early Detroit strings are awful, and were probably not union players. . . . Motown didn't start contracting union players until 1963 or 1964, which is when all of the glorious [Detroit Symphony Orchestra] strings start to appear." This shift can be heard on such tracks as the July 1964 "Baby I Need Your Loving" by the Four Tops or the December 1964 "My Girl" by the Temptations.[48]

As both Robert Fink and Flory suggest, Gordy's interests in class, upward mobility, and racial market crossover are tied in part to his roots in a Black bourgeois value system.[49] Flory has noted a 1949 *Color* magazine image of Gordy entertaining his family at the piano with the sheet music of Edvard Grieg clearly visible, writing that "it is doubtful that . . . refined art music permeated the room, as Berry, Jr. could not perform from a written score at the level of Grieg's writing. It is more likely that Berry was entertaining . . . with boogie-woogie . . . , creating a conflict between a visual impression of respectable entertainment and the reality of vernacular sound."[50] Morris similarly suggests connections between this same middle-class, aspirational milieu and 1970s self-images of "Black masculinity and the sound of wealth" in the symphonic soul of Barry White, Hayes, the Temptations, and so forth.[51]

In his 2013 book, *Persistence of Sentiment: Display and Feeling in Popular Music of the 1970s*, Morris discusses a range of orchestral pop that parallels and intersects with repertories studied in this book. My work builds on areas of Morris's monograph, and in certain areas we consider similar (or identical) examples of elevated musical topics related to the popular music use of both "classical" instruments and musical gestures that invoke "classical" associations in the popular imagination. We diverge somewhat in the language that we use for these practices, however. I aim to illustrate that there was a long, largely self-standing tradition of vernacular orchestral-pop arranging whose practices extend across the twentieth century, building generation by generation, with little direct engagement in the actual compositional and scoring traditions of classical music, whether serious or light. I contend that the associative chain of how one hears luxe pop strongly relies on popular music made in reference to other popular music productions, even if that music can occasionally involve textural topics invoking "classical" music. Note the setting of this latter term in quotations. This is precisely the framing that Morris uses, though it is clear in the context of his book that he is referencing many of the musical practices that I discuss as luxe pop. In his consistent use of the in-quotes "classical," he is predominantly referring to referential musical gestures or textures that might summon vague popular-culture notions of "classical" culture, rather than genuine art music references. But he never fully states this or clearly defines what he means by "classical," though his references are often well made in relation to the loose way that period American popular-music audiences broadly employed this term. Only in Morris's index does he refer to "classical" as a "super genre."[52] By this I read the in-quotes "classical" as referring not to Western art music but a much looser meta-idea within American popular culture. The latter includes popular-music adoptions of classical-instrument textures (e.g., strings, woodwinds, harpsichords, etc.) without necessarily relying upon musical/textural topics that point specifically to Western art music. This is, of course, the territory of much luxe pop. I find the latter term to be a more concrete, tradition-specific reference. Moreover, Morris does not overtly delve into this music's engagements with "brow" discourse, nor does his book consider its lengthy tradition (instead, its focus concerns other important critical issues in 1970s pop). With pop's self-referentiality in mind, and with an eye toward the tradition of luxe-pop topics tied firstly to long-standing American conventions of musical glamour, glitz, and sophistication, I thus find the loose use of "classical"—with or without quotes—to be obfuscating in contexts like the aforementioned comments of "fusions of soul with various breeds of more 'classical' music."

The invocations of "classical" and especially "classicistic" are, however, useful in reference to musical topics that directly invoke associations with classical (Western art or concert) music.[53] Without this more bounded use, dialogue around orchestral pop is reduced to an essentialist binary pop-classical divide, thereby obscuring the broad *spectrum* of fascinating American discourses that intersect in luxe pop. The evidence and analyses I present across this book—with attention to conventions of musical glamour, glitz, sophistication, and so on, as well as the varied types of large-ensemble entertainment orchestras—undermine an essentialist reading that presupposes most luxe pop was interpreted via "classical" referentiality (both as art music or meta associations with classical aura, culture, and practice). Nonetheless, I do agree with Morris's reading that "classical" referentiality was a part of this culture at differing levels of awareness. Centrally, there is important class-based aura transference in luxe pop's symphonic opulence. Massed musicians, particularly orchestral string players, signify production indulgence and extravagance, as well as access to capital. In live performance, displays of opulence, capital, and power are materialized in the juxtaposition of a "formal" backing orchestra and the demotic performers out front.

Gordy highlights similar tensions in his own productions. He characterizes arranger Paul Riser's "string and horn arrangements" as having "merged classical traditions into Motown funk."[54] Gordy also puts Motown's orchestral sound into the lineage of luxe pop, the result of working firsthand with producer Dick Jacobs in 1959 sessions for Jackie Wilson. (Though Jacobs worked in rock and roll production, like Riddle, his formative arranging years were tied to both Dorsey and Sy Oliver.)[55] Gordy recalls the "drama" of recording with horns, strings, flutes, bells, harp, background singers, and "Jackie's powerful voice," adding, "I knew that was the way great records should be made."[56] The album, Wilson's *Lonely Teardrops*, epitomizes the hi-fi production aesthetic Zak identifies as key to American pop music of the 1950s, albeit with R&B and doo-wop set alongside Mitch Miller–like novelties. Gordy later notes that "never having forgotten that big orchestral sound" from this session, he "tried to re-create it" with "string players from the Detroit Symphony."[57] The arrangements for the album, such as "Someone Who Needs Me," which includes strings, have little to do with classical music despite Gordy's middlebrow inspiration to hire "symphonic" musicians.

Marvin Gaye, "I Heard It Through the Grapevine" (1968)

The Norman Whitfield–produced hit, "I Heard It Through the Grapevine," recorded by Marvin Gaye and arranged by Paul Riser, represents the mature realization of Gordy's Motown sound. This 1968 single predates *Hot Buttered Soul* by eleven months. Example 1.4 is based on a string and horn score

EX. I.4. Excerpt 1 from Marvin Gaye, "I Heard It Through the Grapevine" (arr. Paul Riser).

re-created by Riser and transcribed material from a 2008-leaked multitrack file for "I Heard It Through the Grapevine."[58] The eight tracks of the latter include lead vocal, three-part female backing vocals, two guitars, a distorted Wurlitzer electric piano and a Hammond B3 organ, electric bass, conga and tambourine, drums, and strings and French horn. According to Motown engineer Ken Sands, rhythm tracks and certain overdubs were handled at Motown's Studio A, while the offsite Studio B was used for strings, horns, and lead and background vocal overdubs.[59] Unlike some contemporaries (e.g., Spector), Motown had always favored crisp high-fidelity recordings. Like Spector, Motown typically recorded the backing band-and-rhythm section track first, but "everything was done piecemeal," dividing the initial session and overdubs between engineers and studios, as was commonplace multitrack practice by 1968.[60] Despite the jazz pedigrees of the studio's Funk Brothers collective, Motown likewise avoided arranging, stylistic performance, and harmonies and voicings that might evoke jazz. As Sands notes, for example, Gordy initially rejected Gaye's later "What's Going On?" single (and album) on the grounds that it was "too jazzy."[61] There are notable stylistic connections between the sound of this latter recording and Hayes's work of the era, and following Hayes's *Hot Buttered Soul* and *Shaft* (among other influences), big-band-plus-strings textures become a staple of early 1970s soul.

The template for Motown's string arranging was luxe pop. In 1950s and 1960s luxe-pop craft, there are many common traits in the roles of strings and sectional scorings. The basis of this postwar pop practice was traced in 1946 by Tom Bennett, an NBC radio staff arranger, to the layout of Paul Whiteman's famous orchestra as foundational: trumpets, trombones, doubling saxophonists, a rhythm section, and strings.[62] Though they might expand to "symphonic" proportions, such ensembles generally varied in size between eighteen and forty-five instruments and might include a harp, French horn, or tuba. In describing the role of the strings, Bennett notes both that the violin section has primary focus, and that strings are "almost entirely used for embellishment" of the other sectional textures. He explains that violin subdivisions are related to "the complexity of harmonies in modern [jazz and popular music] writing" made up of "four, five, or six notes" without duplication. He outlines proportions for various string combinations and comments that "in radio orchestras, . . . fewer strings are used," thus, "the additional harmonic notes enable this smaller group to produce sounds similarly rich and full."[63] Similar advice is passed on by Nelson Riddle in his 1985 arranging book through charmingly mixed metaphor: the utilitarian strings are both "the putty of an orchestra" and "a velvet cushion . . . to display the sparkling woodwinds or the rich brass."[64] Riddle points out practical reasons for placing strings high above the horn sections: "Strings, buried in open brass, are another helpless situation, especially if the string section is small. This problem can sometimes be alleviated by having the strings play an octave or two higher" than the brass, and such textures require a "skillful [recording] engineer" to bring out the timbral warmth of high-register violins, as the instrument tends to "thin out."

Example 1.5 shows these techniques in action in another excerpt from "Grapevine." Here strings move primarily by sustained half- and whole-note motion akin to what was typically used in the Sinatra-Riddle model. Note the standard high-register, arch-shaped countermelody that prepares the statement of the title phrase and how the unison violin countermelody is set

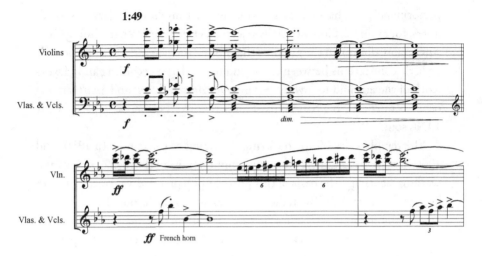

EX. 1.5. Excerpt 2 from Marvin Gaye, "I Heard It Through the Grapevine."

above the treble stave, well more than an octave above the violas. The violas and cellos are thus buried behind the rhythm section in the mid-register of the mix soundscape despite the clarity of the final mix and Gordy's self-described obsession with mixing perfection.[65] It is surprising to note how lush the lower strings are in the score, with at times seven-part voicings that span two or more octaves. Riddle was correct; these harmonies are buried in the mix and can only be heard when the original string tracks are isolated. But what one hears in the mix is the high-register violin section offset from the soul background.

At times in the isolated strings-and-horn track, however, the small string section almost evokes chamber music. Such brief details involve classicistic string writing. This sort of texture is heard in the overly accentuated neighbor-note gestures in Example 1.5, which function as exclamation marks to the vocal line. These gestures are complemented by tremolo, a French horn response, and an upward-sweeping, chromatic scalar run. All of this is self-consciously melodramatic. The French horn doublings and melodic interjections, however, also show both classicistic tropes and an influence from contemporary "baroque pop" production trends. Such textures are not a norm for—but are not entirely foreign to—1960s orchestral soul. Textures like these involve a slightly stiff performance style that drags in juxtaposition against the backing-track groove. The timbre, counterpoint, straight rhythm, and performance approach all speak self-consciously in a "formal" register in the context of groove-based soul, thereby briefly invoking "serious" music, which in turn stands in contrast to the R&B-native, luxe-pop string/reeds/ brass idiom predominantly heard in these recordings.

HAYES AND SYMPHONIC SOUL

Rock culture of the late 1960s into the 1970s witnessed both orchestral and chamber pop ranging from the Beatles to singer-songwriters (e.g., Van Dyke Parks, Leonard Cohen, Scott Walker, and Nick Drake). In turn, these pop-music (as opposed to art-rock) trends took on self-conscious qualities of theatricality and camp (with T. Rex, ELO, and others). Such white pop was complemented by the symphonic soul of Black musicians like Hayes, White, and others, music that soon ushered in the lush sounds of disco and MOR. Much of this music—white and Black—is marked by scoring gestures that sound classicistic. In most instances though, classicistic gestures merely decorate a scoring practice inherent in high-class pop. Moreover, orchestral pop had so long used such classicistic decoration—orchestral code-switching dates back to ragtime—that by the 1970s, the gestures sound native to pop, even if they give a momentary nod to "serious" music as well.

This trend is ideally illustrated in Hayes's "The Look of Love," a track that clarifies Jay-Z's dialectical relationship to symphonic soul. The 1971 album ... *To Be Continued* followed the successes of *Hot Buttered Soul* and *The Isaac Hayes Movement*, both from 1970, and the 1971 *Shaft* soundtrack album.[66] Hayes stretched out the signature soul of the Bar-Kays rhythm section (the Stax in-house band) and the earthy reeds and brass of the Memphis Horns, and added soulful organ work, crooning baritone vocals, and extended spoken "raps" (as he called them), topping the whole confection with jazz-derived flute-work, as well as strings, French horns, and woodwinds borrowed from the Memphis Symphony Orchestra. Each of these albums feature epic-length tracks, including reimagined song covers not associated with early Stax soul. In 1972, Hayes remarked that "pop music doesn't set any restrictions any more. . . . You can use anything you want."[67] He also contended that his music was "like a sponge and I'm just now squeezing myself. . . . I've absorbed country[,] blues, . . . classics, jazz, pop. It all came in and now I'm letting it out."[68] He later noted that "My influences were all over the map. Sure, I was inspired by [Motown's songwriters] Holland-Dozier-Holland, but I also dug [the Brill Building adult pop of] Burt Bacharach. . . . Whatever I heard,

I took it down to Soulsville and sung my way."[69] Hayes thus later claimed that "people recognize me as one who has put polish on soul music, put it on another level."[70]

This "higher" level was defined by lush strings and jazzy big-band textures. The tensions of these luxe sounds against what Hayes described as "raw" Memphis soul was the goal "to combine the feel of a big symphony with the nasty funk."[71] Moreover, on his spoken introductions to early 1970s tracks, Hayes noted that in "my raps there are grammatical errors which I don't care to change. . . . Music is the one language [in which] grammatical errors are accepted. . . . I don't even think about trying to speak correctly."[72] As this suggests, the pungent non-classical musico-grammatical errors—or tensions—in Hayes's symphonic soul are embedded in the sustained style, race, and class oppositions of this music. These oppositions are visually evident in 1973 footage of Hayes and his band with an orchestra.[73] In "The Look of Love," the tuxedo-clad white symphony in the orchestra pit is juxtaposed against the (ghetto-)fabulous image of Hayes behind his B3 organ in dark sunglasses, bare-chested with gold-chain vest, and his band in the finest, Black-urban street fashion of 1973. The contrast of high and low, of Black and white, was meant not to transcend popular music but to impart an *aura* of musical sophistication via textural and timbral juxtaposition.

These very contrasts are clearly audible in the Hayes samples that Jay-Z appropriates and in the sustained cultural tensions directly evoked in Jay-Z's (and later Kanye West's) performances. For instance, "Can I Live" juxtaposes topics on jazz flute, funk bass, DJ scratching, and full orchestral hits. The harmonically rich scoring later in the song (Example 1.3) reveals a Vegas-luxe big-band topic present in both the Jay-Z performance and the Hayes original. (The lushly scored harmonies here—moving from B9, to B9/A, to G♯min9, to C♯min9—are characteristic of dense postwar big-band scoring.) Jay-Z juxtaposes agile, word-dense rap against the thickened-unison jazz-flute line (underscored with reeds and brass doublings), the funk-fueled backbeat of the drums and the minor-key groove of the electric piano and bass, the classicistic harp arpeggiation, and the strings (Example 1.2). The debt of the Hayes and Jay-Z strings here to the old-school arranger's craft documented by Bennett is palpable in the archlike, intensifying, high-register violin-section countermelody, supported by a close-voiced, seventh-based sustained harmony performed in tremolo. As Riddle advised, a luxurious string countermelody is ensconced securely two octaves above the street-level noise of the funk groove ("presidential suites my residential for the weekend"). Jay-Z is a master of "confidentially speaking in codes," and the use of strings here stands in for a whole series of dialectical juxtapositions: high versus low, white versus Black, wealthy versus working-class, conspicuous bling (privileged "haves") versus hardscrabble hustle (aspirational "have-nots").

The sonics of "Can I Live" thus draw on social juxtapositions that defined Hayes's 1970s image and the use of his music in films like *Shaft*. In 1970, *Ebony* described Hayes's entertainment persona as "decked out in fur, silk, velvet and looking like a mogul from some ultra-scopic-multi-million dollar movie spectacular."[74] Hip-hop bling culture clearly took a lot from Hayes-era Black entertainment fashion and its cinematic portrayals of Black culture. Hayes's own 1990s publicity emphasized the importance of his 1970s "Black Moses" persona; his "uncompromised" ethnic pride, the promo copy noted, continued "the tradition of Duke Ellington, writing tone poems about his own people," while acting as a "symbol of black masculinity" and "setting a precedent for generations to follow."[75] The self-conscious class, culture, and gender tensions in this promotional material ground Hayes's persona in racial discourse around spectacle and entertainment glamour, but they also position his efforts in an elevated artistic lineage extending back to jazz. As the proliferation of hip-hop-meets-orchestra events demonstrates, Hayes's legacy was indeed "a precedent for generations to follow," but in pop-culture memory, such imagery—whether sourced from cinema, stage, album and promotional art, or fashion—is firmly associated with the distinct set of musical timbres outlined here under the rubric of luxe pop.

Other elevated musical registers beyond symphonic timbres can be present in much of this luxe music. As demonstrated later in other chapters, across luxe pop history, including these Jay-Z and Hayes examples, there is also a post-1950 elevated "jazz register" in operation. The soul-meets-big-band-jazz pop invocations of a jazz register are especially important to understanding the connections between Hayes and Jay-Z discussed throughout this chapter. In countless live symphonic soul and hip-hop presentations—including Jay-Z's Radio City concert and Isaac Hayes's 1970s tours—the jazz-trained brass/reeds sections are offset from the performers as tuxedo-clad, anonymous "orchestra" musicians, whereas the performers and core backing band typically present themselves in street fashion. This was the case in the 1973 Hayes video. It is from a postwar repositioning of jazz as "serious" adult music that another layer of musical hierarchy emerges in luxe-pop practice—that of a roughly hewn, youth-culture soul, funk, and R&B foundation set against a *culturally elevated* big-band polish, urbanity, and musical glamour. And this sophistication typically signifies adult African American urbanity, just as Count Basie and Quincy Jones provided a Vegas-luxe sound for Sinatra.[76] These connections inform the rich tonal references to 1970s symphonic soul in Jay-Z's Radio City performance.

The connections of music to image are likewise important here. A central part of the post-1950 Sinatra image of the urbane, swinging bachelor is its relation to mid-century hipness, and these associations have been purposefully "reimagined" by Jay-Z, West, and Diddy. For instance, Jay-Z's fedora, Italian finery, and cigar are straight out of Rat Pack fashion as filtered through mafioso films. Jay-Z specifically avoids reimagined 1970s pimp evocations of West Coast rap figures like the mid-1990s, Afro-ed Snoop Dogg (whose 1994 "Gin and Juice" video begins with an unidentified but very Hayes-style symphonic soul "8-track" underscoring intro). The Rat Pack—the New York–Las Vegas social clique of Sinatra and his hard-drinking, glamorous friends—was a pure product of mass entertainment, but they projected a sense of hip superiority through their depictions of glamour and wealth. This urbane, mixed-class image of sophisticated, romantic machismo is central to this music's generations of fan appreciation, including the hip-hop mogul generation of Jay-Z, West, and Diddy.

That said, there is also an important midcentury Black crooner—or "sepia Sinatra"—tradition (Billy Eckstine, Sammy Davis Jr., Nat "King" Cole, and numerous others) that held other popular racial ideas of access to capital, and displays of glamour and power, to many African American entertainers and audiences up through the 1970s. This is relevant here. Hayes remarked in 1971 that when growing up he "wanted to sing pop" and "Nat Cole was my idol."[77] (This is a common trope among that era of African American male performers.) His early 1970s albums thus suggest a reimagining of the sounds of mid-1950s Cole, Billy Eckstine, and Sinatra for the 1970s, a hypothesis that is reinforced by Hayes's 1972 production work for Eckstine, where Hayes claimed that he was bringing the older crooner "to where we're *at*, but with his same sound."[78] However, as "Look" covers a Bacharach tune, and in light of the "inspiration" he took from producers like Norman Whitfield at Motown, he clearly adapted several generations of luxe pop to "Soulsville." In turn, this sound became the quintessential 1970s model for underscoring the Black urban experience in film. In addition, *Shaft* is often seen as a Black, American, urban reworking of the James Bond franchise.[79] Hayes's film score thus might be seen in part as a similar translation of Barry's Bond scores, somewhat in the way that Hayes recast Bacharach's "The Look of

Love" (from a film that also tried to reimagine Bond). These cross-Atlantic, cross-race, and cross-style connections are further augmented in Jay-Z's later reimagining of Hayes's music. In sum, with Hayes's symphonic soul, you hear three sustained class registers: low Soulsville funk; the middlebrow Vegas-luxe big band; and middle-high cinematic luxe pop. This combination is emulated and expanded—with contemporary rap and hard hip-hop beats—in both the Kanye and Jay-Z performances.

CONSPICUOUS SYMPHONIZATION, TOPIC THEORY, AND REGISTER

Many manifestations of luxe pop are tied together by entertainment manifestations of conspicuous symphonization. I have compared this idea to ostentatious hip-hop culture bling displays. But bling swerves away from melting-pot homogenization through ironic juxtapositions of pop culture and high-status symbols. A similar tension permeates most luxe pop, including the Jay-Z and West orchestra events. Tuxedoed orchestras followed on from the adoption of designer suits, Cristal champagne, luxury automobiles, and upper-class consumer signifiers that were routinely set in juxtaposition with street-level lyrics, thematic content, and cultural posturing.

Most luxe pop involves similar juxtapositions of disparate musical topics. Topical theory builds on the work of Robert Hatten and Leonard Ratner, the latter of whom aptly described musical topics as "characteristic [musical] figures" associated with specific social and cultural ideas, practices, entities, and musical traditions.[80] While both Hatten and Ratner focus on the semiotics of classical music repertory, this theory has found relevance to studies of other musical traditions, including Leydon's study of hip-hop.[81] Such pop-embedded associative traits are equally relevant to Michael Long's ideas on musical register and Philip Tagg's museme theory.[82] Long's concept refers to musical materials whose texture, contour, instrumentation, and/or gestures congeal as a *musical register* that provides "embedded fragments" of meaning in "vernacular" music. He is specifically concerned with a "classical" register in popular-culture musical media. Long's work draws from the concept of semiotic "musemes." Tagg described musemes as *minimal* units of expressive musical meaning and somewhat analogous to the linguistic building block of a morpheme.[83] While Long acknowledges that cultural register suggests a vertical, high-to-low cultural continuum, he invokes register in a way that links "cultural products to the expressive value" of registers via "acculturated styles and genres in which [expressive register] functions as a [cultural] signal and a marker."[84]

The theoretical differences between topics, registers, and musemes may be a matter of analytical perspective and scale. While musemes mark the smallest semiotic level of musical material with associative meaning, a topic can involve two or more musemes that collectively reference more complex stylistic, cultural, and social associations. In this framing, a topic is equivalent to Tagg's idea of museme stacks (museme composites where individual meanings combine to a greater unit of meaning). By contrast, register involves the *linear* and *interactive* juxtapositions of multiple topics that collectively impart specific class-hierarchy, taste subculture, and expressive values. This interpretation is based on Long's idea of "nested matrices of vernacular registers."[85] He refers to such texts as hybrid expressions, but beyond invoking postmodern bricolage or pastiche, Long does not really examine the varied ways that cultural hybridity has been theorized.[86]

At the risk of oversimplifying Long's work, the signature of his classical register in popular culture is a sort of lofty mode of address that invokes "serious" matters in a manner akin to classicistic gestures (as I have defined this term). In Long's examples—which range from Max Steiner's film scores to hip-hop—his identifications of classical register are primarily based on idiosyncratic hearings without recourse to historical, ethnographic, or survey evidence that support his understandings of "serious" musical textures in pop-culture products. I contend that alternate interpretations are suggested, for instance, with much Hollywood film music. For instance, with Steiner's score to the 1933 film *King Kong* (RKO), I strongly believe that most audiences might describe the underscoring as a distinct category of pop-culture orchestral music, as *Hollywood music* rather than "classical" music. Such distinctions are dependent on cultural literacy and the variable specificities of symbolic tones *in the context* of specific media and genres. Also notable, though, is the unavoidable variability in—and subjectivity of—interpreting associative musical signifiers.

Such subjectivity is certainly present in various references to classicistic signifiers, aura, and aspirations among creators and critics in luxe pop. When discussing "Barry White's mode of crossover," Morris considers the role of the "domain of timbre." He states that "Barry White's orchestrational choices" on his 1973 debut, *I've Got So Much to Give*, "scream 'classical,' but it is doubtful that they are meant to do so directly." Morris also draws connections between "White's orchestration and another grown-up style" in which a certain "combination of instruments evokes a particular tradition of easy-listening music popular during the 1950s and 1960s.[87] The White album Morris discusses here is unusually dense with classicistic gestures when compared, for example, to a trademark White hit like the 1974 "You're the First, My Last, My Everything." Even with White's 1973 Love Unlimited Orchestra instrumental, "Love's Theme," most of these sorts of classicistic textures are more native to the string arranging idioms of contemporary soft soul and proto-disco. Beyond exceptions like *I've Got So Much to Give*, such idiomatic classicistic flourishes in soul do not routinely "scream classical," and they were not heard as—nor were they typically meant to be heard as—culture-aspirational concert music. Rather, as Morris also underscores, they are indexes of class, glamour, luxury, wealth, and so on. A listen through the mountain of string-laden AM Gold recordings of 1970s radio (see chapter 6) reinforces the observation that there is a long history of luxe pop that has its own rules and topical associations, including minor uses of classicistic textures. This is generally how White is interpreted, even when he is fronting an orchestra. For example, the *New York Times* reviewer John Rockwell noted the "Muzak-support of the orchestra" at Barry White's 1976 Radio City event.[88]

This first chapter has illustrated a range of important orchestral pop associations beyond classical register; although, as noted, classical register—or classicistic gestures—can unconsciously inform meaning around luxe pop sounds. However, while a "Hollywood" music register may involve a residual *aura* from classical register, that does not mean that such music will be commonly understood through classical register. Such problems arise in Long's reading of Busta Rhymes's "Gimme Some More," which uses a sample from Bernard Herrmann's score to *Psycho*.[89] Long's analysis builds on his valuable idea of "cinematic" popular musics. Contrary to the assumption of hearing classical register in such sampled "past classic referents" (Herrmann's score), however, I contend that Long overlooks Mark Katz's persuasive argument that "sampling is most fundamentally an art of *transformation*," where a "sample changes the moment it is relocated." Katz adds that "any sound, placed in a new musical context, will take on some of the character of its new sonic environment."[90] Zak further notes that the ever-increasing, "infinite [sonic] palette" of popular music is built on rich networks of historically accumulated meaning, where "sounds carry . . . entire stylistic legacies" and "the rhetorical sense of sounds develops through . . . cultural practice" and "a constellation of associations" that has grown with time.[91] Thus, by too quickly identifying a rhapsodic string flourish as a classical referent, or classicistic, one ignores a history of more relevant pop practice and cumulative associations.

My six-degrees map (Figure 1.1) offers a hypothetical outline for one historical constellation of stylistic associations, but this exercise in turn suggests how we subjectively find meaning in the style, culture, and image accretions of popular music. A colleague commented about an earlier version of this chart, saying it suggests "a way of looking at how we listen to pop music. . . . Even if you don't know who all those guys are, or that there's a long tradition . . . that capitalize[s] on the juxtaposition[s] of funky, lowdown, street American vernacular and high art style, if you jump in at any point of the network . . . it will conjure the rest of the network into memory."[92] Zak similarly notes that the "rhetorical aspect of timbre involves . . . conventional associations that . . . allow them to stand as symbols suggesting . . . resonances beyond the boundaries of [a] track." He further notes Luciano Berio's contention (in 1967) that orchestral pop arrangements can "move beyond the 'idea of *song* and develop into a sort of sound drama . . . [and] *collage*'" of musical and stylistic referents.[93] This maps quite nicely onto how certain orchestral borrowings function within hip-hop, such as the music of the Jay-Z or West events, or Long's example from Busta Rhymes. Indeed, Long astutely notes that register juxtapositions are primarily taken in and heard all at once. The perspective of historical context is likewise important in terms of understanding both production intent and potential audience reception. Zak observes that influential sounds—such as the orchestral pop of the Beatles' *Sgt. Pepper's Lonely Hearts Club Band* album—quickly become part of rock's ever-expanding recording-production lexicon.[94] Again, I am talking about recombinant pop that invokes earlier pop music. Thus, while passing orchestral pop textures (a "cinematic" string intro, for example) might invoke potential classical-leaning *topics*, from the broader perspective of hearing a track or an album as a whole, the overall expressive register is better described as *luxe pop*, as these sounds typically invoke pop-music history.

In the stylistic bricolage of luxe pop, expressive textures, topics, or musemes, are part of a larger signifying system. Such music involves *hybridity*, but I mean to evoke a more exclusive meaning here for that term than simply cultural mixing. Diana Taylor stresses the botanical definition of *hybridity*, which she notes "refers to the engineered . . . grafting of two dissimilar entities."[95] Taylor interprets such mixings as a "collision" of identities that reference juxtaposed "signs, systems of power, [and] spaces"[96] through a maintained sense of *sustained heterogeneity* rather than a homogeneous, integrated fusion. Similarly, evocative luxe-pop juxtapositions—Black and white, high and low, luxury and street, conservative and counterculture cool, lush and edgy, hipster slang and highbrow posturing—reveal the core aesthetic, social, and cultural discourse themes embedded in the rich, multi-layered semiotic constructions of such musical arrangements and recording productions. Such cultural tensions and meaningful sustained contrasts of expressive register are how this music speaks to audiences.[97]

CONCLUSION

Despite the frequently presumed irrelevance of classical music in modern mass culture, and despite a long history of luxe pop, both Jay-Z and West describe their conspicuously symphonized performances as rap-meets-classical-orchestra events, and each invokes the cliché that he took rap to "a whole 'nother level of respect." Indeed, while both artists identify orchestral strings with high culture and the "classical," their music is built on emulations of well-known models of orchestral pop. Both artists emphasize their performances' high-low juxtapositions, and Jay-Z even notes a certain ironic humor—what he calls "sarcasm," meaning likely "wit" rather than "contempt"—in the fact that a highbrow orchestra was employed to speak in the street dialect of hip-hop. To paraphrase West, everything about these events involves conspicuous juxtapositions of "pop and luxury" or, rather, luxe pop. Regardless of the stylistic idiom performed by the backing ensemble, the performance involves key transferences of prestige, luxury, and even high-culture aura from the supposedly classical and jazzy elements of the ensemble—as well as from the high-esteem venues—to these artists. This middlebrow transference of aura is central to most luxe pop. Since the beginning of the recording era, artists have sought to position orchestral pop projects as innovative class-culture violations, despite the long luxe-pop history that provides the infrastructure for their efforts. Glorified pop regularly seeks to invoke the violin as an antipop token musical icon of highbrow, white European Culture-with-a-capital-C—a form of posturing particularly curious in light of the decidedly non-cutting-edge postwar radio format called MOR, where string arrangements abound, along with a distinct lack of cultural prestige.

The power of such pretensions lies in public image constructions. In its borrowings from the 1971 film *Diamonds Are Forever*, West's "Diamonds from Sierra Leone" owes an obvious debt to Barry's trademark James Bond scores. Similar Bond-Barry connections are suggested in the Jay-Z-Hayes-Bacharach "Look of Love" thread. These mixed orchestral backgrounds emulate aspects of Barry's trademark melodramatic-but-hip Bond sound of lush, high-register strings (on key tension tones with tightly voiced, minimal harmonizations), above earthy, big-band brass and reeds. The Bond soundtrack formula regularly annexes "contemporary" musical topics in order to juxtapose them against the timeless and "classy" string, reed, and brass sections. With the Jay-Z arrangements, hip-hop beats and rap take the contemporary position originally occupied by surf-rock guitar. As we have seen, equally important stylistic touchstones for West and Jay-Z can be found in the soul-plus-strings sound of 1970s blaxploitation film scores and symphonic soul, another trove of pop-culture imagery and cultural associations tied to epic, grand, cinematic visions. These dual stylistic sources have spilled over into adjacent album projects. For example, this cinematic-soul, danger-with-glamour vision is directly seen in Jay-Z's 2007 *American Gangster* album, which was promoted with reference to Ridley Scott's Harlem-themed film (also 2007) of the same name. As film and album, *American Gangster* transfers gangsta-rap culture's fascination with Hollywood's mafia crime-film tradition to 1970s Harlem drug wars. Jay-Z's album lyrics also imply other possible influences, including Sinatra and Motown. Likewise, in his song "Threat" from the 2003 *The Black Album*, he compares his circle to the Rat Pack and directly refers to himself as a Black Sinatra. One year earlier, he also adapted Sinatra's signature tune "My Way" on his *The Blueprint 2* album. This world of symphonic soul timbres thus readily conjures up recombinative connections to blaxploitation narratives and both Bond- and Sinatra-like fashion, high-living, and posturing.

For Jay-Z, West, and even Diddy, the inspirational connections to Sinatra and his high-living Rat Pack pals are spelled out in lyrics, critical reception, and video, including notable 2008 and 2011 advertising campaigns in which "Diddy Channels Frank Sinatra to Promote Ciroc Vodka."[98] In this campaign, Diddy and his entourage are portrayed as a modern-day Black Rat Pack (inverting the original racial ratios by including one white member as a counterpart to Sammy Davis). They are shown living the high life, drinking champagne in glamorous settings (in evening wear) with a lushly scored jazz-pop Sinatra track playing in the background. Likewise, in his hit single

"Empire State of Mind," Jay-Z renews the boast "I'm the new Sinatra." This is precisely the cross-generation, cross-race, cross-class nexus of heterogeneous cultural codes that I have identified around the mediated timbres of luxe pop, where image constructions, tonal worlds, performance spectacle, and juxtaposed cultural markers create a greater, glorified whole. Postwar middlebrow criticism arrived arm-in-arm with a jaundiced highbrow view of mass culture and attempts to democratize high culture for the masses. For instance, at mid-century, Dwight Macdonald warned that mass culture breaks down all cultural distinctions to produce a scrambled, homogenized culture. Middlebrow culture was even more troublesome to Macdonald because it displays "the essential qualities of [mass culture]—the formula . . . the lack of any standard except popularity—but it covers them with a cultural fig leaf pretend[ing] to respect the standards of High Culture while it vulgarizes them."[99] For Macdonald, the middlebrow is thus a Trojan Horse that threatens high culture through a potential confusion between art and entertainment—in other words, the home territory of luxe pop.

While much luxe pop indeed sounds middlebrow, not all of it works neatly to glorify bourgeois culture. Jay-Z's Radio City concert celebrated the disruptiveness of class mobility, while the street-hustler, Mafioso rap of the *Reasonable Doubt* album—threaded through a plethora of luxury-brand signifiers—speaks of the betrayed promise of class mobility for Black American youths, even as hip-hop music was embraced by both white middle- and upper-class youths (and academia). While the culture, class, race, economic, and branding strategies of the Radio City event suggest a debt to brow discourse, and while its meaning is partly derived from this legacy, it should be observed that there is no pretension here to "respect the standards of High Culture," no overarching claim of art for art's sake. Indeed, the subversive act of vulgarizing these lofty standards, of relishing the musico-grammatical errors Hayes noted, tears away the middlebrow cultural fig leaf that masks luxe entertainment as art. Instead, rapping in front of an orchestra is a playful inversion and skew(er)ing of traditional class, culture, and race assumptions through a range of Black signifying practices. These practices repurpose a style—and a sound—that in turn invokes the sonic history of luxe pop. This is the history that will be explored across the following chapters, retracing in expanded detail the six-degrees pathways outlined here.

TWO

The (Symphonic) Jazz Age, Musical Vaudeville, and "Glorified" Entertainments

The Melting Pot of Music: America Is a Melting Pot of Music Wherein the Melodies of All Nations Are Fused into One Great New Rhythm JAZZ!

—INTERTITLE CARD IN THE *KING OF JAZZ*
(UNIVERSAL, 1930)

IN APRIL 1930, Universal Studios released its musical revue, *King of Jazz*, an opulent feature for the bandleader Paul Whiteman. The film's title is borrowed from Whiteman's common epithet in the press. More accurately, Whiteman was the king of *symphonic jazz*. Similarly, in the epigraph quotation above, the "jazz" reference is best read as a reference to interwar symphonic jazz, which was indeed a "melting pot of music" but also a foundation for the luxe-pop practice of the twentieth century. This film provides a rich example of these ideals, as *King of Jazz* was designed as a potpourri entertainment extravaganza and a frame for Technicolor scenic innovation and spectacle. The studio spared no expense. They had hoped to secure Florenz Ziegfeld, the impresario of *Ziegfeld Follies* fame, as director, but he was unavailable. The studio thus hired John Murray Anderson, widely considered to be Ziegfeld's closest competitor, and also the director who had produced Whiteman's film prologue shows (i.e., the lavish live stage revues that preceded film presentations in many deluxe movie theaters).

The film progresses through various musical interludes, songs and song medleys, dances, and vaudevillian comedy sketches. The centerpiece is a grand production number based on George Gershwin's *Rhapsody in Blue*, which had been commissioned and premiered by Whiteman in a 1924 showcase concert at New York's Aeolian Hall. In the film, this number is lavishly overproduced and sets the Whiteman band atop an enormous piano with multiple pianists and richly costumed dancers, many of whom were Roxy-ettes borrowed from New York's Roxy Theater.[1] Though it was a box-office failure due to the double blow of the Depression and the public's sudden distaste for Hollywood's derivative musical revues, the film received quite favorable critical reception, as seen in the bold-faced headline that "Universal's *King of Jazz* [Is a] Triumph in Screen Aesthetics . . . [and] Showmanship: Whiteman's Super-Production Is Both [a] Great Concert and Great Show."[2] This description highlights central symphonic-jazz traits, including notions of high-class entertainment expressed via codes and practices of glamour, sophistication, and spectacle, mixed with period showmanship and jazzy popular music.

While jazz-history narratives have marginalized Whiteman as an eccentric musical phenomenon outside the core jazz tradition, more recent writings have moved from this partisanship to consider Whiteman's important role in American popular music. For example, Elijah Wald's 2009 contrarian "Alternative History of American Popular Music," *How the Beatles Destroyed Rock 'n' Roll* (the title is a red herring), presents a convincing—but not overstated—argument for Whiteman's immense pre-rock influence as being akin to the vast influence of the Beatles on rock-era popular culture.[3] By avoiding the assumptions and biases of genre histories, by carefully considering race, class hierarchy, taste cultures, gender, technology, and show business, among other themes, and by attempting to make sense of mainstream music that was widely popular, Wald seeks to take seriously music that has not always received critical attention. Like Wald, I aim to reevaluate Whiteman through a broad-view, historical-entertainment perspective, focusing on his role as a touchstone of a rich entertainment tradition. I seek to understand "Whitemanesque" musical entertainment in a manner that is not essentialized ("Is Whiteman's music *jazz* or *not*?") but contextualized and historicized, and to view this subject via multiple perspectives, including attention paid to the middlebrow aesthetics of symphonic jazz.

This chapter first broadly considers the ways in which symphonic jazz closely relates to the entertainment ideals of both vaudeville and higher-class stage revues. Then, returning to *King of Jazz*, I will suggest how symphonic jazz was positioned as a musical node for several interwar entertainment traditions. The idiom was fundamentally a popular music arranging tradition that spread from dance bands, to stage entertainments, to the orchestras of radio and film. As such, a single song arrangement—the Whiteman orchestra's 1924 "By the Waters of the Minnetonka"—is studied to articulate how the vaudeville aesthetic was musically employed in the arranging practices that were shared across these entertainment traditions.

THE MELTING POT OF MUSIC
AND THE VAUDEVILLE AESTHETIC

In the previous chapter, I touched upon a working definition of sustained "hybrid" qualities in luxe pop. The Whitemanesque "melting pot of music" ideal underscores the centrality of such cultural mixing to symphonic jazz. In the 1920s, the offerings of dance orchestras and musical theater closely adhered to the era's variety-entertainment model. The Whiteman orchestra's 1920s repertory epitomizes this aesthetic. In a reflection of Tin Pan Alley, vaudeville, and Broadway trends, the orchestra performed syncopated/jazzy popular songs; novelty/comedy numbers; sentimental ballads; Oriental/exotic numbers and other ethnic stereotype songs; mammy/minstrelsy numbers; arrangements of novelty piano music; entertainment spirituals; numbers from musical theater, revues, and operetta; dance arrangements of light concert music; waltzes, fox-trot, and jazz renditions of popular classics; and arranged renditions of hot blues and jazz numbers. All were enhanced via the symphonic jazz arranging idiom, which was celebrated in its day for its hybrid collisions of musical styles and idioms. After his orchestra's 1924 Aeolian Hall concert, which premiered Gershwin's *Rhapsody* as specially scored by Whiteman's arranger, Ferde Grofé, the orchestra's eclectic repertory additionally involved both extended instrumental concert works and elaborate concert-style arrangements of popular music.

Hybridity needs to be viewed here through a specific understanding of the term. Rather than focus on homogeneous, integrated fusions, Diana Taylor's aforementioned description of cultural hybridity frames certain cultural mixings through both their *collisions* of disparate identities and their *sustained heterogeneity* between these areas of difference. Here is where "cultural memory" (Taylor's phrasing)—or, in the present study, artistic invocations of distinct mixed cultural ideas—is central to understanding the meanings generated in hybrid expressions. Such cultural memory involves the invocation of the embedded and embodied cultural dispositions and understandings of habitus. In popular music, these cultural codes are embedded in musical scoring textures, which function as signs for guiding relevant cultural readings. As discussed later, symphonic jazz arranging greatly depended upon "characteristic scoring effects." These effects were fundamentally referential musical topics—meaning "patches of music that trigger clear associations with [musical] styles, genres, and expressive meanings," as Robert Hatten defines this concept.[4] The juxtapositions of such topics function in a manner akin to humor, where the tensions between relevant cultural literacy and personal habitus allow insight and appreciation for the wit of the artful collisions within this sort of hybrid entertainment expression. Through her reference to "systems of power" and social and cultural "spaces," Taylor underscores the relevance of cultural hierarchy and valuation discourses. Luxe pop engages silent and not-so-silent habitus dispositions of social and cultural power, whether artistic and cultural class (meaning the brows, high, middle, and low, and the spectrum between entertainment and art), socioeconomic class, race, or gender. Cultural, economic, and social power relations are embedded even in the lightest, most innocuous commercial entertainment. Similarly, as detailed in literature on social networks and affinity communities in musical practice, as well as literature on cultural and musical geography, conceptions of space and place are inherent in understanding and interpreting music and power discourses within music, and inherent in both musical creativity and consumption.[5] By adapting this delimited definition of hybrid culture for describing luxe-pop aesthetics, I call attention to the audibility of this music's juxtapositions of distinct, disparate topics and styles—elements that later jazz proponents and highbrow critics disparaged—as positive artistic qualities. This merit resides specifically in the conflicts, tensions, and interactions between any given arrangement's referential musical topics.

In her outline of conceptions of cultural fusion in *The Archive and the Repertoire* (2003), Taylor centrally distinguishes between *hybridity* and *mestizaje*. This book examines the roles of performance and embodied memory across select cultural and political events, theater, and other activities from across the Americas, building valuable hemispheric and transnational perspectives on South and Central American mixed-culture exchanges and the transmission of cultural knowledge. Taylor notes that in this context, these two expressions for describing cultural mixing are "often used interchangeably" but are "not synonymous." These terms "tell us different things" about the "heterogeneous, multilayered" constructions of mixed-culture artifacts.[6] While each term implies both a fusion and juxtapositions of discrete cultural expressions, the concept of *mestizaje* in Chicanx, Latinx, and Mexican cultural studies has a complicated social and political history in its racial-discourse applications in Latin American and Latino cultural history. As

Taylor observes, "mestizaje (mestizagem) refers to a concept of biological and/or cultural fusion. As used in the Latin/o Americas, it has a history, it tells a history and it embodies a history," and "its root, from mixtus," predominantly references "the child of racially mixed parents."[7] For example, the Mexican (female) mestiza is "mapped by racialized and gendered practices of individual and collective identity"; through her racial and cultural "mix of indigenous and Spanish stock," the mestiza "simultaneously signal[s] gender, race, ethnic background, and the cultural positioning of liminality: European and indigenous, betwixt and between, central to Mexico's national identity yet politically marginalized."[8] In this racial discourse, the *fusion* is important both in the sense that mestizaje is thought to improve disparate borrowings, and specifically in that this fusion is an act of normalization, acculturation, and absorption, with a resultant homogeneity. There are thus troubling race and identity politics embodied in this term, with key acts of erasure, absorption, and homogenization of Blackness and indigeneity being central to many *mestizaje* narratives of racial mixing.

This tangent into distinctions between discrete conceptions of cultural mixing is useful for underscoring the social, racial, and cultural politics inherent in the sorts of performative cultural juxtapositions in much of the music discussed across this book. While a speculative (and decontextualized) comparison between Latin/o American *mestizaje* discourse and the Anglo/white American music discussed here is beyond the aims of this chapter, there is a suggestive resonance between this problematic conception of cultural hybridization and the erasure, absorption, and homogenization of Black and "Latin" musical inspirations in much of the stylistically hybrid, middle-of-the-road (MOR) and easy-listening luxe-pop progeny of symphonic jazz across the 1920s through 1970s. For example, the white erasures, absorptions, and homogenizations of Blackness within Whitemanesque aesthetics and performance practice are certainly entwined with the glamour and sophistication discourses explored here. And in a manner similar to the mestizaje narratives of Latin/o cultural fusion, criticism has viewed these 1920s glorified American popular music ideals as having led to luxe-leaning pop idioms built from homogeneously bland cultural mixings—merging white mainstream pop ideals and idioms with evocations of Black jazz, soul, R&B, and disco, or various "Latin" idioms—for white mainstream consumption. (Latin-flavored, mixed-culture mainstream pop, for example, includes the luxe pop of Xavier Cugat in the 1940s and the "exotica" mood music of Les Baxter or Yma Sumac in the 1950s, as well as the Tijuana Brass in the 1960s.) That said, much of this later MOR pop heritage lost the 1920s cultural tensions that were inherent to appreciating and *hearing* Whiteman's music. The period's variety entertainments foregrounded and relished the cultural collisions of the sort that were polished away, smoothed down, and overlooked in later MOR, music that rarely inspired the sorts of debate and elevated cultural attributes ascribed to symphonic jazz of the 1920s and 1930s.

Despite the aspirational implications embedded in symphonic jazz's elevated textural topics, post-1930 jazz criticism viewed this arranging idiom as a bastard, commercial dilution of jazz. In 1938, for instance, Winthrop Sargeant described this idiom as "lush movie-house spotlight jazz" designed "to astound musical yokels" with "gilded orchestral effects." He felt this hybrid sound was "the very essence of musical vulgarity" and it "achieved the perfect fusion of the pretentious and commonplace that defines bad taste."[9] In sum, such hybrid collisions of high and low recall the era's Hollywood film-musical gold digger cliché where blue-blooded old fogeys go slumming with red-blooded, young chorus girls for a little lowbrow entertainment. This plot cliché is realized, for example, in the 1933 film musical *42nd Street* (Warner Bros.), which was arranged by Ray Heindorf, former protégé of Arthur Lange, a key architect of symphonic jazz arranging. The symphonic jazz sound is readily heard in the movie's main title cue, which uses the song "42nd Street" as its first theme. After a concert-style, brass-heavy opening fanfare, the instrumental cue segues into the high-low juxtaposed swooning strings and blaring, jazzy brass and reeds of the title song's opening chorus. The (unsung) lyric of this tune beautifully articulates the cultural juxtapositions of symphonic jazz: "Little nifties from the Fifties innocent and sweet. Sexy ladies from the Eighties who are indiscreet. They're side by side, they're glorified, where the underworld can meet the elite—naughty, bawdy, gaudy, sporty Forty-Second Street." These place- and space-centered interminglings of elite culture and lowlife crime, of respectable ladies and prostitutes, and so on, all imply a glorified greater whole that bubbles forth from the vibrant cultural collisions of urban life in glamorous New York City. In sum, hybrid conceptions of class, place, identity, and collisions of social power are richly entwined in both film narrative (e.g., these collisions are acted out in the narrative of the "42nd Street" production number) and the luxe-pop scoring of the music.

As I have noted elsewhere, the attributes that post-1930 jazz critics considered essential to the tradition of what was called "hot" jazz (which emphasized

African American musical aesthetics, improvisation, the blues, swing, etc.) were not nearly as commonplace or prominently featured in this music until the later 1920s.[10] Across the 1920s and 1930s, such hot music—as played by Black or white performers—was viewed by its proponents to be in stylistic opposition to both "sweet" jazz and syncopated dance-band, theater, hotel, and radio orchestra music, as well as the jazzy, syncopated popular songs of Tin Pan Alley. Despite this widely circulated hot-versus-sweet jazz essentialization, in practice, popular culture of this era regularly encouraged variety-entertainment stylistic confluences, and the dance music business was one such arena for stylistic miscegenation (with cross-racial implications being central to the music as well). Thus, for example, many of the so-called sweet ensembles—including Whiteman's orchestra—regularly employed hot soloists, and many of the large orchestras, hot or sweet, included a wide diversity of styles in their performing repertories, as did the era's nightclub floorshow revues and theater entertainments. This variety-entertainment musical culture was the most troubling concern for post-1930 jazz critics—including Sargeant and figures like Roger Pryor Dodge, Hughes Panassié, Frederic Ramsey Jr., and Charles Edward Smith, among others—who felt that 1920s journalism was far too inclusive about what actually constituted jazz and which elements in this novel music contributed to its infectious vitality.

Symphonic jazz dance band arranging, both in terms of its formal models and instrumentation, grew out of several intersecting variety-entertainment traditions that coalesced in the melting pot of 1920s New York. These practices included sweet-style dance orchestras; Tin Pan Alley commercial arranging; and the musical traditions of vaudeville, novelty ragtime, and the production numbers of film prologue entertainments and Broadway musicals and revues. There are prestige hierarchies within these idioms, and symphonic jazz aspired to the high-class cultural prestige of Broadway, which in fact subsumed the idiom as a characteristic sound for its own jazzy entertainments. I suggest that there is an overriding ethos that binds the music of these traditions together, and it relates to what the film scholar Henry Jenkins has termed "the vaudeville aesthetic."

Jenkins examines the relation between Hollywood's so-called anarchistic comedies of the early 1930s (e.g., films of the Marx Brothers), and the roots of this tradition in American vaudeville.[11] Jenkins's study concerns both comedy traditions and the negotiations that occurred in early sound films between New York's ethnic-based entertainment, and Hollywood's target audience of the American masses beyond urban centers. While Jenkins acknowledges the presence of musical numbers in his film subjects, he makes no effort to examine the role of music in these entertainments, even while holding up *King of Jazz* as his exemplary model of the transitional film musical revue.

Jenkins's "vaudeville aesthetic" provides a model of the precepts governing 1920s variety entertainments:

> the underlying logic of the variety show rested on the assumption that heterogeneous entertainment was essential to attract and satisfy a mass audience. . . . The vaudeville program was constructed from modular units of diverse material, no more than twenty minutes in length each. These individual acts were juxtaposed together with an eye toward . . . the highest possible degree of novelty and variety rather than toward the logical relationship between . . . components. . . . The program . . . offered no consistent message. . . . What vaudeville communicated was *the pleasure of infinite diversity in infinite combinations.*[12]

This latter italicized credo was manifest on large and small scales in an evening's entertainment, and within individual acts. Symphonic jazz arranging closely followed this ethos. With Whiteman, for example, the vaudeville aesthetic operates both on the smaller scales of compressed diversity within symphonic-jazz popular-music arrangements and the orchestra's diverse repertory recorded in the 1920s, and on larger scales like performance programming, as in his "Experiment in Modern Music" concert series, which—especially in the 1920s—was organized via a variety-entertainment diversity template.[13]

In the institutionalization of vaudeville entertainment, as Jenkins notes, "formulas for constructing and arranging acts originated and were refined." Ultimately, "every conceivable form of mass entertainment assumed a precise position upon the variety bill."[14] Vaudeville's goal was to create intimate appeal to a broad audience. Entertainments were built on the era's underlying cultural tensions of societal change, particularly via melting-pot ethnic humor, the collapse of the older generation's barriers between respectability and the risqué, the weakening divide between high and low cultures, and the public's increasing interest in classy, sophisticated entertainment. Jenkins observes that the time pressures of the vaudeville stage ultimately shaped how individual acts were designed:

> Moments in [a] performance were more or less fixed and inflexible. The introduction needed to quickly establish the characters . . . situation or . . . theme from which the variations would be derived. The act sought to build toward a "Wow Finish" that would top all preceding gags and end on . . . peak

emotional intensity. Closure was of little importance . . . but climax was . . . [since it assured] the audience's [enthusiastic] final response. . . . Other elements could be added, subtracted or rearranged . . . , having little to do with the act's overall structure or logical development.[15]

This model accords closely with the three- to five-minute, variety-based arranging routines of symphonic jazz. Such arrangements similarly relied upon episodic construction via which "elements could be added, subtracted or rearranged" with little concern for "overall structure or logical development," and building in ever-shifting scoring variations toward a "wow finish." Despite the music's veneer of sophistication and class—early symphonic-jazz arrangements were even hyped as being "almost in symphonic form"[16]—this arranging tradition depended on its ties to both vaudeville's and Tin Pan Alley's multifarious song genres. The commercial appeal of the latter was their foundations in broad familiarity and generic entertainment categories. While vaudeville circuit agencies pressured performers into producing genre acts that fit comfortably on a standardized bill, act competition encouraged performers to individualize performances within these genres, and to seek out novelties and "specialties" to add to their acts. According to Jenkins, variety theater became the "theater of the expert" because acts were "designed to focus attention upon the performer's [specialized] skills."[17] Such spectacle-oriented acts "appealed to a fascination with showmanship for its own sake," and "fed a desire to be impressed by the skill of the performer."[18] Jenkins adds that "the consummate entertainer" displayed the broadest range of specialties "within the shortest period of time."[19] Such aesthetics likewise defined areas of symphonic jazz.

Whiteman represented the epitome of such a spectacle-oriented, "consummate entertainer" among the 1920s dance bands, and this vaudevillian emphasis on virtuosic showmanship, diversity, and spectacle manifested itself in musical presentations, and the precepts of symphonic-jazz arranging—and especially this arranging model's emphasis on spectacle through artful symphonic stylizations and virtuosic instrumental display. While the connection between symphonic-jazz arranging and theatrical production numbers was certainly made explicit in *King of Jazz*, this was not merely a concoction of Hollywood producers. For instance, the revue setting of *King of Jazz* had been presaged by Whiteman's 1928 collaboration with Anderson in their coproduction of film prologue shows for the Paramount Publix theater chain. Film presentations at the deluxe movie palaces—for example,

Samuel "Roxy" Rothafel's Roxy Theater or Radio City Music Hall in New York, or Sid Grauman's Chinese and Egyptian theaters in Hollywood—were preceded by live stage revues with orchestral backing and performances. For one Whiteman engagement, the promoters touted: "The Paramount Theatre is going to top any previous . . . popular entertainment. Not only is Paul Whiteman . . . with his full orchestra, but . . . the whole act will be surrounded by a stage show that is the last word in Broadway entertainment. Special costumes, scenic designs, special talent, special songs, chorus girls, and all the accompanying elements that go to make up a big Broadway revue will find a place on the Whiteman program."[20] The classy revues of this engagement included comedy and "eccentric" dancing teams, a tenor singing sentimental ballads, tango dancers, and a military march–themed production number with chorus girls as soldiers. These acts were all underscored by Whiteman. The band's solo performances included specialty instrumental numbers, accompanied vocal solos and trios, concert works, and medleys. In the prologue *Rainbow Rhapsody*, there was the extended medley, *Shades of Blues*, which was based on "a potpourri of indigo-titled themes including the *Blue Danube Waltz*, a snatch of the *Rhapsody in Blue*, the *Waltz Bluette* with violin quintet interludes, *Wabash Blues*, *Alice Blue Gown* (saxophone septet arrangement) . . . [and] *St. Louis Blues* climaxed by Mike Pingitore at the banjo." It was suggested that this "unique" prologue was "worthy of becoming a Whiteman trademark."[21]

The stylistic diversity in the Whiteman Publix engagements suggests that ear-catching scoring effects played a large role in the effectiveness of the band in a revue setting. Here, characteristic scoring is equivalent to the ethnic- and class-based topical humor of vaudeville and musical revue melting-pot entertainments. Entertainment interest in ethnic and class stereotypes was part of a commercial culture that had emerged in the first decades of the century. This culture extended to a national interest in New York's symbolic role as the quintessential, modern-American, urban melting pot. Gavin Jones builds his research on vaudeville dialect humor out of an examination of the national interest in "New Yorkese," as this colorful dialect was termed. Jones illustrates that New Yorkese was a thoroughly modern, hybrid urban dialect.[22] This mongrel dialect represented the future of American language under the melting-pot ethos. For some, this was a horrifying disfigurement of the sacred English language. For others, it represented American cultural vitality.

In 1920s US popular-music journalism, a similarly horrifying melting-pot disfigurement of proper language—the language of music—was regularly blamed on "jazz" acts like the Original Dixieland Jazz Band (ODJB). By contrast, Whiteman's refinement of this melting-pot music was celebrated as the musical counterpart to American linguistic vitality. This journalism was thoroughly fascinated with Whiteman's entertaining mix of vernacular wit, cultural irreverence, mild vulgarity, suave urbanity, and sophistication. Such attributes were manifest through the playful manipulation of the "synthetic" and conventional cultural markers of the characteristic scoring effects of symphonic jazz. Like vaudeville, the Whiteman formula's greatest commercial achievement was its ability to bridge urban entertainment styles and the consumer interests of the masses beyond urban America. This formula's basis in familiar scoring effects and its veneer of respectable sophistication (without too many overtures to highbrowism), made jazz-like music respectable to an otherwise wary mass audience.

Regarding vaudeville's conventionalized social representations, Jenkins observes that "characters and situations needed to be immediately recognizable" through an "elaborate system of typage" with "exaggerated costumes, facial characteristics, phrases, and accents [that] were meant to reflect . . . traits viewed as emblematic of a particular class, region, ethnic group, or gender."[23] Retrospectively, the most problematic part of this entertainment was the continued presence of minstrelsy-derived blackface. By the 1920s though, this Black stereotype was merely one ethnic caricature among a repertory of stock characters that included Jews, the Irish, the "Dutch" (i.e., Germans), the Chinese, Italians, New England Yankees, and so on. Jenkins further observes the widespread practice of the layering and playful manipulation of these stock caricatures.[24] The vaudevillian aesthetic of affective immediacy gave audiences rapid, intense, and diverse stimulation through this elaborate system of typage. Similarly, Whiteman, Grofé, and other arrangers and orchestras employed symphonic-jazz conventions in a transparent, layered manner based on a 1920s "jazz" sensibility—meaning enlivening the music or making it exciting—that delighted in playful cultural mongrelization.

The post-1930 anti-Whiteman bias of jazz critics had critical roots in the 1920s. For instance, in his 1924 review of Whiteman's first "Experiment in Modern Music," the New York Times music critic Olin Downes criticized Rhapsody in Blue for its "technical immaturity" and Gershwin's naive "attempt to rhapsodize in the manner of Franz Liszt."[25] By contrast, in reviewing the 1928 "Third Experiment" concert, Downes nostalgically claimed that his first "Experiment" concert had charmed its audiences to "rejoice in [the] racy patois" of Whiteman's "jazz" through his music's "humor" and "fine disregard of the musical respectabilities."[26] Downes had also come to believe that the earlier praise of Whiteman and Gershwin's efforts at Aeolian Hall had "been instrumental in an ominous decline in the quality" of Whiteman-style "jazz." For Downes, Whiteman and his imitators had come to see themselves as overly "important and self-conscious," and had "begun to put on outrageous airs." Downes's concert review was especially damning of Grofé's concert work, *Metropolis*, which he derisively characterized as "high-hat jazz" and a work "out of its own element, endeavoring to emulate the ways of its betters, to talk portentously of deep and grave things." Despite the reported "stormy applause," Downes argued that "the concert of last night was not important . . . for its music."[27] Instead, the music was of

> trivial quality . . . [and] an exhibition of the remarkable virtuosity and precision in [the] ensemble of his players. They can do almost anything with their instruments . . . a thing no doubt good for *musical vaudeville*, but not . . . significan[t] as music. It is not that we abjure . . . good American popular music; but . . . [this] was *mannered, uninspired, and sophisticated* [in a negative sense]. The first title on Mr. Whiteman's list was "Yes, Jazz Is Savage." *Our objection is that it was not "savage" at all!* . . . It merely wore clothes more pretentiously cut than ever before, and tried to use long words, with [a] learned accent.[28]

Here, from his perspective as a cultural defender of classical music, Downes foreshadows many of the anti-Whiteman themes of post-1930 jazz criticism.

THE SYMPHONIC JAZZ AGE IN CONTEXT

Symphonic jazz was a product of the 1920s, a period nostalgically remembered as "The Jazz Age," after F. Scott Fitzgerald's colorful characterization. This epithet is a misnomer, though, because the dominant syncopated musics of this era owed much more to symphonic jazz than they did to the Black, "hot" jazz tradition of improvisation, a tradition that was explained as the "jazz problem"—to invoke an oft-cited 1924 *Etude* magazine issue.[29] The hermeneutics of the 1920s have significantly affected many post-1930 critical accounts of this music up until more-recent reassessments of Whiteman. While this chapter will not revisit such jazz historiography, some understanding is necessary to frame the reception of symphonic jazz. My interest in this anti-Whiteman jazz criticism concerns the cultural associations and brow discourse this reception implied rather than building up straw men for arguments about the jazz canon. Central here is Whiteman's role in mainstream pop, and this criticism illustrates—for positive purposes—the cultural impact of symphonic jazz in popular culture. The aforementioned criticism of Sargeant, especially his 1938 book, *Jazz: Hot and Hybrid*, is representative of this anti-Whiteman discourse, and he was notably also central to midcentury anti-middlebrow discourse, which is relevant to this larger study of luxe pop.[30]

Sargeant's aforementioned diatribe condemned this music as garishly theatrical and commercial, and he further compared this idiom to the architecture of its so-called native environment, the gaudy 1920s movie palace theaters. Sargeant primarily focuses on three signal exponents of these trends: Whiteman, Grofé, and the commercial arranger Arthur Lange.[31] Again, despite Sargeant's vilification, such commentary is astute in relation to this music's cultural associations. In a Venn diagram of American 1920s popular culture, the sphere of symphonic jazz influence extends well beyond overlaps with jazz even as Whiteman and his peers employed and featured musicians from this tradition. But again, jazz was merely one element in the variety-entertainment portfolio of symphonic jazz.

The gilded, pretentious luxe-pop traits that Sargeant and his peers disparaged were in fact celebrated 1920s mainstream entertainment aesthetics. Symphonic jazz arranging endowed popular music of the day with an aura of glamour, elevated refinement, sophistication, and "class." According to the social politics of the era, and to use period-appropriate phrasing, this "glorification" of popular music had to occur under a sophisticated stylistic and formal veneer that emulated the symphonic tradition. Whiteman and Grofé had many sweet/symphonic-style orchestra peers. These outfits included the ensembles of Art Hickman, Isham Jones, Roger Wolfe Kahn, Vincent Lopez, Leo Reisman, and Ben Selvin, for example, alongside various European orchestras. The major recording labels likewise had their own in-house orchestras—such as Nathaniel Shilkret and his Victor Orchestra and Louis Katzman and the Brunswick Orchestra—that rivaled the size, musicianship, and repertories of the Whiteman orchestra.

The symphonic-jazz arranging and concert work idioms were also popular in the entertainments of the large orchestras of vaudeville, Broadway, and film-prologue revues of the deluxe movie palaces. Each of these venues additionally featured many of the aforementioned orchestras onstage in elaborate production numbers and as guest replacements for a house pit orchestra. The symphonic jazz idiom and orchestra model also played important roles in the new media of radio and sound film. Early radio programming included such popular, Whiteman-styled ensembles as Willard Robison and the Deep River Orchestra and B. A. Rolfe and the Lucky Strike Dance Orchestra. Further, commercial arrangers central to the symphonic jazz vogue were recruited to found the music departments of both radio and film companies, and the arranging idiom formed a backbone for the popular music in these media. This larger milieu defines the concept of "Whitemanesque" musical entertainment. That said, the contextual development of the Whiteman orchestra and its aesthetics is illustrative of symphonic jazz ideals as a whole, as well as the accuracy of Sargeant's characterizations of this music.

In late 1919, Whiteman formed a nine-man orchestra for the Alexandria Hotel in Los Angeles. This foundational orchestra included such long-standing Whiteman musicians as trumpeter Henry Busse, banjoist Mike Pingitore, and, shortly after formation, Grofé. In early 1920, the band relocated to the East Coast with financial help from a film director who had encouraged them to audition with Ziegfeld for a Broadway show. It was three years before they appeared in a Ziegfeld revue. The band's first extended East Coast engagement was at Atlantic City's Ambassador Hotel. In spring 1920, the band signed with Victor Records, and in August they recorded the band's most popular dance numbers, "Avalon," "Japanese Sandman," and "Whispering."[32] "Whispering" sold 2.5 million records, a figure seen as the turning point when recordings began to outsell sheet music.[33] This sudden fame led to a long-term engagement at New York's Palais Royale, a high-profile Broadway dinner and dancing club.

The band grew in size across the 1920s. The L.A. ensemble included Whiteman on violin, Grofé as pianist/arranger, one trumpet, one trombone, two doubling reed players (on clarinet/alto sax and soprano sax/alto sax/flute), banjo, tuba, and drums. By August 1921, the band had twelve musicians, including a second trumpet, a third sax, and another violinist. After the 1924 Aeolian Hall concert, Whiteman's recording and dance orchestra grew to fourteen or fifteen musicians with two trumpets, two trombones, three to four reeds, two violins, two pianists, banjo, tuba, and drums.

By the mid- to late 1920s, Whiteman had a unique collection of musicians who were renowned for virtuosity and versatility in doublings, including a violinist-accordionist, brass doublings (between trumpet, flugelhorn, and euphonium), and four reed players who doubled on an arsenal of instruments. The most famous sideman was Ross Gorman, who performed on up to fourteen instruments, sometimes even in one specialty number. Whiteman also added the virtuoso violinist and trombonist, Wilbur Hall, a performer famous for a vaudeville novelty act that included "The Stars and Stripes Forever" and "Pop Goes the Weasel" on a wheezing bicycle pump. In 1926, the critic Henry Osgood marveled at Hall's use of comic trombone mutes (e.g., a lamp shade), but also his "double-tonguing, triple-tonguing and false positions," and his capacity to "manipulat[e] the slide with a speed that seems physically impossible."[34] Hall's routines were integral to Whiteman's concert and vaudeville performances.

Whiteman's orchestra was one of the highest-paid acts in variety entertainment. The orchestra starred on Broadway in *George White's Scandals of 1922*, in the *Ziegfeld Follies of 1923*, in Ziegfeld's 1928 hit *Whoopee!*, in prologue entertainment revues of the Roxy and the Paramount movie theaters, and in variety spectacles at the New York Hippodrome. Beginning as early as 1921, the band also regularly performed extended engagements at the premiere venue for high-class vaudeville, New York's Palace Theatre. Following the Aeolian Hall appearance, Whiteman also regularly engaged in concert work, including his 1925 and 1928 "Experiment in Modern Music" concerts, and the band's three "Transcontinental Concert Tours" (in 1924–25, 1925–26, and 1928–29).[35] On these tours, Whiteman traveled with his "Greater Concert Orchestra," an ensemble of twenty-five to twenty-seven performers that expanded his band through additions of a small string section, three French horns, and even a cimbalom player. On recordings, it was further enlarged (primarily through additional strings). Lastly, in early 1928, Whiteman also entered radio when his band was a featured musical ensemble for the landmark, coast-to-coast broadcasts of the NBC "Dodge Victory Hour." From February 1929, Whiteman's orchestra starred in their own weekly CBS variety program, the "Old Gold Paul Whiteman Hour."[36]

Whiteman's most protracted efforts to bridge the hot- and symphonic-jazz idioms were in the mid- to late 1920s. From 1924, when Black bandleader Fletcher Henderson brought the young Louis Armstrong to New York to augment his orchestra with a star hot soloist, white and Black orchestral dance bands began to incorporate hot-jazz stylizations and, in some cases, improvisation. The most successful dance orchestras, however, still closely adhered to the revue-derived ideal of stylistic versatility and variety. Hot-jazz instrumentalists were thus initially another stylistic ingredient among many in dance-band repertories. From 1926, Whiteman also employed Black arrangers, including Henderson's chief arranger, Don Redman, and William Grant Still (1929). And from fall 1927, Whiteman augmented his orchestra with top white jazz instrumentalists, including Jimmy and Tommy Dorsey, Frank Trumbauer, Joe Venuti, Eddie Lang, trumpeter Bix Beiderbecke (Whiteman's answer to Henderson's hiring of Armstrong), and others. The orchestra thus offered a potpourri of musicians, from "formally trained" musicians to hot specialists to Tin Pan Alley composer/arranger/ pianists (Grofé, Roy Bargy, and Hoagy Carmichael, etc.) to Broadway theater musicians to instrumentalists from vaudeville and variety theater. The entourage was further diversified through a stable of crooner vocalists, including the young Bing Crosby. For post-1930 jazz critics, it was this "commercial" variety-entertainment model that degraded the art of "non-commercial" jazz.

As I have discussed elsewhere, symphonic jazz further reflected the era's discourses on race and gender.[37] The gendered discourse on the idiom's reception are rich, as can be observed in period statements claiming that Whiteman and Gershwin sought "to make a lady of jazz." The roots of this phrase lie in Walter Damrosch's introduction to the 1925 premiere of Gershwin's Concerto in F, where the conductor spoke of "Lady Jazz," Gershwin as a "knight" who enabled her to be received as a respectable member in musical circles . . . by dressing this . . . up-to-date young lady in the classic garb of a concerto." Henry Osgood's 1926 book *So This Is Jazz* widely disseminated the connection of this phrase with Whiteman's symphonic jazz.[38] The book further suggests that "the New York Historical Society . . . [should] erect a significant tablet" at the Palais Royal where "Whiteman first conceived the idea of making an honest woman out of Jazz."[39]

The gendered politics of "making a lady of jazz" embodied a wealth of cross-cultural transgressions, evoking metaphorical transformations from a red-light prostitute to a blue-blood socialite; from lowbrow to highbrow; from ragged, impoverished street clothes to *haute couture*; from provincial to cosmopolitan; from obscurity to international renown. Recall again the high-low collisions invoked in the lyric to "42nd Street." These sustained tensions are at the heart of symphonic jazz and were repeatedly invoked in the entertainments it was employed in. The arranging- and instrumentation-based notion of "dressing" jazz and jazz-like music is central here. In the pre-Whiteman late teens, "jazz" meant raucous, early improvised white jazz modeled after the Original Dixieland Jazz Band. This is what was elevated in "classic garb." This does not mean that jazz *had become* classical music, nor that Whiteman was trying to position jazz-like music *as* classical music (though such rhetoric was in his concert promotion strategies), nor that he sought to appropriate formal models from highbrow music. While these transgressive metaphors imply a one-way elevation from low to high across brow hierarchies, mongrelization, stylistic heterogeneity, and glorification are far more accurate descriptions of the resultant amalgam.

Several prominent dance-orchestra leaders—most notably Whiteman, Jones, and Lopez—were reticent to identify their highly arranged syncopated music as "jazz" because of this term's ongoing attachment to the hokum and rough improvisation (colloquially called "faking") associated with white, ODJB-inspired small-group jazz. Jones asked that his music be called "American Dance Music."[40] While in 1925 Whiteman proclaimed that his concert orchestra was "not a jazz band" but a "Modern American Orchestra," he conceded that he did "not object to the term 'jazz' if it help[ed] to popularize what I am doing."[41] In his 1926 book *Jazz*, Whiteman describes his music simply as "modern American music" (he apparently preferred this description, despite the book's title).[42] This observation is notable because while "symphonic jazz" was in public circulation, it appears nowhere in Whiteman's book or the earlier promotional literature of the Whiteman camp.

Whiteman-style dance band arranging was one of several intersecting American entertainment traditions of the (Symphonic) Jazz Age. These included: (1) "sweet"-styled orchestral dance music; (2) Tin Pan Alley commercial arranging for vaudeville, hotel, theater, film house, and dance and recording orchestras; (3) contemporary "novelty" ragtime in both piano and orchestral settings; and (4) the jazz-styled production numbers of live film prologue entertainments and Broadway musical theater. One name ties all these activities together: Arthur Lange. Though not well-known to the public, Lange's reputation was enormous in the popular music industry, and he was a pivotal figure in the transition from Tin Pan Alley and Broadway to early Hollywood sound films, working as a commercial arranger, composer, conductor, and pianist from 1906.[43] It was not until 1917, however, with his arrangement of the "instrumental novelty" "Dardanella: An Echo from the East" (by Felix Bernard and Ben Black) that he arrived at the forefront of Tin Pan Alley arranging.[44] The catalyst for this success was the 1919 hit recording of this arrangement by Ben Selvin's orchestra. Selvin's "Dardanella" was the most successful dance band recording prior to Whiteman's 1920 hits with "Whispering" and "Japanese Sandman."[45]

To capitalize on the immense popularity of the social dancing craze of the early teens, Tin Pan Alley was publishing rudimentary arrangements of popular tunes by the mid- to late teens. These ragtime-era "stock" arrangements provided only a simple scoring routine based on a two- to four-measure introduction and one statement each of a song's verse and chorus. In pre-"Dardanella" performance practice, dance orchestras played the choruses of these "arrangements" as many times as needed, without contrast. For Lange, the importance of his "Dardanella" arrangement was both its relative musical sophistication and that it was the first commercial dance-band chart not derived from a song arrangement.[46]

In conceiving "Dardanella" as an "instrumental novelty" for dance orchestra, Lange took creative license to jettison key orchestration conventions of the day. As a dance number, this arrangement was unusual in its flowing, arpeggiated, ostinato bass rather than an oom-pah-style accompaniment; its exotic, Eastern-styled, characteristic scoring effects; and its sweet-styled, subdued tone. These generically innovative elements derived from salon and theater orchestra traditions, but this approach was new to the dance-band business. The work's more elaborate three-strain form and its use of modulation were likewise not typical for dance orchestrations of the late teens. In light of this stock orchestration's tremendous market success with audiences and other orchestras from coast to coast, the dance-band industry and publishers quickly learned that there was a vital market for sophisticated arrangements that borrowed from other popular orchestral traditions of the day. Thus, this novelty was a foundational predecessor for Whitemanesque symphonic jazz.

In the early- to mid-1920s, Lange provided arrangements for most of the major Tin Pan Alley publishers, was an active arranger and conductor for Broadway shows, and provided special arrangements for Whiteman's competitors, particularly the Lopez band. From 1922 to 1924, Lange also led a popular dance orchestra under his name. From 1924, his ensemble continued under Roger Wolfe Kahn (son of the financier, Otto Kahn). This incarnation became a central competitor to Whiteman (with Lange as director).

The mid- to late-1920s were a busy period for Lange's symphonic jazz-style arranging. In 1924, Lange founded Arthur Lange, Inc., a venture that published his arrangements and provided contracted arrangements for orchestras, Broadway productions, Tin Pan Alley firms, and movie houses. In a 1925 *Billboard* article on dance band arrangers (which includes one of the first printed instances of the term "symphonic jazz"), Lange was proclaimed "king of 'em all."[47] In 1926, Lange, Inc. published his influential book, *Arranging for the Modern Dance Orchestra*, a text that was the primary manual for symphonic jazz arranging.[48] In the late 1920s, Lange's career involved arranging and conducting for shows on Broadway and film prologues at New

York's Capitol Theatre, as well as arrangements for national radio programs, including the *Lucky Strike Dance Hour*, a landmark program hosted by the Whiteman-inspired orchestra of B. A. Rolfe. In February 1929, Lange joined the great Broadway migration out West after he was recruited to head MGM's music department at the dawn of the sound film era. Lange's career thus spanned dance bands, Tin Pan Alley, Broadway, film prologues, radio, and Hollywood film—in sum, the breadth of symphonic jazz in popular culture, thereby reinforcing Sargeant's characterizations of the territory of this idiom. An examination of the Grofé-Lange arranging idiom thus provides an umbrella understanding of symphonic jazz as a whole and its role as a foundation for twentieth-century luxe pop.

THE ANATOMY OF (SYMPHONIC) JAZZ

In *Jazz*, Whiteman provides only a short characterization of the arranging conventions he and Grofé had developed for the orchestra: "[Our approach to] orchestration is that after the tune is set the instrumentation shall be changed for each half chorus. In between, the keys are shifted, with a four to eight bar interlude to get into the new key. The new demand is for change and novelty . . . [and] there must be at least two rhythmic ideas and sometimes more."[49] Whiteman cautions, however, that it was important "to avoid overcrowding the material, for the melody must not be lost." He further emphasizes building "change and novelty" through ever-shifting stylistic diversity.

Lange expounded in greater detail. His manual is devoted to explicating the task of a dance-orchestra arranger: the scoring of three- to four-minute instrumental arrangements of popular songs. Nevertheless, Lange additionally discusses arranging for "concert situations"; that is, arranging for concert jazz, theater, or movie palace orchestras, contexts that allowed for "greater rhythmic complexity, tempo variation, and the use of non-dance oriented" scoring effects.[50]

Lange describes a Modern Dance Orchestra comprised of "violin[s], saxophones, trumpets, trombones, banjo, bass, piano and drums."[51] Like Whiteman, Lange emphasizes the importance of complementing this basic ensemble through auxiliary instrumental doublings.[52] The reed, brass, and rhythm sectional divisions comprise the foundation for commercial stock arrangements; the other parts—including strings—were optional. While Lange does not elaborate on the era's more exotic doubling practices, he does stress that a well-stocked percussion battery includes a Chinese gong, bells, chimes, vibraphone, xylophone, marimba, tympani, and special effects (e.g., slapstick, cow moo, dog bark, duck quack, etc.). He likewise emphasizes the color resources of a range of brass mutes.

Lange stresses the function of the rhythm section to act as a rhythmic background for the ensemble scoring effects. This unit's function is to impose the "tempos" (characteristic rhythmic textures) of "all types of American Dance Music," such as fox trots, Charlestons, hot dance music, blues, waltzes, and so on.[53] Lange purposefully avoids the term "jazz" and refers instead to the "hot style," which, to him, was but one category of "rhythmic" American dance music. Symphonic jazz was based on the juxtaposition of continually varied scoring effects against such underlying rhythmic backgrounds. Both Jones and Lange emphasized the importance of an arrangement's appeal to the feet, regardless of its appeal to the head (i.e., an arrangement's artfulness).

Lange places great emphasis on instrumental scoring effects. Each effect involves distinct features of melody and accompaniment, a certain palate and distribution of tone colors, and specific textures of counterpoint and harmony. Lange addresses three basic categories: (1) common rhythmic dance band textures, (2) "trick effects." and (3) "effect ensembles." Any given arrangement will likely involve combinations of all three of these categories as well as straightforward, first-chorus rhythmic scoring that emphasizes both the melody and the characteristic traits of the song's genre. Direct evocations of hot jazz are generally avoided until a later chorus.

While trick effects refers to non-standard instrumental effects that take liberties with melodic and harmonic material, effects refers to textures that suggest recognizable aural phenomena or styles. The most important effect topic is "characteristic effects," a subject that is especially helpful for understanding the cultural dynamics of this tradition. Characteristic effects reference ethnic and nationalistic musical styles. The most "useful" effects are said to be evocations of "Oriental, Irish or Scotch, [American] Indian, Chinese, Italian, Russian, [and] Jewish" music.[54] "Characteristic effects" also include aurally imitative effects, such as chime effects, arpeggio effects, and "rhythmic color" effects. Arrangements then were based on combinations of sweet and/or hot jazz and popular dance band styles with a variety of these effects. For large-scale design, Lange notes that an "arrangement consists of . . . composition . . . instrumental effect . . . [and] routines."[55] The term "routine" denotes an arrangement's ordering of popular-song sectional components (the verse, patter, and chorus strains), the repetitions of these elements, their combination with instrumental effects and modulation, and the use of an introduction, interludes, and/or a coda.

This manual was the first formal text on American popular music arranging, and it had an influence on dance-band and jazz arranging until at least the swing era. Outside of its lack of discussion concerning improvisation, for post-1930 jazz writers, the major problems with Lange's manual were his emphases on scoring effects, on the significance, frequency, and length of introductions, interludes, and codas; on the importance of auxiliary instruments (including strings); and on modulation, extended harmonies, and counterpoint. In sum, the book's central concerns epitomized the "variety," "complexity," and "elaborate recipes" that Sargeant had attacked. In fact, Sargeant derived his description directly from Lange's text.[56] Sargeant's disdain, though, relates to complaints he had with both the commercialism and products of Tin Pan Alley: "Popular music is mass-produced music, created, like bathtubs, automobiles or Grand Rapids furniture, to fill the needs of the average bourgeois American. . . . It is efficient, standardized, sometimes inspired, but usually lacking in individuality and artistic distinction. It usually gets its artistic coloring, like most Grand Rapids furniture, by nostalgically imitating various styles."[57] While not directly applied to symphonic jazz, this quote articulates the fundamentals of Sargeant's attack on Lange's "recipes," and resonates closely with Sargeant's later attacks on middlebrowism.

The significance of the Grofé-Lange arranging model is its relation to subsequent radio and film arrangers who saw this tradition as a cornerstone for their craft. For instance, in 1946, the radio arranger and composer Tom Bennett wrote,

> Without Grofé there would be no radio orchestra as we know it today. True, there would still be symphony orchestras heard on the radio . . . but that type of orchestra which is peculiarly indigenous to radio would not have been known without Grofé. In this category fall such orchestras . . . which play popular music in a concert manner rather than in a dance tempo. . . .
>
> The present radio orchestra is an outgrowth of Ferde Grofé's innovation[s] and . . . based on saxophones and . . . [the use of] strings for embellishment. . . . The radio orchestra plays popular and light pieces in a style that is neither dance nor concert music. It is created to make the sometimes banal and trite music of the day interesting to listen to rather than interesting to dance to.[58]

The connections to the Grofé-Lange model can be seen in Bennett's description of the standard interwar radio orchestra, which I noted in chapter 1. This is the same hybrid show-band orchestra that Whiteman developed and that Lange discusses at length in his book.

Bennett also comments on arranging for production numbers, which Lange calls "concert" arrangements, and Bennett calls "the big, spectacular arrangements" or "attention getter[s]"—"that piece on a program which makes the listener lay down his newspaper and give heed to the music." These types of arrangements "are usually of some length, running four or five minutes . . . and they are of varied treatment. . . . [They] present a tune, or several tunes, in a startling variety of treatments . . . designed to attract the attention of the listener.[59] The models for these practices are found in the Grofé-Lange tradition, but there are also close connections here to Broadway's, and later Hollywood's, musical production numbers.

While Grofé left little discussion of his approach to arranging, he, like Whiteman, stressed the effectiveness of custom arrangements "made to fit the talents of a special [and specific] group of men or instruments."[60] Whiteman's orchestra score manuscripts routinely display orchestrations based on individual performer talents, and such customized arrangements were standard in the top-flight orchestras with their own arranging staffs and stables of star musicians.

Paul Whiteman, "By the Waters of the Minnetonka" (1924)

Osgood's *So This Is Jazz!* articulates Grofé-Lange-style orchestration practices through a study of Grofé's 1924 arrangement of Thurlow Lieurance's 1915 "By the Waters of the Minnetonka: An Indian Love Call." Osgood provides an unprecedented, ten-page discussion of a popular dance orchestration. Evidence suggests that this derived directly from Grofé's manuscript. (He did not, however, listen closely to the recording in preparing his examples—he repeats details verbatim from the manuscript, where the recording reveals discreet deviations.) Osgood's "Minnetonka" book chapter first appeared in 1926 as an *American Mercury* article titled "The Anatomy of Jazz."[61]

The transition of "Minnetonka" from a light-classical piano piece of the 1910s to a dance orchestra hit of the 1920s illustrates a number of cultural points. Lieurance's "Minnetonka" represents an early-1900s fad for parlor music based on Native American–styled themes. "Minnetonka" was the most popular of these works, but models for this vogue are heard in compositions from Victor Herbert and Charles Wakefield Cadman. Osgood cites the latter composer as an authority on this faux-Indian style when pointing out the use of a characteristic "Scotch snap" figure in "Minnetonka," a detail "which . . . Cadman says is as indigenous to American Indian music as to Scotch."[62]

"Minnetonka" aspires to the same musical sphere as that occupied by Edward McDowell's "To a Wild Rose" (1896), another supposed classic that was a favorite object of jazzing in the 1920s. "Minnetonka" is built on an ABA design in a 16 + 8 + 16 measure form. Osgood rightly notes the work's "conventional, restricted harmonies" and its nature as a "simple, unpretentious tune."[63] The "tune" is characterized by its recurrent accompaniment pattern of thirty-second notes and by the Scotch-snap rhythmic figure (a sixteenth note plus a held note) of its melody. Both are shown in Example 2.1. While the thirty-second-note flourish is somewhat of a Lisztian art-music signifier, Lange's book presents a similar figure that he identifies as an "Indian flute call." The Scotch-snap figure further contributes to the Indian musical caricature, alongside a pentatonic melody, a drone bass, and simple tonic/dominant harmonies. These clichés are key to this work's popularity as a fox trot, and they further align this music with period ethnic-based, melting-pot entertainment forms. As the vaudeville scholar Robert Snyder notes, these two entertainment arenas were intimately intertwined: "Tin Pan Alley and vaudeville lived off each other: vaudevillians took songs from Tin Pan Alley, and Tin Pan Alley used vaudeville to boost song sheet sales."[64]

The manuscript to Grofé's orchestration includes the following handwritten, pre-compositional routine outline:[65]

Int.	6
Refrain	32
Mid. Strain	16
2nd Refr.	32
Interlude	8
3rd Refrain	32
4th Refr.	16
Interl.	8
4th Refr.	16
	166

This plan-of-work provides clues to Grofé's approach to arranging. Obviously, he sought to fit the timing constraints of a standard 78 rpm disc, as this attention to score length demonstrates. The routine is built via an introduction,

EX. 2.1. Accompaniment figuration for Thurlow Lieurance's "By the Waters of the Minnetonka: An Indian Love Call" (1915).

four choruses, and two interludes, and each strain (i.e., the melodic sections of a song) is scored for one or more changes in instrumentation and character. Modulation is used more sparingly than Lange advocates, though the arrangement's half-step modulation up in the second half (A2) of the fourth statement of strain A corresponds with Lange's final-chorus advice, where such a modulation of "one tone higher" for the last chorus is said to add "brilliancy."[66] Table 1A charts the final form of Grofé's arrangement.

Lieurance's score is reinterpreted as a cut-time fox trot in thirty-two-bar song form. The original A section is expanded first by doubling the note values of Lieurance's melody, and second by a lengthening of the sixteenth note of the Scotch snap. Grofé also interpreted the B section as a separate sixteen-bar strain. He seemingly approached this arrangement design through the model of a multi-strained, novelty piano piece.[67]

In the manuscript, Grofé's "Minnetonka" is scored for three reeds (flute, clarinet, and sopranino, soprano, and alto saxes), two trumpets, two trombones, two violins, two horns, banjo, piano/celeste, tuba, and percussion. On the recording, the band performs a reduced arrangement that excludes the horns and most of the percussion (likely due to the sensitivity of contemporary acoustic recording technology). Considering its inclusion of horns and a 1 June 1924 date, this score was likely intended for Whiteman's first "Transcontinental Tour" of 1924–25, though its initial function was material for a 10 June studio recording date.

The introduction and second interlude each include the Indian-styled scoring of a "tom-tom" drone set in parallel octaves on even quarter notes with a half-step grace note. Example 2.2 shows the Introduction. These episodes further include shrill, high-register violins and woodwind trios. This stereotyped Indian scoring also adds a melodic setting of *marcato* brass chords that

Measure	Time	Section	Key	Dyn.	Primary Melody	Accompaniment
1	0:00	Intro	A♭	ff	Trombone(s)	(1) Soprano sax trio + vlns on Indian motif; (2) Open brass. NO RHYTHM
7	0:07	Strain A, 1st	A♭	f	Sopr. sax trio + trpts on harmonized melody	(1) Trbns + banjo arp. figure; (2) Comping rhythm section
39	0:39	Strain B	A♭	mf	Violin duet (call)	(1) Celeste (response); (2) Comping rhythm section
55	0:54	Strain A, 2nd (part 1)	A♭	mf	Solo legato trbn	(1) 2 altos on arpeg. fig.; (2) Horn/trbn on pedal; (3) Comping rhythm section
71	1:09	Strain A, 2nd (part 2)	A♭	mf	Muted trpts (Harmon mutes?)	(1) Obbligato vln solo; (2) Comping rhythm section (1) Clars + muted trpts (resp.);
87	1:26	Interlude 1	seq.	ff	Open trbn + tuba (call)	(2) Celeste (cadence). NO RHYTHM
93	1:32	Strain A, 3rd	A♭	f	Alto trio on melody (call)	(1) Vlns (response); (2) Comping rhythm section
123	2:03	Strain A, 4th (part 1)	A♭	f	Muted brass, piano + tuba (call)	(1) Celeste. Stop-time. NO RHYTHM
141	2:20	Interlude 2 (Intro var.)	A♭	ff	(1) open trbn solo (2) Tutti on last mm.	(1) Clar. trio on Indian motif NO RHYTHM
149	2:28	Strain A, 4th (part 2)	A	ff	Open brass + vlns	(1) Clar. trio / new accomp. figure; (2) Comping rhythm section; (3) Temple block

emphasize simple tonic-to-dominant, parallel minor chord motion—basic motifs for the primitive, which when combined with the tom-tom drone motif, signify "American Indian" in the Broadway and Hollywood musical lexicon. Lange illustrates similar Indian-effect examples. Like Grofé, Lange relies upon soprano saxophones as a timbre for creating the texture he calls an "Indian yell." This effect similarly scores its melody in percussive, open brass, harmonized in parallel octaves and fourths, and underscored with an all-purpose, Indian-style drum cliché of a straight four-beat pulse on tom-tom with strong-beat accents of bass drum (and tuba).

In measures 4–6 of Grofé's Introduction (Example 2.2), the Indian effect adds "modern harmony" via ninth chords, a sus4 chord,[68] and the chromatic,

TABLE 1B Cumulative Harmonic Complexity
in Grofé's "Minnetonka" Arrangement

Measure	1	2	3	4	5	6	7	8
R1	Ab	Fm→Ab	1	2	1	2	1	2
R2	Ab	Fm→Ab	1	2	1	2	1	2
R3	Ab	Ab	Fm	Fm	Cm	Cm	Fm	Fm
R4	Ab→Fm	Fm	Cm	Fm	Bb9→Bb	Eb7	Ab→Fm	Fm→Ab

Measure	9	10	11	12	13	14	15	16
R1	Cm7→Gdim7	Gdim7→Eb7	9	10	1	1	1	2
R2	Eb7	Eb7	9	9	1	2	1	2
R3	Bb9	Bbdim	Eb7	Eb7	Ab	Fm→Ab	1	1
R4	Ab→Fm	Fm	Cm	Fm	F7	Bb	Cm→Eb7	Ab

"R" indicates each sixteen-bar refrain. The numbers in the chart indicate other measures within the refrain from which the harmonies of the later measures derive.

EX. 2.2. Introduction to Ferde Grofé's Minnetonka arrangement.

descending counterpoint of measures 4–5 (moving from the G♭9/D♭ sub-dominant, through a series of nonfunctional chords, to a dominant-ninth chord). Such Tin Pan Alley musical modernism is frequently employed in introductions and interludes. A similar "modern" novelty-ragtime-type passage can be seen in the sequential structure and whole-tone patterns of the first interlude.

The placement of the second interlude (starting 2:20) is unusual. Because the primary strain involves a sixteen-bar melody and its varied restatement, Grofé exploits this structure by inserting the interlude into the middle of the A strain. The interlude's placement creates a quickened episodic pacing between chorus statements. This effect is heightened by the modulation up (from A♭ major to A major) for the final sixteen bars. As the tom-tom motif shifts from an open-fifth dyad to tritones, an E7 harmony (a tritone away from the previous tonic harmony of A♭) suddenly appears and modulates the work into A major.

Grofé's arrangement closely reflects Lange's model of a regularly varied routine. Example 2.3 presents the first three measures of the first statement of strain A (0:07). Building upon the "primitive" brass of the Introduction, the primary theme is presented in a homophonic texture of widely voiced primary triads. The flourish is transformed into a virtuosic but comic, double-tongued trombone run (by Wilbur Hall) with banjo doubling—a setting that transforms a classical signifier through vaudevillian overtones. This texture is underscored with a banal "oom-pah," fox-trot accompaniment (piano and tuba). The new textures are likely meant as mildly mischievous juxtapositions of high and low music.

Strain B (0:39 ff.) appears only once. Because of its placement between the first and second statements of the primary strain, the composition's original ABA structure is retained within the routine. Strain B's function as melodic contrast between the first and second statements of strain A is heightened with a shift from the reed/brass/rhythm texture of the first strain, to the call and response of a violin duet and celeste in this strain.

The second strain A (starting 0:54) builds upon the B strain's sweet-styled orchestration, albeit via a contemporary saxophone scoring. The saxophone accompaniment takes over the arpeggiated figure and performs this passage in straight eighth notes. This sweet dance-band style is also felt in the open-bell, legato trombone solo on the primary theme, as well as a third textural shift (at part 2, from 1:09) to a muted-trumpet duet with a rhapsodic violin obbligato solo.

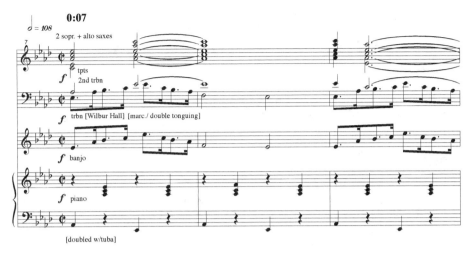

EX. 2.3. Excerpt from strain A1 of Ferde Grofé's "Minnetonka" arrangement.

For the third strain A (1:32 ff.), Grofé avoids a flashy "arranger's chorus" (as Lange termed it) and instead retains a sweet dance-band texture of a call and response (between the violins and celeste) and an alto sax trio. The arpeggiated accompaniment pattern is absent. Also, where the first and second strain A statements followed the simple harmonic framework of the original, the third and fourth strain A statements increasingly include third-relation substitutions and triad extensions of sevenths and ninths. The arrangement thus builds in harmonic complexity as it progresses to the final chorus (see Table 1B).

The fourth strain A (starting 2:03) is interrupted midway by the second interlude (starting 2:20). The first sixteen measures of the fourth strain A are set as a stop-time chorus constructed from a call and response between the brass and celeste. Following the modulation to A major, the final sixteen bars (2:28ff.) are set as a *fortissimo* passage with the main theme stated by two cornets and trombone. This variation adds a vibrant, two-measure rhythmic ostinato in the high registers of both the violins and a clarinet trio (Example 2.4). The ostinato is further articulated by a chromatic melodic motive set in the third clarinet and violins. This passage also introduces percussion through an ad lib temple block accompaniment and a final cymbal crash. In early 1920s Grofé-Lange arrangements, this final chorus is often set as a hot out-chorus, regardless of the characteristic style of an arrangement. This final hot chorus acted as a melting pot of whatever characteristic effects

EX. 2.4. Excerpt from strain A4 (part b) of Ferde Grofé's "Minnetonka" arrangement.

may have come previously. While this arrangement avoids hot-jazz polyphony here, it does set the jazz-derived textures of the rhythm section against a jazzy, biting clarinet trio, and a full-throated brass choir on the melody.

. . .

Sargeant and his jazz-proponent peers disparaged the "overloaded," "gilded" orchestral effects of symphonic jazz, hoping to carve out an elevated space for the music they valued, but such concerns mattered little to the audiences who bought this highly popular recording: jazz or not, this was the height of high-class popular music, and it did in fact pack its arrangements with gilded, exotic orchestral effects. The notion of applying characteristic effects to dance music likely emerged as an extension of the sideline work of many musician-arrangers providing descriptive music for silent film, vaudeville, and variety theater, each of which employed a widely circulated lexicon of descriptive musical effects. In particular, it is in the silent film era's catalogs of descriptive "moving picture music" that one finds direct parallels with many of the characteristic effects espoused by Lange.[69] Symphonic jazz figures with such backgrounds included Whiteman, Grofé, and Lange, and arrangers such as Domenico Savino and Nathaniel Shilkret. Conversely, from the mid-1920s through contributions from such top silent-film arranger-directors as Erno Rapée, Hugo Reisenfeld and J. S. Zamecnik, the major movie palace orchestras—many of which added saxophones and dance-band musicians—regularly performed elaborately scored popular tunes as part of their variety offerings.

GLORIFICATION AND GLAMOUR

Symphonic jazz proponents centrally aimed to "glorify" American popular music. The term glorify is employed here as a paraphrase of the slogan of the Ziegfeld Follies, the revue series that since 1922 had used "glorifying the American Girl" as its motto. In *Ziegfeld Girl: Image and Icon in Culture and Cinema*, Linda Mizejewski explores the symbolism and cultural phenomena of both the Ziegfeld Girl tradition and its stylistic progeny in film and media.[70] Mizejewski focuses on the discourses that surrounded the over-the-top Ziegfeldesque tradition of female pageantry and this tradition's reflection of consumerist desires. As an icon of (white) beauty, the Ziegfeld Girl functioned as a cross between a fashion model and a showgirl. The chief purpose of the Ziegfeld Girl was her entertainment role as both a treasured object and as untouchable art—that is, an embodiment of inaccessible "glamour." As Mizejewski explains, entertainment glamour involves the "public visibility of a desirable object . . . and its resulting value as class marker or commodity."[71] Ziegfeld's extravagant revues represented the epitome of contemporary style and fashion. Although the prized Ziegfeld Girls provided visual background or chorus support for other acts, as Mizejewski notes, these women "were the raison d'être and centerpieces of the [revue's central] grand parade and tableau productions," and for many, "the variety acts were simply fillers between the Girl parades."[72] Mizejewski observes that as the "glorification" rhetoric developed, the revue structure came to suggest an ideology as well as a style. Thus, in the variety context of the revues, Jewish, African American, and other ethnic-based comedy (including blackface) in effect "functioned as the 'contrast' to the Glorified American Girl."[73]

In a manner akin to the "glorification" of female beauty in Ziegfeld's revues, symphonic jazz sought not so much to position popular music as high art, but rather to dress such music in lavish arrangements that conveyed an aura of contemporary sophistication, glamour, and refinement. The term glorified is appropriate for describing the relation of symphonic jazz arranging to the popular music that it elevated or glamorized. For example, in 1928, B. A. Rolfe—Whiteman's replacement at the Palais Royale restaurant on Broadway—promoted the sound of his Lucky Strike Dance Orchestra's Whiteman-modeled music as "Glorifying American Jazz." Likewise, in reviewing Whiteman's 1928 Carnegie Hall concert, *Variety* critic Abel Green captures the entertainment essence of Whiteman's "jazz": *"Whiteman is always box-office. . . .* For all the concert hooey and high-hat aura of the sainted precincts of Carnegie, [Whiteman] is *too much the showman* to concern himself about such things. . . . After all, Whiteman is primarily a rhythmic exponent . . . attuned to the jazz tempo. If this tempo is *symphonized* and *glorified* to approach [the style of a] symphony, it is still basically jazz, and it is manifestly in error to judge Whiteman by any other standards."[74]

Lloyd Whitesell theorizes musical "style modes" in Broadway-Hollywood, glamour-focused arranging practices employed in interwar film musicals. This idiom developed much from symphonic jazz, and the connection was direct: Hollywood's transition to sound via musical films included considerable contributions from former symphonic jazz talent, including, for example, Arthur Lange and his even more successful protege, Ray Heindorf. Heindorf's long list of Hollywood orchestration, arranging, and musical direction credits start with such symphonic-jazz indebted musicals as the *Hollywood Revue of 1929* (MGM) and *42nd Street*. This jazzy sound was, of course, one stylistic idiom among several in Hollywood musical practice, but symphonic-jazz-trained arrangers and orchestrators—and the style mode in this vein—were central to film underscoring and musicals in Broadway and Hollywood from the 1930s through the 1950s. Whitesell describes film-musical style modes as discursive fields associated with distinct musical styles and their components. For Whitesell, it is the stylistic treatments in musical numbers—"the *how* of representation" and "connotative expression"—that project glamorous qualities of "ethereality or sophistication by way of deportment, sensuous textures, elevated styles, and aesthetically refined effects." Whitesell relates style modes to musical topic theory, but be observes that they can also function as "background modalities" that "interact with specific musical topics."[75] He argues that some balance of the four "contributing aesthetic qualities" of "sensuousness, restraint, elevation, and sophistication" is imperative for a "true glamour experience."[76] Such traits are relevant to the glamorous qualities of symphonic jazz discussed here and luxe pop in general. In luxe pop, such stylistic artifice is heard in the connotative tensions between vernacular/popular and "legitimate" textural, performative, stylistic, and timbral signifiers, with the latter embodying various levels of restraint in contrast to the bodily physicality of "rhythmic" popular music. Furthermore, the latter territory—idioms that were glamorously glorified both through symphonic jazz arranging and the practices Whitesell describes—relied upon the new American variety-entertainment practices that emerge in full flowering across the 1920s. Tin Pan Alley popular song, symphonic jazz, jazz and pop recordings, and Broadway and Hollywood productions were important arenas for these new vernacular modes of mixed-register/mixed-class glamour expression.

In describing the interwar era, historian Ann Douglas has commented that Americans' were "newly fascinated with their own cultural resources," repudiating "European traditions and their genteel American custodians as emblems of cultural cowardice," and in turn finding pride in "learn[ing] that they spoke, not English, but "The American Language," as H. L. Mencken officially named it in a monumental but witty study of 1919.[77] Douglas's reference to Mencken's calls for an artistic rehabilitation of American vernacular idioms is relevant to considering the period's interests in mixed race and mixed class (highbrow-lowbrow) expressions. Mencken was renowned for his satirical battles against the stultifying "Genteel Tradition" (George Santayana's characterization) and American Puritanism. These writings presented an entertaining mix of vernacular wit, irreverence, vulgarity, urbanity, and sophistication—attributes that reflect the ideals Mencken espoused in *The American Language*. His illustrations of innovation in "novel Americanisms" are culled from popular culture (dime novels, film, musical theater, popular song, tabloids, and press sources like *Variety*).[78] His fascination with the colorful qualities of American "mongrelization" (between Black and white, and high and low, cultures), as Douglas terms it, was central to many cultural products of the era.

The symphonic jazz idiom's indiscriminate mixtures of vernacular and elevated topics derive from the ideals that Mencken espoused as the American penchant for creating colorful new slang and locutions through cultural appropriation, juxtaposition, modification, and playful contextual manipulation.[79] The "jazz" of symphonic jazz invokes 1920s journalistic uses of this term as both an adjective and verb for acts of mischievous cultural "mongrelization." This understanding is immensely important for the legacy of symphonic jazz in luxe pop, which in its more adventurous forms relies precisely on the entertainment qualities inherent in such cultural collisions and mongrelizations, middlebrow or otherwise.

In the era following World War I, there was an ever-increasing American trend toward cultural democratization—or "homogenization," as the critic Dwight Macdonald later termed it.[80] It was this very trend that prompted midcentury cultural critics such as Clement Greenburg, Macdonald, and numerous others, into their defense of highbrow cultural authority against the onslaught of mass culture and the predisposition of Americans toward middlebrow, or *entertaining*, art.[81] Whereas symphonic jazz had been hotly discussed in the critical and popular press of the 1920s as a promising new challenge to "serious" art, only a small number of symphonic jazz concert works from this era survived as "pops" concert staples by the late 1950s, as the majority of this repertory was largely relegated to our cultural trash heap as frivolous, middlebrow kitsch.

As Joan Rubin observes in *The Making of Middlebrow Culture*, the critical backlash against middlebrowism emerged as an eleventh-hour barrier against the erosion of highbrow authority.[82] In the spirit of Van Wyck Brooks's bifurcation of American cultural life into the highbrow/lowbrow castes, the midcentury's further stratification of American culture into a tripartite structure—adding middlebrowism, and later upper and lower middlebrows—allowed cultural critics to bolster the avant-garde's claims to the legacy of Euro-American art cultures.[83] In literature, Rubin argues, this new hierarchy allowed the elevation of some writers into "major" figures and provided fuel for "the exclusion and marginalization of others . . . on the basis of social, political, and ideological assumptions."[84] Such has been the case of symphonic jazz in jazz historiography.

In describing symphonic jazz and its progeny as middlebrow, I do not mean to denigrate this music in the manner that many interwar and mid-century critics had. The anti-middlebrow discourse raised in this book offers valuable sources of cultural reception, though this negative discourse need not carry its original presumed authority as to the cultural worth of the luxe music it aimed to defame. Indeed, the artful entertainment aesthetic of this music has a great deal to tell us about American culture. Through symphonic jazz, one can see the "middleness" of American middlebrow musical culture.

Under the glorified entertainment—and middlebrow—aesthetics of symphonic jazz, elaborate popular music arrangements function as both a type of aural spectacle and a form of variety entertainment. Each of these qualities saturates *King of Jazz*. The epigraph quotation for this chapter is taken from the grand finale of the film, the "Melting Pot of Music" sequence, an extended bipartite medley meant to suggest the wealth of traditions that merge into Whiteman's music. This over-the-top production number realizes—thematically, visually, and musically—key symphonic jazz aesthetic ideals. This sequence also screams of middlebrow spectacle and artful aspiration, both in production and music.

The "Melting Pot of Music" is filmed on a vast, stadium-sized set far beyond the reach of a normal theatrical stage. The centerpiece of the number is the prop of a huge, steaming black kettle—or melting pot—set atop an immense Roman-style altar that forms the proscenium arch of a smaller performance space. On both sides are two immense banks of steps, each functioning as stage areas for several hundred chorus members and dancers who perform synchronized marches, drills, and formal figurations. The set is backed by towering stone pillars capped with eagles, providing an almost militaristic sensibility. Though not of a style directly evocative of Busby Berkeley's emerging film musical spectacles, the camera work in this sequence is quite cinematic in scope. Through such editorial techniques as hidden cuts (creating seamless ensemble transformations) and both the alternation of closeups and detail shots of solo performers, on the one hand, and extended and crane shots of the massed performing units, on the other hand, the number merges spectacle and multiple levels of cinematic perspective.

The first two-thirds of the "Melting Pot of Music" sequence provide a lavish display of cultural diversity through an extended medley of European folk and national tunes. These themes are depicted as raw elements to be mixed into Whiteman's "jazz." The musical melting pot of this number, however, conspicuously excludes one central jazz ingredient: an African American presence.[85] This initial medley is presented in an overtly "straight" (non-jazzy) style with ever-changing groupings of the chorus who perform with appropriate nationalistic costumes, dancing, and pageantry. The extravaganza of old-world traditions continues for eight-and-a-half minutes and includes highlights like the Roxyettes performing as brightly colored flamenco dancers, massive configurations of bagpipers alongside Roxyettes garbed as short-skirted Highlands dancers, and a Ziegfeldesque waltz sequence (evoking high-class entertainment?) with showgirls parading in lavish, flowing gowns.

Then, following a brass fanfare, the number presents Whiteman madly stirring the steaming "melting pot" of musical traditions. Trick photography superimposes shots of Whiteman, the hot steam, rising neon halos, and other effects, all underscored with agitated, chromatic music in the strings and brass. The passage builds up to a brief frenzied pastiche of jumbled snippets from the earlier medley. Suddenly this musical brew coalesces, just as a massed army of saxophonists marches down the steps. Whiteman's band breaks into a reprise of the chorus from the preceding Broadway-tinged, cowboy production number of "Song of the Dawn," a number that mixed Wild West imagery with an entertainment-spiritual musical style. Shortly thereafter, the doors to the smaller stage burst open with a parade of dancing, leggy Roxyettes in red-sequined cowgirl outfits. The arrangement then proceeds through an up-tempo, jazzy medley-reprise of songs from other earlier film numbers as the chorus girls give way to a parade of novelty dancers. This subsection ends on the close-up of a chorus girl in a patriotic top hat, after which the alter/stage rotates to reveal the Whiteman orchestra. The band again reprises the introduction to "Song of the Dawn," but as they emerge to full view, they segue to "Stars and Stripes Forever." This American "melting pot" signification then gives way to a chorus from the film's hot dance number, "Happy Feet," with massed Roxyettes stomping away. The number concludes with a third reprise of "Song of the Dawn." At the final lines of the chorus ("Sing 'Hallelujah!,' for the dark night is gone. / The world is singing / the Song of the Dawn"), the band platform rolls forward and an extended shot reveals hundreds of performers fervently waving their hands in the air as if they were part of an old-time Southern camp revival. The film then closes with a double-forte statement of the main theme to *Rhapsody in Blue*.

Both this film and its grand "Melting Pot" finale raise the question of what relation the 1930 film public saw between the cultural project of Whiteman's music and such over-the-top Broadway/Hollywood performance spectacle. The answer is simple: everything! Whitemanesque symphonic jazz was intimately derived from the defining modern-American, classy aesthetic principles of these entertainment traditions, and the Whiteman orchestra's performances were characterized by the role of musical, performance, and staging spectacle within a revue-derived, variety entertainment format.

CONCLUSION

Such spectacular, glorified production arrangements were everywhere in late 1920s entertainments, especially the nascent media of radio and sound film.

The cross-industry interactions between Broadway, Tin Pan Alley, Hollywood, and national radio played an important role in the larger dissemination, reception, and understanding of symphonic jazz-derived music. In the exodus of New York musical talent to Hollywood, Broadway and Tin Pan Alley arrangers played a key role in the founding of music departments in film studios, and this transition to sound occurred around the vehicles of film musicals and musical revues. Lange was brought west specifically for the purpose of founding the MGM music department. Upon settling in Hollywood, he imported a stable of arrangers who became major Hollywood music figures of the 1930s. This exodus from Broadway also included two individuals who soon became cornerstone composers of classical-era Hollywood movie music, Max Steiner and Alfred Newman. Newman was notably the conductor, musical director, and arranger for John Murray Anderson's popular *Greenwich Village Follies*, well before that director worked with Whiteman. Newman wrote a number of film scores indebted to the symphonic jazz idiom, as heard, for instance, in the hit 1931 film *Street Scene* (United Artists) which was published as a Whiteman-styled concert work by Whiteman's publisher, Jack Robbins. (Steiner's film-music career had fewer ties to symphonic jazz stylizations, though this sound does appear in his scores.) In sum, Hollywood's transition to sound is indelibly marked by the film industry's vigorous promotion of both Broadway- and vaudeville-styled entertainments with soundtracks that were openly indebted to symphonic jazz.

The characterizations of Whiteman's performance presentations as jazz raise important questions about how the jazz label could be stretched to include such extravagant stage and film entertainments, let alone music that, at times, displayed only tenuous stylistic connections to such now-accepted Black-jazz cornerstones as the late 1920s big band music of bandleaders like Duke Ellington or Fletcher Henderson. That said, Jeffrey Magee's books on both Henderson's orchestra and Irving Berlin's embrace of ragtime and jazz elements in Broadway musical theater, John Wriggle's study of the world of New York arranging in the swing era, my own work on Ellington's early concert-jazz compositions, and recent studies of the genre boundaries of jazz all illustrate important musical and professional connections that did in fact exist between the worlds of hot and sweet dance/jazz orchestras, Black and white, across the interwar era.[86] These connections, and subsequent post-1930 efforts to elevate jazz, ultimately lead to orchestral jazz textures becoming another luxe-pop textural topic in the postwar years. In sum, I contend that the postwar lens of what Scott DeVeaux has called the core jazz tradition, or "the essence of the idiom as we have [commonly] defined it"[87] (meaning the tradition canonized in post-1930 jazz writing), is not the most appropriate lens through which to assess the contemporary content, meaning, value, or aesthetics of symphonic jazz and the entertainment model that Whiteman embodied. This relatively well-defined core jazz tradition simply does not do justice to providing a full picture of how this music was heard and understood as mainstream classy entertainment.

The lush big-band-plus-strings textures of symphonic jazz represent a quintessential modern American entertainment sound. This broad family of popular music shared glorified entertainment ideals under which popular music was imbued with a luxuriant aura of sophistication, glamour, showmanship, and spectacle. For Whiteman's proponents—and there were many—he was the absolute pinnacle of contemporary musical entertainment. A typical 1920s critical response can be seen in the following bedazzled account of a 1926 San Francisco theater performance by Whiteman and his twenty-eight-man Concert Orchestra: "The grand young man of jazz is hitting on all twenty-eight cylinders. . . . The stage was suffused with indigo, dotted with white suits, the highlight being the banjo in the middle, with a red light under [the instrument's] parchment [drumhead]. . . . It was great stuff. Vital, full of orchestral color, chalk-a-block [sic] with unusual effects, sensual and glamorous, yet curiously legitimate."[88] This report suggests several key traits of Whitemanesque musical entertainment: stage spectacle, showmanship, glamour, and a "curious" balance between entertainment and artful musical sophistication. *And* this report aptly underscores the modern American view that this is somehow "legitimate"—a word typically reserved for serious art and culture. This 1926 review's enthusiastic emphases on spectacle and entertainment, and particularly both its praise of artful entertainment and the identification of this entertainment practice as "jazz," suggests the complicated relation of Whitemanesque music to the traditional narratives of jazz, the culture of concert music, musicals, and film music in the United States. The hybrid entertainment heritage of symphonic jazz, which had Venn-like partial overlaps and intersections with each of these music traditions, notably fell between chairs in the genre histories of these traditions, escaping much commentary outside the defenders of the core jazz tradition and anti-middlebrow discourse.

In the wake of the touchstone luxe-pop aesthetics of Whiteman's 1920s orchestra, American popular music continued to "glorify" itself with visual and instrumental references to social class, economic affluence and its associative glamour, and concert music. In closing, it should be stressed again that Whitemanesque symphonic jazz did not entirely originate with Whiteman, Grofé, or Lange; these figures were merely high-profile transmitters of larger traditions. Rather, there were mutual paths of influence among New York's arranging traditions in the 1920s that each led into the 1930s and 1940s, as explored in the next chapters.

THREE

Jazz with Strings

BETWEEN JAZZ AND THE
GREAT AMERICAN SONGBOOK

IN THE 1940S AND EARLY 1950S, there were several important trends in popular music that merged standard big-band instrumentation with lush, urbane, string-based backgrounds. These trends were first evident in the early 1940s when a number of bandleaders expanded their ensembles by adding strings and other orchestral instruments. Such jazz-ensemble extensions derived from earlier traditions, including 1930s radio, Hollywood, musical theater, and dance-band orchestral traditions, as well as the roots of such traditions in 1920s symphonic jazz practice. These midcentury popular-music trends formed the roots of a highly successful commercial canon of both "jazz-with-strings" recordings and lush "American Songbook" vocal recordings. This broad jazz-with-strings repertory is closely related to midcentury American middlebrowism, a connection that is prominent in this music's glorified entertainment aesthetic and its presumed dilutions of "legitimate" highbrow music. While the expression first emerged in the early 1930s, middlebrow only gained its negative connotations in the 1940s when the term was adopted by white cultural critics as a means to describe the pervasive hybridization of mass and highbrow cultures, or rather the watering down or vulgarization of high-culture standards and symbols in popular culture. This contempt for both commercialism and stylistic hybridity is a direct outgrowth of midcentury class politics, and these debates are reflected in the negative critical reception of much of the jazz-with-strings repertory. Through considerations of select artists, arrangements, contemporary cultural discourses, and criticism, this chapter articulates the aesthetic issues and cultural conditions that shaped the hybrid, middlebrow ideals of these postwar jazz-with-strings subgenres.

Concurrent with the multitude of popular manifestations of the symphonic-jazz sound well into the 1940s, the early 1930s marked a turning point in its critical reception in the nascent fields of jazz criticism and historiography. This shift occurred just as jazz-styled concert music had been largely dropped from the interests of contemporary art music circles. The lack of highbrow respect or interest, in tandem with the idiom's growing commercial associations (particularly in its connections to the more jazzy scores of Hollywood and Broadway) and the tensions between earlier critical claims that the idiom was elevating or legitimating jazz, only helped to make white symphonic jazz a critical target during the rise of a new, post-1930 jazz criticism tradition that defined the music through the rich African American jazz legacy, the art of improvisation, and Black musical aesthetics. While the term middlebrow was not in broader public circulation until the mid-1940s, the highbrow reception of such middle-culture activities as "high culture diluted for mass sales and consumption" was definitely present.[1] And for many music critics, symphonic jazz was a primary manifestation of such activities. For better or worse, in pandering to the American anti-intellectual tradition, many of the proponents of symphonic jazz promoted their activities as a cultural middle ground and as an entertaining art. In general, however, most of the later critics of interwar middlebrowism would likely agree with critic Dwight Macdonald's midcentury assessment that "there is something damnably American about Midcult" (his term for middlebrow culture).[2] The colorful criticism by jazz-proponent figures like Winthrop Sargeant, who sought to distance symphonic jazz from *both* "authentic" jazz and the field of classical music, unintentionally reveals the highly seductive and "damnably American" entertaining nature of this popular idiom—even despite the fact that this criticism was employed in the efforts of an aesthetic war against such culturally homogenizing trends from popular culture.

John Szwed has noted that the core jazz tradition's boundaries, which he characterizes as "jazz," or jazz-in-quotes, represent a large family of "jazzy," syncopated popular musics that extend from Tin Pan Alley and symphonic jazz to stage and film musicals, Hollywood jazz-derived film underscoring, 1950s jazz-styled mood music, and the jazz stylizations of various modern pop subgenres, among other trends.[3] The boundaries of the core tradition encompass a wealth of music that musicians, critics, and aficionados have resisted calling jazz, *but* much of this music nonetheless overlaps with core jazz practice in performance, style, and arranging conventions, and even in the participation of musicians from the core tradition. Moreover, less ideologically invested contemporaries among the public, promoters, and the press characterized much of this music as jazz, depending on the era and context. Thus, the terminological semantics around the genre boundaries of jazz date back to 1920s, but such muddied genre boundaries extend to varying degrees as far as the 1950s (and beyond).

At the height of the swing era across the late 1930s and early 1940s, many of the same professional and stylistic divisions between the hot-jazz, sweet-jazz, and commercial dance-band idioms continued to blur because jazz—used here in a broadly inclusive definition—was mainstream, commercial popular music. Jazz was an integrated part of an interwar American pop culture that was centrally defined by a variety-entertainment aesthetic and a myriad of cross-cultural, democratizing trends. This situation can be seen in the era's music-trade magazines, such as *Metronome* and *Down Beat*. Present-day histories of interwar jazz can give the impression that these periodicals were solely devoted to coverage of jazz and swing. However, in the 1930s and early 1940s, both magazines covered a large cross-section of musical activities. Over its first several years in the mid-1930s, the title banner of *Down Beat*, for instance, proudly proclaimed that its coverage extended to "Ballroom, Cafe, Radio, Studio, Symphony and Theater." *Jazz* is not even mentioned. Moreover, both magazines routinely reported on a wide range of hybrid, cross-class (and even cross-race) American music, much of which stylistically fell in or near the symphonic-jazz idiom and its progeny.

From a broader historical perspective, the spectrum of interwar jazz-related idioms can be described as operating roughly between and among three stylistic poles: *jazz*, meaning the core tradition; *jazz-pop*, meaning what Szwed defined as a jazz-in-quotes family of commercial popular music traditions; and *glorified jazz*, which includes much of the jazz-with-strings repertories (ranging across jazz and jazz-pop). In practice, none of these stylistic poles was exclusive and many times it is difficult to articulate precise boundaries in the gray areas between the poles. For example, the core jazz tradition could be dressed up in orchestral arrangements and marketed as jazz-pop, and jazz-pop recordings (whether in small combos, big bands, or glorified big bands with strings arrangements), particularly by singers, could include performances by instrumental jazz artists. Together, these overlapping repertories and music practices represent the extended family—the uncles and aunts, cousins, second cousins, nephews/nieces, and offspring—of the core jazz tradition, and there was a lot of interbreeding and socialization going on in this broad family. Most of the post-1930 instrumental jazz-with-strings trends discussed in this chapter include performances by at least a few musicians associated with the core jazz tradition, but their jazz instrumental voices are employed in a hybrid stylistic context alongside the performances of non-jazz dance-band, theater, and concert-music musicians in largely non-improvised, score-based performances.

An abbreviated, post-1920s outline of strings in jazz orchestration reads something like this: At the onset of the Depression, many of the large, Paul Whiteman–style, symphonic jazz dance bands were forced to downsize or eliminate string sections. Radio, theater, and film orchestras nevertheless continued to present music in the Whiteman mold, most commonly backing the still-thriving male crooner trend following the models of Rudy Vallee and Bing Crosby (the latter emerging from Whiteman's organization). Then came the 1935 boom in the big-band business following the rise of Benny Goodman's orchestra. This period saw a near-exclusive adoption of the brass, reeds, and rhythm band model for dance orchestras. Yet by the spring of 1942, the pendulum had swung back. *Metronome* magazine remarked on the "mounting number of bands that are adding strings."[4]

One model for the early 1940s big-band-plus-strings vogue lies in the arranging conventions of interwar radio orchestras. A fine example of the growing popularity of elaborate radio production numbers can be heard in Adolph Deutsch's arrangement of Gershwin's "Clap Yo' Hands" for Whiteman's orchestra in a 1934 broadcast of the *Kraft Music Hall* program. Table 2 shows an outline of the extravagant arranging routine for this number. The arrangement unfolds over four different key areas. It displays a wealth of varied scoring textures that rapidly change at every four to eight bars. The arrangement includes 1920s Broadway orchestral textures, pre–swing era, big band sax soli, Dixieland-jazz textures, various hot-style solos, a vocal solo by Johnny Mercer, pseudo-spiritual choral passages, and even vocal contributions from the band. In sum, the whole displays an abundance of connections to the symphonic-jazz practices of the 1920s.

Many other bandleaders of the big-band-plus-strings outfits of the early 1940s had extensive work experience in 1920s symphonic jazz radio, theater, and dance orchestras. Tommy and Jimmy Dorsey—who were members of Whiteman's orchestra in the late 1920s—briefly recorded grandiose, Whiteman-style arrangements as the studio-based Dorsey Brothers Concert

TABLE 2 Formal Outline to Adolph Deutsch's 1934 Radio Arrangement of George Gershwin's "Clap Yo' Hands" for the Paul Whiteman Orchestra.

SECTION	Intro (A)	Intr (B)	Chos 1 (A1)	Chos 1 (A2)	Chos 1 (B)	Chos 1 (A3)
MM.	4	4 + 4 + 4	8	8	8	6 (truncated)
KEY	A-flat major					
TEXTURE	Broadway show music. Trpts + trmbns exchange with reed background.	Gershwinesque tutti.	Sax soli. Pre-swing big-band texture with sustained string backing. Brass exchange into next phrase.	Varied repeat of (A1).	Bix-like trumpet solo (paraphr. improv. based on written). Sustained strings and reeds background.	Slight variation on texture of (A1).

Interlude-Ext. 1	Vamp/Verse 1 (*not* from orig. verse)	Verse 2 (*not* from orig. verse)	Chos 2 (A1)	Chos 2 (A2)
4	8	8	8	8
	C minor		E♭ major	
Tutti.	"Moaning" trombone solo (Teagarden) with pizz. strings and reeds background.	Vocal solo (Mercer) with shouted band/choir responses and a solo vocal response (Teagarden). Repeats background to Verse 1.	Solo vocal (Mercer) with Gershwinesque tutti backing and a jazz-styled trumpet section into next phrase.	Varied repeat.

Chorus 2 (B)	Chorus 2 (A3)	Interlude/ Extension 2	Interlude/ Verse 3	Chorus 3 (A1 var.)
8	(6 truncated)	8	4	8
			C major	
Quasi-oriental scoring effect with oboe lead backing vocal ("On the sand of time…")	Vocal cont. Prominent string backing, often in unison with vocal. Sustained reeds.	Repeated choral "Hallelujah" passage with light tutti backing and pedal strings.	Vocal solo and chorus (including band) exchanges. Loosely related to original song verse materials. Background largely based on rhythm section w/guitarist on prominent banjo part.	First four mm. extends previous section and then shifts to final 4 mm. of (A1). (Same backing.)

(*continued*)

TABLE 2 *(continued)*

Chorus 3 (A1 var.)	Chorus 3 (B)	Chorus 3 (A3)	A3 Extension (varied repeat)	Coda
8	8	8	4	4
Varied repeat.	Dixie-style big-band texture with "hot" clarinet solo (paraphrase improv. on written solo). Strings out.	Out-chorus big-band texture (trbn lead).	Trbns and saxes continue riff texture (with string backing on beats 2 and 4).	Rising choral "Hallelujah!" ending with tutti backing on beats 2 and 4.

Orchestra circa 1928–29. On at least one recording, the young conductor Eugene Ormandy directed the ensemble. Despite this self-conscious classical connection though, the orchestra was packed with future swing-era musicians such as Glenn Miller, Phil Napoleon, Chauncey Morehouse, Hal Kemp, and Skinny Ennis, among others.[5]

With the onset of the Depression, these sorts of massive popular orchestras folded due to economic necessity, and musicians like the Dorsey brothers found work in countless studio recordings and the burgeoning field of radio orchestra work. A similar trajectory can be seen in the early career of Artie Shaw, but the initial stylistic leanings of Shaw's mid-1930s career shift to bandleader also rightly suggests a lingering swing-era interest in the deluxe orchestral sound of symphonic jazz among Shaw, the Dorseys, and some of their peers. Shaw is often said to have gained "overnight" success in 1936, but this sudden fame came not with his famous big band but rather with a hybrid ensemble that consisted of his clarinet, a string quartet, and a rhythm section. This transition to bandleader was facilitated by his participation in a 1936 New York concert held in Broadway's Imperial Theater. In his 1952 autobiography, Shaw notes, "Up to this time American dance music had always been a sort of bastard child of 'real' music [i.e., classical music]—good enough to be danced to but hardly to be taken seriously as anything to listen to." He further suggests that in this concert, there was the "rather revolutionary concept" that "'swing' music, as an American idiom, was something to be listened to for itself."[6] With this high-minded intent, Shaw introduced his "Interlude in B-flat," which was written for clarinet, string quartet, rhythm section, and a "little big band" of tenor saxophone, trumpet, and trombone.[7] At this premiere performance, however, Shaw performed the number without the added "little big band." Shaw's "Interlude" is scored with a self-conscious, chamber-style quintet texture that initially features the string quartet alone, followed by a suitably rhapsodic clarinet cadenza over the held strings. But at m. 13 of the manuscript score, modern swing bursts forth in a hybrid chamber-jazz scoring for solo clarinet, a lightly swinging rhythm section, "little big band" interjections (by trumpet, tenor saxophone, and trombone), and sustained strings.

Shaw was one of a growing number of musicians concerned about the social and class stigma of performing in commercial dance bands. The string quartet obviously was added to impart an air of sophistication that tapped into the highbrow aura of classical music. While Shaw's account of the genesis of the piece emphasizes this work's inspiration in "the clarinet-and-string literature" of Mozart and Brahms, the form of this arrangement comes directly out of the three-strain Whitemanesque Modern American Music popular concert work tradition of the 1920s and 1930s.[8] Nevertheless, Shaw's "Interlude" is an early example of the idea later embodied in the Charlie Parker sessions with strings.

According to Shaw, there was not a sustaining audience for this unusual ensemble, and he was soon encouraged to organize a conventional big band. In December 1938, however, Shaw's Whitemanesque aspirations were rekindled when he was invited to be the featured soloist in a bluesy concert number at Whiteman's 1938 Carnegie Hall concert.[9] By March 1939, Shaw had disbanded his standard big band. In February 1940, the trumpeter/bandleader Harry James likewise briefly added a string quartet to his big band for movie prologue revue work. James waited until late 1942, however, to hire a full-time string section for his band. That said, it was Shaw who most fully popularized this trend. By the spring of 1940, Shaw and a newly enlarged studio orchestra—with a full woodwind section and strings—were recording in Hollywood. A version of that orchestra was shown in the 1940 film *Second Chorus* (Paramount). Shaw's cameo role features rehearsals of his Concerto for Clarinet as well as a dance production number in which Fred Astaire's character guest-conducts a bestringed Shaw orchestra in a bluesy, symphonic-jazz concert number. This Hollywood studio outfit had ties to the 1920s Whiteman band in that it included such former Whiteman musicians as Charlie Margulis on trumpet, Bill Rank on trombone, and Mischa Russell on violin, as well as arrangements by the sometime Whiteman arranger William Grant Still. Within several months, Shaw reduced this outfit to a standard big band plus strings, with saxophones doubling on other woodwind instruments, in the fashion of the Whiteman orchestra. (There were also occasional studio additions of other orchestral woodwinds and French horns.) This ensemble was billed as Shaw's "Symphonic Swing" band. As the critic Paul Grein argues, in Nelson Riddle's later choice to mix "strings with swing orchestra" in his influential work for Frank Sinatra, the arranger "developed an idea that the band leader Artie Shaw had experimented with a decade-and-a-half earlier." Grein also rightly notes that "Riddle's swing-with-strings fusion was more elegant than Shaw's."[10] But the success and sophisticated arrangements of Shaw's Symphonic Swing ensemble inspired other top-tier 1940s bandleaders to follow suit with string-section expansions.

Despite the occasional concert-style work recorded by these 1940s outfits, the bulk of their repertory was popular-song arrangements. According to Shaw, "a string section provides a broader musical palette, just as a wider spectrum of color enables a painter to do more complex things." He likewise broadened his band's instrumental palette through the hiring of the ex-Count Basie trumpeter and singer, Oran "Hot Lips" Page, who acted as "kind of a spark plug" to this ensemble.[11] Shaw's interracial, hot-and-sweet jazz mixed with a string section formed the aesthetic heart of the symphonic swing band sound, and this ensemble model is a forebear to the Sinatra-Riddle sound that emerged in the mid-1950s. Despite the popularity of his outfit, Shaw broke up the band and joined the Navy after the December 1941 attack on Pearl Harbor.

Artie Shaw, "Blues in the Night" (1941)

Example 3.1 presents an excerpt from the bridge to the first chorus from the 2 September 1941 recording of "Blues in the Night," a number that features the trumpet work and singing of Hot Lips Page.[12] From the first notes of Page's opening trumpet solo, it is clear that Shaw's ensemble intended to infuse this big-band-plus-strings texture with a distinctly "hotter" swing than Whiteman had featured in the 1930s. (The Whiteman orchestra of this later period, however, employed a number of star swing soloists, including trombonist Jack Teagarden, as well as the author of "Blues in the Night," Johnny Mercer.)

In this bridge passage, the string section is employed as a fourth texture for contrast to the brass, reeds, and rhythm sections. Here, the strings replace the saxes in what might have been a typical texture with reeds backing a vocal alongside blues-based responsorial interjections by the trombones. That said, this textural substitution is not direct in either melodic and harmonic

EX. 3.1. Artie Shaw, "Blues in the Night" (arr. Sy Oliver).

content or phrasing. The use of the strings here displays various idiomatic commercial string textures, as seen, for instance, in the swooning glissandi between key harmonies in the progression. Likewise, note that Shaw sets the three-note harmony voicings in the violin section with prominent octave-spread outer voices set in dissonant diminished and augmented fifth relations with an internal voice. The strings are set homophonically as a section, thus the octave-based countermelody of the violins is quite prominent, and even more so since it favors both chromatic movement and dissonant intervallic leaps in its melodic contour. The mock-modernist effect of this dissonant, non-linear string arrangement distances the string texture here from the saccharine commercial style of string writing found in contemporary radio orchestras, yet it is also different from the typical saxophone voicing that one might expect to underscore this number in Shaw's earlier big band. The string scoring conventions seen here, then, are key components in Shaw's efforts to create a concert-style band for listening rather than dancing, and they resonate with similar string textures in the concert-style numbers of this outfit.

. . .

Following the success of the newly expanded Shaw and James bands, a number of major swing orchestras added strings across the early 1940s. For instance, the 1944 big band of the famous Black pianist and bandleader Earl Hines featured for several months an all-female string section and a harp.[13] During this period, Hines notably told *Metronome* of his long-standing desire to "do something like . . . Whiteman [but] along jazz lines."[14] Like the Whiteman band in the 1920s, these swing-era hybrid ensembles were employed as multidimensional musical units. While these outfits featured hot-style big band arrangements, they equally emphasized sweet-style ballads and occasional concert-style numbers, thereby building an ensemble and band book that was suitable for both dance dates and theater, hotel, or radio work. Such groups also usually included a coterie of singers, and often featured a small group-within-the-group that performed hot jazz. These all-in-one types of symphonic swing bands of the early 1940s—especially Tommy Dorsey's outfit—form the foundations of the later Sinatra-Riddle sound, and this lineage is fairly direct, as many Capitol Records studio musicians on Sinatra's mid-1950s recordings were alumni of the 1940s Dorsey orchestra.

The full potential of these symphonic swing orchestras was chiefly realized in the critically overlooked big-band venue of movie theater prologue-revue shows. These jobs were prized among both white and Black bands, with or without strings. Most of these revues featured bands set amid extravagant stage settings, with performances of current hits; ballads and up-tempo hot-style numbers; event-specific extended production or medley arrangements; instrumental soloist features; and backgrounds for vocalist features, novelty numbers, comedians, acrobats, and dancers. In vocal-heavy, sweet big bands like Tommy Dorsey's, singers were also featured in what critic Will Friedwald has aptly termed "movie-style production numbers—three-ring circuses that involved several spotlighted singers, a vocal group, and any number of instrumental soloists."[15]

In early 1942, Dorsey annexed Shaw's violin section en masse. At that time, Dorsey's main arrangers were the ex-Jimmie Lunceford arranger Sy Oliver, an up-tempo specialist, and Axel Stordahl, who specialized in romantic ballads for the young crooner Frank Sinatra. Oliver's arranging in the 1930s defined the sound of Lunceford's orchestra. When he left this celebrated Black band for the monetary rewards and broader audience of the Dorsey ensemble, Oliver's arranging, trumpet work, and distinctive vocals infused this first-tier white orchestra with a greatly valued quality of hot Harlem-style jazz. This interracial collaboration was not without precedents, since Benny Goodman's breakthrough swing band was built on the arrangements of Fletcher Henderson and other Black arrangers, and Goodman had hired Black musicians for small-ensemble work. Likewise, Artie Shaw's Symphonic Swing orchestra included Hot Lips Page as a central instrumental voice. The interracial texture of sweet-style white swing and Black instrumental voices is yet another important model that points to the later Sinatra-Riddle sound, with musicians like Count Basie's one-time star trumpeter, Harry "Sweets" Edison, performing the comparable role to Page and Oliver in most mid-1950s Sinatra-Riddle recordings.

This connection is not coincidental. Both Sinatra and Riddle looked back to Oliver's work for the Dorsey band-plus-strings configuration as the foundation for their 1950s collaborations. According to Riddle, he and Sinatra had numerous discussions about their "mutual admiration for Tommy Dorsey." He noted that "In planning [the landmark 1956 Sinatra-Riddle album] *Songs for Swingin' Lovers*, Frank commented on 'sustained strings' as part of the background to be used. Perhaps unconsciously my ear recalled some of the fine arrangements Sy Oliver had done for Tommy, using sustained strings but also employing rhythmic fills by brass and saxes to generate excitement. The strings . . . add to the pace and tension of such writing. . . . It was a further embroidery to add the bass trombone . . . plus the . . . fills of Harry "Sweets" Edison on Harmon-muted trumpet."[16] This description outlines the characteristic up-tempo idiom that Riddle employed for Sinatra's Capitol recordings.

Tommy Dorsey, "On the Sunny Side of the Street" (1944)

The opening of Oliver's celebrated 1944 arrangement of "On the Sunny Side of the Street" for the Dorsey Orchestra demonstrates the band-plus-strings texture that Riddle admired in Oliver's writing.[17] This recording was Oliver's biggest hit with this ensemble. Despite the string section, the disc under-scores Oliver's assertion that Dorsey "wanted a Swing band," and that the bandleader had "changed personnel until he got the guys that *could* do it." Oliver was one of these additions, and his hiring highlights that Dorsey spe-cifically wanted to infuse his orchestra with key elements of the trademark Lunceford sound. As Oliver noted, "when I moved from the Lunceford band to Tommy Dorsey, I didn't change my writing approach."[18] While this state-ment holds some truth, it also neglects to note the expansion of his style to include his use of strings. This added texture, when combined with the musi-cal identities of both Dorsey and Oliver, created a somewhat gentler version of the two-beat rocking, rhythmic swing of the Lunceford band. Many of the Oliver swing and popular-song arrangements for Dorsey are built on a soft, two-beat rhythmic feel that is borrowed directly from Oliver's Lunceford work. This sensibility is immediately felt in the "Sunny Side" arrangement. Likewise, Oliver's trademark Lunceford-era interests in novelty effects and extreme textural and dynamic juxtapositions and contrasts is evident in the eight-bar introduction's layering of *sforzando*, two-chord brass and reed punctuations (brass on the first note, the reed color dominating the second), that are set against a *mezzo forte* baritone sax tonic pedal-point ostinato, occasional arpeggiated obbligato piano interjections, and an even softer foun-dational layer of strings that harmonically cushion the whole episode. At the entry of the instrumental statement of the first chorus, the strings segue to a harmonic background of saxophones and guitar-dominated rhythm section, all of which underscores the muted-trumpet-section melodic statement.

While the string section adds a pleasant contrapuntal line against the melodic materials of the introduction, the strings are not given a distinctive melodic line themselves. Rather, they take on the "sustained" quality that Riddle appreciated. Throughout the chart, the string part generally moves in a step-wise rising motion, primarily following the harmonic rhythm in half-note shifts or by sustaining across chords on common tones between chords. The rising contrapuntal line of the string part, to borrow Riddle's later comments on scoring strings, adds to the "pace and tension" of the episode "without getting in the way." The part infuses the introduction with a sense of dramatic shape melodically and harmonically. The harmony is fundamentally built on an elaborated I–IV–V–I progression. Dramatic tension is built through the dissonances created between the tonic pedal and the primary melodic notes of the violin section. Melodically, the four notes of the string part form a rising arc. The first note of mm. 1–2 is the third of the tonic, which in turn moves up a half step in mm. 3–4. The new note becomes the root of the subdominant chord but forms an eleventh with the baritone-sax dominant. The arc then peaks as the violin line moves up to a flat 9th tone for the dominant chord, which forms the dissonance of a flat thirteenth or augmented fifth above the tonic pedal in mm. 5–6. In mm. 7–8, the strings subtly reduce dynamics and the line moves a half step downward to a resolution on the fifth note of the tonic chord. This introduction and its segue to the first chorus show Oliver's craft in designing a rich musical fabric built from a series of simple elements. The introduction, for instance, derives maximum dramatic effect from a very spacious, and aurally transparent, setting of a few discrete elements. Such a sensibility is of central importance to Riddle's later postwar, jazz-pop swing style.

LUSH POP IN THE 1940S: FROM SINATRA AND STORDAHL TO MOOD MUSIC

An early outgrowth of the 1940s big-band-plus-strings vogue was the rise of melodramatic, quasi-symphonic ballad orchestrations for popular vocalists both male and female, but at the center of these trends were crooners like Frank Sinatra. Sinatra began his solo career in September 1942. This post-Dorsey period of the singer is defined by the arrangements of the ex-Dorsey arranger, Axel Stordahl.

In comparing the 1940s Columbia recording and persona of Sinatra with the 1950s Capitol Records rebirth of the singer, the New York Times critic John Rockwell has noted,

> The musical style captured in this Columbia Sinatra set will strike most non-nostalgists and non-Sinatra cultists as bland and sticky-sweet. . . . Everything is insistent ingenue vulnerability, pretty at the expense of almost every other emotional or musical virtue.
>
> The arrangements [of the Columbia era], mostly by Mr. Sinatra's standby during this decade, Axel Stordahl, have dated badly, however much we may try to be sympathetic to the conventions of yesteryear. Twinkling harps, swooning strings and above all those terrible mewling [vocal] choruses all subvert even the strongest performances.[19]

Rockwell's comments reveal a typical post-1960 critical assessment of the differences between Stordahl's work and the Riddle arrangements for Capitol. The idiom of the earlier period is heard to be dated, while the latter continues to be held up as a timeless cornerstone in American popular culture—indeed, the latter idiom is now held to be "traditional pop." Rockwell's remarks reflect a stylistic predilection rather than a characterization of arranging skills, as close attention reveals Stordahl to be one of the most adroit vocal arrangers of the 1940s, a figure who crafted finely tuned backgrounds for the era's defining pop music voice.

Frank Sinatra, "I'm Walking Behind You" (1953)

Despite this Columbia/Capitol division, an ideal example of this sound can be found in Sinatra's first recordings for the latter company in 1953. The lack of commercial sales for these Capitol sides ultimately led to the singer's celebrated partnership with Riddle, who had also worked for Dorsey. Example 3.2 shows the lush, melodramatic opening of the 1953, Columbia-style arrangement of "I'm Walking Behind You."[20] This chart, too, abounds in the sort of "twinkling harps" and "swooning strings" that Rockwell abhorred. The ensemble also features such overtly symphonic instruments as French horns, flutes, oboes, and harp. The melodramatic arrangement further employs string glissandi as part of the swooning, romantic effects that likely were meant to underscore the vocal portamento effects that Sinatra employed to send bobbysoxers into amorous delirium. Stordahl places great emphasis on constructing richly harmonized sectional countermelodies that complement the non-doubled vocal part. Despite the classical aura his string writing might impart, I suggest this association has more to do with the cultural- and class-based aura of the instrument family rather than the writing itself. If reduced to simply a piano part (which seems to be how Stordahl approached arranging), one can readily hear a similarity to the quasi-orchestral piano style of the era's cocktail piano traditions. In fact, the entire arrangement can be transcribed note-for-note to be comfortably played by a single pianist.

Despite the densely harmonized and frequently moving string parts, Stordahl leaves plenty of room for Sinatra's voice. Accompanimental motion regularly slows when the vocal part moves, and it provides ornamental fills where Sinatra's part pauses. Harmonically, the arrangement is rather straightforward when compared to the riches of the big-band arranging tradition. Dissonance is used sparingly for dramatic effect, such the D♭9/♯5 (circa 0:38, under "me") harmony that Stordahl introduces for a "pained" effect in response to the lines "Though you may forget me." The aforementioned semi-classical textures are heard in the introduction's rubato call-and-response

0:00

EX. 3.2. Frank Sinatra, "I'm Walking Behind You" (arr. and cond. Axel Stordahl).

between the sweeping strings, complemented with two clarinets, an oboe, and harp glissandi, on the one hand, and the horn on the other—all of which is performed sans rhythm section, which only enters subtly under the vocal chorus.

. . .

Another major figure in the continued commercial expansion of the 1940s big-band-plus-strings vogue was the ex-Dorsey arranger Paul Weston. By

1944, Weston was musical director for the newly formed Capitol Records. Along with Stordahl, Weston's arrangements for Capitol singers like Jo Stafford and Peggy Lee epitomize the pop vocal arranging conventions of the day. However, it was Weston's instrumental albums that created the successful new genre of "mood music." This latter development has ties to earlier trends, such as the sweet-style dance orchestras of the swing era, the rise of the Muzak corporation in the mid-1930s, and the 1930s light music repertories of certain radio orchestras. The Weston mood music model favored pre-war hit songs from the 1920s through early 1940s—that is, the repertory that we now call "standards." Weston later described his arranging and big band performance formulas for these recordings as "underplayed," "underarranged," and "on-the-melody."[21] This approach can be heard in Weston's 1946 arrangement of "You Go to My Head."[22] Here, Weston employed the sort of subdued big-band textures that were held to have fallen out of favor with postwar audiences: slower tempos, no blaring brass, and an emphasis on lush, Glenn-Milleresque five-part, close-position sax voicings. These settings further include a restrained, piano-less rhythm section. Weston's charts also typically involve lush introductions featuring strings, harp, and reed textures. The arrangements leave only a small amount of room for ornamental improvisation from soloists. In contrast to the design-intensive "sophistication" of the symphonic jazz tradition, Weston's arranging routines are regularly reduced to one or two choruses with no modulation and at most only a few additional measures for either an introduction, single interlude, or tag coda.

MAKING A LADY OF MODERN JAZZ

In a postwar environment that saw both the decline of the dance-band industry and an increase in concert-setting performances of jazz, various bandleaders and arrangers began to experiment with new harmonic and formal devices, as well as further symphonic-leaning ensemble augmentations. In contrast to the overtly commercial intent of Weston's "underarranged" mood music, several arrangers began to explore comparatively complex textures that emulated the music of prewar modernist composers such as Igor Stravinsky and Paul Hindemith. By the late 1940s, this new, self-consciously complex big-band music was called "progressive jazz," but its roots lay several years earlier. In 1946, the producer Norman Granz began to commission recordings for his landmark album, *The Jazz Scene* (which was released in 1949).[23] Two of the artists to use strings in this project were the arrangers Neal Hefti and George Handy, both of whom were associated with the idiom that came to be called progressive jazz. Significantly, saxophonist Charlie Parker's first performance with strings occurred in the 1946 recording of Hefti's composition "Repetition." Handy's contribution to *The Jazz Scene*, his composition "The Bloos," illustrates several intersections between progressive jazz and the big-band-plus-strings vogue. As seen in Table 3, this work is built from three strains, one of which is a blues chorus that is repeated twice for an improvised tenor sax solo. Like "Clap Yo' Hands," Handy's arrangement for "The Bloos" restlessly shifts scoring textures at every four- to eight-bar phrase. Beyond his use of dissonant harmonic extensions, Handy's progressive textures are built from melodramatic, widely varying tempi and performance gestures, a hyperactive palate of dynamic shadings, and smatterings of ritards and rubato cadenzas.

While progressive jazz originally received front-page press coverage, and while progressive bands won readers polls (e.g., Stan Kenton's orchestra won top band honors in the 1947, 1950, and 1951 *Down Beat* readers polls, and his arranger, Pete Rugolo, won his category across 1949–1952), many critics remained wary of the idiom's contributions to jazz.[24] This concern was expressed by the jazz scholar Marshall Stearns, who suggested in 1956 that progressive jazz "reversed Paul Whiteman's formula by adapting jazz to academic [modernist] music," thereby resulting in a negative "diffusion of [real] jazz." This anxiety about the mutual watering down of both modern jazz and modern classical music reflects period concerns about middlebrowism. *Down Beat*'s record reviewer saw similar middlebrow modernist pretensions in the "[Warner Bros.] big movie brass effects" of "The Bloos," though he read these elements as indications of "a brilliant . . . satire."[25]

Stan Kenton, "Lonesome Road" (1950)

These suspicions of middlebrow intent were most prominently leveled at the high-profile career of Stan Kenton, the bandleader who popularized the term "progressive jazz." In 1949, Kenton unveiled his Innovations in Modern Music Orchestra. The Innovations Orchestra was a standard big band augmented by a sixteen-member string section, an expanded woodwinds section, French horns, and harp. A 1950 concert program notes that with this group, Kenton had "grown into manhood—and with manhood comes . . . musical maturity."[26] This "mature" repertory ranged from atonal concert-style works with occasional bebop episodes, to more traditional big-band

TABLE 3. Formal Outline for George Handy's "The Bloos"

SECTION	Strain 1 (A1)	Strain 1 (A2)	Strain 1 (B)	Strain 1 (A3)	Strain 1 (C1)	Strain 1 (C2)
MM.	8	8	8	8 + 2	8 + 8	8 + 8
KEY	C maj/min			G maj		
TEXTURE	Oboe lead w/strings + celeste background (rhythm out). "Progressive" 2 mm reed + brass answer to phrase.	Varied repeat.	Brass-heavy, extension of the answer to A phrase. Single vln + oboe emerge out of held chord and bridge into next phrase.	Variation on A phrase with added solo vln + oboe. Includes 2 mm. extension.	Brass-heavy concert jazz antecedent (no rhythm sect.) and a symphonic-style consequent phrase led by woodwinds.	Varied repeat (with new French horn soli).

Interlude, pt. 1	Violin Cadenza	Interlude, pt. 2	Strain 2	C3 phrase var.
8	3	6	20 (6 + 6 + 2 ext. + 6)	4 + 4
—	—	—	[unstable]	G maj
Variation on motives from phrase C over high vln pedal. Call-response between concert-jazz and symphonic textures. Gives way to sustained *Tristan*-Prelude-type string texture.	Overt "classical" effect. Vln cadenza over held "symphonic" chord in reeds + strings.	"Progressive," jazzy chord stabs in response to cadenza. Dovetailed into jazz trbn solo (over strings + celeste).	Jazz trbn solo over shifting harmonic progression. Melodramatically backed by oboe + strings (ref. both pop and symph orch traditions) with alternately subdued and bombastic big band. Closing 4 mm trbn cadenza.	Repeat of opening Strain 1 (C) phrase, w/improv jazz sax solo ending backed by rhythm section and pizz. strings.

Blues Chorus 1	Blues Chorus 2	Interlude	Strain 1 (A1)	Strain 1 (A2)	Coda
12	12	4	8	8	3
D		C maj/min			
Improv. sax solo with rhythm section only.	contin.	Screeching big band interjections followed by odd "symphonic" oboe cadenza.	See prev.	See prev.	Varied repeat of phrase A2 material with ominous ensemble swell.

arrangements with room for improvisation. The orchestra also featured elaborate vocal arrangements by Pete Rugolo written for June Christy. The February 1950 recording of "Lonesome Road" offers an ideal representation of the hybrid art-meets-entertainment aesthetic of these arrangements.[27] The arrangement's introduction (see Example 3.3) displays a bombastic,

0:24

EX. 3.3. Stan Kenton, "Lonesome Road" (arr. Pete Rugolo).

dissonant, "progressive" texture with Christy's vocalise on top, and a slow, rubato tempo. Chorus 1 develops this melodramatic pop-modernist texture through scoring shifts at each phrase and phrase turnaround. Big-band jazz fully enters at the double-time interlude.

The progressive textures of "Lonesome Road" are largely scoring effects superimposed on top of a standard vocal arrangement routine. But Rugolo's design-intensive approach recalls the production arrangements of symphonic jazz dance bands and radio orchestras. This sort of connection was not lost on Kenton's detractors. One reviewer noted that he had "the terrifying thought that maybe . . . [Kenton] was the Paul Whiteman of the day."[28] This reception was ultimately the undoing of Kenton's position in the modern jazz canon.

PARKER, GRANZ, AND JAZZ SOLOISTS WITH STRINGS

Unlike Kenton's progressive jazz, which has mostly faded into obscurity, the recordings from this period of Charlie Parker with strings sell remarkably well to this day. Despite the commercial success, however, and despite their influence on generations of jazz-soloist-with-strings recordings and events, they have had a problematic critical reception in jazz historiography. Notwithstanding their intention to showcase the "modern" improvisational voice of Parker, the "with strings" backing charts are fairly conventional, radio orchestra–style arrangements with only rare touches of Rugolo-leaning "progressive" textural coloring.

Charlie Parker, "Just Friends" (1949)

The 1949 recording of "Just Friends" notably became the best-selling record of Parker's career.[29] Jimmy Carroll arranged this chart for Parker's alto along with five strings, harp, oboe, and rhythm section. As seen in Example 3.4, the arrangement begins with a four-bar, Stordahl-style mock-concert texture of a cello solo backed by swelling tremolo strings and sweeping harp arpeggios. At the fifth bar, Parker enters in double-time with cadenza-like flourishes over a sustained, shimmering tremolo string backing. Parker then seamlessly glides into his embellished statement of the chorus melody. In the manner of the "glorified" arranging models discussed earlier, the backgrounds of the initial chorus are varied with each eight-bar phrase. Carroll's work on "Just Friends" has been singled out by jazz critics as the highlight of these Parker

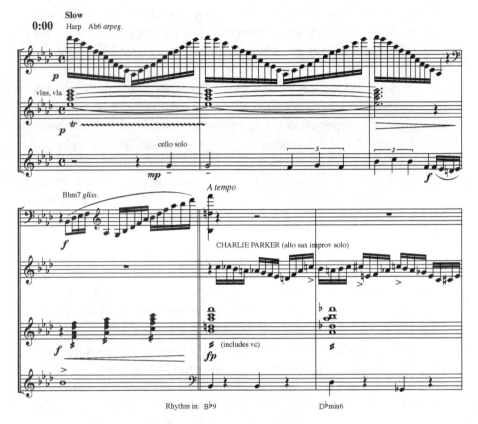

EX. 3.4. Charlie Parker, "Just Friends" (arr. Jimmy Carroll).

recordings because, unlike many of the other "with-strings" charts, it gave Parker ample space for full improvisation across another chorus and a half plus the coda.

. . .

In interviews of this period, Parker regularly expressed his keen interest in the music of various prewar modernist composers (Stravinsky, Hindemith, etc.). With these statements in mind, many critics have been puzzled by the commercial sound of the "with-strings" arrangements. Some have suggested that Parker was contractually coerced into making these recordings. In response, Parker noted that "my friends said 'Oh, Bird is getting commercial.' That wasn't it at all. I was looking for new ways of saying things musically. . . .

I asked for strings as far back as 1941."[30] This claim is backed by Parker's producer, Norman Granz. In 2001, Granz remarked that "I'm most criticized for . . . *Bird with Strings*, like this [project] was a crime against humanity. . . . Charlie . . . virtually put a gun to my head, insisting he wanted . . . strings. . . . [Likewise] . . . Lester Young . . . Ben Webster . . . [and] Johnny Hodges [all] wanted strings."[31] The negative reception in jazz-critic circles may have been sparked by Granz's liner notes for the original LP release of these recordings. In these notes, Granz wrote

> Unfortunately . . . , the [mass] public has been slow in its acceptance of [Parker's music]. . . .
> All of the music in this album shows a new Parker to most listeners. He plays the melody very closely and it's good that he does, for the tunes are truly beautiful. . . . Some of the harsh effects achieved heretofore by Parker's [bebop] ensemble are nowhere noticeable here, [with] the strings softening and prettying Parker; and Parker, for the first time, plays with truly great [legitimate] musicians, which meant he had to be . . . on his best musical behavior.[32]

These gendered, classist comments about "softening and prettying" Parker with a backing string ensemble of "great musicians" resonate loudly with historical commentary around jazz-with-strings endeavors. In the 1920s, it was a popularly held notion that Gershwin "made a lady of jazz" and that Whiteman was the musician who had brought dignity and highbrow respect to this supposedly lowbrow music. In the opinion of mid-1930s jazz critics like Winthrop Sargeant, however, the symphonic jazz idiom was seen as a pretentious, commercial vulgarization of "true" jazz. Damning claims of this sort foreshadow the "criminal" characterizations of the 1950s and 1960s jazz-with-strings vogue, which was critically received through class-hierarchy culture filters that read the music in terms of the never-to-be-combined cultural roles of modern jazz, middlebrow musical kitsch, commercial entertainment, and "legitimate" concert music. To paraphrase the Whiteman camp, it sounds like Granz was worried that he might be accused of "making a lady" of modern jazz—a metaphorical notion that post-1930 jazz critics would likely have equated with a sort of musical emasculation, and as a clear cultural opposite to highbrow, legitimate music. This class-oriented and gendered reading stands in contrast to the hypermasculine, modernist arranging strategies of Kenton and his progressive jazz peers, musicians who sought to avoid associations with the new, culturally devalued (read "overtly commercial") sounds of mood music and *Hit Parade*–style radio orchestras. While this self-described, "musically mature" *progressive* (instead of "regressive"?), often bombastic sound ideal sought to evoke the highbrow cultural aura of then-current notions of modernist concert music, Kenton's clear ties to popular music (e.g., "Lonesome Road"), jazz, and huckster-style showmanship (which is apparent in various Kenton poses on his publicity literature and several albums covers), repositioned these trends squarely back in the territory of mid-century middlebrow culture.

THE COMMERCIAL JAZZ-POP CANON
BECOMES TRADITIONAL POP

This chapter's focus has been the critically disparaged gray area that lies between two traditions. On one side is the core of the canonic instrumental jazz tradition ("the essence of the idiom as we have defined it").[33] On the other—at the so-called boundaries of this core jazz tradition—is the emerging sound of the celebrated midcentury vocal recordings, now identified as the "Great American Songbook" repertory. The music trends discussed here ultimately led to a highly successful *commercial* jazz canon that includes both jazz-soloist-with-strings recordings and the vocal American Songbook repertory and its requisite big-band-plus-strings arranging conventions. While the post-1950 emergence of the latter tradition is the subject of chapter 4, it is useful here to briefly consider the terminological, stylistic, and genre problems that emerge in any attempt to accurately define the boundaries of the core jazz tradition in this era from a historically grounded perspective on 1940s and 1950s popular culture. Such insights are valuable in articulating this jazz-with-strings boundary between jazz and mainstream pop, or more precisely the shaded spectrum between jazz, jazz-pop, and jazzy pop at midcentury. One window on how to parse such muddy stylistic boundaries is found in the genre categories of contemporary industry-oriented periodicals like *Down Beat* and *Billboard*, and particularly in the genre distinctions made in these magazines' recording reviews, readers/critics polls, and sales charts. What becomes obvious in such materials is that across this period there was a gradual but steady growth in the breadth of genre distinctions that each magazine made.

Despite my observation on the diversity of music covered in *Down Beat*, this periodical still functioned as the primary organ of the jazz and swing industries. Their readers polls distinguish between only three stylistic genres—swing, sweet, and corn—among the popular bands and musicians they polled their readers on. In this cultural context, swing is understood to mean "hot jazz," or the core jazz tradition, and corn—with its negative connotations—is understood to mean a variety of overly sentimental or novelty commercial music trends; thus, the magazine's view on dominant genres only slightly updates the hot/sweet/commercial distinctions of the 1920s. The polls also recognize the performance categories of bands (meaning *big* bands), arrangers (non-style identified), soloists (divided into both a non-style-identified instrumentalist category and corn), and vocalists. (Vocalists were typically not independent stars but rather supplemental band members.) By the early 1940s, small combos had been added, as well as separate "male" and "girl" singer categories, each marking new distinctions in how popular music was increasingly being performed. Again, however, the big bands still functioned as self-contained variety entertainment businesses, so orchestras like those of Tommy Dorsey and Claude Thornhill, which won a number of best sweet band awards, routinely included arrangements and instrumentalists that were otherwise associated with the core jazz tradition. By 1944, two years after Sinatra began his solo career, the magazine further subdivided the singer categories into "Vocal Group," and "Male" and "Girl" singers "With Band" and "Not Band." Sinatra won the latter, illustrating that a central area of the "Not Band" category was music from the ballad-driven, male-crooner vogue (meaning orchestral, gently-swinging music in the vein of the Stordahl-Sinatra Columbia recordings).

In 1952, the poll inaugurates a "Hall of Fame" category (won first by Louis Armstrong). This new category partly reflects the emerging trend of prewar nostalgia in jazz and jazz-pop production, consumption, and marketing. More telling, however, is the 1953 inauguration of the magazine's critics poll, marking both the first time that the genre categories are significantly refined and expanded and the first time that the term jazz is specifically mentioned in the magazine's genre-based music polls (though, of course, the word jazz had appeared in the magazine's pages since its first issue). In the 1953 readers poll, the new genre- and performance-based categories include "Best Record-Popular," "Best Record-Jazz," "Best Record-Rhythm & Blues," "Best Record-Classical," "Dance Band," "Jazz Band," and "Combo-Instrumental." While the stylistic forebears of all of these trends were covered in the pages of the magazine (like the music of the core and boundary jazz traditions), the poll's articulation of these subgenres reflects the magazine's adjustments to new music trends, including the rise of hi-fi culture, the aging of the magazine's original audience, the importance of newly dominant popular musics outside the core tradition of jazz, and the new postwar distinction between the core jazz tradition and "pop," as mainstream popular music was increasingly called across the decade (though the term "pop" dates back to the 1920s), among other trends. In 1954 "Personalities of the Year" (indicating a recognition of the growing focus on celebrity status in popular culture) was added, to complement the categories of "Popular," "Jazz," "Latin American," and "Rhythm and Blues." By contrast, the early critics polls (e.g., 1953–1956) focus exclusively on categories defined by the core jazz tradition, thus underscoring this period's role as a historiographic moment in the critical elevation of jazz from its popular culture roots.[34]

Billboard magazine's reviews, columns, and sales charts represent another, broader facet of American popular culture's refinements in genres across this period, a trend that reflects both industry refinements in marketing and changes in the music industry and its market across the postwar years. These topics are beyond the scope of this chapter, but a few points and examples should suffice to make several observations.[35] As is well-documented, the music industry of the 1920s and 1930s primarily divided the popular recording markets into national, race, and regional (such as "hillbilly") subcategories.[36] The national market remained largely dominated by jazz-related recordings that American-music scholar Charles Hamm identifies as mainstream syncopated music "performed by white musicians for white audiences within the context of white American culture," and, to a lesser extent, the category of jazz and blues "performed by black musicians for white audiences within the social context of white American culture."[37] *Billboard*'s pages document the industry's continued refinements to this meta-framework for marketing music. While largely focused on national popularity—on the "Music Popularity Chart"—and large-scale regional sales (East, West Coast, Midwest, and South), as well as the distinction between national (white-focused) and race market sales (the latter through a "Harlem Hit Parade" column), through much of the 1940s, the magazine's coverage of recording sales and media play reflects the same sort of jazz/jazz-pop genre framing that was seen in *Down Beat*. Around 1945, they added "Popular Record Reviews" and "Folk Record Reviews (Hillbilly, Race, Cowboy Songs, Spirituals)" sub-columns to the "Music Popularity Chart" section. The stylistic breadth of these distinctions can be seen, for instance, under the "Pop Record" section of the 27 January 1943 issue, where the reviewer considers recordings by Duke Ellington, the sweet dance band of Horace Heidt, the blues of Roosevelt Sykes, and the close-harmony vocal stylings of the Four

King Sisters.[38] Across 1946–48, the magazine was also tracking "England's Top Twenty"; "Best-Selling Popular Retail Records" (singles); "Best-Selling Popular Record Albums" (LPs); and single and album categories for classical music, songs from film soundtracks, and "Children's Music." It had also separated "race" records from the "folk" category (now "Cowboy and Hillbilly Tunes"), thereby nodding to the rising postwar music markets for what the magazine would soon rename (in 1949) "Rhythm and Blues" and "Country and Western." Around 1951, they begin to track "Latin American," "Sacred," "Spiritual" (meaning Black gospel), and "International" recording sales.

Only in 1953 did *Billboard* finally include a "Jazz" recording sales column, which is notably titled with the old-fashioned epithet, "Hot Jazz," despite the fact that the column most commonly covered modern recordings of bebop artists like Charlie Parker. By 23 April 1955, however, the magazine deemed it timely to educate its readers—primarily industry and sales people—with a primer on "Categories of Jazz Disks," in which the writer outlines modern jazz ("West Coast jazz, East Coast jazz, bop, progressive, cool, and others"), "instrumental jazz" (meaning recordings that are devoted to individual soloists), "swing," "Dixieland," and "cocktail piano." In examining the breadth of recordings in the latter trend, the magazine notes, "There are solo efforts by other jazz men that can qualify with the blue-lights or mood-music fanciers. Among them are presentations of certain horn men with strings—for example, the recent Ben Webster and Benny Carter issues. . . . All are perfect antidotes for the pop listener's jaded palate [for jazz]." This page-14 article was paired with a front-page announcement that "Jazz Disks, Paced by LP, Hit Cool 55% Jump in Hot Year," as well as an article on "Buying, Selling, Programming Jazz Records, Tunes, and Talent: The Billboard 1955 Review and Preview Section," an editorial titled "The Jazz Renaissance," a section on jazz DJs, and other such companion material. For *Billboard*, this mid-1950s "Jazz Renaissance" boom marks the very moment that jazz became a marketing category distinct from popular music.[39] This market-based interest in following jazz is distinctly targeted at the booming hi-fi adult consumer subculture, as implied in the aforementioned headline, and in the fact that in the previous year (1954) the magazine also introduced a "High Fidelity" column. The above comment about the jazz-soloist-with-strings trend offering "perfect antidotes for the pop listener's jaded palate [for jazz]" perfectly frames the gray jazz-pop boundary territory of the jazz-with-strings repertory across the early to mid-1950s. It is fascinating to observe similar class-conscious jazz-pop commentary and genre review placements in the *Billboard* reviews of many of the artists discussed in this chapter, and particularly those artists who intersect with the aforementioned postwar nostalgic "standards" trend. For instance, despite their similarly pop-marketed, soft-swinging presentations of standards repertory, in the 2 June 1956 issue of *Billboard*, the big-band-plus-strings Dinah Washington album release of sung standards, *Dinah!*, was filed under the jazz reviews, while the Granz-produced album, *Ella Fitzgerald Sings the Cole Porter Song Book*, was reviewed as popular music, despite Fitzgerald's present-day canonic elevation to "the quintessential jazz singer."[40] It was noted, however, that the Fitzgerald release would be a "bonanza for jocks [disc jockeys], for jazz fans and for the [popular song] sophisticates to whom this Cole [as opposed to Nat Cole] is 'King.'"[41]

What these accounts of *Billboard* and *Down Beat* reveal is that jazz only emerged as a *marketing* category distinct from popular music *after* jazz was no longer a popular music for the dancing and youth markets of the swing era. Nevertheless, even in the 1950s, the distinctions between jazz, jazz-pop, and glorified-jazz/jazz-with-strings trends remain a slippery slope for the many gently-swinging, standards-leaning releases—both vocal and instrumental—that were marketed to the exact same adult consumers, and often under some form of a "Songbook" marketing strategy. Since the late 1980s, first following the reemergence of the Sinatra-Riddle sound and song repertory in Hollywood musical comedies (after the success of the 1989 *When Harry Met Sally*, among other films), and then with the rise of the rhetoric of the "Great American Songbook" after both the Lincoln Center performance series of the 1990s and the journalism it inspired, Sinatra's and Fitzgerald's midcentury recordings for Capitol and Verve, respectively, came to embody the quintessential sound of what the National Academy of Recording Arts and Sciences has characterized as "traditional pop." This term first appeared as an album-based Grammy category in 1992, the year when the first award was given to Natalie Cole for the digital technology–enabled ghostly duet she sang with her long-deceased father, Nat Cole, with Riddle's original orchestration. In the next few years, the category was dominated by Tony Bennett (1993–95 and 1997–98) and Sinatra himself (1996). NARAS has provided the following description of the award:

> This category is for performances of a specific type of song that cannot properly be intermingled with any other past or present form of "Popular" music. This is basically the body of music, often identified as the Great American Songbook, that was first created by the Broadway, Hollywood and Tin Pan

Alley songwriters and is still being written by the artistic successors to those writers. . . . The term "traditional" . . . [is] a reference, equally, to the style of composition, vocal styling and the instrumental arrangement, without regard to the age of the material.[42]

While the "songbook" idea dates back to Granz's Verve "Songbook" tribute recordings to famous popular composers by artists like Ella Fitzgerald and Oscar Peterson, among others, the arrangements of these 1950s and 1960s recordings reflect the idiomatic ideals established by Riddle in his work with Sinatra and Nat Cole, among others. As shown, this sound emerged among a family of related jazz-with-strings trends, much of which—with or without "vocal stylings"—can be labeled "traditional pop" if viewed from period understandings of such music prior to the mid-1950s, and regardless of their performance and stylistic proximity to the core jazz tradition, since much of this music was marketed either to pop-song "sophisticates" (adult aficionados of the standards repertory) or as "perfect antidotes for the pop listener's jaded palate [for jazz]."

While the Parker "with strings" recordings have long been appreciated among both the record-buying general public and lay jazz fans, the post-Parker model of jazz soloist with strings has routinely been situated as a commercial, bastard stepchild of jazz proper (i.e., the core tradition) by many aficionados, critics, and jazz historians. Even so, through sheer sales numbers and their back-catalog staying power in the marketplace, the Parker "with strings" recordings represent an anomaly—commercial success—in the history of postwar jazz. Despite the occasional critical appreciation afforded some other "with-strings" efforts—like those by trumpeter Clifford Brown (e.g., his 1955 album, *Clifford Brown with Strings*) or saxophonist Stan Getz (beginning with the 1960 album, *Cool Velvet*)—the most prominent popular/commercial success in this tradition after Parker is likely found in the many "with-strings" contributions of pianist Oscar Peterson, which in some cases sound conspicuously close to being updates on the Weston mood-music formula for easy-listening ballads. Like many jazz-with-strings record releases of the 1950s and 1960s, there are fairly obvious connections between certain Peterson with-strings albums and postwar mood-music trends. Such connections can be heard and seen, for example, in a release like the 1957 Peterson album, *Soft Sands*, which features gentle piano-plus-orchestra arrangements of ballads as well as a typical period "vinyl vixen" album cover, the latter of which reflects a widespread, midcentury mood-music marketing practice that featured gauzy cover images of alluring women in alluring and romantic poses. (In this case, the album cover involves a close-up head shot of a young blond beauty lying in the sand with a sultry red flower in her hair.) This marketing trend began at Capitol Records in the early 1950s with the jazz-inflected mood-music albums of Jackie Gleason.[43] While these sorts of images appeared on album covers for many music genres, they were absolutely central to the fashionable jazz-inflected mood music and "Music for [fill in the activity; e.g., 'a Rainy Day']" easy-listening albums of the 1950s and 1960s. Indeed, there are a host of big-name jazz artists—such as pianist George Shearing (his 1956 *Black Satin* and *Velvet Carpet* albums, for instance) or saxophonist Sonny Stitt (e.g., *The Sensual Sound of Sonny Stitt* from 1961)—who released such commercial jazz albums in this vein (vinyl vixen covers and all).

One goal of this chapter has been to articulate a greater, and more nuanced, historical context for the emergence of the jazz-soloist-with-strings tradition(s). An overriding side point that needs to be made is that while these improvising-soloist-with-strings albums seem to form a mass-market/popular/commercial canon of jazz recordings, they are decidedly *not* deemed to be part of the accepted core jazz canon that is taught in classrooms or that has been the traditional concern of jazz historiography. Even if some might argue that the Parker "with strings" releases could be considered as part of the jazz canon (unlike the big-band-plus-strings efforts of Kenton or Paul Weston, for example), they have been viewed this way solely because of Parker's indisputable canonic role in jazz history and the considerable strengths of his inspired solos in these recordings. In fact, the backing textures (the "with strings" part) of these releases have been routinely characterized by critics as extraneous, dispensable, irrelevant, and/or embarrassing facets of these recordings, and not something worthy of the jazz canon or worthy of "serious" critical consideration, even despite the recurrent historic popularity of similar backing textures among core jazz artists. Such a mixed-message critical stance—wherein a critic praises Parker's performance while simultaneously disdaining the schmaltzy character of the arrangements—can be seen in the comments of prominent writers like Gary Giddins, for instance, who once wrote that Parker's string arrangements "were painfully banal in several instances; [but] they seemed to enervate his playing with their pseudo-serious melodrama."[44]

As both Riddle's early career history and his comments (cited above) confirm, there are undeniable (and even obvious) connections between the core jazz tradition and the emerging Great American Songbook tradition, on the one hand, and, on the other hand, the broad, midcentury jazz and jazz-pop practices that blossomed in the fertile popular musical culture that lay between these two bounding (and now-venerated) traditions. In fact, the cultural idea of the cherished canon of popular song standards represented in this latter territory seems to have arisen across the 1940s and 1950s through the mood-music and vocalist-plus-orchestra branches of the jazz-with-strings legacy. In terms of sales and marketing presence, the jazz-with-strings tradition has ironically come to function as one the most prominent representatives of the jazz legacy in popular culture.

Beyond 1930, jazz historiography has been based largely on the cornerstone premise that authentic jazz is an art form. After World War II, this debate was historically framed in terms of midcentury cultural politics that recognized only a similarly rigid division between the cultural spheres of art and entertainment. As such, the jazz canon came to be built with questionable boundaries based on rigid cultural binaries such as art versus commerce and pure versus contaminated—that is, ideas that are wholly based on the devaluation of, and subjective assessments of, commercial and entertainment intent. In turn, this hard-won consensus of jazz as art continues to carry an essentialist policing mechanism that does not often acknowledge the many gray, pluralistic middle areas that exist in American culture, our identity politics of race, gender, commerce, and class, and our social sites of racial interchange. What the narrative of a core jazz tradition has ignored is the extensive dialogue, interchanges, and musical overlaps among a large family of American popular music that grew out of these midcentury jazz-with-strings trends.

FOUR

Defining Populuxe

CAPITOL RECORDS AND THE
SWINGING EARLY HI-FI ERA

THIS CHAPTER CONSIDERS the 1949–53 vocal jazz-pop roots of the post-war sound associated with what we now call the "Great American Songbook." This period parallels the first flush of broadly circulated American writings on middlebrow culture, and much of this music was indeed entwined with middlebrow-adjacent discourse. I employ adjacent here in the sense of sharing common meeting points or adjoining elements. While efforts at democratizing concert music are central to the midcentury musical middlebrow, the intersections of the middlebrow and the expanding middle class also included aspirational *entertainment* traditions that glamorized affluence through consumer fantasies of luxury and jet-set cosmopolitanism.[1] A long, interwar, cross-class mythology tied to glamorous music (as seen and heard, for example, in many interwar Hollywood musicals) has abided in American entertainment.[2] But the intersection of entertainment with lifestyle consumerism trends at midcentury was uniquely pervasive. This essay explores this territory through Capitol Records recordings, with the orchestral jazz-pop of both Nat "King" Cole and Frank Sinatra as primary examples.

While mid-twentieth-century middlebrow literature says much about consumerism, it has surprisingly little to say about popular music. This situation is particularly true of "highbrow," anti-middlebrow writings up to Dwight Macdonald's 1960 essay, "Masscult and Midcult," and his related 1962 book, *Against the American Grain*.[3] Such Frankfurt School–indebted criticism involved protectionism *against* cultural democratization and middlebrow, or *entertaining*, art. At this time, Macdonald was resident film critic for the male (middlebrow) lifestyle magazine, *Esquire*. He admitted he knew little about music, particularly beyond classical music.[4] Such ignorance of popular music and classical music snobbery—and often oversight of music in general—characterize midcentury middlebrow discourse on music. For instance, in the 1957 volume, *Mass Culture*, there is amazingly little discussion of popular music beyond one essay that positions itself against "gifted Europeans" (i.e., the Frankfurt School) who are "horrified" at both American "vulgarization[s] of taste" and "middlebrow 'culture diffusionists.'" Nevertheless, the chapter's author, sociologist David Riesman, concludes that teenagers have "undiscriminating taste in popular music," surmising that pop music merely provides "training in the appropriate expression of consumer preferences."[5] The author's taste predilections as a jazz-loving, white-male adult academic are hardly questioned, nor are the invisible social mechanisms of habitus. Yet recent scholarship has underscored the significant relevance of middlebrow culture and discourse to understanding broad areas of twentieth-century popular culture and media, including popular music. Nonetheless, despite a predominant post-2000 scholarly focus on middlebrow aspirational relations to highbrow cultural capitol, aesthetics, practices, and taste values, I am wary of a unitary middlebrow conception defined solely by such highbrow-aspirational parameters.[6]

The relevance of middlebrow-adjacent, *class*-aspirational popular music— with *class* and *classy* being understood as glamour-based stylistic adjectives relating to aspirational, socioeconomic status, rather than high-culture pretension—can be seen in two famous 1949 articles, from *Harper's* and *Life* magazines. The presumed highbrow dominance is evident in the essay "Highbrow, Lowbrow, Middlebrow," by Russell Lynes, which describes a "new cultural class order" notable for its distinction between upper middlebrows, the "purveyors of highbrow ideas," and lower middlebrows, who consume "what the upper middlebrows pass along."[7] Lynes's arguments were widely circulated through a *Life* article that included an illustrated lifestyle chart with notable music references.[8] The distinctions on the chart imply that one key difference between the upper and the lower middles is found in the aspiring high-cultural-capital pretensions of the upper middles: they have the economic means but not the refined taste of the highbrow. By contrast, the depictions of lower-middle taste suggest a less self-consciously aspirational consumption of lifestyle goods and experiences, leaning toward goods that could be appreciated (in the right contexts) by both upper middles and lowbrows. For lower-middlebrow musical tastes, the illustrated chart suggests "light opera, popular favorites," depicting music by Victor Herbert, vocalist Nelson Eddy (an operetta-style vocalist), Ferde Grofé's *Grand Canyon Suite*, and albums by crooner Perry Como and radio conductor André Kostelanetz (who positively embraced his middlebrow characterization).[9] As Keir Keightley notes, all five were identified as "easy listening," a broad category of middlebrow-adjacent hybrid orchestral pop.[10] None of this maps easily onto notions of tastes driven by highbrow cultural pretensions/aspirations or cultural molding from the upper middles. Rather, these musical goods align with postwar middle-class notions of aspiring to the "good life," prosperity, and cosmopolitanism. The historical evidence suggests that the aspirational modes of the orchestral pop explored here are centrally determined by social and economic factors tied to glamour, cosmopolitanism, and affluence, rather than by high culture or classical music per se, though "elevated" associations derived from classical or classicistic music (via an aura transference facilitated by orchestral instruments) may be present.

Keightley has defined 1946–66 as the "Easy Listening Era," a period in which an aesthetic of "music for middlebrows" spanned "radio programming," "background music," and "adult-oriented pop."[11] The era was a high-water mark for luxe production, most of which had ties to the easy-listening aesthetics Keightley articulates. (The easy-listening, sophisticated-pop aesthetics of countrypolitan music, which developed from the bestringed Nashville Sound of the 1950s, is discussed in chapters 5 and 6.) Capitol's period catalog is a synecdoche for this pop aesthetic, as heard through Jackie Gleason's mood music, Les Baxter's exotica, Stan Kenton's progressive jazz, and the vocal jazz-pop of Nat Cole, Frank Sinatra, Peggy Lee, and others. These idioms emerged alongside the postwar "class"-focused cocktail lounge, which famously included such venues as the Copacabana in New York, established in 1940, and the Las Vegas casino lounge the Copa Room, established in 1952. Here, "class"—as employed in *Variety* and *Billboard*—connotes lifestyle, decorative, and consumer signifiers for sophistication, luxury, and glamour. The central musical entertainment for such venues was "swoon-croon" vocalist "personalities like Sinatra" and "the school of Perry Como, . . . Dean Martin, et al."[12] In the bigger, more prestigious venues, such artists were increasingly backed by bestringed hybrid ensembles that recalled period radio, theater, and recording orchestras. Such conspicuous symphonization practices were central to "class" entertainment—practices that paralleled wider trends of "conspicuous consumption" and consumerist displays of social status, wealth, and/or sophistication. I adopt the term populuxe, coined by Thomas Hine to characterize consumerist trends of 1954–64, to describe this midcentury orchestral jazz-pop idiom. Hine's term is a synthetic word "created in the spirit of the many coined words of the time." It "derives, of course, from populism and popularity, with just a fleeting allusion to pop art.... [I]t has luxury, popular luxury, luxury for all ... [a]nd ... contains a thoroughly unnecessary 'e,' to give it class."[13] The earlier period, 1946–54, saw an increasing market trend for aspirational, upscale goods/experiences for the expanding middle class, inviting consumers "to indulge in [such] luxuries" through "an overlay of fantasy, of personalization, of style."[14] Within popular music, Capitol's populuxe recordings, their promotional imagery, and a new upmarket nightclub-lounge culture focused on glamour were also likewise central to this trend.

CLASSY COCKTAIL LOUNGES AND THE 1940S SWOON-CROON VOGUE

In early 1942, *Variety* reported that the new "show business" model of the "'Cocktail Lounge' Is Classier" than earlier club designs "because of its appeal to women."[15] This trend included the opening of high-end nightclubs like the Copacabana, as well as the rise of Las Vegas lounge entertainment in the 1950s, with venues like the Copa Room at the Sands Hotel and Casino. *Variety* routinely characterized such venues as "class," "swank," or "plush." For instance, in 1944, they trumpeted "Cocktail Lounges Now Big Business," and "Terrific N.Y. Nitery Biz," with musical entertainment from "name band" acts and "personalities like Sinatra." The latter generated "terrific traffic" at the Waldorf-Astoria's Wedgewood Room, a "class calibre" venue similar to the Copacabana. This was evidence that "the swoon-croon cycle" (the male-crooner-plus-orchestra trend) was "a continued vogue for the school of Perry Como, ... Dean Martin, et al."[16] Despite wartime economic hardships on the home front, this vogue quickly became central entertainment for these new class lounges. In 1943, for instance, *Variety* trumpeted crooner Perry Como's booking at the newly opened Copacabana, just following the "start of the radio-singer trend with Frank Sinatra" at New York's Riobamba.[17]

While reeds-brass-rhythm dance bands were certainly employed, with the bigger, more-prestigious venues, artists were increasingly backed by bestringed hybrid ensembles that recalled radio, theater and recording orchestras. In 1946, *Variety* compared the new upscale, aspirational retail trend for the masses to these new "class spots," which similarly found "an influx of mass trade whose dollar was just as good," allowing such "plush niteries" with "class style" entertainment, white and Black, to "collect those fast fives and tens faster from the bourgeoisie" creating a mixed clientele of "the great and the grates" ("ingrates," meaning lower classes).[18] On the heels of glorified/luxe popular music idioms of the 1920s and 1930s, this post-swing-era shift back to orchestral-backed crooners—an offshoot of the late 1920s and early 1930s crooner pop—relied upon the same overall veneer of luxuriant and respectable orchestral sophistication. In this stylistic pendulum swing back to sweet jazz-pop, the press noted the tensions between fans of mainstream easy-listening pop, and enthusiastic supporters of core jazz idioms, from New Orleans–style traditional jazz (i.e., "Dixieland," which was returning to popularity), swing, modern jazz (bebop), or even new, lighter cocktail-lounge piano jazz. There were further divisions between the taste subcultures of youth and young adults, and along gender lines. For example, *Variety* reported a 1943 "Pop-Symph [Sinatra] Concert" at Hollywood Bowl, where Sinatra's lush music is said to have bored male "jive addicts" but wowed female "adolescent Sinatriacs." The entertainer "sang intimately, personally, like a guy parked with his gal on Lovers Lane," and his pop-song arrangements ("Night and Day," etc.) are described as "the happy merging of swoonism with classicism in the art of music."[19]

Postwar easy-listening idioms owed much to the sweet-styled dance bands of the swing era, a context that extended the crooner idiom of the late 1920s and early 1930s into the swing idiom. The former led to the 1940s dominance of solo singers, male and female, following Sinatra's solo-career lead. In her study of crooning, Alison McCracken considers the implications of Bing Crosby's shift from his early crooner falsetto to baritone register, alongside the subsequent promotion of Crosby through a masculine everyman image. She contends that through Crosby the gendered politics of male crooning shifted from Rudy Vallee–era "Vagabond Lover" sensitivity toward clearer hetero-normativity and masculinity to counteract earlier male audience resistance against this perceived feminization of popular music. The 1940s swooner-crooners, including Sinatra, were in the latter mold, though in some cases—and centrally with the young Sinatra—the young female fans ("bobbysoxers") were more fanatical, and in greater numbers, than with the first-wave, Vallee-era crooners. However, their music was still widely associated, particularly in male jazz-enthusiast circles, with a perceived feminization of popular culture, albeit without the heterosexuality of male stars coming into question. The achievement of this cross-gender and cross-ethnicity appeal allowed for unprecedented recording sales across gender lines, appearances in mainstream motion pictures and hosting of radio programs, and national-tour and extended engagements in theaters and nightclubs. And, by the mid-1940s, there were even a number of Black male crooners dubbed as "sepia Sinatras," including Billy Eckstine. Alongside areas of 1940s jazz-with-strings trends, particularly the advent of mood music, there was a broad spectrum of adult-market easy-listening music at the 1940–49 height of the crooner vogue.

As early as 1946, *Variety* announced "Swoon-Croon [Is] on the Wane."[20] New jazz-pop trends emerged through mergings of orchestral popular music, easy-listening, and jazz-indebted idioms, some being tributaries for Capitol populuxe. With the 1953 partnership of Sinatra and Riddle, such emergent trends led to a reworking of the earlier Artie Shaw and Tommy Dorsey big-band-plus-strings jazz-pop models, but this compromise between orchestral easy-listening and swinging-sweet jazz was manifest in other ways too. For instance, *Variety* noted the "tremendous" impact in 1947 of Cleveland's "class," "swank" Continental Cafe, with its "gilt-edged" "pop concert" formula showcasing a "21-piece symphonette" playing "urbane but catch[y]" programs of "light-keyed symphonic syncopation" for "middle-brow fans" of "good music." The lineup of "nine violins, a tuba, eight reeds, harp and piano," also had "cheesecake appeal" involving female violin and harp soloists. The group would further reconfigure as a "10-piece dance band" to play "urbane but catchier rhythms for customer hoofing" using "lushly-orchestrated, ear-soothing" arrangements "airmailed weekly" from "Frank DeVol, the Capitol recording maestro."[21] DeVol is central to Nat "King" Cole's Capitol transition from trio-based jazz-pop to lush, mainstream orchestral pop (i.e., populuxe) backings, and he becomes a 1950s easy-listening artist and traditional-pop/populuxe arranger for top artists of the day.[22] As the African American Cole held jazz bona fides, his late 1940s move toward jazz-pop, and then to pop in the 1950s, was somewhat of a fence-sitting act between the two worlds of jazz and mainstream popular music.

NAT COLE AND THE EMERGENCE
OF EARLY CAPITOL POPULUXE

The Cole Trio signed with Capitol in 1943. With Cole featured as a genial vocalist/pianist, the group benefitted from the postwar cocktail lounge boom as their act successfully rose to the top tiers of national entertainment. Around 1948–49, in near parallel to the *Harper's* and *Life* articles,

Capitol led the industry in the embrace of new high-fidelity technologies, thereby positioning the label at the forefront of the "hi-fi" vogue.[23] Cole became the label's premiere artist and a Black vocalist with both cross-race appeal and significant success on the national supper club and lounge circuit (which largely catered to white audiences). His recordings were at the center of Capitol's shift in 1947–48 to the new technologies that were showcased in their then-unusual choice of employing lush orchestral arrangements for backing an African American artist. This music stands as a cornerstone for 1950s Capitol hi-fi populuxe—in sound, orchestration, fidelity, and studio personnel—and the success of these efforts in turn positioned Cole well for both the highest-class (and highest-paying) supper club venues and related career markers of his celebrity.

The orchestral-Cole hits, from "Nature Boy" (1948) to "Christmas Song" (1953), delimit a foundational, pre-Sinatra era during which the Capitol populuxe sound emerged and formed key associations that subsequently became central to our cultural understanding of this idiom. In April 1953, Sinatra began his recording career with Capitol, and his pivotal early session with Riddle—the 30 April "I've Got the World on a String" (big band only)—shows the beginnings of a hi-fi, mid-century pop reinvention of swing that would reach its iconic full fruition in the 1956 album *Song for Swingin' Lovers*. These recordings were "class" consumer goods with new postwar, middlebrow-adjacent aesthetics distinct from more common understandings of middlebrow aspiration. The codes of glamour in these recordings parallel aspirational lifestyle codes seen in Hine's midcentury populuxe consumer-goods trends. Their melodramatic orchestral veneer—as in other easy-listening pop—invites consumers to indulge in the hi-fi audio luxury (to paraphrase Hine) of the recordings' vibrant, life-like orchestral renderings (cutting-edge fidelity for that time).

The associative style and textural topics in this music invoke the luxe material stagings of "class" entertainment of the day, whether in relation to glamorous nightclub lounges or media depictions of such venues and their entertainment. This is akin to the musically "mediatised cosmopolitanism" that Tom Perchard identifies in intersections of jazz-related music and midcentury luxe consumer materialism.[24] Moreover, midcentury American populuxe, at Capitol and elsewhere, was complemented by the promotion of glamorous media personalities presented via the same discourse that Stephen Gundle, in his study on glamour, describes for the Hollywood celebrity system.[25] These intermedia connections between populuxe and "the good life" as evoked by Hollywood and Madison Avenue defined this music's postwar connotations, shifting such lifestyle fantasy associations to a glamorous, classy entertainment register within postwar popular music. Such classy lifestyle fantasies—which bind together conceptions of glamorous entertainment venues and accompanying decor, fashion, and luxe-music idioms—are widely seen in *Variety*'s reportage on the midcentury nightclub/lounge business.

Gundle observes that postwar "Americans were drawn to European ideas of sophistication, class, taste, and sex and to the products that somehow embodied them."[26] He identifies the "upmarket," glitzy hotels and nightclubs as being central to this new glamour discourse. Lloyd Whitesell has theorized the glamour-focused "style modes" of Hollywood musicals.[27] These modes closely relate to the orchestral-pop aesthetics discussed here in that both employ the "contributing aesthetic qualities" of "sensuousness, restraint, elevation, and sophistication" to project glamorous "ethereality or sophistication by way of deportment, sensuous textures, elevated styles, and aesthetically refined effects."[28] In these populuxe Cole and Sinatra Capitol recordings, or the orchestral populuxe music of these lounges, such artifice is heard in the connotative tensions between popular idioms and such glamorous textural, performative, stylistic, and timbral signifiers.

Cole had three of Capitol's biggest sellers from its first decade, including "Mona Lisa" (1950) and "Too Young" (1951), both arranged by Riddle. The DeVol-arranged/backed third hit, "Nature Boy" (1948), similarly featured the Cole trio alongside brass, reeds, and strings. With the latter, *Billboard* noted Cole's "usual simple, relaxed [vocal] manner," the "haunting, rich" melody that could be a theme for "a magnificent piano concerto," and the "spellbinding" "pastoral music mood" of the "semi-classic arrangement."[29] Such "semi-classic" textures were key to the subsequent Cole tracks with arranger Pete Rugolo, such as "Land of Love" (1949), which is said to have the "same fancy orking [orchestrating] with strings" and a "pash [posh] . . . big ork scoring."[30] Initially these qualities were employed at the expense of the upscale lounge jazz-pop elements of the Cole Trio recordings.

The "fancy" melodrama of "Nature Boy" is heard in the intro, with its minor-key French horn motive, which lands on a bed of low strings with an upward harp glissando. This transitions to an English-horn response, and then a register-expanding, flute-led, orchestral texture. Following another harp-sweep, the music slows over held low-strings, which soon undergo another harmonic shift, over which a fluttering flute (evoking exotic birds) is foregrounded. The music ultimately gives way to an easy-swinging orchestral lilt, but the "posh" scoring never transcends into jazz, even while Cole's voice is grounded in Black jazz-pop. The track is more 1940s Hollywood underscoring than post-Romantic modernism (for example in the lush string sweep following "over land and sea").[31] *Billboard* once referred to these Cole arrangements as "production background[s]."[32] This phrasing references elaborate production numbers in radio, film, and recording. Recall NBC arranger Tom Bennett's 1946 description of production arrangements setting "banal and trite" pop in a "concert manner," with a "startling variety of treatments" "to attract the attention of the listener."[33] This goal is a clear foundation for both 1940s crooner arranging and later populuxe practice.

Nat Cole, "Lush Life" (1949)

The transition to swinging Capitol populuxe briefly included Cole's pairing with Rugolo, starting with their 1949 recording of Billy Strayhorn's "Lush Life." Cole's trio musicians, alongside Stan Kenton's bongo player, Jack Costanzo, are central to a newly prominent jazz foundation for Rugolo's orchestral Cole setting, which touches on Kenton's progressive jazz. Kenton's Capitol career paralleled Cole and press clippings document their familiarity prior to 1949. Kenton's progressive jazz incorporated some of the best West Coast modern jazz players and mixed their voices into dissonant hybrid jazz-classical arrangements that borrowed from prewar chromatic and atonal concert music idioms. As a former student of the French modernist composer Darius Milhaud, Rugolo was at the center of this change.

While elements of modernist Kentonia are heard in the Cole-Rugolo "Lush Life," the collaborations of Cole-Rugolo were not promoted as progressive jazz. The lyric invokes the protagonist's dubiously glamorous "lush" (with double meaning) lifestyle of "jazz and cocktails" in "all the very gay places" (with double meaning) or "a week in Paris." The track arrangement, following Strayhorn's formally complex song, is the height of production-number sensibility, with consistently shifting textures and style modes across an unorthodox formal design with numerous modulations. The arrangement, which mixes the jazz trio with a studio orchestra (strings, harp, flute, bassoon, French horn, oboe, bass clarinet, etc.), takes the following structure: Intro–A^1–A^2–B^1–B^2–C–D^1–D^2–D^3–E^1–E^2. The first 30 seconds capture its restless essence. The three-bar recorded introduction (0:00–0:09; there were cuts from the manuscript score) features modernist "symphonic" textures including chromatic melodic movement (e.g., the horn line employs all twelve tones) and block and chromatic harmonic movement, all juxtaposed against a bongo roll, and ending on a D♭9(♯11) harmony. The semi-rubato A¹ section (0:10–0:25) reduces instrumentation down to piano with Cole's entry, thereby foregrounding his almost spoken-word vocal delivery (a crisp, closely miked diction, often slightly ahead of the beat). This passage includes two harp glissandi accentuations. Section A² (0:26–0:30) jumps to a lounge-jazz mode after Cole swings the words "jazz and cocktails." This is followed by a brush-snare drum pickup, a brief *a tempo* swinging groove with a jazzy orchestral hit, and cascading Hollywood strings with a slackening tempo. The shifting textures underscore lyrical and interpretive elements, though Cole maintains a jazzbo-distanced cool in his delivery.[34] There is a kinship with other Capitol early 1950s singers, such as the former Kenton singer, June Christy, whose vibratoless, speech-indebted jazz phrasing is later dubbed "vo-cool" to indicate a kinship with midcentury West Coast cool jazz aesthetics, something which Cole's trio is not too far from.

Example 4.1 shows a swinging hybrid populuxe texture from this arrangement. As heard from 2:30 forward (section E¹), Cole's spoken-swung phrasing floats above an improvised small-group rhythm section, with shuffling-sputtering, bop-indebted drum work and wide-ranging bass work, all undergirding luxuriant, swinging Hollywood strings. The phrase closes with jazz reed-section woodwind doubling of dissonant, close harmonies (C9♯5–B9♯5–B♭9♯5), and the accent of a solo flute run. The textures are akin to Gil Evans's *Birth of the Cool* charts from the late 1940s (also on Capitol). This section's mixed-style modes point toward mature populuxe, which involved a shift toward Riddle's emerging aesthetics and away from Rugolo's Kentonian modernism. In "Lush Life," musical glamour is conveyed through the sensuousness of key-juxtaposed textures, including lustrous strings and the cool emotionality of the jazz trio. There is a graceful quality that stands at a restrained distance from "progressive" excesses and bop-indebted mainstream jazz, providing a sophisticated, bespoke formal wear for its lounge jazz-trio foundations.

• • •

In 1950, the bandleader Les Baxter commissioned Riddle to ghostwrite two arrangements for Cole, including "Mona Lisa." The uncredited Riddle had previously been an arranger/trombonist for Dorsey, as well as an NBC radio

EX. 4.1. Nat "King" Cole, "Lush Life" (arr. and cond. Nelson Riddle).

arranger.[35] Riddle's first credited arrangement for Cole was "Unforgettable" (1951), which owes much to Riddle's deft adaptation of the lounge-jazz sound of pianist George Shearing's quintet. Shearing voiced his group's piano, vibraphone, guitar, and bass in a manner akin to what he describes as "the Glenn Miller saxophone section" being "scored for piano, playing all five

EX. 4.2. Nat "King" Cole, "Unforgettable" (arr. and cond. Nelson Riddle).

voices, [adding doublings] with vibes playing the top [melodic line], [and] guitar playing an octave lower than the vibes."[36] Shearing's "locked-hand" piano style consisted of a three-note-harmonized melody in the right hand, while the left hand doubled the melody in octaves below. Example 4.2 shows an excerpt from Riddle's adaptation, with the locked-hand piano voicings complemented by guitar and celesta (evoking vibes) doublings, brushwork on drums, and rudimentary bass, alongside a lower cello doubling and responsorial pizzicato strings and harp. While this subdued hybrid-instrumentation aesthetic partly foreshadows mid-1950s West Coast cool, the textures also evoke glamour modes similar to those of "Lush Life" (without progressive textures). Though distinct from Riddle's forthcoming big band arrangements for Sinatra, "Lush Life" retains a similarly cool, swinging aesthetic in accompaniment and easy, swinging vocals. Beyond his reinvention of jazz-pop swing with Riddle, Sinatra's early Capitol hi-fi recordings also notably foreground his employment of baritone chest resonance, particularly in interpretive verbalizations that modulate the grain of his voice (enhanced by hi-fi recording technology). Similar subtleties permeate Cole's vocals, and both vocal styles and their lush backings embody the glamorous, but middlebrow-adjacent, aesthetics of a luxe life of jazz and cocktails.

The luxuriant string backgrounds Riddle provided for Cole's ballads are useful for contextualizing this idiom in the populuxe lifestyle aesthetics of this era. As Riddle's biographer Peter Levinson has noted: "Nat Cole's collaboration with Nelson Riddle fit the context of 1950s America. The Eisenhower era saw the effects of the return of the veterans of World War II. . . . 'Conformity, conservatism, consensus' . . . the suburban house, the six o'clock cocktail shaker, and the regulation gray flannel suit. . . . Beautiful love songs served up with lush string backgrounds perfectly reflected the . . . serenity of the decade."[37] Levinson's description resonates with Hine's account of midcentury consumerism, albeit via suggestions of an association between the music's deeply mainstream, middle-of-the-road (MOR) images of midcentury middleclass consumer glamour and prosperity.

This "conformity" perspective needs to be contextualized through a contrast with midcentury hipness discourse. Levinson portrays Cole's output as a positive reflection of mainstream values, and, indeed, Cole's reputation has rarely been disparaged in the manner of easy listening and MOR pop— particularly mood music and lounge exotica—from the Capitol catalog. Much of this latter repertoire, despite its glamorous cover images, which strongly suggest associative connections to aspirational "good life" trappings, is undeniably "square." Originating in swing-era jazz culture (first as a Black slang term, then used more broadly), in opposition to the positive, fashion-forward characterization of "hep" (hip), the derogatory use of square—as a noun and adjective—characterized someone or something that embodied overly conventional (possibly old-fashioned) tastes, and/or that was out of touch with contemporary culture. By the late 1930s, such notions were widely circulated cross-racially, as can be seen, for example, through Black bandleader Cab Calloway's 1939 "Hepster's Dictionary," which provides the following interconnected set of hip-versus-square definitions:

> Got your boots on—you know what it is all about, you are a hep cat, you
> are wise.
>
> Hep cat (n.)—a guy who knows all the answers, understands jive.
>
> Hip (adj.)—wise, sophisticated, anyone with boots on.
>
> Icky (n.)—one who is not hip, a stupid person, can't collar the jive.
>
> Jive (n.)—Harlemese speech.
>
> Square (n.)—an unhep person (see icky . . .).[38]

In the "Hepster's Dictionary" and the pop-culture circulation of jive slang, there is a Black-indebted, midcentury update on H. L. Mencken's "novel

Americanisms" from popular culture. Black expressions of postwar hipness were increasingly an influence on white popular culture, so much so that it led to the 1957 publication of Norman Mailer's inflammatory essay, "The White Negro: Superficial Reflections on the Hipster."[39] Such trends hold implications for understanding Sinatra's mid-1950s "swinger" reinvention at Capitol. Likewise, however genteel and refined his image might have (necessarily) been in white-dominated media, Cole retained a modicum of Black hipness that derived from his insider status as a Black jazz musician. And, indeed, the lyrics to his pre-luxe Capitol hits like "Straighten Up and Fly Right" or "Frim Fram Sauce" (1946) offer clear hipness phraseology.

While not strictly racial in its connotations, white consumerist culture—meaning middle-of-the-road, however glamorous and aspirational in its musical textures and marketing imagery—was and is by definition, square. Midcentury saw the emergence of bebop and a jazz avant-garde, nonconformist resistance to mainstream America in trends like the Beat subculture, an increasingly cross-racial interest in Black R&B, and a generation gap exposed with the rise of youthful rock and roll. As such, mainstream pop consumer culture was deeply marked both by its whiteness and square, conformist sensibilities. The sweet-styled, swing-oriented idioms of much mood music epitomized square, white, out-of-touch adult music to many hip, and want-to-be-hip, music listeners.

However artful in its veneer, midcentury MOR pop holds troubling aesthetic connections to the period's far-from-venerated "beautiful music" vogue. In the latter, I am specifically referring to the string-laden easy-listening subset of instrumental music that arose as a radio and recording format at midcentury, intersecting in the mid-1950s with the arrival of Muzak and background "elevator" music. Keir Keightley discusses such utilitarian, "aural wallpaper" music, much of which was part of the "Music for [fill in the activity]" album trend (henceforth "Music-For") initiated by Paul Weston's Capitol mood music. In resonance with Hine and Levinson's references to midcentury aspirational-lifestyle consumerism/marketing, Keightley quips that the "'classical' appropriations" of this music (strings, various symphonic instruments, and select "orchestral" textures and gestures) "contributed a sense of 'classiness' and bourgeois luxury that meshed with both the populist consumer promises of an 'easy' life and the middlebrow sensibilities of the era."[40] As Keightley notes, however, critics saw this music as degraded, unashamedly commercial product rather than elevated artistic expression—this latter criticism, which includes Theodor Adorno's damning critiques of "passive listening" among compliant, mass-market music consumers—situates MOR, "beautiful music," and mood music as a node between both this aforementioned binary of hip versus square as well as between midcentury brow discourse and the ideologies of art music. There are thus artistic valuation tensions between consumer interests and cultural/critical reception, and also likely tensions between media and corporate applications of mood music (e.g., as elevator music) as opposed to the potential artistic intentions of some top recording artists. For example, with Weston and Jackie Gleason, both leading mood-music artists, their limited historical commentary suggests their own artistic sincerity and interest rather than merely marketplace opportunism. Regardless, this "wallpaper" mood music lacked postwar sensibilities for hipness. In mid-1950s popular culture, this increasingly desirable sensibility denotes *nonconformity* and freedom from mass consensus, adhering centrally to what Phil Ford identifies (following Thomas Frank's study of hip culture) as the "countercultural idea."[41] The dominant, nonconformist aesthetics of counterculture—a term that does not enter circulation until the early 1960s, despite 1950s counterculture precedents—hold little connection to 1950s Capitol populuxe, which is a decidedly mainstream commercial product. The mood music of Weston and Gleason, just like the media personalities of these artists, represented the uniformity and conformity of white mainstream American values—Weston and his wife, singer Jo Stafford (a swing era star), had their purposefully unhip (and nearly unmusical), bad-lounge comedy-music act of Jonathan and Darlene Edwards; Gleason played the working-class everyman, bus-driver Ralph Kramden, in the hit 1950s sitcom *The Honeymooners*. That said, with the rise of the swinging bachelor image of Sinatra, as well as the early 1960s emergence of Sinatra's "Rat Pack" (with Dean Martin, Sammy Davis Jr., Peter Lawford, and Joey Bishop, but inclusive of others), Capitol promoted a new area of hip populuxe for the adult mainstream market. Riddle's early arranging style for Cole thus laid the groundwork for both his up-tempo and ballad arrangements for this new, hip image of Sinatra.

THE CAPITOL HI-FI REINVENTION OF SINATRA

In contrast to the crooner-plus-melodramatic-orchestra aesthetic of Sinatra's Columbia years, a newly jazz-indebted idiom emerged for the singer in his 1953 *Swing Easy!* sessions with Riddle. The title is apt: it references easy listening, and it refers to a tempo, groove, and aesthetic of jazz-indebted hip-ness in music, image, and a way of life. This is the LP in which the swinging Sinatra-Riddle idiom emerges, minus the strings. Riddle had been subcon-tracted to arrange and conduct for the session. He scored two numbers in the manner of Capitol arranger/bandleader Billy May (who was originally contracted for the session), as well as two in his own arranging voice. The latter charts included "I've Got the World on a String." The Capitol session was part of the comeback project for reinvigorating Sinatra's career. Levinson quotes the photographer Sid Avery (present at the session) as saying "When Frank listened to the playback . . . he was really excited about it and said, 'Jesus Christ, I'm back. I'm back, baby, I'm back!'" Avery describes this as "an upbeat style that Sinatra wasn't used to" and "a totally new sound" for the singer, adding that "everybody seemed to sense it."[42] In vocal terms, there is a shift toward a looser, casual swinging sense of text accentuation and phras-ing, with passages that are closer to the jazz-hipness and Jersey-indebted vocal mannerisms of Sinatra's everyday speech than his earlier affected, emotional, breathy crooner stylizations. With these easy-swing numbers, Sinatra reduces sensual intimacy in favor of a cool emotional distance. There's passion in the performance and arrangement, but a movement away from the crooner's feminine-market target toward a postwar ideal of "swinger"/jazzbo mascu-linity. (Alongside this swinging repertory, ballads remained a core part of his output, though often in the new interpretive vocal manner.)

The most iconic Sinatra Capitol albums appeared after 1955, the period that is mythically celebrated as the moment in which rock and roll swept aside all other forms of pop music. The marketplace reality is more complicated than this myth, however, as can be seen in the fact that Sinatra's Capitol albums proved to be major commercial successes well beyond the rise of Elvis Presley. These albums were at the forefront of new commercial schisms—between the generations, and between competing new media formats—within the recording industry across the 1950s. Sinatra's career comeback with Capitol coincided with the breakthrough years of long-play (the twelve-inch LP) and extended-play (ten- and seven-inch EPs) high-fidelity vinyl records, media that were initially reserved for what was called "good" music—meaning typically classical or concert-music albums, but including areas of jazz, "light music" (including mood music), and popular music such as Broadway cast albums. Because of economic disparities between generations, this medium was initially marketed to adults, while the increasingly booming teenage music market for singles—particularly rock 'n' roll—was dominated by the 45 rpm, seven-inch medium. Sinatra's albums were central to this new adult, hi-fi recording market, and Riddle's arranging style is a product of this medium.

As biographer-critic Will Friedwald has noted, the Sinatra-Riddle sound has "become what we think of when we think of Sinatra; the pre-Riddle period can be reduced to a prelude, the post-Riddle period to an after-thought."[43] Beginning with "I've Got the World on a String," this idiom continued to be refined over Sinatra's first two album releases for the label, including, *Songs for Young Lovers* and *Swing Easy!*, both from 1954. In 1955, they released the first of their celebrated ballads albums, *In the Wee Small Hours*. And in early 1956, Sinatra and Riddle recorded an album that has been celebrated as the apex of the Capitol-era "swinging" Sinatra, *Songs for Swingin' Lovers*.

Sinatra's legacy is central to the company's own artistic narrative in the aforementioned Capitol autobiography. This 1992 volume, written and edited by *Billboard* magazine columnist Paul Grein, with senior-editor guidance from Capitol public relations executive, Bob Bernstein, was published as a "limited edition for promotional use only—not for sale."[44] This book amounts to in-house publicity copy for both how Capitol wanted their legacy to be portrayed, and how they wanted their artist roster to see their own ties to the company's legacy. The volume offers a glossy deep-dive into its own image and document archives, with Nat Cole and Sinatra being presented as the pillars of the 1940s and 1950s chapters. Cole and Sinatra are the only pre-1960 artists who are given extended overview space on a par with the Beach Boys, the Beatles, and a handful of other iconic Capitol rock-era artists. Both are thus emblems of Capitol's own glamorous self-image, which, as the volume shows, is built on the bedrock of Hollywood's mystique of glamour and celebrity glitz. This reading is suggested in the volume's characterizations of Sinatra, and particularly in the six-page essay (with extensive photos) by contributing writer, Stephen Holden. Holden adopts Capitol's colorful promotional voice rather than the objective critical voice of his own primary work as a critic at the *New York Times*. He contends, for instance, that Riddle's arrangements merged "the worlds of the Hollywood soundstage and swing band to cre-ate cosmopolitan musical canvases against which Sinatra embodied urban romantic sophistication."[45] Perhaps uncharacteristically for Holden, a leading pop critic, he prefaces this framing with reference to "filtering the musical impressionism of Ravel and Debussy through the worlds of the Hollywood soundstage," a turn that reveals an intended highbrow-aspirational framing for this promotional material. Nonetheless, this art-music comparison holds more substance with Riddle than with Stordahl because Riddle had in fact pursued studies in composition and orchestration in the late 1940s—just prior to his Capitol association—with the Italian ex-patriot composer, Mario Castelnuovo-Tedesco. Castelnuovo-Tedesco was one of the most sought-after compositional teachers in Hollywood music circles.[46] Riddle claimed this was the most important facet of his musical training and that these lessons were central to the foundations of his large ensemble orchestration skills. The influence of this training increasingly emerges in the delicate scorings of many of his ballads of the 1950s and 1960s for Sinatra. Such suggestively "impressionistic" textures are far less evident in the swinging Sinatra repertoire, though this area benefitted from lessons learned from Castelnuovo-Tedesco, albeit perhaps more on the side of the string-orchestra film score qualities of these charts. This training also likely informed the clarity and relative complexity of the instrumentation and harmonic voicing in these up-tempo swing charts, which do not slavishly adhere to obvious swing-era models but expand upon these inspirations. Though not discussed here, Riddle's ballad arrangements extend and develop aesthetics found in Stordahl's ballad style, although often with a greater inclusion of jazz-indebted materials.

Holden also suggestively adds that the Sinatra-Riddle partnership "reinvented swing music for the 1950s."[47] This idea of a 1950s revamping of big-band swing for a postwar market is central to understanding the Sinatra-Riddle legacy. Sinatra's Capitol albums progressively refine his ideals for the high-fidelity record medium. These collections were constructed as "concept" albums. Holden contends that Sinatra

> explored various adult approaches to love and its alternatives and different personas. Among them were a fun-loving hedonist (*Songs for Swingin' Lovers*), a jet set playboy (*Come Fly with Me*), a loner (*Where Are You?*), and a hardened sensation-seeker (*Come Swing with Me*). More than assumed attitudes, these roles suggested the many sides of a volatile singing personality that was complicated enough to represent the spirit of an American everyman.
>
> That spirit encompassed . . . a yearning for an Old World sophistication [classical music] by re-imagined American style [jazz and popular song], symbolized by the gaming tables of Las Vegas, Hugh Hefner's *Playboy* philosophy, and a flashy Broadway-to-Vegas-to-Hollywood lifestyle of drinking, smoking, and partying.[48]

This quotation reads remarkably close to the typical liner notes from Capitol's mood-music catalog, as seen in the Gleason album copy discussed later.

Here is the *classy* Sinatra image of the swinging bachelor that I will explore. In Holden's narrative, the comeback years are charted as a series of stylistic accomplishments that lead to the "popular music revolution" in which "Sinatra defined his 'swinging' mode."[49] In brief, *Songs for Young Lovers* is said to introduce "an intimate pop-swing style that used swing-band instrumentation to suggest the texture of a classical chamber ensemble" (another elevated comparison), *Swing Easy!* added "a tougher rhythmic fiber," and *Wee Small Hours* is an "artistic *coup de grâce* that re-established Sinatra as the foremost [ballad] singer of his generation" by introducing a "primal *angst*" that reinvented and "personalized" both the "stylized" "smoothie" crooner practices of the 1940s, and an "operatic-level" singing that recalled the style of the "stentorian Italian-American balladeer emoting grandly a la Mario Lanza" (yet another elevated comparison, this time somewhat exoticized). All these characteristics are framed as tributaries to the big-band-plus-strings "high-living sensualist" persona typified in "I've Got You Under My Skin," the "greatest swing recording of Sinatra's career."[50] In sum, Holden's commentary displays Capitol's retrospective, canonized understanding of Sinatra's accomplishments, but it does so in a manner that tightly adheres to both Sinatra and class-focused populuxe discourse of the 1950s.

Frank Sinatra, "I've Got You Under My Skin" (1956)

The 1956 *Songs for Swingin' Lovers* offers the definitive album representation of Sinatra the swinger, and this LP's recording of "I've Got You Under My Skin" ideally illustrates the Sinatra-Riddle swing sound. Porter's original chorus is unusual with its AA′BC design of sixteen, sixteen, eight, and sixteen bars each, respectively. Riddle's arrangement begins with a six-bar introduction for rhythm section, celesta, trumpets, and bass clarinet, which features a notable bass and bass clarinet ostinato motive. This material provides core material for many areas of the chart. The arrangement then proceeds to a vocal chorus statement. In Example 4.3, which shows this chorus, note the gradual adding of forces, starting with rhythm section and strings (which quickens in harmonic rhythm across the passage in an arch-shaped semi-countermelody); adding a response to the vocal by Harmon-muted trumpets in a higher register than the strings to that point; and then the unison saxes enter in response to the title line above a lush harmonic bed of held strings, just as the baritone sax reintroduces the introduction's ostinato motive. In its final two bars, chorus 1 dovetails over the first two bars of the instrumental interlude. The crescendo

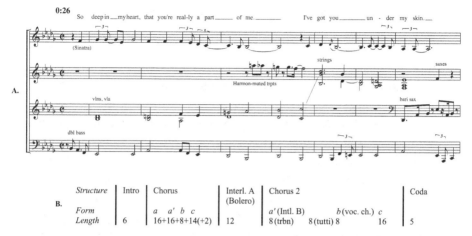

EX. 4.3. (a) Excerpt 1 from Frank Sinatra, "I've Got You Under My Skin" (arr. and cond. Nelson Riddle); (b) structural layout for the arrangement.

of the first part of the instrumental interlude is based on ever-increasing instrumental forces and harmonic tension, and layers of Afro-Cuban-derived polyrhythmic patterns. The "Bolero" stylizations of the middle interlude were first suggested by Sinatra, but it was the ex-Kenton bass trombonist George Roberts who suggested this interlude emulate the Afro-Cuban polyrhythmic patterns from Kenton's "23 Degrees North, 82 Degrees West." At the peak tension of this crescendo, the passage arrives at not the first A strophe of the chorus, but at the A′ strophe. Here the instrumental interlude bursts forth as the big band of the ensemble shifts to a 4/4 meter and takes over to back a passionate eight-bar solo by the ex-Kenton trombonist Milt Bernhart. Bernhart builds on the previous musico-dramatic tension before he gives way to a hard-swinging full ensemble passage in which the orchestra blares out a richly harmonized melodic paraphrase of the second half of the A′ strophe before stepping back dynamically, right before Sinatra and the string section reenter on the song bridge. This half-chorus vocal entry begins yet another musico-dramatic building process. Over this second vocal chorus, Sinatra displays new, fully swinging chops as a jazz-indebted vocalist by introducing far greater liberties in melodic, rhythmic and textual content. This passage peaks at a high F, Sinatra's highest note, on the "Don't" of "Don't you know little fool," by which point the orchestra—with prominent soaring strings now—has returned to a hard-swinging, full-out ensemble accompaniment. This swing passage appropriately comes to a full stop just after Sinatra sings "makes me stop, before I begin." Sinatra is given a one-bar a cappella spotlight before the band reenters in the soft swing of the opening chorus. The arrangement closes with a light six-bar coda for vocal, rhythm section, bass clarinet, and celesta. This texture and its melodic material naturally reference the introduction, but it now underscores a vocal repeat of the final line of text (the title phrase) before the bass, guitar, and drums close the final cadence alone.

The Sinatra-Riddle swing formula innovatively expands on both (white) sweet swing from the earlier bestringed Dorsey orchestra alongside (Black) hot-jazz elements derived from the post-1952 "second testament" Count Basie band, and a "two-beat" rhythmic groove (emphases on beats 1 and 3 in a 4/4 meter) adapted from the Jimmie Lunceford Orchestra.[51] The latter elements are heard in this arrangement's opening with a gentle, Basie-style groove merged with the laid-back swing of a 1930s Lunceford chart. The string work emulates Sy Oliver's sustained string writing and its use in building musico-dramatic tension. This can be heard in the first vocal chorus (Example 4.3), and especially in the use of the strings in building the harmonic tension—as well as texturally expanding—in the first twelve bars of the interlude leading up to the trombone solo. "Skin" adheres to Dorsey's advice to his arrangers that they employ accompanimental motivic materials as a way of creating form. For example, the introduction and coda are related both by instrumentation and motivic materials. Similarly, the interlocking bass and bass clarinet ostinato motives of the intro return throughout the arrangement in various guises. Lastly, this formula displays a great interest in multi-stylistic and melodramatic textural and dynamic contrasts. Such contrasts range from the delicate textures of the intro and coda to Afro-Cuban-inspired polyrhythm to the blaring brass of ex-Kenton musicians to the hard- and soft-swing styles of the 1950s Basie band to Hollywood-style pop strings. This synthesis was designed to enhance Sinatra's rich vocal interpretation, but its model introduced an influential arranging tradition to this repertory of song.

THE SWINGING POPULUXE BACHELOR

This melodramatic swing formula was part of a larger reinvention of the public image of Sinatra for the hi-fi era. The swoon-inducing vocal and arrangement style that Sinatra's music embodied in the 1940s was a direct outgrowth of the "crooner" legacy of early 1930s singers like Rudy Vallee and Bing Crosby. As Allison McCracken has observed, following the model of Rudy Vallee, 1930s crooners were "largely non-ethnically marked white men, [who] sang intensely emotional music softly, using the microphone to create a sense of intimacy with their audiences. . . . They presented themselves directly to women as objects of desire."[52] For its many male detractors, the "soothing sound" of the intensely romantic singing style of the 1930s crooners "represented popular music's furthest step yet away from dominant standards of white masculinity."[53] This gendered fan/non-fan dynamic was still present for Sinatra, though to a different degree, as seen in *Variety*'s aforementioned 1943 reportage on the tensions between the non-fan male "jive addicts" and swooning female "adolescent Sinatriacs." In both the 1930s and 1940s, the crooner's primary medium was radio. In the earlier part of this tradition, male crooners were typically backed with the Whiteman-derived, sweet-jazz style radio orchestras. The new female audience for this music, and their passionate enthusiasm for their purportedly effeminate and purposefully vulnerable singing idols, resulted in a significant male backlash prior to the mid-1930s arrival of the swing bands. Just prior to this, however, Crosby transformed the dominant model of the romantic crooner into his more "natural" baritone vocal range. His revamped hetero everyman image, as McCracken suggests, sought to "legitimize crooning by connecting it to traditional notions of white masculinity: a good work ethic, patriarchy, religious belief, . . . and contained emotions."[54]

Following the model of Crosby, in the 1940s, Sinatra's publicists cultivated a boyish, family-man image that appealed to the young female audience who followed the singer. The swooning, emotional ballads that Sinatra became famous for with Stordahl instilled a new sensual and romantic aesthetic that was largely absent in the song repertoire and patriarchal image of Crosby. In comparing the 1940s and mid-1950s music and public personae of Sinatra, the critic John Rockwell astutely noted that in the 1940s, "Sinatra was perceived not as a safe and maternally-approved comfort in a time of war . . . but as overtly *sexy*." However, according to Rockwell, Sinatra and Stordahl "still had not discovered the eroticizing power of the big [swing-oriented] beat. It was smooth and dreamy and consoling—female sexuality, if you will, rather than the [later] masculine energies of Elvis's rock-and-roll."[55] As noted, this earlier, crooner-based musical style is often characterized as "bland and sticky-sweet" due to its heightened sensuality and its emphases on emotional vulnerability and lush, swooning orchestral backgrounds. Aspects of this reception were already present, however, in the 1940s. As *Life* magazine noted in its 1943 report on Sinatra's national tour with various regional symphonic orchestras,

"the swooner-crooner" was "a kind of musical drug . . . an opium of emotionalism."[56] This same crooner emotionalism likewise permeates Weston's
mid-1940s model for mood music and this connects deeply to melodramatic
period musical idioms in radio and classical Hollywood film. These associations between luxe-pop heritage, the crooners, mood music, and easy listening are not circumstantial connections—there is a notable luxe-pop lineage
here. For example, as noted, Crosby's first career breakthrough was with
Paul Whiteman's orchestra, and Vallee was an employer of Paul Weston as a
radio-show arranger prior to Weston joining Dorsey in 1936, not long after
Stordahl joined the band (1935). Weston also did freelance work for Crosby
and Whiteman in the later 1930s, and ultimately joined Capitol in its early
years with his mood-music albums becoming one of his initial successes on
the label before also he also scored several Hollywood films.[57]

Sinatra joined the Dorsey band in 1939, and started his association with
Stordahl in that band before striking out as a solo artist (with Stordahl) in
1942. He started a Hollywood film career roughly in tandem with this move.
Despite his peak 1940s successes in both arenas, his career unraveled in the
early 1950s, along with his wholesome image. For instance, Sinatra left his
wife to pursue Ava Gardner, and his not-so-wholesome connections to Mafia
figures were revealed.[58] Capitol's 1950s comeback reinvention of the image of
Sinatra played off the newly outsider elements of these developments—that
is, the aura of the jet-setting womanizer, and the tough businessman with
gangster overtones. This swinging 1950s image taps into other cultural myths,
particularly the bachelor mythologies promoted in both *Playboy* and *Esquire*
magazines, and the marketing of other 1950s Capitol orchestral jazz-pop.

Riddle's arrangements were but one reinvention of 1940s big-band-plus-
strings jazz-pop in this later era. Beyond vocal arrangements, the next-most
successful manifestation is found in Capitol's instrumental music for the
adult market. Beginning with the mid-1940s mood-music albums of Weston,
a wealth of jazz-pop instrumental subgenres emerged. By 1952, on the heels
of the considerable market interest in Weston's mood music, as well as Riddle's arranging successes with Nat Cole, Capitol's head of A&R would crow
in bold headline print in the entertainment trade journal *Variety*, "Giant
Market of Adults Should Be Disk Target."[59] Despite their branching out into
artists from folk, R&B, and country, the main target market that Capitol
pursued at the mid-to-late 1950s dawn of rock and roll (an idiom that they
were late to follow) was this young and middle-aged adult demographic.
Weston left Capitol in 1950. Despite the blow of this departure, Capitol

nevertheless expanded on the "adult" equation of the new mood music market. First, Les Baxter (for whom Riddle ghostwrote at one time) introduced a subgenre called "exotica" with his hit 1951 album *Le Sacre du Sauvage*.[60] This label addition sold well, but it marks an interesting departure from the conformist mainstream. While still based on a big-band-plus-strings foundation, Baxter—or more accurately his primary ghost arranger, Rugolo—infused the "soft, smooth, shimmering" sound of Weston's mood music with quasi-exotic melodies and instrumentation (conch shells, bamboo sticks, jungle drums, etc.), as well as prerecorded jungle sounds like tropical birds. The idiom held important ties to evolving lounge culture, such as the tiki cocktail-lounge vogue seen in venues like the Trader Vic's restaurant-bar chain. This trend grew across in the 1950s and relied upon the same faux-tropical, tiki-lounge-primitivist decorations and marketing seen on the Baxter album covers. (That said, by the mid-1990s lounge-music revival, Baxter's then-retro exotica had actually become hip.)

While Baxter's exotica is clearly central to the burgeoning cocktail-lounge-meets-hi-fi culture of the mid-1950s, even more important was the comedian Jackie Gleason's direct extension of Weston's mood-music model. Like Weston, Gleason's idea was to record albums of dreamy, romantic mood music in a big-band-plus-strings texture. Like both Weston and Riddle's orchestra, Gleason augmented his ensembles with distinctive jazz soloists, and Gleason especially featured the ex-Glenn Miller trumpeter Bobby Hackett. Though not an actual musician, with the help of a professional arranger (Pete King), Gleason conducted, directed, and occasionally composed for these efforts. Beginning in 1953, especially with the Gleason-penned "Melancholy Serenade" that became the theme song of his television show, the comedian became one of the best-selling recording artists of the mid-1950s with his Capitol albums. As Grein colorfully noted for Capitol's autobiography,

If you were born between 1953 and 1958, you may owe your very existence to Jackie Gleason. That's because Gleason was the master of mood music . . . the man who would put the "boom" in the baby boom. The titles of Gleason's albums tell the story: *Music for Lovers Only, Music to Make You Misty, Music to Remember Her, Music to Change Her Mind, Music for the Love Hours.*

Gleason's first Capitol album, *Music for Lovers Only*, was released in January, 1953—just in time for Valentine's Day. It spent 17 weeks at No. 1 and remained on the charts for more than two years. It also went gold, a rarity for albums released in the '50s. Gleason's 1954 album *Music, Martinis and Memories* (a 1950s title if there ever was one) also hit No. 1 and went gold.[61]

The music is a clear extension of the aforementioned utilitarian Music-For album vogue. Like Weston, Gleason favored recording nostalgic hits from the 1930s and 1940s, many being now-standard Broadway and Tin Pan Alley tunes that were part of the Sinatra repertory. In the words of Gleason's biographer, these were songs that Gleason "liked to drink by at 2 a.m."[62]

Gleason's mood music was more melodramatically orchestrated than either Weston's or Riddle's arranging styles, but it is related to each. The "melody first" aesthetic of these Music-For albums functions as a commercial reductionist turn on the artful Sinatra-Riddle arranging approach, and certainly—based on the simultaneous presence of both Sinatra and Gleason releases on *Billboard*'s 1950s "Best Selling Popular Albums" charts—there were many consumers who bought albums from both areas of the Capitol catalog. Moreover, Riddle himself contributed albums to this trend in the mid- to late-1950s, including, for instance, *The Tender Touch of Nelson Riddle and His Orchestra*, a 1956 luxe instrumental Capitol mood-music album of standards—with a sensual cover of a suited beau kissing the bare shoulders of a beautiful, welcoming brunette.

Gleason's Capitol albums have come to be held as definitive models of 1950s mood music, more so than Weston's earlier examples. (Gleason's trademark sound was typically more restrained than the exaggerated style of "Melancholy Serenade.") Gleason's formula was described as simply "soft soulful music, with no vocals . . . for use as background accompaniment in love-making."[63] This wholly "adult" utilitarian intent was paired with an influential means of marketing the music, most specifically through sexually suggestive album covers. For instance, his first album, the 1952 *Music for Lovers Only* (see Figure 4.1), has a cover showing two burning cigarettes on an ashtray, an apartment key, a ladies handbag and gloves, and two wine glasses. This image was backed with the liner note explanation: "A wisp of cigarette smoke in the soft lamplight, the tinkle of a glass, a hushed whisper . . . and music for lovers only. This is love's entrancing setting. For music, in a thousand ways, describes each glowing facet of romance. In this album Jackie Gleason has chosen a group of love's most appealing melodies . . . tender ballads that have special significance for all of us. Here is tuneful, sentimental music for your most relaxed listening." The sexually suggestive design of the album cover and its notes is entirely absent in the 1940s albums of Weston, but not from their 1950s reissues.

While the utilitarian intent of this music is obvious in these descriptions and images, soon after this suggestive but discreet cover for *Music for Lovers Only*, Capitol and Gleason spearheaded the trend for "vinyl vixen" covers that

FIG. 4.1. Cover to the 1952 Jackie Gleason Capitol Records album, *Music for Lovers Only*.

featured images of alluring women in seductive poses.[64] While these sorts of sexy images appeared on album covers for many music genres, they were absolutely central to the fashionable Music-For albums of the 1950s and 1960s. As early as 1954, this album cover trend would be discussed in such venues as the *New York Times*, which remarked: "How to gain the attention of the [record-buying] public? Music-For is one way. . . . Most effective are the cover designs that feature bosomy models in leopard-skin underwear or transparent, flowing negligees."[65] Later, in July 1958, *Playboy* ran the article "Music to Make Your Eyeballs Pop (Jacket Art Hath Pulchritude to Soothe the Savage Breast)."[66] As these descriptions and images suggest, Capitol's orchestral jazz-pop was largely marketed at the postwar male subculture that celebrated a sophisticated bachelor lifestyle—real or imagined. Their frequent mixture of high-culture posturing and popular-culture aesthetic interests align neatly with the lower-middlebrow, classy, lounge-culture trends discussed earlier. This is precisely the sort of aesthetic that was culturally coded within the Sinatra-Riddle and 1950s mood-music appropriations of classical instruments and various concert-style musical gestures. These intentionally hybrid musical qualities parallel the self-conscious mix of high and low cultural signifiers in Sinatra's contemporary hipster image of a fashion-conscious, jet-set playboy with a streetwise Hoboken accent, Mafioso mannerisms, and a penchant for jazz-derived slang.

This lower-middlebrow male idolization of the white hipster-bachelor-swinger and his mythically glamorous lounge lifestyle found its ideal voice with the arrival of Hugh Hefner's *Playboy* magazine in 1953. This connection can be reiterated through the 1950s "mantra" of *Playboy*: "We like our apartment. We enjoy mixing up cocktails and an *Hors d'oeuvre* or two, putting a little mood music on the phonograph, and inviting a female acquaintance for a quiet discussion of Picasso, Nietzsche, jazz, sex."[67] The Capitol-era Sinatra was embraced by the magazine as an embodiment of these aesthetics. This connection is especially apparent in a 1958 *Playboy* essay where the magazine called the singer "the love god of our time" and highlighted his new public virility by asserting that he embodied a "hip brand of love god, so different from the lush and limpid-eyed love gods of yore"—an odd claim that disparages the type of crooner Sinatra embodied in the 1940s.[68]

As sociologist Barbara Ehrenreich and critic Reed Johnson have observed, "the magazine's contents added up to a kind of consumer profile of the newly enlightened male: the cars one should drive, the books one should read, the discs one should listen to, the clothes one should wear, even the bachelor pads one should covet."[69] According to Ehrenreich, the early magazine gave "the means of status to the single man."[70] Moreover, as Johnson has noted (when writing on Hefner and the magazine's fiftieth anniversary), the early "Playboy was never really about naked women." Johnson contends that

> Hefner, knowing that his male readers needed a little more spit and polish if they were to triumph in the coming Wars of Sexual Liberation, saw his magazine as a "civilizing influence." Anti-intellectualism, no less than sexism, racism or homophobia, was firmly ingrained in American life. But *Playboy* went ahead and began publishing serious fiction and serious criticism about art, literature, culture, food, fashion and design.... *Playboy* was showcasing such esteemed ... [men of letters] as Erskine Caldwell, John Steinbeck and Evelyn Waugh, right alongside ads for a $16.95 set of bongo drums ... [and] previously unpublished Picasso drawings.

In *Playboy*'s aesthetically promiscuous pages, the hipster argot of the emerging Beat generation mixed with the Squaresville idiom of mainstream advertising like strangers at a cocktail party. Classy black-and-white wood-cuts by John Held, a longtime illustrator for the *New Yorker*, brushed elbows with gauzy photographs of seminaked women.[71]

The eclectic, syncretized mixture of high and low cultural subjects, and both hip *and* square aesthetics, described here brings to mind key cultural criticisms in Macdonald's midcentury "Masscult and Midcult" essay. Macdonald damns similar high/low juxtapositions in *Life* magazine, including such affronts as "nine color pages of Renoir paintings followed by a picture of a roller-skating horse." He argues that "somehow these scramblings together seem to work all one way, degrading the serious rather than elevating the frivolous. . . . Just think, nine pages of Renoirs! But that roller-skating horse comes along, and the final impression is that both Renoir and the horse were talented."[72] For both its midcentury critics and proponents, the Capitol populuxe repertories seem to have functioned in much the same fashion for either the purpose of glorifying pop or degrading the presumably noble sound of an orchestra. This is precisely the commercial, popular-culture territory that Russell Lynes had referred to as the lower middlebrow. I have referenced the idea of "syncretization," which implies an attempt to unite and harmonize different stylistic languages and ideological beliefs. While such traits certainly resonate with the musical lower-middlebrow expressions discussed in this chapter, in most instances, the low-high juxtapositions of such music are not meant to involve melting-pot unity but rather ever-present sustained stylistic contradictions and tensions.

The 1940s crooner-era Sinatra was promoted via a sensitive, boyish-lover image that was seen by men as "for women," and thus worthy of less notice. By the mid-1950s, Capitol's toughened, street-smart, adult-swinger image of Sinatra (still in his pre-Rat Pack career) reframed his relation to women—his role as an object of female desire—as being central to his appeal to men. In the 1950s, his alpha male personality was central to his appeal for male consumers as a fantasy celebrity role model. This role is seen in the early *Playboy* coverage of Sinatra. In its first years, *Playboy* was a decidedly middlebrow publication in which both Sinatra's swinging Capitol recordings functioned as the ultimate mood music, and his image represented the ultimate playboy, man's man, ladies man, and man about town. While this "scrambled together" (to invoke Macdonald), dually high-low image of Sinatra the playboy—that is, the sophisticated, streetwise, hard-drinking, high-living

FIG. 4.2. Cover to the 1954 Frank Sinatra Capitol Records album, *Swing Easy!*

swinger with his snap-brim hat, a crisp dark suit, and a loosened tie of the finest silk—is initially presented on the covers of his Capitol albums (see, for example, the cover of *Swing Easy!*, Figure 4.2), this persona is most vibrantly documented in several films of the period, such as the 1955 *The Tender Trap* (MGM) and 1957 *Pal Joey* (Columbia Pictures). Each of these films adapted earlier Broadway productions, a process that reveals important facets of the cultural origins of the Sinatra swinger image. For instance, in both play and film, *The Tender Trap* concerns a New York theatrical agent (named Charlie Reader) who lives a seemingly idyllic bachelor life managing the beautiful women who clamor to share their lives with him in his swanky bachelor-pad apartment. One reviewer proclaimed that the film "is going to create a whole new respect for the joys and delights of bachelorhood."[73] From just after the opening credits where Sinatra the swinger sings the Riddle-arranged title song in Technicolor, the establishing scene features Gleason-style mood music based on this tune which underscores an apparent filmic re-creation of the *Music for Lovers Only* album cover. After the camera pans across a coffee table with half-empty whisky glasses and a well-used ashtray, a seductive female hand flicks a cigarette before returning to pleasure the reclining sultan whose every whim is being catered to. (Though the main title track was scored by an uncredited Riddle, the film's soundtrack was scored in the Riddle/Billy May idiom by Jeff Alexander.)[74]

Pal Joey originated as a Rodgers and Hart Broadway musical from 1940. The film greatly reduces the original score and augments it with other hit Rodgers and Hart numbers, including "The Lady Is a Tramp." The transformation of Joey from the 1940 play to the Sinatra film-vehicle of seventeen years later underscores key aspects of the new Sinatra persona and midcentury America's changed cultural mores. In its original 1940 stage incarnation, reviewers called the show "an odious story" saturated in "depravity," and an overall "ugly topic." One reviewer described the basic plot as follows: "Joey is a punk or a heel . . . [or] a rat infested with termites. A night club dancer and singer, promoted to master of ceremonies in a Chicago dive, he lies himself into an affair with a rich married woman [who was once a burlesque strip artist] and opens a gilt-edged club of his own with her money." In the end, the society woman discards Joey because of his disreputable character. In 1957, five years after a far more successful Broadway revival, Columbia cast Sinatra in the lead and Rita Hayworth in the role of the rich society woman. Many changes were made: Joey's talents were changed from dancing to singing; the setting was shifted to San Francisco; a smaller bit part of the original play was turned into a full-blown love interest (apparently done to please the Production Code, the moral police of Hollywood in that era); and rather than being dumped by the society woman in the film, Joey gives up his dream of running the club, both because "nobody owns Joey but Joey," and because of this love interest. From Broadway 1940 to Hollywood 1957, Joey went from being received as an ugly, unredeemable heel and moral rat, to being a morally weak, complicated, but charming man-about-town, and high-living playboy type who is somehow able to reject the allures of Rita Hayworth for a complicated but conformist, "true" love. This revised image and the doctored dialogue adhere closely to the Sinatra image promoted by Capitol, where his ballad concept albums intentionally mean to convey heartfelt, intimate romantic sentiments, even despite the fact that the opposite side of this public image was the swinging bachelor. As with *Tender Trap*, Riddle was brought in to arrange Sinatra's numbers for *Pal Joey*. The high point is the interpolated production number of "The Lady Is a Tramp." After having outlined his "system" for managing the attentions of women to the bar owner who employs his band, this is the scene in which he demonstrates his sexual prowess through a seduction of Hayworth by treating the supposed "lady" as a "dame." Numerous critics have remarked that this sequence ideally captures the Sinatra "swinger" image of this period. At the close of the sequence, the morally deprived lovers leave the club together. The entire band cheers the success of the conquest, as Sinatra puts on his trademark hat to complete the screen re-creation of the Capitol cover image of the singer. This particular arrangement, which closely adheres to the formula heard in "Under My Skin," is nearly as celebrated as its model.

Lastly, it is further useful in mapping out music-and-image connections around the Sinatra-Riddle and Capitol populuxe idioms to note that in 1953 (the year of Sinatra's Capitol signing and the first *Playboy* issue), UK author Ian Fleming released the first of his James Bond spy novels, *Casino Royale*. The novel's tuxedoed, lounge-native, ladies-man antihero clearly overlaps with many of the midcentury masculinity ideals that shape the new Sinatra image and the male ideals espoused in Hefner's magazine. More importantly for arguments here, there are suggestive similarities between the midcentury masculinity image and musical style of the Bond films and both Sinatra and Capitol populuxe. The chart-topping throbbing brass, soaring strings, and easy-swing of Gleason's "Melancholy Serenade" is remarkably similar to the brassy-jazz-with-strings crime/noir film and TV scores emerging in the period, an idiom that is now often called "crime jazz" underscoring. There are strong resonances between Capitol populuxe idioms and Sinatra's new image, on the one hand, and both midcentury Hollywood's flawed antihero protagonists in urban crime/noir films and the underscoring of these films, on the other hand. These connections are seen in Sinatra's film roles of the period, from the hustler/gambler Nathan Detroit in *Guys and Dolls* (MGM, 1955) to the ex-con drug addict Frankie Machine in the noirish *The Man with the Golden Arm* (United Artists, 1955); his role in *Pal Joey;* and his classy ringleader-thief character, Danny Ocean, in the Vegas heist film (with his Rat Pack buddies), *Ocean's Eleven* (Warner Bros., 1960). Riddle provided scoring to the latter two films. Beginning in 1953, this midcentury crime-drama, hard-drinking, hard-living loner/ladies-man antihero stereotype found its most enduring UK iteration in Ian Fleming's cosmopolitan character James

Bond, who was brought to the big screen in the early 1960s. There are strong similarities between certain Riddle scores in this film subgenre area and the slightly later construction of the trademarked James Bond scoring sounds of John Barry. The latter merge "cinematic" tremulous, high-register sustained strings with piquant internally dissonant close voicings; Kentonesque brass; and progressive jazz voicings with showband textures, symphonic scoring details, and contemporary pop (surf rock guitar in its original iteration).

Nelson Riddle, "The Untouchables" (1959)

Example 4.4 presents Riddle's original orchestration for the well-known theme music to *The Untouchables* TV series that began in 1959. In this chart's repeating one-bar, chromatic-dyad progression (F/E♭—G♭/D—G/ D♭—G♭/D) in violins and trombones, bleating bass trombone pedals on the offbeat, swinging ride cymbal, crime-show trumpet line, electric guitar, and sustained, high-register cinematic strings, we see Riddle's late

EX. 4.4. Theme from "The Untouchables" (comp., arr., and cond. Nelson Riddle).

1950s Vegas-style luxe idiom transformed into a cinematic language that is extremely suggestive of being an inspirational seed for John Barry's famous orchestration of Monty Norman's Bond theme, first heard in the 1962 *Dr. No* (Eon Productions). Moreover, the tuxedoed cosmopolitan spy glamour of Bond is not too far from the Rat Pack, Mafia-tinged, cosmopolitan Vegas glamour of Sinatra, and their trademark sounds are merely an evolution of a small constellation of aural sounds and symbols.[75]

. . .

An important part of the long cultural fascination with this Sinatra image of the urbane, swinging bachelor is its relation to midcentury dialects of hipness. The subject of Sinatra reveals at least two conflicting 1950s ideals of hipness. With a group like the Beat poets, hipness was based on an outsider relationship to establishment culture. Sinatra's hipness, by contrast, widely represented insider cultural power. Across the late 1950s into the 1960s, this aura was further refined into the harder-edged "Rat Pack" aesthetic. Unlike the Beats, who saw the general populace as mindless mass-culture consumers, the Rat Pack was a pure product of mass entertainment. The Rat Pack projected a sense of hip superiority, not in terms of countercultural irony and posturing—as you might find within 1950s jazz and Beat circles—but in terms of their displays of relative glamour and wealth.[76] There is an outsider sensibility here, but not in the traditional sense of hip. As *Playboy* characterized them in 1960, the Rat Pack was "the innest in-group in the world," and Sinatra was "the king of the hill."[77] This outlook is central to the swinging bachelor aura of the Riddle sound; Sinatra's image and its cultural mythology; and, by extension, areas of Capitol's mood music and orchestral jazz-pop of the 1950s. The hybrid aura of classy, glamorous, romantic machismo is central to this music and its appropriation as an imaginary soundtrack for the aspirations and lives of several generations of Sinatra fans.

CONCLUSION

The above reading of Capitol-era Sinatra's image and music needs to be further articulated in the contexts of both period pop and consumer trends. There was plenty of non-luxe pop on 1950s charts to foreground populuxe's elevated, classy style mode. As noted, this music's having-it-both-ways brow fluidity—as mass pop with "fancy orking" (to echo *Billboard* vernacular)—neatly reflects glamour-aspirational consumerism. Such midcentury luxe consumer goods inherently involve a range of sustained tensions between their mixed-class markers. Academic literature on brow discourse frequently mentions the *Harper's* and *Life* articles but has yet to consider the original reader responses. While *Life* briefly observes that the "differences are often blurred" between the brows, letters to the editor emphasize this point, with readers proposing "all-around brow," among other variations, to describe their broad consumption habits.[78] Such mixed-brow interests are captured—all-in-one—in populuxe consumer goods.

In 1974, sociologist Herbert Gans observed that in real life, "people do not limit their choices to one [taste] culture" and they "often make culture choices from many menus."[79] He underscores that the indices of education, occupation, and income, alongside age, gender, and race, form vital factors in brow affinities, thus suggesting the need for nuanced criticism and that some cultural/brow exchanges may be more (democratically) horizontal than (hierarchically) vertical. (See chapter 5 for greater discussion of Gans.) Music trade magazines display a similar brow-eclecticism, as seen in *Billboard* album "popularity" charts in 1950 in which music by Arnold Schoenberg ("not suitable" for jukeboxes; "moments of chromatic schmaltz") is reviewed alongside easy-listening orchestral pop by Black crooner Billy Eckstine, each being ranked by points according to "Production Idea," "Name Value," and so on (Eckstine 85, Schoenberg 68).[80] As the music industry ramped up postwar promotion practices, trends in classy entertainment circulated among marketing of "the good life" to the lower middlebrows. Gans characterized the postwar lower middlebrow as being more interested in "cosmopolitan sophistication" than high culture per se.[81] Here, the focus shifts from class/brow aspirations to classy entertainment, with luxe artifice and stylization resulting in middlebrow-adjacent consumer goods (recordings) where the imagined cultural fig leaf hiding commercial intent (to paraphrase Macdonald) has more to do with significations of affluence, glamour, and Hollywood-style elevation than with high culture.[82]

FIVE

Phil Spector, Early 1960s "Teenage Symphonies," and the Fabulous Lower Middlebrow

PRODUCER PHIL SPECTOR's early and mid-1960s "Wall of Sound" recordings are illustrative of how the lush, adult-pop production ideals of the mid-1950s, which were largely absent in early rock and roll, came to dominate the American teen music market over 1959 to 1963. This period in rock-pop was marked by a media schism, where the 45 rpm single was marketed centrally to teens and the long-playing hi-fi album was still seen as a predominantly adult medium. On the charts, the latter was dominated by the traditional populuxe idiom of artists like Frank Sinatra, Judy Garland, Johnny Mathis, and Andy Williams, along with extensions into the early bestringed "countrypolitan" sound of artists like Patsy Cline (e.g., "Sweet Dreams [Of You]" and "So Wrong," both 1963 and produced by Owen Bradley, a key figure in developing the "Nashville Sound") and Ray Charles (*Modern Sounds in Country and Western Music*, 1962), the instrumental soundtrack albums of Henry Mancini, and the MOR easy-listening of artists such as Billy Vaughn and Bert Kaempfert. The early teen-oriented rock and roll and R&B of the mid-1950s, on the other hand, typically involved pared-down, "roots" instrumentation that greatly contrasted with this luxe mainstream adult pop. Nonetheless, from 1959, teen rock-pop increasingly embraced luxe production in a "teenage symphony" production trend. Likewise, from the early 1960s, record labels, including Spector's Philles Records, progressively built a rock-pop teen market for the LP medium. Such developments emerged from several directions, starting with the increasingly luxe R&B production work of Leiber and Stoller, as well as contributions from a number of young artists—for example, Connie Francis, Bobby Darin, and even the albums of the Black singer Sam Cooke—who were in part positioned as the new generation's representatives for traditional pop entertainment, so much so that they soon worked the same glamorous cosmopolitan nightclubs and Vegas casinos as established adult acts.

By reworking 1950s populuxe markers of class, sophistication, urbanity, and musical melodrama for a new generation, this early 1960s teen music sought to impart a new commercial marketability on the previously rebellious, youthful character of rock 'n' roll and R&B. Following his breakthrough 1962–63 singles with the Crystals and the Ronettes, Spector—soon dubbed the "tycoon of teen"—rose to the forefront of this trend. Spector's recordings extended the territory of postwar, lower-middlebrow entertainment, but his productions built upon the legacies of other producers, particularly Leiber and Stoller. What emerges is a further democratization of traditional taste markers, thereby creating newly sophisticated youthful rock and roll and R&B idioms that were "popular but had a bit of a brow," to paraphrase a comment from Louis Menand concerning later 1960s rock-pop.[1]

This period marks a high point in the visibility of a range of colorful public intellectuals across media, from print to television, many of whom—as respected cultural authorities—pontificated about American consumer culture and entertainment. In parallel, at a less public level, certain conservative critics focused their attentions on popular or "mass" culture. The latter included the anti-middlebrow Dwight Macdonald, his academic peers in sociology and history, and contributors to small-circulation "little magazines" (e.g., *Partisan Review*), who fretted over aspirational/middlebrow consumer trends marketed at the middle and lower-middle classes. This class- and taste-studies literature, often pioneering academic attempts to engage with modern popular culture, mixes scholarly objectivity with unabashed protectionism (alongside white male privilege) against the debasement of high culture in postwar American society.

Though such brow discourse was increasingly out of public view by the early- and mid-1960s, middlebrow-adjacent, glamour-aspirational popular culture—often with elements suggesting a "bit of a brow"—thrived in American entertainment. Similarly, the New Journalism—a later coinage by writer/journalist Tom Wolfe—celebrated such American entertainment pleasures, from glamour to kitsch. Wolfe employed lengthy, stylized accounts of the status symbols that his essay subjects projected, created, and acquired as part of their "statusphere" (also his coinage). Wolfe describes statuspheres as worlds of self-creation, "each with its own rules of engagement and hierarchies based on fame, style and imagination, rather than [an] archaic . . . established social order."[2] He characterizes the modern world as a Venn diagram of intersecting, overlapping, and divergent statuspheres in which mass affluence and cultural change had replaced class hierarchy with "new, unofficial but elaborate status hierarchies."[3] In New Journalism, the hard objectivity of traditional commentary shifted to a subjectivity that "combined journalistic accuracy with a novelist's eye for description, theme, and point of view."[4] Applying this technique, Wolfe's early 1960s essays touch on statusphere subjects that are highly relevant to this chapter, including Phil Spector ("The First Tycoon of Teen") and the glitzy lifestyles of early 1960s nightclub scenes in New York ("The Peppermint Lounge Revisited") or Las Vegas ("Las Vegas (What?) Las Vegas (Can't Hear You! Too Noisy!) Las Vegas!!!!").[5]

This chapter explores the relationship between Spector's luxe-pop productions and early 1960s glamorized entertainment aesthetics. These themes are framed in relation to the betwixt-and-between nature of early 1960s popular culture, particularly in the interplay between both lingering 1950s and early 1960s mindsets of what critics characterized as lower-middlebrow taste culture, on the one hand, and the emergent statuspheres that Wolfe finds in American youth culture, on the other.

With respect to Spector's most celebrated act, the Ronettes, in the context of early 1960s glamorized entertainment, consider the November 1964 album image of *Presenting the Fabulous Ronettes Featuring Veronica*. The cover, seen in Figure 5.1, shows an iconic presentation of the Ronettes, with their exotic mixed-race glamour; towering hair and thick mascara and eyeliner; cantilevered breasts; and facial expressions that indicate inaccessible distance, sexuality, and the invitation of fun. This "fabulousness"—an exaggerated, glamorous presentation aesthetic that relates to many other period entertainments—invokes the nightclub jet-set glamour of New York, Los Angeles, Miami, or Las Vegas. It is a youth-centered statusphere image not inconsistent with either the traditional glamorous pop of the contemporaneous (adult) Rat Pack or areas of pre-Invasion American rock and roll and R&B. Descriptors like *fabulous*—and synonyms like *classy*—extend to many lower-middlebrow entertainment qualities of production, promotion, reception, and fashion. There are further elements of cross-racial discourse and exaggerated camp in this 1963 Ronettes image. This look first coalesced when they began their careers as dancers and singers at New York's fashionable Peppermint Lounge and its sister club (same name) in Miami Beach. Each of these elements will be considered in relation to Spector's productions and their distinct merging of lo-fi youthful rock and roll and R&B with 1950s' hi-fi orchestral adult pop.

FIG. 5.1. Cover of the 1964 Philles Record album . . . *Presenting the Fabulous Ronettes Featuring Veronica.*

Spector's Wall of Sound presents a dense, diffuse, reverb-heavy recording ideal built on massed instrumentation. It was employed predominantly on R&B-based girl-group pop of the early and mid-1960s. This chapter builds a multifaceted understanding of this idiom through considerations of the 1962 "Zip-A-Dee-Doo-Dah," and three 1963 releases—all arranged by Spector's collaborator, Jack Nitzsche—that were recorded within a month-plus of each other: the Ronettes' "Be My Baby," the Crystals' "Then He Kissed Me," and "Lonely Surfer," a symphonic surf-rock instrumental by Nitzsche. All of the latter appear on the 28 September 1963 *Billboard* and *Cash Box* popularity charts, with "Be My Baby" arriving at number 3 after five weeks on the *Billboard* chart, "Kissed Me" holding at number 6 after seven weeks, and "Lonely Surfer" dropping to number 54 after peaking at number 39 after eight weeks.

Over a month-plus, these tracks—which then sat at numbers 4, 6, and 63, respectively, in *Cash Box*—competed with a wide range of hits. The top eleven tracks include two non-orchestral Tamla records ("Heat Wave" by Martha and the Vandellas and "Mickey's Monkey" by the Miracles), Bobby Vinton's "Blue Velvet," the Angels' "My Boyfriend's Back," and the Beach Boys' "Surfer Girl," which is on the charts just as Brian Wilson begins his lifelong infatuation with the production of "Be My Baby." Outside the ongoing girl- and boy-group and surf-rock trends, these pre-British Invasion charts are all over the stylistic map: from the comic, orchestra-backed novelty song "Hello Muddah, Hello Faddah" of Alan Sherman to the eccentric, harpsichord-backed "Blue Bayou" of Roy Orbison, the string-laden traditional pop of Wayne Newton's "Danke Schoen" (featuring his gender-bending alto voice), the kitsch film-music instrumental cover of jazz trombonist Kai Winding's "More (Theme from Mondo Cane)" (with surf-rock guitar, transistor organ, and jazz brass), and the live big-band-backed R&B of "Fingertips" by teen harmonica virtuoso Stevie Wonder. These singles illustrate the eclecticism of the 1963 charts, which span from non-luxe standard pop, rock and roll, and R&B, to luxe big-band or orchestral extensions of adult and teenage pop. This is the context that framed how audiences heard these Spector and Nitzsche tracks, but the rhetoric of this music's promotion and reception carries class-aspirational—or statusphere—sonic qualities that are unique for this era.

MIDDLEBROW SYMPHONIES FOR TEENS

Spector biographies have routinely perpetuated middlebrow intentional and interpretive descriptions around the producer and his productions. These include both symphonic and operatic analogies, with particular reference to nineteenth-century opera composer, Richard Wagner. Central here are elevated associations of the massed instrumentation of Spector's productions, and the brow and value implications of the tropes of artistic "seriousness" and durability versus "cheap," throwaway pop. This discourse seeks to praise the pop achievements of this music, setting it somehow outside and above the "commercial," "degraded" efforts of its pop-chart peers. For example, the first page of Mick Brown's 2007 Spector biography states, "When most people . . . regarded pop as disposable ephemera, Phil Spector alone dared to believe it could be art. Marshaling armies of guitars and keyboards and brass and drums, celestial sleighbells, and voices keening like angels, he made records of a hitherto unconceived-of grandeur and majesty, elevating ... teenage love and heartache to the epic proportions of Wagnerian opera—'little symphonies for the kids,' as he put it."[6] This juxtaposition of aggrandizing rhetoric, aura transference, and pop sensibilities emerged in 1963 in Spector interviews and reviews that resemble the Billboard description of "Kissed Me" as "a first-rate piece of teen material ... by Phil Spector, with the Crystals backed by a big, splashy ork that sounds like the New York Philharmonic."[7]

Spector and Nitzsche rose from underprivileged and lower-middle-class homes, respectively, to upper-middle-class (or higher) prosperity during the golden age of postwar marketing of classical music to the masses via the LP medium. Their humble origins do not seem to have involved high-culture exposure beyond (perhaps) postwar radio programming. Despite this, by 1963, in their early twenties, each characterized their success via class codes of cultural mobility and affinities for higher-taste cultures than their professional stations as R&B/rock-and-roll producers. From the perspective of authorial intention—or *self-promotion*—when asked to articulate their pop-industry success, both Spector and Nitzsche framed their music and themselves via highbrow, cross-genre analogies and aspirational references. For example, in 1963, on his first trip to Great Britain, Spector remarked to a reporter that "I've been told I'm a genius," that his productions were "like art movies," that his records aimed to "make a sound that was universal" (e.g., like classical music) and were "built like a Wagner opera ... start[ing] simply and end[ing] with dynamic force and purpose." The writer complements this self-aggrandizement by dissecting the successful "Spector Sound" with its "100 violins, fuzz boxes and pianos, all churning away at great speed." The article further notes his dandyish hipster-meets-baronial fashion sensibility, "which alone would have made him famous," and marvels over both the monetary rewards of his success, and the jet-set conspicuous consumption it affords him.[8] Nitzsche was a likeminded enabler in Spector's production team. For instance, in 1965, he announced in an interview: "What I want to do" in these recordings "is combine the commercial techniques ... [of] rock 'n' roll with classical traditions. I write with a classical progression—I try to build everything to a great, big peak. My biggest inspirations have been Richard Wagner and Frederick Chopin—Wagner's music and Chopin's life."[9]

While neither the Ronettes nor their fans spoke of the music in such terms, these records were repeatedly described by Spector and Nitzsche, and to a slightly lesser degree, promoted by Philles (via liner notes, for example) and the press through a rhetoric combining pop sensibilities with tones of middlebrow adjacency. The Spector productions are the only pop tracks I have seen *Billboard* and *Cash Box* make comparative reference to both the New York Philharmonic and Philadelphia orchestras. The latter ensemble was in its Leopold Stokowski era, which popularized classical warhorse repertory for the mass hi-fi LP market—and they were notably criticized for these middlebrow democratization efforts. For example, in the 1960 opinion of Macdonald, a highbrow who never stooped low enough to consider youth music (let alone Spector), "It is one thing to bring High Culture to a wider audience without change, and another to 'popularize' it by sales talk . . . or by hoking it up as in Stokowski's lifelong struggle to assimilate Bach to Tchaikowsky."[10] The aspirational Wagnerian rhetoric around Spector's productions is adjacent to this brow discourse, but it operates in an independent statusphere. However, if the anti-middlebrow critics were to listen to Spector's recordings, and if any orchestral aura was perceived (a big "if"), it would likely be heard via the lens of "pops" orchestra associations, "light" concert-music fare (e.g., Tchaikovsky), or middlebrow popular orchestra leaders such as André Kostelanetz. Indeed, this is the context that *Billboard* interpreted the Wall of Sound through: the "pops" configuration of the Philadelphia Orchestra is the Robin Hood Dell Orchestra, which released a 1950 Tchaikovsky Columbia "Masterworks" album under the direction of Kostelanetz, only three years after his open embrace of his middlebrow characterization.[11]

These productions involve a *conspicuous symphonization* aesthetic relating to *earlier luxe pop*. Attention is drawn to the ostensibly "foreign" orchestral instruments and "symphonic" strings that are employed to heighten the melodrama of these pop tracks. This is a production-based status display that sonically parallels conspicuous consumption, under which luxury items—in this case symphonic instrumental sounds—are employed as class markers. Such sonic qualities were juxtaposed against corresponding mixed-taste image constructions, as seen in the pop fabulousness and glamour of the Ronettes.

Some caution should be taken to avoid anachronisms in talking about middlebrow and middlebrow-adjacent pop-culture aesthetics in the 1950s and early 1960s. The term middlebrow was often used very loosely, and often pejoratively, despite the wealth of proponents and consumers of middlebrow-related and -adjacent culture. Recall from chapter 4 the conclusions of sociologist Herbert Gans and the 1949 *Life* readership commentary, both of which underscored that consumers often partake in cultural consumption outside their class/taste cultures. Spector and Nitzsche both display such mixed-brow tastes, with passions not only for rock and roll and R&B but also traditional classical music. Nitzsche's family archive includes his notebooks on private music listening, and classical music was central to his interests. (Although this same evidence suggests that rather than being a dyed-in-the-wool highbrow, his concert-music interests were tempered by the practical, inquisitive mindset of an omnivorous arranger/composer seeking to expand his craft in symphonic orchestration—a trait that led him to film scoring.)

From the vantage of 1950s and early 1960s middle-class consumerism, there was a considerable range of middlebrow-ish cultural expression in media. This included the hi-fi album boom in canonic classical music, light concert music and orchestral easy listening, jazz (as art rather than entertainment), Broadway show albums, film-score albums, and so forth, all of which appeared alongside other "serious"-minded entertainment in film, television, and radio, as well as on the stage. Such middle-ish entertainment blended varied degrees of making "culture" available to mass audiences via the business models of postwar American consumer culture. This territory is part and parcel of the postwar American mainstream—recall Gans's account of America's lower middlebrows as the "dominant taste culture" with a greater interest in "cosmopolitan sophistication" than high culture.[12] It is in this larger middle-ish mainstream that the elevated airs of Spector's self-presentation are best understood.

Spector cultivated a "pop-genius" mythology for the purpose of promoting an elevated perception of his role as a savvy pop businessman and producer of self-described "symphonic" teen-pop chart hits. This image was abetted and augmented by the media. It conflated oppositional taste and class categories, situating Spector as a unique teen-pop paradox. Spector positioned himself as a tastemaker and passionate defender of pop, rock and roll, and rhythm and blues, while his cross-brow image blurred the assumed differences between a hit-maker pop mogul and his airs of elevated cultural and artistic authority. The latter are projected via Spector's professions of his own artistic genius (derived from Romantic ideals of genius) and his high-culture affinities and tastes displayed in the simultaneous conspicuous consumption his (new) wealth granted him. Such pretensions combined with his pop centrality to form an image of genius eccentricity, a quality further displayed via fashion and personality in his tastemaker role in youth-culture hipness. He was at the American forefront of mid-1960s male "peacock" or "modern dandy" fashions in youth culture, balancing modern hipness with a range of retro-historical borrowings. For Spector, this fashion sensibility combined elements of both youth-pop hipness and musty "adult" markers of cultural and wealth aspiration.

It is highly likely that the press received carefully groomed promotional manuals ahead of appearances by Spector. In a period where pop producers were normally behind-the-scenes figures, Spector is foregrounded as a celebrity personality in his own right. In his 1964 trip to London, for instance, press coverage focused on the conflicting pop-mogul, class-aspirational, and oddball-genius traits I have outlined. One article admiringly notes his "reputation for eccentricity," noting that he traveled in a "dark suit, lined in scarlet, a black brocade waistcoat with a pattern standing a quarter-of-an-inch off the surface, a pin-tucked mustard yellow shirt, and mustard silk handkerchief." The reporter adds that "at the end of the tight trousers were long pointed brown shoes with spats to match. In his tie was a pearl stickpin; looped across his stomach a gold watch chain. And he carried a small brief case with the word 'Philip' tooled in gold." There is keen interest in his wealth, noting his "Cadillac," "three apartments—two in New York, one in Los Angeles."[13] This presentation—redolent of idiosyncratic hipness and wealth—was captured in both Wolfe's 1964 article, "The First Tycoon of Teen," and period television appearances.

Wolfe's article is a widely referenced source, but it builds upon well-circulated image themes. It even reports on London's celebrity welcome for Spector: "He is all over the center fold of the *London Daily Mirror*, the biggest newspaper in the Western World, five million circulation: 'The 23-year-old American rock and roll magnate.' He is . . . the 'U.S. Recording Tycoon.'"[14] The Wolfe article's seductive, subjective writing echoes the legacy of "novel Americanisms" that H. L. Mencken identified in the popular press of the 1910s. This sensational, subjective writing voice helped to forge New Journalism. The Spector article also suggests an early example of Wolfe's later notions of statusphere.

Wolfe's writing builds on repeated and varied riffs on cultural, economic, and celebrity status. At one turn, he mock-dismissively shouts in all caps: "STATUS! WHAT IS HIS STATUS? HE PRODUCES 'ROCK AND ROLL,' and, therefore, he is not a serious person."[15] At other points, he obsessively returns to variations of motives, underscoring that the only "serious" mark of American social status is success. This theme is captured in the central iteration that "He is something new, the first teen-age millionaire, the first boy to become a millionaire within America's teen-age netherworld."[16] This is Wolfe's core claim for Spector as "the bona-fide Genius of Teen."[17]

Central to this essay is Wolfe's account of Spector's participation in a 1964 episode of the talk show, *The Open End*.[18] This program was built around multi-guest discussions of timely, controversial topics. Led by the host David Susskind, this 1964 episode featured the disc jockey William B. Williams as an authoritative opposing (adult) voice speaking against rock and roll and youth culture. Susskind apparently sided with Williams. Wolfe characterizes Williams as an "old-nostalgia [radio] disc jockey" (he was a proponent of older jazz and the crooner idiom).[19] This middle-ish syndicated show was renowned for its "serious" conversations around Cold War politics (famously interviewing Nikita Khrushchev in 1960, for instance), civil rights, and other topics of the day.[20] When announced in late 1963, the episode had just been taped and was neutrally named "Record Charts and the Pop Record Sound." The installment promised a "serious" discussion of contemporary popular music, with Spector positioned as an industry architect of the modern pop "sound." Sources indicate that the episode—retitled as "Rock N' Roll: The New Loud Sound from Tin Pan Alley"—was broadcast in August 1964, as the British Invasion was in full swing. This program theme updated the jazz-centered 1940s "Moldy Figs versus Moderns" debates and radio programs. The latter included several radio broadcasts and articles that juxtaposed the jazz writers Barry Ulanov (a proponent of the new bebop) and the older Rudy Blesh (a proponent of traditional jazz and swing), wherein real-world taste-culture tensions between adults and upstart youth were enacted for witty, pointed mass entertainment.[21] With Ulanov and Blesh, while their opinions were real (though exaggerated), dialogue was civil. On *The Open End*, the confrontations were less civil, with Spector being cornered and taking great offense. The new title reflects this divisive generational entertainment. This potential was anticipated in *Billboard*'s December 1963 article: "advance reports . . . indicate that it'll be one of the wildest verbal free-for-alls in the history" of the show. *Billboard* notes that Spector was joined by "Murray (The K) Kaufman, for the Top 40 deejay group," as well as "pop artists Leslie Gore and Bobby Vinton," and adds that the "two and a half hours" of the session "wound up with Susskind and Williams, who questioned the 'dumb sounds' of today's pop disk hits, being swarmed under by rebuttals of the others."[22]

Wolfe focuses on the tensions between youth-market dominance and the entrenched adult, white conservative industry ("the universe of arterio-sclerotic, hypocritical, cigar-chewing, hopeless, larded adults, [and] infarcted vultures" that "one meets in the music business").[23] Race is largely absent as a topic. The teen market—with white, Black, and mixed-race artists mentioned but not culturally identified—is painted as a whole cloth of integrated threads woven together by the contemporary "beat" and the "the pop record sound." Regarding the polluting commercialism of the older "cigar-smoking sharpies" who dominated the record business, Spector contends "they look at every-thing as a product. They don't care about the work and sweat you put into a record."[24] Here, the artistry, craft, and expressive passion of pop are claimed. Throughout, Spector argues that the best pop should be seen as a new ideal of "good music." Wolfe, after depicting the ignorance of Susskind and Williams, adds, "Spector says the hell with it and, being more . . . hip . . . than Susskind or . . . Williams, starts cutting them up . . . asking Williams how many times he plays Verdi on his show—Monteverdi?—D. Scarlatti?—A. Scarlatti? . . . Why don't you play that, you keep saying you play good music. . . . Spector tells Susskind he didn't come . . . to listen to somebody tell him he was corrupting the Youth of America—he could be home making money."[25] This account underscores Wolfe's framing of Spector's "pure American voice" via the power of his native New Yorker, street-smart one-upmanship, its unabashed dual intellectual/artistic-credential display, and especially Spector's use of capital-ism as a trump card. The cultural power of hipness—a quality founded on Black cool—is further underscored as a key to Spector's upper hand against the white, out-of-touch conservative tastes of Susskind and Williams. It is a seductive hipness embedded with inherent contradictions.

Wolfe also foreshadows the more fully articulated 2019 arguments made by the music critic Wesley Morris. Morris reflects on questions around the long history of stylistic and racial "amalgamation" and "miscegenation" in American popular music, contending that the realities of hybridity and inter-sections of much of this music are "more than a catchall word like 'appropria-tion' can approximate. The truth is more bounteous and more spiritual than that, more confused. That confusion is the DNA of the American sound." Morris argues that this miscegenation is "the American birthright of cultural synthesis," and that this tradition of "mixing feels historical." He adds a twist of musical Manifest Destiny by underscoring that this birthright inevitably includes a pop-cultural synthesis/expansion that can lay claim to any and all cultural territory "from California to the New York island," purposefully quoting Woodie Guthrie's "This Land Is Your Land." Bear in mind, though, the song's less-commonly known verse about a "No Trespassing" sign, where on the "other side it didn't say nothing, [and] that side was made for you and me." In discussing American pop miscegenation, Morris identifies a mutually—both Black and white—"dismaying range" of lack of consent. Under this pop ethos, permission is rarely asked. Spector abides by this pop birthright, positioning the stylistic miscegenation and amalgamations of his luxe pop and its mixed-class promotional rhetoric to create a cultural synthesis node for class, taste, and generational discourse. Wolfe's account of these collisions via statusphere is echoed later in the cultural collisions and scrambled racial, cultural, and class miscegenation that Wolfe celebrates in the Americanness of Las Vegas, which I discuss later.

THE BRICKS AND MORTAR FOR THE WALL OF SOUND

Spector's Wall of Sound was built up from the foundations of Nitzsche's charts. In their early 1960s production work, Spector and Nitzsche's written arrangements were material to be manipulated in the production process. The relations of Spector's production process to Nitzche's charts will be explored in the next subsection, which closely considers the iconic 1963 "Be My Baby" ("Baby"), among other tracks. "Baby" was apparently Spector's first use of strings in both Gold Star (his preferred L.A. studio) and in a Nitzsche-arranged session.[26] As critics routinely suggest, "Baby" represents the first full flowering of the orchestral "Wall of Sound" aesthetic. In addition to the roles of Spector and Nitzsche, the engineer, Larry Levine, is likewise central to the crafting of this iconic sound.

Early symphonic soul and R&B emerged in the productions of the Philles and Motown record labels across 1963–1964, but as noted in chapter 1, the production sounds of Spector and Motown's Berry Gordy, respectively, were in turn influenced by the 1959–1960 Atlantic Records orchestral R&B productions of Jerry Leiber and Mike Stoller. The "Wall of Sound" ideal first emerged in the August 1962 sessions of the Bob B. Soxx and the Blue Jeans recording of "Zip-A-Dee-Doo-Dah," and then was expanded with strings in their July recording of "Baby." That said, Spector had worked with string-related sessions numerous times prior to this. His first work as a producer with R&B and strings was on the September/October 1960 "Corinna, Corinna" by Ray Peterson. Several of Spector's Philles and non-Philles recordings after this, mostly from New York studios with arrangements by Arnold Goland, include string arrangements, and he produced the bestringed February 1962 Crystals hit of "Uptown" just prior to Nitzsche and Levine's employment.

As noted in chapter 1, Spector worked as a studio assistant for Leiber and Stoller when all three cowrote the 1960 Ben E. King luxe hit, "Spanish Harlem." This recording sounds like the model for the "Uptown" production, and in fact, Stoller claims that "by watching us in the studio, Phil developed many of his production ideas."[27] Chapter 1 further commented that Nitzsche was interested in Stan Applebaum's arrangements of "choral groups and strings and horns on rock and roll records" by Lieber and Stoller.[28] As Stoller tells it—echoing the hi-fi/lo-fi generational schism in 1950s pop—"the difference . . . between Spector's production approach and ours was this: While we went for instrumental clarity, Spector went for a sound that was anything but clear."[29]

Spector's Philles recordings are closely tied to Gold Star Studios. Levine is often quoted on the producer's process and how his sound was achieved. In a 2009 documentary, for example, Levine remarks: "The 'Wall of Sound' is a function of . . . Studio A at Gold Star. . . . The echo chambers never made the sound acceptable. They enhanced the sound, but the fact that the room was filled with musicians—and it is a small room . . . everything bounced off of—and we got all of this meshing going on, you know? And then you added the chambers to it. So you got this sound that all became this WALL. It was a room saturation, where you had it all melded together."[30] Levine underscores here that room saturation and body-based damping of this specific overflowing, low-ceilinged live room was ideally "enhanced" by the Gold Star echo chambers—which are described as not quite normally acceptable except for this "Wall" sound.[31] (The two echo chambers were located directly behind the control room, and their early setup simply involved a ribbon microphone at one end with an eight-inch speaker at the other.) The echo chambers and limited equalization options were their only effects.[32] But the studio's rudimentary twelve-channel console, other equipment, and live room ("the more people you put in the room, the better the sound is. The bodies provide dampening") provided vital coloring for building the Wall.[33] The Wall was a combination of these room and echo properties with specific placements and combinations of microphones (limited to twelve mic inputs for a large ensemble session), the unique resultant audio imprint from the physical compression affecting the room acoustics and its reverberation patterns and ambience (by maximally packing twenty to thirty musicians with instruments into a small, low-ceilinged room, twenty-two by thirty-two feet), mic bleed (microphones picking up audio from more instruments than the source they were focused on), the microphone and speaker arrangements in the echo chambers, and

Nitzsche's complementary approach to arranging the music (heavily using doublings or triplings of instruments) for performances in this context.

The studio, performers, and engineers were employed as Spector's creative instrument, and he was renowned for pushing his musicians—top session players who rarely made mistakes—to run through materials repeatedly while he worked to build the performance he wanted. Levine contends that "Phil's routine almost never varied":

> He would start off with the guitars—usually three or more—and have them play the figure that was written on the lead sheet. Jack Nitzsche built the lead sheets, and that was the thing—it all got built. I'm not sure that Phil had the sound in his mind as to the finished product. . . . [Spector] would have the guitarists play eight bars over and over while the rest of us were listening, and then he might change the figure. Once he thought it sounded OK, he would bring in the pianos. Then, if all of that didn't work together, he'd go back to the guitars, return to the pianos, and when everything fit he'd bring in the bass. He always brought in the instruments piecemeal . . . and the guy who worked the least . . . was the drummer Hal Blaine, because he didn't . . . start playing until everything else was right.[34]

Levine theorizes that Spector wanted to exhaust musicians before he would record in order to subdue personal instrumental voices (so they "lost their individualism") to create a "blended," massed sound.[35] Based on posthumously released studio outtakes, I am skeptical of this conjecture. First, the above quotation outlines a process, and these outtakes document many run-through takes.[36] For example, the "Baby" sessions involved at least thirty-three takes to capture the backing track. Many were likely used as reference recordings for developing work in progress, as many takes involve just slight (but observable) adjustments in audio and mix balance, adjustments and changes in parts (as noted above), all alongside mistakes and misstarts. Beyond this backing-track development, there were also overdubbing takes for the vocalists, as well as a later session for the strings. The mutable score material Nitzsche developed—alone, in consultation with Spector, or as part of the in-studio process (likely all three, but there is little evidence of such specifics)—was central to building the Wall.

Other collaborators have commented on this process. Songwriter Jeff Barry, a key contributor to the Wall catalog, observed:

> It was basically a formula. . . . You're going to have four or five guitars lined up . . . and they're going to follow the chords, nothing tricky. You're going to

use two basses in fifths, with the same type of line, . . . strings . . . six or seven horns, adding the little punches, and there would be the formula percussion instruments . . . bells, the shakers, the tambourines. Then Phil used his own formula for echo, and some overtone effects with the strings. . . . There was a formula arrangement to create a formula sound.[37]

Here, Barry underscores the comparative simplicity behind the Wall sound. He stresses "formula," but likely out of a desire to give the facts rather than derision. Levine, Barry, and other sources (including manuscript sources) uphold the point that Spector achieved success with a "sound" that developed from "Zip-A-Dee-Doo-Dah" forward. He further insisted on working with the same studio, arranger, engineer(s), process, and musicians. The latter were the loose circle of in-demand younger L.A. studio musicians who came to be known as the "Wrecking Crew" (a studio musician community responsible for thousands of L.A. recordings over the 1960s and 1970s). This is central to the success of this music as teen pop. He did, however, increase grandiosity, as heard, for example, by comparing the Ronettes and Crystals to his subsequent success with the 1964 Righteous Brothers' hit, "You've Lost That Lovin' Feeling" (arranged by Gene Page in Nitzsche's absence) and one of his last big Wall productions (with this team), Ike and Tina Turner's 1966 "River Deep—Mountain High."

BUILDING LITTLE SYMPHONIES FOR KIDS

Nitzsche's first professional studio opportunity to arrange for strings appears to have been for his own first commercial single, "Lonely Surfer," a track that illustrates his inclinations toward Wall aesthetics outside Spector's direction. "Lonely Surfer" also suggests connections of the Wall to other trends that are less discussed in Spector literature. The track was released by Reprise Records, which was founded by Sinatra in 1960. According to union session charts, the single was recorded on 31 May 1963, a month and a half before the "Baby" and "Kissed Me" sessions.[38] The colorful sleeve to the single—which includes an introspective head shot of the bespectacled Nitzsche—trumpets "Jack Nitzsche's First as an Artist / Exclusively for Reprise" and prominently lists ten "hits" he has "arranged and conducted" for various artists, including Spector's "Da Doo Ron Ron," "Zip-A-Dee Doo Dah," and "He's a Rebel." The second session for the Nitzsche album was months later, on 22 July, just before the "Baby" and "Kissed Me" sessions,[39] and before "Lonely Surfer" had entered the charts in August.

This track was the centerpiece for the September 1963 *Lonely Surfer* album. The release updates the aspirational cosmopolitanism of 1950s instrumental mood music and show and film music models for a younger generation (hence the surf-rock theme). It presents a mix of styles—even in single tracks—spanning self-penned Southwestern/Mexican/surf instrumental exotica, a reworking of a Spector hit, and covers of a standard ("Ebb Tide") and film themes. *Billboard*'s review remarks on this "flock of material drawn from diverse sources," but adds that "the big strings and tympani sound of the hit [single] is there on all the tracks."[40] *Cash Box* notes the "potent teen-angled instrumental selections" that together "offer a tasteful program of standards, flick items and . . . self-arranged . . . pop hits."[41]

There were two key additional figures involved in the project: cowriter Marty Cooper and producer Jimmy Bowen. Both the single and album were produced by Bowen, who soon produced successful mainstream albums and singles for Sinatra, Dean Martin, and Sammy Davis Jr.—at the peak of their Las Vegas fame—amid the British Invasion. He had even greater success as a country music producer in 1970s Nashville, at the height of the countrypolitan vogue, working extensively with former Wrecking Crew regular Glen Campbell. Bowen's career thus embraced guitar-centric rock-pop, a penchant for lush, string-heavy orchestral-pop production, and instrumental MOR (including production for Bert Kaempfert and disco-era David Axelrod).[42] "Lonely Surfer" was thus a cornerstone for the orchestral-pop side of Bowen's career.

Cooper and Nitzsche had a long friendship. Cooper notes that Reprise and Bowen "said [Jack] can do anything [he] want[s] and [he] can have as many musicians as [he] want[s] . . . I suggested that he make a giant symphonic surf record. The title 'The Lonely Surfer' is a vague play on the Tijuana Brass, 'The Lonely Bull.' Jack was influenced by Wagner. Note the French Horns. . . . [It was recorded at t]he old RCA Victor studios on Sunset Blvd. Same studio as Mancini."[43] The elevated-entertainment topics here map out a nexus of intersecting middlebrow-/MOR-adjacent themes: the notion of a "giant symphonic surf" record; the associative reference to Mancini, the king of instrumental-pop and film soundtracks; the reference again to "genius" and high-aura affinity for Wagnerian drama; and the calibration of production to market trends (instrumental pop; surf rock; and beat-era exotica from the Tijuana Brass).

These reworkings of contemporaneous pop inspirations are multilayered. For example, "Lonely Surfer" is apparently a reworking of Cooper's "Lonely Highway." The latter was written under the pseudonym Jay Martin, with Cooper listed as producer. The title was originally recorded in 1960 by a surf guitar band called Del Ray and the Roamers (a.k.a. the Jayhawks) on Cooper's Capella Records label.[44] In addition, Nitzsche documentarian Kristian St. Clair heard from producer H. B. Barnum that he considered it a reworking of his song for the O'Jays, "Lonely Drifter."[45] Regardless, the single is part of a trend in "Lonely [fill in the blank]" titles on the charts over 1963.

· · ·

Jack Nitzsche, "Lonely Surfer" (1963)

The session charts for "Lonely Surfer" suggest that the instrumentation budget was gradually increased, the single being the smallest session with twenty-four musicians, fifteen of whom were Wrecking Crew regulars or musicians tied to Spector. At the second session, the strings increased from twelve to a standard sixteen studio strings (adding four cellos), alongside other musician additions (e.g., two trumpets and two trombones).

This was not the first "symphonic surf" recording. One such instrumental symphonic-surf hit of 1962 was the John Barry Seven's recording of "The James Bond Theme," a follow-up to a number of their less-brassy tremolo-heavy, proto-surf-guitar-with-strings recordings, often more in a lounge-pop style, such as the 1960 "Hit and Miss." While it is unclear whether Nitzsche had knowledge of either of the two latter hits, the Beach Boys' *Surfer Girl* album—with the lesser-known, strings- and harp-laden filler track "Surfer Moon"—entered the charts in parallel with, and outperformed, the Nitzsche album.

The manuscript score to "Lonely Surfer" is written on paper stock printed with Nitzsche's name. Based on other extant charts, it appears that he acquired personalized paper just after or before starting work with Spector, sometime in late 1962 or early 1963. The paper suggests dance-band instrumentation akin to a Nelson Riddle session, *minus the strings* and adding three guitars, like Lieber and Stoller had used. It includes staves for voice, three trumpets, four reeds, three trombones, guitars, two percussion, bass, drums, and piano. This was his standard score paper with Spector, even after Nitzsche began his film-score work with the "giant symphonic surf[-rock]" soundtrack to the 1965 *Village of Giants* (Berkeley Productions), a sci-fi teen surf film with giant, ransacking, toga-clad teenagers. The movie's main theme, "The Last Race," is an extension of the instrumental-pop idiom of the *Lonely Surfer* album.

The heart of "Lonely Surfer" is the driving eighth-note rhythm section groove heard in the track opening (see Example 5.1). This includes a low-register, dry electric guitar on the melody (the score calls for tremolo effect, but it is not heard) set over a second, muted, eighth-note, single-line guitar part on chord roots. (Nitzsche specifically scores both parts for the rich sound of a Danelectro baritone electric guitar, then popular in country and surf rock.) These are complemented by four-to-the-floor bass drums, clacking percussion of muted castanets and beat-three, finger-cymbal accentuations, low piano chords, and two bass parts (electric and acoustic) in fifths set on each whole note. The chord progression is guitar-like (note the parallel-fifth writing), and the piano's voicings similarly move in block motion emulating the voicing of an "E"-type guitar barre chord between C (the tonic), B♭, and G major harmonies. The whole is founded on a duple-based, bolero-like groove (♫♩♫♩♫♩♫♫). For sectional accentuation, this part expands from octave-and-a-fifth voicings to nearly two octaves and then contracts again.

The arrangement dramatically builds from this opening, with most parts increasing in activity over the track's two-plus minutes. In this building process, the strings enter in a high, unison tremolo played ponticello (with the bow kept near the instrument's bridge) over a first repeat of the chorus (0:25). The violins lead the third chorus (0:47) with an emphatic varied melody, and with violas providing harmonic support and responsorial phrases. The recording drops French-horn octave glissandi that were written for this chorus. Instead, the horns enter at their statement of the main theme—complemented by the lead guitar—for chorus 4 (1:04), with high-register strings providing beat-three accents. A nine-bar, string-led modulatory bridge follows (1:27) with violins taking the melody and horns accenting the downbeat. F major arrives at chorus 5 (1:46), with harmonized horns (with pitchy flubs) and lead guitar again stating the theme. Ethereal, unison violins return on a held high C pedal (and violas on a countermelody octaves below). The big out-chorus sets the high-register strings on the main theme (again with countermelody violas), above the original lead-guitar twang below, and the horns jumping in with urgent, octave glissandi.

This overview illustrates the music's distance from the "Wagnerian" qualities that the Nitzsche-Spector circles routinely referenced. The closest

EX. 5.1. Basic groove of Jack Nitzsche's "Lonely Surfer" (comp., arr., and cond. Jack Nitzsche).

analogue might be the assertive, classicistic brass textures—here, the horns—that some lay persons might associate with Wagnerian brass writing (e.g., as heard in the pops Wagner staple "Ride of the Valkyries") in the context of this over-the-top orchestral-pop production. While this is not the sort of pop-tune "classical progression" foundation that Nitzsche spoke of in 1965—as noted, a guitar-like chord progression underscores this chart—the arrangement clearly "build[s] everything to a great, big peak." This chart demonstrates the fine work of a competent young arranger working for the first time with "symphonic" ensemble additions. What he does is effective and well within genre norms, even if it is not as rich as a Riddle or Mancini chart. But this work matches and out-dramatizes the simplicity of many

1950s mood music albums, a tradition that this album was meant to extend into rock and roll. This chart also reveals a model of Nitzsche's skills and artistic choices outside of Spector, just prior to "Baby."

· · ·

The Wagner and "symphonic" tropes require some reflection in relation to the emerging Wall of Sound aesthetic across 1962–63. As observed, an aggrandizing rhetoric and efforts at high-culture aura transference were present in the promotion and press reception of Spector and Nitzsche from early on. While I take the professed passion of Nitzsche and Spector for Wagnerian opera seriously, and while I respect their pop production artistry, I see no direct way of connecting Wagnerian influence and the Wall of Sound beyond Nitzsche's sparing uses of brief classicistic scoring effects like the French horns in "Lonely Surfer." These are musico-dramatic—or cinematic— narrative-building effects. The mere presence of eight violins, four violas, and two French horns likewise forms a second, loose musical topic with associative connections to classical music, regardless of the music they are applied to. Nitzsche clearly privately studied classical scores. When he started to do so is uncertain, but his archive contains pocket scores for Hector Berlioz's *Symphonie fantastique* and Aaron Copland's *El Salon Mexico*, as one might expect a Hollywood composer or orchestrator to own. That said, Wagnerian chromatic harmony; expansive formal scale; emotional breadth; and structural, philosophical, and poetic complexity, are absent from *Lonely Surfer*— thankfully. Nitzsche, Cooper, and Bowen would likely admit that such traits were not compatible with this commercial project, even if their intent was a "giant symphonic surf record." With no brow slight intended to Spector or Nitzsche, it is hard not to read their interest in Wagner and classical prestige via the lens of the hi-fi era boom in classical warhorse-repertory marketing for the masses. Nevertheless, even if Nitzsche were given a green light to score pop in a Wagnerian fashion, it would not have fit the market. There is an ocean applied here to watering down any intended classical influences. If they exist, they are merely a few dashes of seasoning (like the French horns) in a larger production recipe. The greater whole more clearly references other pop productions rather than classical music per se.

Spector and his collaborators point to the August 1962 Bob B. Soxx and the Blue Jeans recording of "Zip-A-Dee-Doo-Dah," Philles no. 107, as the origin for the Wall formula. The "teenage symphony" sound is said to have emerged across 1963, particularly in Philles Records 115, 116, and 118, which includes the July recordings of the Ronettes' "Be My Baby" (116) and the Crystals' "Then He Kissed Me" (115), and the November Ronettes' track, "Baby, I Love You" (118). "Kissed Me" entered the *Billboard* Hot 100 charts on 17 August and rose to number 6, "Baby" entered the Hot 100 on 31 August and rose to number 2.[46]

DISCOVERING THE WALL

Bob B. Soxx and the Blue Jeans, "Zip-A-Dee-Doo-Dah" (1962)

When Levine began work at Gold Star in July 1958, the venue was a one-room demo studio. Spector had at least one session with Levine at Gold Star that year, as well as in 1961, but their professional association began in earnest with the 1962 Crystal's "He's a Rebel" session that brought Nitzsche into their fold. Three weeks later, the three were in the studio for "Zip-A-Dee-Doo-Dah" with an ensemble of Spector regulars dubbed as Bob B. Soxx and the Blue Jeans. Levine has commented on their discovery of the room's special massed properties being a result of his negotiations between Spector's unorthodox process, adjustments to limited equipment and studio space, happenstance discoveries from both mixing on-mic clarity and off-mic bleed, and pushing recorded sound to where the tape was bordering distortion (via saturation from too-high audio levels, which Spector insisted on).[47]

Nitzsche recalled that Spector "had this idea in his head to do 'Zip-A-Dee-Doo-Dah.' And . . . the record . . . [that we wanted] to make 'Zip-A-Dee-Doo-Dah' sound like was 'I Know' by Barbara George. So we used . . . that rhythm."[48] His reference here to the 1961 track "I Know" by Barbara George, and the chart's reference to the same groove as "Hully Gully," illustrates an inspirational web. The latter references the 1959 hit R&B song by the Olympics (related to the dance craze of the same name). Both illustrate how the growing hit-making machine of Spector and Nitzsche mined production inspiration from the charts. Nitzsche adds that "some things happened in the session that were just incredible. The [off-microphone, fuzz] guitar sound [by] Billy Strange—god!—[that] was pretty unique in those days and the [opening distorted] Wurlitzer electric piano, that sounds like an explosion, [was] . . . so awesome."[49] Nitzsche captures the unique mixtures of sound qualities that could be part of the emerging Wall aesthetic. The opening of the track is built on an unbalanced mix of muddied and distorting left-hand

Wurlitzer piano stabs, biting (and clear) rhythm guitar stabs in the upper register, a clacking castanet foreground, a muffled bass drum, and backing vocalists sounding as if they have been banished to another room. The Strange guitar part was central to discovering the potential of off-mic bleed. In recounting an incident where Levine cut the faders and brought them up one by one with the exception of the guitar, he comments that Spector suddenly shouted "'That's the sound, that's the sound! Let's record it!' I said 'Well, I don't have Billy Strange's microphone turned on,' and he said 'Don't turn it on . . .' As it happens, you can hear Billy Strange's guitar throughout . . . It just bled onto the other mics."[50]

This introduction readily displays the lack of clarity that Stoller pointed to in Spector's productions, but this quality is used for a lo-fi but highly musical effect, thereby enhancing qualities that both Spector and Nitzsche admired in early rock and roll and R&B.[51] Nitzsche further describes his typical partnership with Spector in relation to this early track, noting that Spector "had a lot of ideas. . . . I couldn't imagine 'Zip-A-Dee-Doo-Dah.' I didn't hear what he was hearing but when he started showing me on the piano, I understood. . . . That's what we had together. . . . I understood what he was trying to get across. And when it came to arrangements, especially like on 'Zip-A-Dee-Doo-Dah,' Phil had a lot of ideas himself. So in many cases, I almost became like a musical secretary. I mean he didn't know how to orchestrate and voice things correctly and so on."[52] While this characterization aligns with how collaborators describe the mogul-production process of Spector, I suspect that Nitzsche in fact contributed quite a lot to the music in his attempts to flesh out what Spector requested.

The surviving charts from "Zip-A-Dee-Doo-Dah" include piano, two basses, drums, trumpet, tenor and baritone sax, and three guitars. The three-guitar lineup suggests Lieber and Stoller minus orchestral complements. There are multiple copies of certain parts, a detail that underscores intentions for instrumental doubling of these parts by additional musicians. Indeed, Spector typically had three to four pianists, two bassists, four guitarists, three or four reeds, two trumpets, two trombones and diverse additional percussion. On the chart, there is an added note (by Nitzsche, Spector, or a guitarist) about the inserted Strange guitar solo. This detail further illustrates the mutability of the charts during development in the studio. And, of course, many non-notated details that define the final recording were discovered through the in-studio rehearsals. For instance, the iconic Wurlitzer introduction is not present in the charts. Lastly, like nearly all charts for Spector, the vocal parts are never found in notated form, unlike with Nitzsche's non-Spector sessions. The producer's hands-on oral process for developing vocals is suggested in studio film footage.[53]

The Ronettes, "Be My Baby" (1963)

A study of how the original Nitzsche chart for "Baby" was adapted into the recording reveals much about the Spector production process circa 1963. Example 5.2 presents a chorus passage derived from both the extant score and transcribed performance material. Neither this chart, thirty-three extant bootleg takes, nor Levine's commentary, hold evidence about the addition of the strings, and I have found no documentation of the string session.

In Spector's early 1960s recordings, the backing tracks were recorded live in mono. Gold Star's three-track machine variously recorded the backing track, and combinations of the lead vocal, backing vocals, and overdubs for additions like strings. Though on "Baby" lead and backing vocals are heard in one bootleg take each with the band, Ronnie Spector's lead and the backing vocals were captured separately.[54] This suggests an intermediate bounce-down of three tracks to two on a second three-track recorder to make room for the string overdub.

Nitzsche's chart is on the same paper stock as "Lonely Surfer," with its big-band-with-vocal layout and no staves for strings. The "Baby" chart is written for a single trumpet, a trombone, and tenor and baritone saxes, along with three guitars, castanets, non-notated shakers, drums, bass, and piano. The horns are a standard four-piece R&B horn section, as evident in their triad-, riff-, and blues-based parts. While this lacks a luxuriant big-band texture, the "orchestral" qualities are enhanced through the large studio band. The mutability of the score is evident in various details. For example, on the recording(s), one hears a new intro and outro, the added famous drum fills before the fade, materials being used in new combinations and places, and various musician contributions. There are also small score details not used. A "low horns with bass" notation on one page seems to be a later addition, and this idea is used in the first chorus. Another page includes a note, "Nite Owl Low Horns," which references the horn-section sound of a yet-to-be identified R&B recording. In the recording, the second chorus uses chart material on the bottom half of page 7, but a string section is added that is not in the score. The strings—violins, violas, cellos, but likely not a standard sixteen strings—double the unison baritone sax and trombone part at octaves.

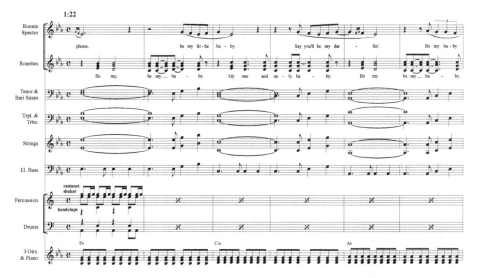

EX. 5.2. Transcription from the Ronettes, "Be My Baby" (arr. Jack Nitzsche, prod. Phil Spector).

The addition provides a melodrama to the pleading chorus, but it lacks the fullness and countermelodies employed on "Lonely Surfer." This suggests choices made by Spector, the producer. The "Wall" mix and instrumental background also notably lacks the sectional clarity of traditional jazz-pop scoring. In "Baby," the strings only step into a clear foreground in the cello/viola-section solo after the second chorus (again, an unharmonized melody, now based on the verse).

While Spector and Nitzsche built this chart on a standard I-vi-IV-V doo-wop chord cycle, they reinvent this cliché through studio artifice that marries Leiber and Stoller–like luxe pop to lo-fi early 1960s R&B production. The latter is evident in several details. For example, a bootleg vocal take with both Ronnie and the Ronettes includes ambient bleed from the playback track (played for the singers via a speaker in the vicinity of the microphone). In mixdown, this bleed double-tracked the Wall backing with further off-mic room ambience. Like Sinatra, Ronnie sang into a Neumann U47 mic, which brought her voice into clear relief at the mix foreground. The higher fidelity of the isolated string tracking is also noticeable. In sum, a core Wall aesthetic is its *blending* of hi- and lo-fi production, and both production- and style-based tensions between the juxtaposed layers of this sonic accretion process. Interestingly, despite later reception of "Baby" as the foundation for Spector's teenage symphony ideals, neither the *Billboard* nor *Cash Box* reviews reference the strings. Rather, *Billboard* emphasizes the track's melodrama: "This is the best record the Ronettes ever made. . . . Spector . . . has transformed the gals into a [powerful] singing group who handle this dramatic piece of material with flair. Backing has a stunning, rolling rock sound that's bound to make the disk score with the kids."[55]

The Crystals, "Then He Kissed Me" (1963)

It is also instructive to consider the Crystals' "Kissed Me" from the same session. Here, Nitzsche crossed out the manuscript paper's trumpet section to write string parts. Throughout, he writes harmonized violin parts almost exclusively in registers above the treble stave (like in "Surfer"), with half-note-based string movement marked both for tremolo and "sustain," and characteristic, end-of-section string glissandi and brief melodic figures. Notably, various written details of the latter sort are absent in the recording, perhaps because Spector deemed them too busy. From the third bar of the bridge (1:10 forward), a later-process addition (written above the string lines in a darker pencil) of a soaring, high-register melodic response to "he kissed me in a way that I've never been kissed before" adds a suitable dramatic effect. Here, underneath the erotic memory of the lyric, Nitzsche expands to four-octave, five-voice, two-bar sustained chords, with three-part violin close voicings at the top. He occasionally even uses seventh chords. It is an artful touch, but amid the dense ambience of the Wall, the lower strings are lost in a mid-range fog. Throughout "Kissed Me," Nitzsche creates a registral division between the tremulous strings and the earthy, low-register R&B horn section. That said, the instrumental break—comparable to the strings solo in "Baby"—includes a passage of classicistic scoring (from 1:49). The latter is uncharacteristic for mid-1960s Spector, but routine on *Lonely Surfer*. In "Kissed Me," the strings and trumpet perform a semi-contrapuntal, two-line call-and-response in a stiff style that drags against the backing groove. The timbre, counterpoint, straight rhythm, and performance approach all speak in a "formal" register that involves a brief evocation of the style of "serious" music in contrast to the R&B-native, luxe string/reeds/brass heard in the track.

The immense echo-based sound—the "big, splashy ork that sounds like the New York Philharmonic"—was a result of an engineering mistake by Levine who had attempted to increase the volume for Spector in the control room. The backing track was recorded using two tracks on the three-track machine for left and right channels, and then later mixing the chosen take down to mono. With "Kissed Me," Levine sought to increase monitor volume by deleting one channel and duplicating the other (to fill left and right channels), but due to the mixer setup, they heard "echo from both [the original] left and right [channels] on the one channel," leaving "a double echo with half the musical presence."[56] This double echo effect became a new part of the Spector sound.

· · ·

In his study of genre, *Categorizing Sound*, David Brackett situates most early 1960s orchestral R&B in the middle "R&B, Consistent Crossover" circle of a Venn diagram that illustrates the overlaps between the poles of "R&B, Inconsistent Crossover" and "Mainstream." This "consistent crossover" includes "Motown Pop, MOR-R&B-Pop, and Brill Building R&B-Pop," the latter of which presumably includes the Ronettes. Indeed, the group and "Baby" were on the November 1963 *Cash Box* R&B chart that is central to Brackett's study of emerging market definitions of soul. This was an unusual moment in which R&B, "one of the tributaries of the mainstream," began "to assume a similar level of stylistic heterogeneity" as mainstream pop "in the pursuit of the broadest audience."[57] Elsewhere in his marketing discussions, Brackett describes areas of "Brill Building Pop-R&B" as "uptown," a New York-derived term that evokes upward class mobility, cosmopolitanism, and glamour in midcentury entertainment. This notion of uptown R&B, or perhaps even cosmopolitan R&B with a New York edge, is useful for understanding the Ronettes.

CONSIDERING THE RONETTES

Cultural interpretation is inherently multivalent. Beyond discourse around Spector, Nitzsche, Levine, and their musicians, and beyond critical and industry reception, an expanded accounting of the field of meaning around "Baby" requires consideration of the Ronettes, including their self-perception, their views on their music and Spector, and the understandings of their fans. The Ronettes—Veronica Bennett, a.k.a. Ronnie Spector, the lead singer ("Ronnie," to avoid confusion with the producer), her sister Estelle Bennett, and their cousin Nedra Talley—have left extended commentary on their image, but little commentary on the sound of their recordings. A 1964 article notes,

"The Ronettes said they could not explain how that . . . sound came to be recorded. 'It's all the work of our record boss, Phil Spector,' said Ronnie. 'He's just a genius. We stand in the middle of the recording studio, in a glass box, like goldfish, and the place is packed with musicians. We just sing when he tells us to—if you want to know how the sound happens, you'll have to ask Phil.'"[58] Speaking of "Baby," Nedra haphazardly lists off the instrumentation, and adds, "They sure made a powerful noise." The group emphasizes, though, that their music is rock and roll, with Nedra adding, "We have always been plain rock-n-roll fans," and Ronnie noting, "None of us goes a lot on jazz [but] [w]e like the bluesy types—Ray Charles and the Miracles."[59] Thus, as seen in a range of interviews, other than brief mentions of violins, Spector's "genius," and the "powerful noise," there is little highbrow-associative *musical* framing from their perspective. This is not true, however, with regard to "class" entertainment (i.e., where *class* and *classy* are understood as glamour-based adjectives not indicative of socioeconomic status), a perspective that neatly ties into their self-image and its relation to entertainment tropes of glamour and wealth.

In her autobiography, Ronnie only makes one reference to the symphonic ideals of Spector and Nitzsche. Despite her admiration for the sound, this commentary offers a brow-corrective that frames "little symphonies" more as a loose analogy. After arbitrarily sketching out the huge personnel and mixed instrumentation for Ronettes sessions, she remarks: "Then he'd record everything back on top of itself to double the sound. Then he'd double it again. And again. And again and again, until the sound was so thick it could have been an orchestra. That's what Phil was talking about when he told a reporter that his records were like 'little symphonies for kids.'"[60] The passage contains little of the aspirational aura that Nitzsche and Spector sought to convey in their accounts.

Rather than sound, the first thing Ronnie chooses to discuss in her auto-biography is the group's connections to mixed race and culture in Spanish Harlem. Here, she emphasizes the culture clash she and Estelle experienced due to their white father and half-Black, half-Cherokee mother. She describes a community of "Chinese laundries, Spanish restaurants, and black groceries stores,"[61] as well as singing lessons from an "old Italian."[62] She discusses the outsider nature of being a "half-breed," even in that neighborhood, and of having mixed racial features and skin tone. Nedra, who was biracially His-panic and Black, was darker complexioned, and thus more closely reflected Black Harlem.[63] Ronnie emphasizes her identity crisis at puberty of not being accepted as Black, white, or Spanish, and of trying to determine which bodily features mapped onto which heritage. These Black-leaning but ambiguous visual aspects of the Ronettes were significant for their reception, allowing them to project different identities to different audiences, though always with qualities of Blackness and New York multicultural cool. This fit well with Spector's vision for the group, as he felt their New York sensibility was central to their appeal. That said, growing up, their community pointed them to the Apollo Theater as the apotheosis of entertainment, with their idols being the "biggest black stars," and with Ronnie trying to "dye my skin darker" to resemble these celebrities.[64] Gender-norm transgression also was a factor: Ronnie viewed herself as a tomboy.[65] She states repeatedly (in her book and elsewhere) that her vocal delivery was indebted to the Harlem teen-age star, Frankie Lyman.[66] This complex of mixed culture, race, fashion, and community is what set the group apart from competition.

Such traits were central to their success prior to their Spector affiliation. By spring 1961, while only seventeen and eighteen, the group was performing at "bar mitzvahs and sock hops," had a manager, and a contract to record bland girl-group material for Colpix Records.[67] The under-age group insinuated themselves into Manhattan's Peppermint Lounge, the center of New York's "rock and roll crowd" at the height of the 1961 twist dance craze. The Lounge hosted the biggest celebrities, politicians, and members of the cultural "in" crowd.[68] With "all the tricks to using eyeliner, blusher, and lipstick," "Kleenex to stuff" in their bras, and "teased hairdos until they were stacked up to the ceiling," the underage trio became featured dancers—with opportunities to sing—alongside the house band, Joey Dee and the Starlighters.[69] This led to the reinvention of group, their naming, and the refining of their image just prior to Spector's interest. The group opened the fashionable Miami Peppermint Lounge, and were popular "beautiful dancing girls" for the teen rock 'n' roll revues of disc jockey Murray "the K" Kaufman.[70] This latter Brooklyn engagement allowed them to further build their image, teasing their hair as high as it could go, and dramatically overextending eyeliner and mascara. Ronnie notes, "We'd look pretty wild . . . onstage, and the kids loved it." The goal was to "make an impression with our style," and this played with perceptions of mixed race. They borrowed their look from

> the girls we'd see on the streets of Spanish Harlem, the . . . girls . . . with thick eyeliner and teased hair. . . . We exaggerated it onstage . . . to be bigger than life. . . . We may have looked like street girls, but . . . under all that makeup, we were really just three innocent teenagers. . . . [The audience] liked that

combination.... We followed our own style.... The Ronettes were what the girls wanted to be, and what the guys dreamed about.... The songs we sang were ... tougher than the stuff the other [girl] groups did.... We weren't afraid to be hot.... [We] squeezed our bodies into the tightest skirts.... and hike them up to show our legs ... [with] slits up the side.... We definitely made an impact.[71]

The group's outfits were often designed by Estelle, who "pag[ed] through *Glamour* magazine" and other sources for inspiration.[72] Also notable, from the perspective of 1990 Ronnie, is her observation that they had a core group of fans circa 1962 who "seemed to be gay men or lesbians. . . . Something about our style . . . spoke to a lot of gay people, because they've always been there for us."[73]

By early 1963, they were associated with Spector. They sought him out because "this guy could produce rock and roll music like no one else," and Ronnie lists the 1962 tracks, "Zip-A-Dee Doo Dah," "He's a Rebel," and earlier "Uptown." Their first meeting came with expectations based on press accounts of Spector. As Ronnie tells it, "Our only image of a rich man came from the TV show 'The Millionaire.'" When the girls met the producer, they "couldn't believe this weird little man" could be Spector.[74] Ronnie added that "for a millionaire, he sure could be cheap."[75] She specifically describes these three tracks as rock and roll, and period fans likely did the same, with their identification emphases placed on the artists' personas and lyrics, and with the "big" production heard as cinematic-style narrative underscoring. My assumption is that the core demographic—teens—likely did not hear the Wall recordings as Wagner-inspired symphonies for kids, just as, I suspect, everyday film fans probably hear classical Hollywood's orchestral underscoring as generic "Hollywood film music" rather than Wagnerian or even classical music. In resonance with this reading, Ronnie describes "Baby" unpretentiously as "a rock and roll classic," that it was a "tough [sounding] record, but it had a sweet side to it, just like the Ronettes. It was the kind of song a street kid would like. And a lot of them did," so much so that "the black and Spanish kids in Harlem nearly had a riot over us." Central again is their mixed-culture, edgy, New York image, as these fans were "fighting over our skin color! Funny thing is, they both were right."[76] They embraced this, but were pleased that "we could pass in the black world."[77]

Before their late 1963 UK tour, their image took on an aura of jet-set glamour, as seen in a September 1963 *American Bandstand* interview where they discuss their exotic and New York—L.A. travels as teenaged stars.[78]

Similarly, the African American middle-class magazine, *Ebony*, featured the group in a November 1966 cover story that describes them as a "rock 'n' roll girls trio," and friends of the Beatles.[79] They are presented not as "street girls" but as fashionable, successful, cosmopolitan young women who are part of Black culture. Notably within this article is an advertisement for Posner "Custom Blends" cosmetics, which touts the cosmopolitan beauty of "that wonderful Exotic Look" available to "only you who are darker than fair."[80] This ad copy accompanies images of three "exotic" beauties, but centrally a mocha-toned Black woman set against a New York nighttime background. The smaller images evoke comparable woman in Venice and Paris—the implication being that young, lighter-skinned African American women have access to an exotic, fashionable, cross-racial, cosmopolitan beauty ideal. These are presented as images of aspirational glamour, and it is this framing that the Ronettes—as modern, hip celebrity representatives of youth—likely represented to fans, whether male or female, straight or LGTBQ. The group was also featured in a 1966 interview in *Jet*; thus, they were clearly seen to be of interest to an aspiring Black middle class.[81] It is notable that Spector is hardly mentioned in either article.

The Ronettes further distinguished their act from the packaging of the Motown girl groups. Ronnie recalls a comment that "you girls could stand to be a little more classy. Just look at the Supremes." Her response argues that sexual overtones were important to the Supremes, but the Ronettes "don't do [that] kind of act." The Supremes are also said to be "not rock and roll. Rock and roll is exaggerated—bigger than life." She continues: "The Supremes wear long, tight gowns and sing about *where-did-their-damn-love-go* in high-pitched voices. That's not sexy. That's Las Vegas!"[82] The latter implies a derogatory attitude, and seems retrospectively revisionist. Evidence suggests that the group did cater to Vegas-style glamour across circa 1963–64, prior to the British Invasion. As Nedra said in the UK in 1964, "When we do cabaret dates we do the night-club type of numbers—the same sort of thing that you'd expect from the McGuire Sisters or the Andrews Sisters."[83]

Despite mild connections to nightclub glamour, in their promotion, the group's streetwise New York background was underscored. The latter appears, for instance, in UK articles, where mentions are made of Ronnie's New York accent being important for her sound as singer. And to a reporter, Spector said "the girls have what I call a 'New York sound.'"[84] This geographical-cultural association and its cosmopolitan pop currency is also played up in a 1965 CBS TV special where the Ronettes were taped parading through New

York's Mott Street neighborhood singing "Baby."[85] This Little Italy locale (not their neighborhood) might reflect either the city's melting-pot, tenement aura (underscoring the American Dream, where immigrant progeny can rise to celebrity), or perhaps represent the youth-culture associations of the 1964 cover to *Another Side of Bob Dylan*. The Little Italy framing also telescopes to the most famous cinematic use of "Baby" as the main title music to Martin Scorsese's 1973 debut, *Mean Streets* (Warner Bros.). Here, the melodramatic longing of the song functions as a cinematic, nostalgic glorification of a street-wise, small-time circle of criminal misfits. The music is juxtaposed against a montage of grainy, 8 mm "home" video shots of the supposedly good times in this Little Italy circle (with baptisms, wedding cakes, celebrations, etc.). Here, the music is connected again to a cinematic New York mythology of gritty, lower-class, mixed-culture perspectives on glamour.

CONCLUSION: AMERICAN CHARACTER, FABULOUSNESS, AND MIDDLEBROW ADJACENCY

The above summaries of intention, reception, image, and self-presentation outline multivalent meanings present in hearing Spector's Wall of Sound and the Ronettes with historically attuned ears. Each perspective reveals connections to period lower-middlebrow taste culture(s) in relation to early 1960s cosmopolitan and celebrity glamour. Within the postwar contexts of both rock and roll and an influential new youth consumer culture, I suggest that the middle-class taste-culture hierarchies explored in this chapter relate less to midcentury writings on middlebrow culture than they do to the somewhat later research of sociologist Herbert Gans. In his 1974 book, *Popular Culture and High Culture*, Gans argues—as Pierre Bourdieu's 1979 book, *Distinction*, would—that cultural tastes, and taste cultures, reflect social, and educational dispositions shared by groups and individuals with similar backgrounds and life experiences. The premise of Gans's study, however, lies in a 1966 essay, thus suggesting foundations in near parallel to the media discussed in this chapter and the cultural mores documented by Wolfe.[86] Gans thus offers an updated perspective on American brow discourse amid the shifting cultural tides of the 1960s.

Via sociological framing, Gans provides a comprehensive consideration of lower-middlebrow culture. His taste-culture study builds in part off of Russell Lynes's earlier writings on brow cultures.[87] With the demographic expansion of the lower middlebrow through postwar prosperity and booming consumer industries, this taste-culture strata had become "America's dominant taste culture" and one that "provides the major audience for today's mass media."[88] In reference to post-1950 America, Gans contends that the lower-middlebrow "public is not particularly interested in what it calls 'culture,' . . . mean[ing] both high and upper-middle culture, but whereas it was once opposed to the cosmopolitan sophistication of both [upper] cultures . . . , this is no longer the case."[89] I contend—in agreement with Gans, and as evidenced in period media—that midcentury characterizations of the social influence of American highbrows at midcentury were markedly out of alignment with the portrayals of this class from a mass-culture perspective.

Gans's commentary on the postwar cultural leveling of both the upward-aspirational influence between the brows, and the expanding interests of lower taste-publics in cosmopolitan consumer interests, aligns with chapter 4's arguments on middlebrow adjacency. While the use and display of (high) culture as a status indicator is relevant across the 1950s and early 1960s, status indicators are also widely found in aspirational consumer culture. In the latter, as defined by celebrity lifestyle and wealth, there is a strong component of aspiration centered around media characterizations—in film, television, and the popular press—of a materialist-centered glamour activated through consumption and public display.

The prevalence of this materialist, lower-middlebrow interest in cosmopolitan glamour is quite different from mid-century characterizations of the dominance of high culture. Even while the latter was common in early 1960s upper-middle media, highbrowism was nonetheless parodied as out-of-touch snobbishness in popular media. For example, Lynes expressed a humorous disdain for highbrow poseurs in his witty 1950 book, *Snobs: A Guidebook to Your Friends, Your Enemies, Your Colleagues and Yourself.*[90] Such butt-of-the-joke characterizations of "square" highbrows were paralleled in entertainment. For instance, the 1963 Annette Funicello film, *Beach Party* (American International), includes a bumbling sociology professor studying "pagan" teenage mating rituals. The square, clueless, and "adult" caricature of this pompous highbrow and his (re)education lies at the center of this lightweight, lowbrow surf, sex, and rock 'n' roll teen film.

It was noted in chapter 4 both that Lynes observed that the "differences are often blurred" between the brows, and that *Life* readers in 1949 described an all-around-brow mode of consumption. Such mixed-brow lifestyles are the lower-middle perspectives that are missing in midcentury middlebrow literature. Gans observes that in these writings, outside high culture, "the standards of the other taste cultures are rarely discussed . . . and are thus implicit, uncodified, and . . . invisible."[91] Nonetheless, the lower-middle's taste predilections were hardly invisible as America's dominant taste culture and the major demographic for mass media. And across the early 1960s, this demographic continued to be all-around-brow consumers. The mixed-brow tastes of Nitzsche and Spector exemplify this mindset, and Spector's own materialist-centered celebrity and self-presentation exemplify lower-middle interests in cosmopolitan glamour. This mixed-brow culture is partly what Macdonald, et al. were so protectionist against.

As a post–civil rights sociology inquiry based on academic critical analysis and data, Gans acknowledges that his study's "apparatus" nonetheless "rests on two value judgements": "(1) that popular culture reflects and expresses the aesthetics and other wants of many people (thus making it culture and not just commercial menace); and (2) that all people have a right to the culture they prefer, regardless of whether it is high or popular." Gans calls his conclusions an "argument for cultural democracy and an argument against the idea that only the cultural expert knows what is good for the people."[92] Like Wolfe (b. 1930), Gans (b. 1927) was roughly a decade older than Spector (b. 1939) and Nitzsche (b. 1937), but all came of age in the postwar era, as opposed to Macdonald (b. 1906) and David Riesman (b. 1909). Both the latter engaged with popular culture from high-leaning perspectives (though, as noted, Riesman's taste-hierarchies favored jazz as an elevated, legitimate popular music). Macdonald was largely an armchair critic peering over the illusory wall that supposedly divided the brows. By contrast, Riesman, a onetime academic adviser to Gans, advocated data-based sociological study of class. He "assured" Gans "that popular culture was a proper topic for a sociologist . . . in an era when it was not considered legitimate by most sociologists."[93]

Two traits among this younger generation are that popular culture was culture that offered something *legitimate* and meaningful, and that there was symbolic elevated status tied to cross-brow taste-culture literacy. This mixed-brow taste proclivity, at least with Spector and Nitzsche, seems akin to the status benefits of what sociologist Richard Peterson identified in 1990s omnivore culture, particularly in music consumption, albeit without the higher-education profile that Peterson identifies.[94] (I suspect, though, that 1950s/1960s middle-class, liberal-arts-educated consumers had some cross-brow consumption tastes, whether or not they purchased rock and roll and R&B.) In 1990 commentary, with reliance upon Peterson, Gans observes that "omnivorous behavior also reflects a finding... [sociologist] Paul Lazars-feld and other pioneers of mass-media research [made]: Those consuming more media or culture content of one kind also consume more of most other kinds."[95] Thus, increased leisure "time, money, and education" allowed some consumers "to choose more culture from several taste levels, making all forms and genres of culture potential" experiences for them.[96] Within postwar prosperity and middle-class expansion, I suspect mixed-brow predilections present in some middle-class consumers of the Wolfe-Gans and Nitzsche-Spector generations are rooted in such trends.

Gans's study reinterprets Lynes's brow framing via "five taste cultures" (for Gans, "high culture, upper- and lower-middle cultures, . . . low," and "quasi-folk low culture").[97] But these distinctions are subdivided "further into conservative, progressive, and other factions," and account for "the youth, black, and other racial and ethnic cultures that came into... visibility during the 1960s."[98] These additional factors influence taste-public variations and associations within each strata. While he notes that these are abstracted, unorganized aggregates, each strata includes some "aesthetic pluralism" of a number taste publics, with "cultures chang[ing] over time."[99] Gans recognizes that "class explains only part of why people choose the culture they do."[100] He points out that, as noted in the previous chapter, "people often make culture choices from many menus."[101] The latter observation is a corrective of pre-1970 discourse, and he observes that such cross-class consumption dates back decades.[102] In a mild critique of the applicability of Bourdieu's theory of cultural capital to US taste cultures, Gans downplays the attraction of "high culture choices as cultural capital" among American wealth, business, and executive classes, noting stronger attractions to lifestyle symbols and some adherence to lower-class values among new-wealth sectors.[103] (He also observes that "Bourdieu's attitudes towards high culture were more positive than mine, and those towards the mass media, more critical.")[104] He further underscores that content regularly "moves between [taste] cultures," and as "cultures borrow from one another, content is often transformed to make it understandable or acceptable to different publics."[105] (The latter is what troubled midcentury highbrow proponents.) Gans's nuanced distinctions here are invaluable for interpreting the populuxe discourse around the Wall of Sound, the Ronettes, and emergent youth culture.

The postwar cross-brow consumption of classical music is central to how one might hear these teenage symphonies with historical ears. For example, in the "Legitimate" section of a January 1956 issue of *Variety*, the article

"Longhair Outgrosses Baseball" highlights this hi-fi, middle-class consumer trend, adding the subtitle: "Symph, Opera and Ballet Big Middlebrow Draw."[106] In citing impressive earnings numbers, the article makes such arguments as opera "has become a mass market venture," and "longhair, long the stepchild of show biz, has now asserted its proper spot in the entertainment scheme." This lower-middle perceived connection, and actual industry connections, of the era's classical and showbiz cultures is valuable for understanding the intersections of class markers and showbiz in Spector's teenage symphonies. It is not surprising that middle-class interests in Wagnerian opera may be a matter of lower-middle cosmopolitan taste cultures. Based on *Billboard* and *Variety*, as well as broadcast programming (such as Leonard Bernstein's *Omnibus* episodes, and the Metropolitan Opera Saturday matinee and Stokowski's "Symphony of the Air" broadcasts), "longhair" music was not the exclusive cultural product that highbrow discourse made it out to be, for all of the reasons for cross-class consumption that Gans outlines. Middlebrow aspiration is a partial explanation in some cases, but the press indicates an increasingly democratic relation to longhair music consumption. There are likely a range of influences, and for some in the middle classes, the relationships may have been more horizontal than vertical in navigating this marketplace. A horizontal, cross-brow relationship may suggest how *Billboard* and *Cash Box* came to describe Spector's sound via longhair music, *even* when strings were not present. This can be seen in a review of the 1963 Darlene Love hit, *Fine Fine Boy*: "It's a wildie with the big Philadelphia Orchestra sound and high-toned choral work."[107] This is a showbiz understanding, and it has to do with the sensational—or rather *fabulous*—qualities of entertainments that aim to invoke postwar Hollywood, or even Las Vegas, notions of glamour.

I have noted Stephen Gundle's identification of the classical Hollywood-era celebrity as America's "most complete embodiment of glamour."[108] This period extends into the 1960s, when the all-powerful studios were still in the business of presenting the "fabulous lives" of their star celebrities, who "were choreographed, pictured, described, and evoked by publicity departments that drip-fed the world's press with news and information.... These alluring personalities were the stuff of fantasy. A fantasy, however, that was somehow accessible . . . [often] as a fabulous everyman or everywoman."[109] Madison Avenue's American Dream promised that through the right attention to the goods, artifice and presentational markers of status—especially consumer codes of luxury—every American could aspire to such a glamorous lifestyle, or the outward appearance of such a lifestyle.

These observations are echoed in post-1990 culture in Lauren Greenfield's 2017 *Generation Wealth*, which examines "the public display of luxury and the celebrities who glamorize it."[110] Greenfield's study—a photo-documentary book—focuses on the sociological framing of consumption, and "the way in which tremors from the epicenter, L.A. celebrity and wealth culture, ripple across classes, regions, and nations."[111] Greenfield examines "the charismatic celebrity accelerants of this culture," meaning Hollywood stars, musicians, athletes, and others who shape the consumer desires, status conceptions, and aspirations of regular people. What Greenfield emphasizes is the *performance of wealth* through which "over-the-top consumerism" is "the expression of . . . personal narrative of success." In this, Greenfield expresses insights that echo Wolfe's conception of statusphere. Greenfield and writer Juliet Schor recognize that this culture has postwar roots in the rise of Las Vegas; new models of marketing, celebrity, and prosperity; and Hugh Hefner's contributions to the increasing "pornification" of middle America. Greenfield describes these trends as "the influence of affluence." This perspective is central to postwar social and economic mobility, in which "the aspiration for wealth . . . bec[a]me a driving force—and . . . and increasingly unrealistic goal—for individuals from all classes of society."[112]

I suspect that Spector's self-presentation of wealth and celebrity, as well as the Wagnerian qualities of his teenage symphonies, are closely tied to the early emergence of this American glamour dynamic. In the early 1960s, the sound and image of the Ronettes display affinities with other areas of Hollywood-Vegas glamorization and evocations of class mobility and status. Both Greenfield and Gundle recognize that lower-middle conceptions of glamour can involve vulgarity, excess, and ostentation. Both likewise observe the broader, multimedia entertainment ecology behind the perpetuation of these notions of glamour, with Gundle commenting that such glamour is

> shaped by a variety of extra-filmic elements. The off-screen lifestyles and personalities of . . . actors were . . . an integral part of what made an actor a star. The aura of stardom was generated as much by magazines, photographs, advertising, and audience perceptions as screen performance. The public image of movie people was derived from [emulating] the super-rich, although its main purpose was not to establish status within the [high economic] group so much as to impress the public. Large houses, private swimming pools, limousines, fine clothes, and an exciting social life were the recurrent features of the Hollywood lifestyle.[113]

Similar extra-musical elements frame period understandings of the Ronettes as glamorous celebrities.

The Ronettes innately knew that emulating such fabulous, exotic, glamorous, and sexually evocative codes within youthful rock-pop culture would have significant resonance with audiences. Their image resonated deeply with the New York and Miami nightclubs they emerged within, as well as on television, within the visual media of record promotion, and even internationally as American pop entered European markets. And the girl-group phenomenon, particularly with sexualized acts like the Ronettes, was a music industry analog to "the culture of woman as spectacle" (to invoke Gundle), and the Wall of Sound formed the sonic spectacular backdrop to such glamorous female spectacle.

In his hunger for both celebrity as a producer-genius and status as the "The First Tycoon of Teen," Spector's youthful wealth allowed for many ostentatious idiosyncrasies, including his hipster-meets-baronial fashion sensibility. The press took great interest in his limousines, wealth, real estate, bodyguards, and industry influence. Spector fed this publicity machine with over-the-top consumption displays such as his Pyrenees Castle in Alhambra, California (about eight miles northeast of downtown Los Angeles). This home features prominently in interviews from the late 1960s forward, and was shared with Ronnie until 1972 (she felt imprisoned). In his 1969 Spector interview, Jann Wenner detailed the kitsch-clutter of "Spectorland," with "20 foot gabled ceilings, sunken rooms, a grand piano, Irish wolfhounds and two Borzoi's . . . chauffeur-bodyguard . . . candy-filled dishes" and "slices of pizza and cokes." After Spector showed up in "outrageous" costume, Wenner remarked "What a show tonight!"[114]

The lower-middlebrow ostentation of Spector's castle foreshadows the displays of Vegas-leaning, garish glamour aspirations seen in Greenfield's brilliant 2012 film, *Queen of Versailles* (Magnolia), which documents the heights and fall of a self-made billionaire couple who rose from low status via their timeshare-property fortune. They attempt to build the biggest house in America, which was modeled on the sort of elite French architecture that attracted Spector. Both examples involve lower-middle taste-culture aspirations for class-mobility expressed via Hollywood and Vegas presentational codes for status, glamour, and wealth. Little of this has to do with highbrow culture.

The midcentury step-child to classical Hollywood celebrity glamour was undoubtedly mainstream pop record promotion under the hi-fi and LP boom. Sinatra's mid-1950s promotional campaigns—managed by Capitol and Hollywood film studios, as well as his publicity agents—are a quintessential representation of this celebrity-based glamour-image marketing of recording artists. Independent labels likewise sought to provide a similar control of image packaging and cultural message for their artists, as can be readily seen with Motown and Tamla Records and their renowned finishing school for artist grooming. While Spector's Philles Records had no such internal department, celebrity image grooming was central to building artists, and the Ronettes themselves had savvy in constructing and maintaining their fabulous image.

In 1985, media scholar Neil Postman foreshadowed Greenfield is in his argument that television and visual media provide "our culture's principal mode of knowing about itself. . . . It is not merely that . . . television . . . entertainment is the metaphor for all discourse. It is that off the screen the metaphor [still] prevails. . . . Americans . . . entertain each other . . . [and] exchange images . . . [communicating] with good looks, celebrities and commercials. For the message of television as metaphor is not only that all the world is a stage but that the stage is located in Las Vegas."[115] He further quips that "There's No Business But Show Business,"[116] which underscores his view of television entertainment, its idealizations and its discourses as a "supra-ideology" in society.[117] Postman's commentary on showbiz aesthetics resonates with the discourse outlined from Greenfield, Gundle, and Gans, and equally holds implications for interpreting Spector's Wall of Sound. He observes that individual media, as well as "interpositions of media," make "possible a unique mode of discourse by providing a new orientation for thought, for expression, for sensibility." Postman cautions that Marshall McLuhan's aphorism, "the medium is the message," can "lead one to confuse a message," which involves a "concrete statement," with a metaphor, which works by "powerful implication to enforce" particular readings of content. He notes: "Our media-metaphors classify the world for us, sequence it, frame it, enlarge it, [and] reduce it."[118] The musical topics of Spector's teenage symphonies, particularly as cross-media interpositions between audio, associated celebrity images, and promotional copy, thus work as mutually reinforcing media metaphors that encourage specific middlebrow-adjacent readings of populuxe textural and visual presentational topics. Postman focuses centrally on the "beautiful spectacle" of television's entertaining parade of images, which require "minimal skills to comprehend," are "exquisitely crafted," and are always "accompanied by exciting music."[119] The promotion of the

Ronettes through television has been mentioned briefly, and their stylized performances on this medium—typically employing backing tracks and/or lip-syncing to Spector's Wall productions (the "exciting music")—were a significant factor in their success. As paired with the Ronettes' fabulous image, Spector's productions—with their emphases on big, exhilarating Wall sound—offered youth-culture, rock-era analogues to adult showbiz populuxe entertainment spectacle and early 1960s Hollywood, Vegas, and television celebrity glamour.

The big-band-plus-strings, MOR pop of the 1950s and 1960s defines a lower-middle populuxe era in which orchestral pop was entwined with both prewar luxe arranging and postwar connections to classy showbiz glamour, swank, and fabulousness. At the turn of the 1960s, rock and roll's embrace of populuxe production simplified luxe showbiz practices for younger generational aesthetics. This shift comparatively limited orchestral additions to melodrama-heightening complementary coloristic textures within rock-pop production—for example, high-register string pads, brief French horn interjections, and interstitial classicistic flourishes amid simplified rock-pop harmonic practice and a foregrounding of the instrumentation and driving rhythms of rock-pop combos and R&B-derived, riff-based horn work. This is often the role of the orchestral complements in Spector's teenage symphonies, for instance. This rock-pop simplification of populuxe arranging was a case of "less is more" in terms of clarity (in sound and intent) and a reduction of the markers of pretension to more centrally foreground the ideals of mainstream pop and rock. Nevertheless, there remains a sustained cross-class tension in this music's populuxe scoring, between lower topical markers for street, authenticity, youth, and race, on the one hand, and elevated (lower-middle) associations of glamour, melodrama, and cinematic aura, on the other hand. It is this sustained low-high topical tension in the Wall of Sound that has long fascinated fans, producers, and musicians. This new rock-pop populuxe sound was evocative of the "exciting" mixed-genre period music of film, television, and advertising (e.g., as heard in the James Bond film scores), but of course, these were two-way exchanges, as popular music increasingly influenced music-in-media practice after 1950.

SIX

Mining AM (White) Gold

THE 1960S MOR-POP FOUNDATIONS
OF 1970S SOFT ROCK

THE LUXE-LEANING, soft-rock sounds of late-1960s and 1970s Top 40 radio later occupied a central role in budget compilations that Time-Life marketed to baby-boomers as "AM Gold." As hawked through magazine and off-prime-time television advertisements, the name "AM Gold" evoked the music's ubiquity, top-shelf production, transistor-radio milieu, and "oldies" market relevance. In the way that Anne-Lise François accounts for 1970s "fashion as 'compulsive artifice,'" this chapter aims to articulate parallel "habit[s] of exaggeration," modes of "wearing excess," types of "banality" in the 1970s "mixing-up of high and low registers, of plain and ornamental styles," and the "uneasy combination of over- and understatement" in late 1960s and 1970s Middle of the Road (MOR) luxe pop.[1]

The advertisements for the *AM Gold* series ran from 1990 (first called *Super Hits*) to the early 2000s.[2] This series has received little critical attention because of its ignominy—it was never hip to purchase such commercial, sentimental, and nostalgic prepackaged music. Such low status was a stigma that resided in this music's heyday despite its success. Central to AM Gold's "soft" textures are the amalgam of a singer-songwriter with deeply personal lyrics set against earnest acoustic guitar strumming. Whether MOR pop or the Laurel Canyon sound (the 1960s and 1970s Los Angeles singer-songwriter community centered around Joni Mitchell, David Crosby, and others discussed later), such textures often include lush, tight-harmony backing vocals, a touch of country-rockish slide guitar, the comping of a harpsichord or electric piano, and lush strings. There might be French-horn, plangent oboe, or English-horn interjections, or crisp brass and/or trumpet solos. This chapter explores what made these sounds of soft rock discursively meaningful to the 1970s American mainstream.

This era follows rock's increasing reception as "serious" music across the late 1960s. Bernard Gendron's 2002 *Between Montmartre and the Mudd Club* traces rock-pop's "cultural accreditation" via its "acquisition of aesthetic distinction" (i.e., cultural prestige) through this criticism. He examines the "high middlebrow" and "low middlebrow discourses" in this journalism over 1963–68.[3] Gendron constructs a two-part "pop into art"/"art into pop" narrative, with the Beatles being central to his study. But while his Beatles chapters fall into the pop-into-art territory (his chief concern), he only briefly considers the flood of 1968–69 pop releases inspired by the Beatles' 1967 album *Sgt. Pepper's Lonely Hearts Club Band*. Within his pop-into-art focus, however, Gendron does note a "popism" discourse that "asserted that mass culture has its own implicit aesthetic that is equally valid with that of high culture."[4]

This chapter considers this popist and supposed art-into-pop milieu as a foundation for luxe AM Gold sounds. Against the backdrop of the mid-1960s, the British Invasion–era boom in adventurous multitrack production, and the late-1960s shift toward harder, countercultural rock, this chapter considers instead "baroque pop" and "sunshine pop," which lay foundations for soft rock in 1969–70. Each were luxe-related expansions of psychedelic and folk-rock trends. Following influential productions of the Beatles, the Left Banke, and others circa 1966–67, baroque pop (a.k.a. "chamber pop," "baroque rock," etc.) references a range of rock and pop that mixed baroque and chamber music textures (harpsichords, string quartets, individual woodwinds, French horns, baroque trumpets, etc.) and styles (often Bach-inspired, contrapuntal, or generally sounding like chamber music) with contemporary rock idioms. The post-1990 subgenre categorization of "sunshine pop" (discussed later) references a range of commercial, highly polished, perpetually upbeat Los Angeles pop of the mid-1960s—from the Mamas and Papas forward—that relate to similar chamber-pop textures without the self-consciously "baroque" or serious-music referentiality. As individuals previously involved in both trends lay the foundations for singer-songwriter and soft-rock production practice, late 1960s popularity charts notably reveal an increasing convergence of tracks that were simultaneously on *Billboard*'s Hot 100 and Easy Listening Top 40 charts. In the summer of 1970, emergent soft rock acted as a nexus for intersecting trends from these rock-pop worlds. This is the heart of AM Gold.

This chapter's synecdoches for AM Gold are early hits by the Carpenters and Bread. Bread, famous for tracks like "Make It with You" ("Make It"; 1970), were—as critic Ben Fong-Torres noted in 1971—"staples of AM radio." Their string-sweetened, guitar-strumming, love-song pop was received by hip rock critics at magazines like *Rolling Stone* (which Fong-Torres wrote for) as derivative commercial pop sounding like "the Hollies as arranged by Bacharach, Crosby, Nash and [the Monkees'] Mike Nesmith."[5] Similarly, critic Tom Smucker *appreciatively* called the "fabulous Beach Boys/Beatles/ Bacharach-inspired" productions of the Carpenters the "forbidden fruits of middle-class culture." Smucker's 1975 conversion to fandom transpired as a transgression against his self-image of urbane hipness as a critic for the *Village Voice*—his shame-inducing attempt to secure a Carpenters album is likened to a teenage boy seeking to acquire condoms. (He received his album in a "plain brown envelope," like pornography sent through the mail.)[6]

Pop guilty pleasure is central to discourse on both bands. There was a tension between America's middle-class suburban/rural love for these groups, and their widespread disparagement from the rock press. As seen in counterculture *Crawdaddy* and *Rolling Stone (RS)*, however, when soft rock and singer-songwriters began to dominate sales, the industry, and AM airwaves over 1969–72, this backlash also included mildly shamefaced appreciation, particularly as apologetic recognition of the high craft in this commercial pop.

The contributory streams for soft rock are multiple, with the idiom forming a node between the singer-songwriter trend, sunshine pop, baroque pop, Brill Building pop, easy-listening (EL) and MOR, as well as folk-rock, country-rock, psychedelia, and convergences of jazz and rock-pop. The Carpenters and Bread illustrate how these threads formed a cohesive, soft fabric. While their mature sound aligns with the Bacharach/Brill Building-lineage of MOR and EL, the Carpenter siblings had dalliances with other late-1960s idioms. Bread represents polystylistic studio professionalism intersecting with singer-songwriter craftsmanship. Their sound comfortably sat in the middle of the road, with group-member backgrounds mapping broadly across the pan-stylistic L.A. pop ecosystem.

Central to this chapter are both how the influential sounds of Bread and the Carpenters emerged in the summer of 1970, and how these sounds were received. A hierarchical reversal is revealed, wherein previously elevated production qualities increasingly signified a debased commercialism or an ironic, sweet, guilty pleasure to hip commentators. This chapter further illustrates Albin Zak's observation that pop recordings in part create meaning through their relations to other pop recordings.[7] As such, the symbolic functions of production textures are examined, with attention to the discourse around derivative commercialism in the music of the Carpenters and Bread.

Against the backdrop of hard rock and protest-pop and -folk trends of the late 1960s, the 1970 top-ten breakthrough of the Carpenters was an outlier that signaled the lush sentimentality of 1970s MOR ballads to come. The group's sentimental, nostalgic love songs foregrounded the intimate, rich vocals of Karen Carpenter atop the studio artifice of overdubbed lush, jazz-pop choral-harmony backing, tinkling harpsichord or electric or acoustic piano, easy-listening jazz-pop trumpet and flute solos, jazzy horn sections, hip-shaking tambourine, big drum fills, responsorial high string lines and lush string beds, and classicistic English horn or oboe solos, all typically set to a square, lilting soft-rock groove.

The Carpenter's chart breakthrough was the Bacharach/Hal David song "(They Long to Be) Close to You" ("Close"), released in May 1970. "Close" entered the *Billboard* Hot 100 in June, achieving number 1 on 25 July. Their cover of the Paul Williams/Roger Nichols song "We've Only Just Begun" became a chart-topping Carpenters hit in the fall of that year, peaking at number 2 on 14 November 1970. Alongside the late 1970 chart histories of these hits, one can see Bread's "Make It" and "Teach Your Children" by Crosby, Stills, Nash and Young (CSNY, and CSN without Neil Young) at numbers 5 and 16, respectively, on the 25 July chart, and James Taylor's "Fire and Rain" at number 3 on the 14 November chart. While the latter two tracks represent the pared-down, folk and folk-rock sides of the singer-songwriter trend, Bread—led by David Gates—fully embraced the lush production side of these same trends. Both these luxe and non-luxe practices are hallmarks of early soft rock. CSNY members and Taylor, however, had ties to a late-1960s luxe singer-songwriter idiom, with Jack Nitzsche providing luxe-arranging productions for members of CSNY, and Taylor's first album being a baroque-pop showcase encouraged by the Beatles' Apple Records. And as the minimal sound of Taylor's hit, "Fire and Rain," was on the 1970 charts (by which time Taylor had relocated to L.A.), Apple reissued their 1968 bestringed production of "Carolina on My Mind" as a single.

The Venn-diagram-like connections between the artists discussed in this chapter were facilitated by the emergence of Los Angeles as a pop center from the mid-1960s. The Carpenter's prehistory illustrates such convergences. Though from Ohio, the Carpenters were centrally a product of L.A., having moved there as teens in 1963. Beginning in 1964–1965, the city's pop-music scenes were transformed through an influx of youthful musicians from around the nation. Following an ongoing folk and roots music revival, this migration further included musicians attracted to early 1960s surf rock, the teen-symphonies of Spector, a burgeoning rhythm and blues scene, and the growing music industry. This paralleled the impact of the British Invasion. By 1966, Los Angeles achieved parity with New York as a music business center. The industry also increasingly engaged in both cross-Atlantic style, talent, and criticism exchanges, as well as innovations in studio technology and production.[8] The soft rock sound of 1970 is thus a result of L.A. as a central node for these trends.

Richard and Karen Carpenter (henceforth using their first names) do not appear to have circulated much with L.A.'s singer-songwriter community, but the latter is vital for understanding soft rock. Barney Hoskyns locates the origins of "the Laurel Canyon era" of L.A.'s singer-songwriter scene in the early 1968 arrival of the then-unknown Joni Mitchell.[9] The frontispiece for Hoskyns's 2005 book, *Hotel California*, is a 1972 *RS* map—"Hollywood's Hot 100"—of this "canyon/Troubador community."[10] Figure 6.1 presents an abridged and amended re-creation of the *RS* illustration. As shown, the map references the Hot 100 chart that dominated Top 40 radio. The canyon/ Troubadour framing foregrounds two sites in the map's musical geography: the artists' Laurel Canyon residential community, and The Troubadour, a West Hollywood nightclub central to showcasing seasoned and breaking acts, and aspiring local talent. This scene included Mitchell, the Byrds, Taylor, Buffalo Springfield (with Young and Stephen Stills), Carole King, Linda Ronstadt, Harry Nilsson, Randy Newman, members of the Monkees, and others.

Across 1968, among the performers at the Troubadour's open-mic "Hoot Night" were Richard Carpenter's band, Spectrum, with vocals by their drummer, Karen. With their vocal-harmony, "middle-of-the-road . . . sound" with both beat- (i.e., period rock) and jazz-inspired originals, the band was "more like a lounge act than a folk group."[11] Along with "crew cuts and blue velvet jackets," as one member described them, they were an "in-between kind of group" with a "pretty" sound that did not fit with period folk or psychedelic rock. The Hoot Nights nonetheless allowed for interactions with the Canyon crowd, and Karen recalled meeting peers like "Jackson Brown and Brewer and Shipley."[12]

Observe that despite the Carpenters' centrality to 1972 L.A. pop, the band was left off the RS map (hence the "absent" indication on the Figure 6.1 map re-creation), even while their label head, A&M's Herb Alpert, and

HOLLYWOOD'S HOT 100

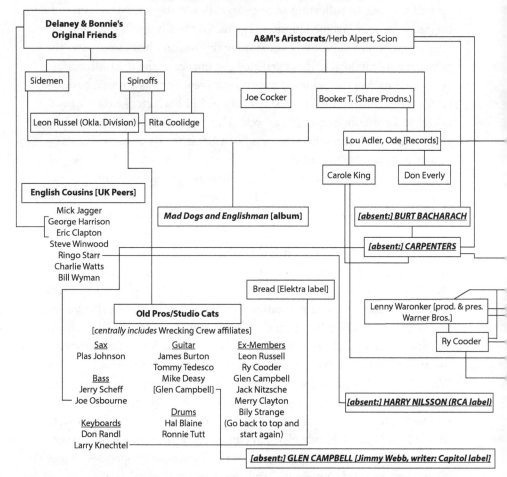

FIG. 6.1. "Hollywood's Hot 100," *Rolling Stone*, 3 February 1972, pp. 26–27, abridged and amended.

fellow soft-rock stars, Bread, are present. By 1972, the Carpenters had won "Best New Artist" and "Best Contemporary Vocal Performance by a Duo, Group or Chorus" at the 1971 Grammys (losing "Record of the Year" to Simon and Garfunkel, alongside competition from Taylor and the Beatles). They likewise won the "Best Vocal Performance by a Duo, Group or Chorus" Grammy in 1972. But the latter event showcased Canyon residents Carole King (her *Tapestry* won the album and record of the year awards) and James Taylor, and soft-rock, East-Coast peer, Carly Simon. Despite the Carpenters'

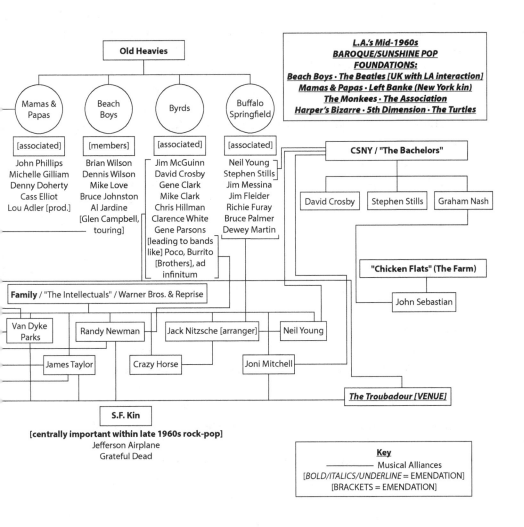

absence, the *RS* map integrates soft rock, its precursors, and its enablers into a rockist-framing of this community, thereby illustrating the bicoastal, cross-generational, and cross-Atlantic elements that intersected in L.A.'s soft-rock and singer-songwriter idioms.

There are several modes within early 1970s L.A. soft rock/singer-songwriter production practice. For instance, the spare strings heard on some early canyon/Troubadour singer-songwriter recordings (e.g., King's "You've Got a Friend") stand in contradistinction to the lavish orchestrations heard on other period albums, as for example, by the Carpenters, Nilsson, Bread, Newman, and others. There was the Canyon-originated rootsy "back to the garden," acoustic-guitar-centered simplicity of Taylor's second album, *Sweet Baby James* (1970) and Mitchell's *Ladies of the Canyon* (1970, with the "Woodstock" line "back to the garden"). The network in Figure 6.1 extends back to "old heavies" such as the Beach Boys, Mamas and Papas, and Buffalo Springfield, all of whom had luxe recordings. There are connections to "intellectual" rock-pop, which includes luxe orchestrations from Nitzsche, but the sparely produced Mitchell and Taylor are also framed as "intellectuals." Period rock "authenticity" discourse informs much of this mapping, but the presence of Bread and "Old Pros/Studio Cats" like the Wrecking Crew also hint at a luxe-pop branch of this perceived singer-songwriter authenticity. It is likely that the Carpenters' "in-between kind" of pop, as well as their image, kept them at a prominent remove from *RS*'s 1972 mapmaking.

The textures of much of this music can be traced back through mid-1960s "chamber pop," "baroque pop," and "sunshine pop," much of which involved Wrecking Crew backing. This chapter explores this sonic lineage over 1966–1969. The music examined includes rock-related easy listening (EL), and the music of Alpert and Bacharach, the Mamas and the Papas, the Left Banke, the Beach Boys, Glen Campbell, and other artists that were prominent on the *AM Gold* releases. This transitional pop era reveals important changes in the classy, glamour, and middlebrow-adjacent discourses discussed across this book. The mixed reception of soft rock reveals much about 1970s taste-public hierarchies, and *whose* opinions were seen to matter.

Several 1965–69 soft-rock tributary trends were originally viewed as evidencing a new sophistication, maturity, and artfulness in pop. Across 1968–1970, there is also an increasing overlap of select hits on *Billboard*'s Top 100 (pop) chart and the Easy Listening chart. The latter chart documents the "best selling middle-of-the-road [MOR] singles." Typically called "good music," one mid-1960s radio programmer described this format as "the wide area between classical and semi-concert music ... and rhythm and blues and top 40."[13] While Top 40 pop was traditionally considered "greasy kid stuff" among the MOR/EL radio stations (the terms were nearly interchangeable), in early 1965, industry discourse illustrates that there was "growing interest in applying the objective approach of the pop operators" to MOR programming.[14] Earlier MOR programmers assumed that "all adults enjoy good music and violently reject rock," that the Hot 100 was "useless as a programming guide," that "advertisers don't want a teen audience," and that playing Hot 100 pop "somehow deprives a station of its respectability."[15] By 1965, programmers describe a new view: the generations might come together with MOR pop. Rock's first generation had become young adults, and thus a potential demographic for the right "moderate" hits. One commentator describes a "chicken 40" policy of balancing "current hits, old hits, new singles, and LP" tracks in the hope of avoiding the loss of more listeners than contemporary hits might gain.[16] These trends opened a lucrative crossover market. However, EL and Hot 100 crossover occurs in parallel with an explosion of "hard" rock subgenres. Alongside the new rock press, the latter music shapes the reception of soft rock.

Eric Weisbard posits MOR as a "rival mainstream" to canonic rock. This chapter echoes Weisbard's observation that "the soft center of American music was often its most diverse province," even while "those in the middle were maligned by rock . . . partisans as debased sellers and mindless consumers."[17] The eclectic range of MOR/EL is illustrative of how production elements are refashioned and recombined in the search for crossover hits. Weisbard describes the Carpenters' label, A&M, and its founders, Herb Alpert and Jerry Moss, as pivotal for such MOR pop aesthetics. MOR/EL embraced two competing models of production: the "commercial" team-based model of songwriting, production, and image-crafting; and the rock model of the self-contained artist in control of the production of their own music and image. Critics essentialized this dichotomy into a rock-versus-pop binary.[18] But there was a spectrum of practices between these poles, and MOR/EL reflected this diversity. Notably, "commercial" songwriters, studio musicians, arrangers, and producers—for example, King, Neil Diamond, Newman, Gates, Campbell, Bacharach, and others—later refashioned themselves into performers, often via soft rock-pop with luxe production. This "soft center" forms the repertory of AM Gold, and its foundations develop across the 1960s.

With roots in earlier surf rock and a catalyst in the Mamas and Papas' hit "California Dreaming," a youth-music migration to L.A. began in earnest circa 1965. The Carpenters and Bread's cofounders, Gates and James Griffin, arrived earlier, the latter in 1962. The Carpenter's breakthrough with "Close" took four years from their start as performing musicians. Gates and Griffin quickly became part of the music scene, with Gates circulating among the Wrecking Crew as a studio musician, and finding success as an arranger, producer, and songwriter. Like the poor-performing eponymous Carpenters debut, the first Bread album failed to generate interest in 1969. Both groups shifted toward MOR for their 1970 breakthrough successes. Bread's origins date to 1967, when Gates was brought in as producer for a baroque-pop band, the Pleasure Fair, of Griffin and Rob Royer. The failure of that album led the three to form Bread. In 1975, Gates reflected to critic Dave Laing that in the psychedelic era "we were getting beaten to death with hard rock music, and I really thought our music would [be] . . . an alternative . . . softer, laid-back approach." Laing observes that "Bread['s] approach . . . was a refinement of the Los Angeles 'sunshine rock' . . . [of] Harper's Bizarre, Spanky and Our Gang and the Mamas and Papas."[19]

In contrast to "commercial" artists like the Carpenters and Bread, "soft" singer-songwriters like King, Mitchell, and Taylor received positive rock-press reviews because of their perceived bona fides as "authentic" artists vetted by the community sketched in Figure 6.1. Bread and Gates's Wrecking Crew colleagues—for example, keyboardists Larry Knechtel and Leon Russell, bassist Joe Osborn, Campbell, drummer Hal Blaine, and guitarist Ry Cooder—are likewise on this map. The latter, plus Alpert, had ties to the Carpenters. The foundations of soft rock were embedded in this Hot 100 community. Thus, while rock's surface roiled from countercultural hard-rock idioms, a reactionary MOR undertow pulled peers toward soft rock.

While both Carpenters followed harder rock, Richard admitted that "I know we're not rock. We're Pop," but adding the qualification: "We're not that kind of bland, unimaginative . . . easy listening [pop]. . . . [W]e are more creative. . . . We do our own arranging, our own orchestration."[20] Craftsmanship is emphasized here, and otherwise-disparaging critics acknowledged the band's professional craft. Richard has often remarked on this negative rock-press reception, astutely picking apart the taste-public culture war in this discourse. In 2018, he notes that countercultural rock writers "really thought that they'd seen the end of pop music . . . , and [then] along we come. We were pilloried . . . [u]nfairly. . . . The 'brother-sister thing' and the 'squeaky clean' way the Carpenters were packaged . . . antagonised . . . countercultural tastes. Parents approved of the Carpenters, which disgusted 'the other side,' but . . . 'it was great for record sales.'"[21]

Central here is the discourse that cleaved rock from Hot 100 pop, and this occurred in parallel with MOR and EL crossover.

By 1966, the pop industry was trans-Atlantic, with two-way "invasions" of artists, idioms releases, and distribution agreements, US trade magazines reporting on European sales, and critical attention paid to all major US/UK music scenes. In the United States, the emergence of the new rock journalism is often dated to Paul Williams's founding of *Crawdaddy* magazine in February 1966. This development was influenced by influential UK rock criticism. Williams's goal was to encourage similarly "intelligent [US] writing about pop music" in contradistinction to the trade press (e.g., *Billboard*), which he criticized for shallowness, inaccuracy, and sales interests as "service magazine[s]."[22] The oppositional construct between rock and pop effaced and ignored the era's dialogic interactions between rock, pop, easy listening, and emergent soft rock. The Hot 100 map reveals this division's fallacies through the professional activities of many individuals who routinely crossed, recrossed, or stood on the broad boundary between "authentic" rock and "commercial" pop. From November 1967, the new rock journalism attained national impact with *Rolling Stone* magazine, which included influential writers like Jon Landau, Greil Marcus, Robert Christgau, Dave Marsh, and Lester Bangs. *RS* too proclaimed opposition to the trade press and the "myth and nonsense" of fan magazines.[23] Here is the epicenter of the pop-versus-rock divide, and *RS*'s 1967–71 pages display only minimal coverage of mainstream pop and soft rock. Only in February 1971 does Taylor receive a cover story (on the "new rock"), after which the magazine increasingly covers soft rock. The Carpenters first received an *RS* cover feature on 4 July 1974, four years after their chart breakthrough.[24]

There are several notable rock journalists who express guilty-pleasure ambivalence about soft rock. For example, despite Bangs's hard exterior as a garage rock proponent, he had an amused soft spot for pop pleasures like the Carpenters, Bread, and the Captain and Tennille.[25] In 1973, for instance, he wrote of the Carpenters: "WHAT ARE WE gonna do with these two? Look, ain't saying I don't love 'em—they've always been one of my favourite swoontracks, especially with them looking so perverted and all. . . . I re-fell in love with my childhood sweetheart to . . . 'We've Only Just Begun' . . . that bugger WAS our song. . . . I had a hell of a lot to thank the Carpenters for." He describes the album *Now and Then* as "just what you needed: more of that nice, syrupy, ultracommercial pap," and cynically—but affectionately—as "wholesome as Wonder Bread" and as reliable as any everyday pop-consumption product.[26] The sustained contradictions in Bangs's guilty-pleasure appreciation of the Carpenters here is inherently an ironic form of popism. Gendron and Keightley both identify 1968 as a high point in the tensions between "popist" proponents and new rock criticism. This is precisely when the Carpenters and Bread both began as acts, and MOR/EL and Hot 100 crossover emerged.

White AM Gold was part of a larger pop-crossover ecosystem. Chapters 7 and 8 address parallel trends found in Black pop, but some generalized comments are helpful here on mid-1960s pop eclecticism. While period *Billboard* and *Cashbox* singles and LPs charts display a foundation for the rock history canon, these sources also reveal an ongoing, overlooked MOR/EL chart presence of older crooners, EL instrumentals, and similar mainstream pop. This omnipresent soft center portends the soft-rock market.

As noted, from 1965, MOR/EL programming increasingly embraced rock-pop hits that might appeal to the "moderate" tastes of a young adult demographic. Some chart-topping traditional pop, such as Frank Sinatra's "Somethin' Stupid" (1967) with his daughter Nancy, suggests MOR/EL generational bridges. "Somethin' Stupid" was produced by Spector's competitor, Lee Hazlewood, and written by Carson Parks, the brother of Beach Boys collaborator Van Dyke Parks, with a backing track performed by the Wrecking Crew. And in 1967, Sinatra's *A Man and His Music* won the Grammy Award for Album of the Year over the Beatles' *Revolver*. Both examples suggest curious interactions between the rock and pop paradigms and generations. As Keightley notes, "Easy listening did not disappear during the rock era; it lived on long past 1966."[27] As "serious" rock emerged over 1966–1968, MOR/EL prominently expanded its inclusive stylistic boundaries. By circa 1970, elements of both traditional and innovative pop meet in soft rock, and this conversion was foreshadowed by the stylistic omnivorousness of MOR/EL.

Despite the music's 1940s and 1950s roots, *Billboard*'s "Easy Listening" chart first appears in November 1961 as a radio programming guide derived from the Hot 100.[28] The accompanying description situates EL as an adult market, links the idiom to mainstream recordings and radio, and makes clear that some "beat"-oriented youth pop and country could fit within the chart's "easy" traditional pop, lighter jazz, mood-music and film-theme instrumentals, and so on. That all these idioms were on the Hot 100 underscores period chart eclecticism. *Billboard* retitled the EL chart in 1962 as "Middle-Road Singles," to reflect music that was "not too far out in either direction."[29] Then the "Top 40 Easy Listening" chart arrived in 1965 to reflect the "best selling middle-of-the-road singles."[30] Keightley observes that "a middle-class avoidance of excess" connects these "middle-of-the-road chart[s] with the middlebrow's anxious suspension between high and low, between snob and slob," but such class anxieties relax from the mid-1960s. By 1965, there is crossover from teen, R&B, country, and UK artists with various luxe production qualities and eclectic arrangements that simultaneously reference several idioms across this broad chart territory.

At the height of the British Invasion, certain LP-chart crossover trends leave one to wonder which demographics the releases were targeted for. Two *Cashbox* "Pick of the Week" single/EP selections of instrumental tracks of Beatles tunes in July 1964 are illustrative. The first, "A Hard Day's Night," by Enoch Light, receives the following review: "The big [sixty-piece] orchestra of Enoch Light is heard on the title from the Beatles film debut.... Lush strings and bright brass are rhythmically combined ... [for] profitable inroads on the singles market." The second review, for George Martin's "And I Love Her," is described as "inventively arranged and orchestrated," noting "this one could be the first big instrumental theme for the rock oriented group" with the potential of "loads of loot to be made here."[31] (Martin was the Beatles' producer.) Note the emphases on profits with these "big," "lush" amalgamations, which offer truly wonderous blends of EL strings, brassy pop, and beat-combo textures. These records foreshadow the eclectic genre-mixings of rock's innovative productions circa 1966 forward.

Enoch Light, "A Hard Day's Night" (1964)

Light was forty-nine at the time of the "A Hard Day's Night" release and a mainstay of the EL market. The arrangement brings big-band idioms into the "now" sounds of early 1960s go-go beat rhythms. Using both stereo for at least two different acoustical perspectives—with the "adult" big band set in a hall reverberation, and the "teen" rhythm section foregrounded in a dry space—Light's track features shifting textural contrasts. The rhythm section overemphasizes backbeats two and four with trebly stabs of the rhythm guitar, alongside snare and bongo accentuations, rock-centric electric bass, and a driving ride cymbal. Ignoring the famous opening chord of the original, the introduction tops the rhythm section with bluesy, riffing country-boogie piano. The first verse shifts to a bright trumpet section alternating with a clarinet trio. Verse two adds shrill, high-register string trills. The middle-eight shifts to high-register violins on melody with surf-guitar single-line riffs as accompaniment, all before a brass turnaround. The third verse melody is scored for saxes with scraping violin and brass-stab interjections. Following a drum break with low-tom striptease fills, the bongos increase activity over a fourth verse with Floyd Cramer–like country piano, backing strings and brass. The guitar solo from the Beatles' original is scored as a lush brass fanfare. Then the final tutti verse ricochets across the stereo field between trilling saxes and brass call-and-response above bongos and a gauze of violins. The recording is a flamboyant, beat-oriented lounge instrumental—teen-friendly EL as Vegas razzmatazz spectacle—from the album *Great Themes from Hit Films in Dimension 3*, which underscores connections to film-theme and hi-fi-hype trends of the early 1960s.[32] Far from being Muzak, this track has the hip hybridity of a James Bond film score. (The same can be said for the Martin track.)[33]

．．．

EL was thus not so "easy," and from the mid-1960s, it increasingly encroached on rock-pop, bridging generation and taste-culture gaps. The lucrative luxe EL recordings that subsumed beat idioms are described by Joseph Lanza as "metarock" because of their abstractions of rock-pop's fundamental textures, topics, and hits "without compromising that *elevated* spirit" of EL instrumentals.[34] This idea of "elevated" music doubly points to elevator Muzak *and* aspirational middlebrowism. Lanza posits that while "generation gap" discourse came to define the era, "many overlooked . . . similarities between the two age groups," which included both youthful pop with familiar melodic and harmonic structures and "EL artists seeking to stay on the blunt end of the cutting edge."[35] The latter foreshadows the 1966 "soundmania" vogue discussed later, where rock and pop increasingly sought out novel sounds or upcycled cultural detritus (e.g., baroque affectations).

A number of pop genres appealed to the MOR market through production "sweetening" with strings and other MOR stylistic markers. For example, the slickly produced "Nashville sound"—as originated by 1950s producers Chet Atkins and Owen Bradley—was increasingly sweetened into the foundations for what became "countrypolitan" (country + cosmopolitan). These idioms aimed to bridge the tastes of both urban and small-town markets—as in the merging of country with cosmopolitan sound markers (pop crooning, schmaltzy vocal ensembles, strings), leading to cross-market MOR sales. Similar US trends occurred with the productions of Motown and Spector, among others, and in Britain—as, for example, with George Martin's 1963 production for Gerry and the Pacemakers, or the work of producer Norrie Paramor with Cliff Richard and the Shadows, each of which include lush, traditional-pop/EL strings. A pivotal aesthetic shift occurred with Martin's June 1965 overdubbing of a string quartet onto Paul McCartney's "Yesterday," a track that inspired mid-1960s baroque pop. At Martin's suggestion of a string backing for the guitar-and-vocal spare first take, McCartney "was adamant about avoiding the 'syrupy' string sound on many contemporary pop recordings," particularly the sound of "Mantovani and Norrie Paramor." In response, Martin suggested "a classical string quartet."[36] As with subsequent baroque-pop, the classicistic affectations of chamber strings suggested an important cultural distance from EL.

In parallel to metarock, there were early 1960s rock-pop artists who released guitar-focused instrumentals with string backing. This included Duane Eddy's 1962 album *Twangy Guitar/Silky Strings*, which showcased film themes, rock-pop hits, Broadway tunes, and an Alpert original—all cast with strings, harp fills, wordless choirs and ethereal soprano countermelodies alongside back-beat drums and surf guitar leads. The sound updates mid-century jazz-with-strings mood music. Nitzsche's 1963 *Lonely Surfer* album relates to this trend. Alongside the Shadows, Britain also heard Stratocaster-meets-strings instrumental hits from the John Barry Seven. From 1962, this sound became the foundation of big band, surf guitar, and strings on which Barry built his James Bond film scores.

While metarock EL rarely entered the Hot 100 and Top 40 programming, this music seems to have influenced "soft" vocal-pop trends that do chart. By 1969, *Los Angeles Times* critic Robert Hilburn would report that "increasingly... the easy listening chart and the Top 100 chart are becoming duplications. Nine of the first 10 on the easy listening chart last week were well within the upper half of the Top 100 chart."[37] That said, while the early 1967 Hot 100 still had Sinatra ("That's Life") and Roger Williams ("Born Free"), increasingly luxe MOR vocal-pop aesthetics were appearing in youthful rock-pop and sweet soul. Two examples of young-adult, non-rock and nontraditional crossover pop—Glen Campbell and Herb Alpert—illustrate this trend. Hilburn notes that "many of the biggest [Top 100] hits since" the emergence of rock in the mid-1950s "have been easy listening records that would be comfortable alongside... pre-1955 material." He mentions Alpert's "This Guy's in Love with You" and "most of the Glen Campbell songs." Both artists also had key connections to the Carpenters and Bread.

Herb Alpert, "This Guy's in Love with You" (1968)

An important bridge between rock-pop and adult MOR/EL lay with the songwriting, production, and solo instrumental album work of Burt Bacharach.

After successes as a composer and producer, and his emergence as a solo artist in 1965, Bacharach signed with A&M in 1967. This brought Bacharach into the sphere of trumpeter and label head, Alpert, who shaped the MOR catalog of A&M. The label's first single was the 1962 EL hit, "Lonely Bull" (number 6 on the Hot 100). "The Tijuana Brass featuring Herb Alpert" was actually a group of Wrecking Crew musicians. While the Alpert-Bacharach association benefitted the early-career Carpenters, Bacharach's collaboration with Alpert on the 1968 "This Guy's in Love with You" ("Guy") opened up a vocal career for Alpert. "Guy" was number 1 from 22 June through 13 July. Bacharach wrote the song for Alpert's April 1968 CBS television special, *The Beat of the Brass*. Jazz critic Leonard Feather commented on Alpert's "easy delivery of the lyrics," Bacharach's "intuitively perfect arrangement with its two false endings," and how the simple electric-piano introduction starts an additive process that "builds in intensity with . . . a dozen strings, four female voices, and Bacharach himself playing piano (nonelectric) in the climactic passages."[38]

The recording of the arrangement largely reflects its Bacharach score, though Alpert changed small melodic and lyric material, and transposed the song down a major third from the lead-sheet he received. Example 6.1 shows the scoring for the emphatic lyrics "I need your love" (changed from "I've looked at love"). This climax involves a string-register shift from lush, mid-low chord pads to high-register violin octaves. These parallel the voice line alongside resounding timpani, low brass, and Bacharach's downward-cascading parallel octave lines and rumbling bass. Melodrama builds additively from a meek opening verse of just piano and vocal. Of Alpert's performance, a critic amusingly describes Alpert as part of a trend in "non-singing singers," with the company of Leonard Cohen, Bacharach, Newman, and Richard Harris.[39]

• • •

The "meta"-EL trend also included Nashville productions. Examples include *Danny Davis and the Nashville Strings Play Instrumental Versions of the Herman's Hermits Songbook* (1965) and *Floyd Cramer Plays the Monkees* (1967).[40] In parallel, the "town and country,"[41] MOR-friendly Nashville star Eddy Arnold spearheaded proto-countrypolitan stylings in hits like the 1965 "Make the World Go Away" (number 1 on the Country and EL charts), which pairs country baritone crooning with lush strings, honky-tonk piano (Cramer), and vocal ensembles. The idiom merges the Nashville sound with cosmopolitan, MOR-pop. One L.A. AM station was soon

EX. 6.1. Herb Alpert, "This Guy's in Love with You" (comp., arr., and cond. Burt Bacharach).

advertising a "New 1967 Countrypolitan Radio Sound Built in So. Calif. by Showmanship."[42]

A 1968 *Billboard* article on Nashville producer Danny Davis notes these emerging luxe tendencies in Nashville's late 1960s embrace of strings; choral backing vocals; French horns and brass sections; and country intersections with pop, rock, and soul. Davis characterizes this aesthetic as "complex simplicity" and "sophistication with retention of basic charm," adding that "just as a simple costume may have enhancing lines, a simple-structured country tune can have its accoutrements. It's only icing on the cake."[43] Even though some "middle-of-the-road jocks . . . won't touch a steel guitar with a 10-foot turntable arm," the writer contended, other "middle-of-the-roaders rebut that this is the sweet story of success" because country has "not been abandoned but rather dressed-up, and that new audiences have been wooed over."[44] This aesthetic ultimately found its way to soft rock.

The Arkansas-born Glen Campbell was a Wrecking Crew regular as a guitarist, bassist, and songwriter. He contributed to many recordings, from Spector sessions, Sinatra, and Dean Martin to the Monkees, Eddy Arnold, Harpers Bizarre, Jan and Dean, and much more. With the Beach Boys, he played on *Pet Sounds* and became a tour-band member. Even after becoming a solo star, Campbell continued studio-musician work, including with Bread, among others who defined soft rock.[45] Campbell signed with Capitol as a solo artist in 1962, releasing instrumental albums that tapped into meta-rock and MOR country, though without strings. His 1963 *Swingin' 12-String Guitar* presents an instrumental mishmash—country, blues, beat, folk—pitting guitars against harpsichord, bass, and drums. *The Big Band Rock Guitar of Glen Campbell* in 1965 added big-band backing for surf-styled covers of the Ventures, the James Bond theme, chart-topping country, the Beatles, the Byrd's cover of Bob Dylan's "Mr. Tambourine Man," and a Tijuana Brass–like original, "Spanish Shades."[46] Arnold's success likely influenced Campbell's opportunity to explore lushly backed, country-leaning production following the modest success of his debut single as a vocalist, the non-luxe "Gentle on My Mind" (1967). After his luxe hit with "By the Time I Get to Phoenix" ("Phoenix"; 1968), the earlier single was rereleased and won Grammy awards.

In 1969, *RS* featured a massive overview of country. Attention is given to country-pop crossover, with a Campbell focus:

> "Sweetenin'" has been around Nashville from the start, but somehow the idea of recording a solo voice and accompanying guitar and rhythm one day and then dubbing in a 30-piece ensemble with voices the next ran against the grain of country music. But Glen Campbell changed all that. . . . Working with Capitol producer Al De Lory, he developed an obviously successful approach. . . .
>
> "For me to get the feel I want on a record it would be pretty hard to go into a studio with a 21-piece band and get it all to sound solid. So on rhythm dates I only do [voice,] bass, drums, guitar, [and] overdub the guitar, . . . and then Al overdubs the strings, the horns, or whatever."
>
> Extensive overdubbing is basic to pop music, but what Campbell did was to use it to package . . . an identifiable country feeling.

The combination was an enormous success, and has been sustained by Nashville, Jimmy Webb's songs, and Campbell's extraordinary popularity.[47]

Glen Campbell, "By the Time I Get to Phoenix" (1967)

"Phoenix" was written by the nineteen-year-old Webb for a 1966 album by Johnny Rivers, as backed by the Wrecking Crew, including Knechtel, later of Bread.[48] Following the success of the Campbell single, Webb wrote several Wrecking Crew–backed MOR hits for Campbell, Richard Harris ("MacArthur Park," 1968), and the Fifth Dimension (a Black MOR pop group), among others. Campbell discovered the Rivers album on a session gig, and recognized the potential of "Phoenix" as a "bona fide pop hit," recording it soon thereafter with Wrecking Crew colleagues in early fall 1967.[49]

"Phoenix" entered the Hot 100 in October, peaking at number 26 on 16 December. At this date, it was number 13 (soon to peak at 12) on the EL Top 40 chart, and number 16 on the Hot Country Singles chart (peaking at number 2 in January). Mid-1967 represents a starting point for MOR-pop crossover on all three charts. The cross-chart success of "Phoenix" is a harbinger of L.A. pop commercialization of rock's sonic innovations and represents unparalleled MOR success at the moment of rock's creative, cultural, and sonic explosion.

Example 6.2 transcribes the introduction to "Phoenix." Note the EL qualities heard both in its simple, melodic string writing for high-register violins, as well as the jazzy, meandering flute, both bathed in spacious reverb. A simple pedal-tone bass introduces the country-rock syncopated pattern that the drums pick up in the first verse. The steel-string guitar introduces slightly more advanced harmonies (seventh chords) than heard in country. The texture represents the complex-simplicity of MOR country-pop, juxtaposing "folksy" signifiers—vocal drawl, a narrative of the road and broken love, strummed and arpeggiated acoustic guitars, a drum shuffle, electric roots-bass, minimal processing—alongside "cosmopolitan" strings, flute (jazzy), English horn, triangle, and so on. The latter textures—with heavy reverb—are a diaphanous tuxedo, "sweetening" the heartfelt, country origins of the song/singer underneath.

• • •

In 1968, Hilburn reported on country-pop crossover trends, pointing out the "steady stream of pop and folk artists" recording in Nashville following "the

EX. 6.2. Glen Campbell, "By the Time I Get to Phoenix" (arr. Al De Lory).

huge success of Glen Campbell."[50] That year, Campbell was named "Entertainer of the Year" by the Country Music Association, had a hit television special, four Grammy wins (two for "Phoenix"), and three albums "pass[ing] the $1 million mark in sales." Hilburn later reported on Campbell's Las Vegas debut, remarking that because of Campbell's "easy listening, middle-of-the-road musical style, some have accused [him] of blandness," but he underscores that these qualities "attract a large and broadly based audience."[51]

In fall 1967, at the release of "Phoenix," Campbell and Webb—then thirty-one and twenty-one—represented older and newer "youth" generations. With cross-generational, cross-chart potential in mind, the industry sought ways of spinning similar AM Gold from the youth market. While the made-for-television Monkees—first backed by Wrecking Crew sidemen—represent L.A. industry unashamedly jumping on the rock (and Beatles) bandwagon, the group appealed largely to youth. Related commercial efforts, though, did reach the sweet, cross-generation, cross-chart MOR markets through "soft" emulations of the eclectic production innovations of the day.

THE BEATLESQUE, SOUNDMANIA!, AND *INSIDE POP*: INGREDIENTS FOR MOR ROCK-POP

The Beatles were central to rock's late-1960s, expanding timbral palette. Alongside "Yesterday," innovations from the 1965 album *Rubber Soul* were likewise models for the trans-Atlantic explosion of production experimentation from 1966. In combination with its "meaningful" lyrics, the album was influential both in its incorporation of acoustic instruments alongside a rock-band core and its quest for eclectic new pop sounds, whether through studio technology and experimentalism, the sitar ("Norwegian Wood"), or "baroque" piano ("In My Life"). The latter involved half-speed overdubbing, which famously sounded like a classicistic harpsichord solo when returned to full speed.[52] Consequently, in 1966, harpsichords entered rock-pop's sonic lexicon.

Gendron outlines how rock was culturally legitimized—rising above its early role as lowbrow entertainment to something more artful and important—in cross-Atlantic critical discourse over 1965. He points first to the emergence of "folk rock" via both the Byrds' and Dylan's shift to rock-combo instrumentation. The Byrds, from L.A., were influential in blending the lyrical conceptions of Dylan with "Beatlesque vocal harmonies and . . . the guitar rock band made fashionable by the Beatles."[53] With *Rubber Soul*, the Beatles took cues from these trends. Ringo Starr calls this a "departure album" for the Beatles "really getting into a lot of different sounds,"[54] including French horn and clavichord ("For No One"), the sitar and Mixolydian mode ("Norwegian Wood"), Greek bouzouki ("Girl"), country stylizations ("What Goes On"), and other textures. To invoke a line from their song, "And Your Bird Can Sing," rock-pop now had license to incorporate "every sound there is."

A May 1966, front-page *Melody Maker* article announced the new era in an article titled "SOUNDMANIA!" The article remarks on the "two years" of UK/US "revolutionary records" that have led to a "fad for using weird sounds and instrumentation." The article asks rhetorically, "how far out can the poppers go?"[55] This report appears three weeks after the release of the Beach Boys' *Pet Sounds*, and ten weeks before the Beatles *Revolver*. Both were cornerstones for the innovative, multitrack productions of soundmania. As Gendron underscores, a "discourse of sounds" spread to the cultural press from the music industry.[56] The soundmania article also appears just as the new rock press emerges.

Jan Butler outlines an emergent dichotomy in this era between recordings that retained an aura of live performance versus recordings that showcased the creative potential of multitrack technology.[57] Butler traces this schism through the L.A. and San Francisco scenes, building an argument for live-sounding studio recordings as a central site for rock authenticity discourse. Conversely, following soundmania, the adventurous sonic confections of

L.A. studio production—with Beatlesque influences, the eclecticism of EL, and so on—gave rise to new commercial pop that later embodied AM Gold. *Billboard* reveals how the industry fed this trend. In June 1967, the magazine advises merchants to stock up on recorders, dulcimers, harpsichords, sitars, bouzoukis, mandolins, kazoos, and amplification for orchestral instruments, to aid bands in their "search for new instrument[al] sounds" in a trend where "anything goes."[58] A 1967 issue on the annual National Association of Music Merchants convention discusses pop's "explosion in sound" alongside Baldwin's announcement for "new amplified harpsichords," and discussions of Danelectro's amplified sitar, new stomp pedals (wah-wah, fuzz and distortion, and treble boosters), and various transistor combo organs and other combo keyboards with innovative sounds—including the Richard Carpenter–favored RMI Rock-si-Chord electric piano.[59] These trends fed production trends in the tributaries to soft rock.

Part of the legitimation process that Gendron identifies in these sonic trends can be viewed in the April 1967 CBS special, *Inside Pop: The Rock Revolution*, hosted by Leonard Bernstein. Soundmania in part allowed rock-pop to bridge both the generational market divide and brow hierarchies.[60] Bernstein was ideal for this meeting of the generations because of his roles as a popular conductor, composer, and a public/broadcast event host who spoke of music in a manner that bridged the classes. Bernstein's television work—on the Young People's Concerts for CBS (1958–72), the *Omnibus* program (1950s), and others—is significant to postwar music appreciation programming (an extension of interwar middlebrow culture). This is the lineage of *Inside Pop*, where Bernstein acted as the hip, older "establishment" interlocutor between conservative adults and liberal long-haired youth. The program allows the latter a platform for explaining their worldview. Bernstein asks two questions: "Why do adults resent" rock music of the youth (defined as ages eight to twenty-five), and "why do I like it?" Despite self-proclaimed open-mindedness, brow partisanship is readily heard, as when Bernstein remarks, "Of course what I like is maybe 5 percent of the whole output," because the majority is "mostly trash." In that good "5 percent," he hears music that is so "exciting and vital—and . . . significant" that it "claims the attention of every thinking person." The Beatles are central to Bernstein's "good" 5 percent, but artists relevant to this chapter are featured as well—acts like the Beach Boys, Left Banke, the Association, and the Monkees, as well as Tim Buckley, Janis Ian, Dylan, the Byrds, Frank Zappa, Graham Nash, and others.

Bernstein uses the Beatles ("always unpredictable, a bit more inventive than most") to illustrate contemporary rock-pop's predilections for "unorthodox" metric shifts, "arbitrary change[s] of key," and "tart, pungent, canon[s]," among other features, adding that "such oddities as this are not just tricks or show-off devices." With Janis Ian's orchestral-pop "Society's Child," he praises the "fascinating sounds both natural and electronic, like a strange use of harpsichord, and that cool, nasty electric organ ... [with] astonishing key changes, and even tempo changes, ambiguous cadences, unequal phrase lengths, the works!" He observes that "in terms of pop music ... they're real inventions." After comparisons to J. S. Bach and Robert Schumann (to illustrate that "it's not only the Beatles who make these inventions"), he discusses the Left Banke, a group central to baroque pop. He praises their "Pretty Ballerina" for its "combination of the Lydian and Mixolydian modes." "Imagine that!" he proclaims. He builds to soundmania-related proclamations, such as: "I like the eclecticism of it—its freedom to absorb any and all musical styles." Here he notes the Beatles' invocations of "old blues" and "a high Bach trumpet," and praises "the use of harpsichord" and "or even a string quartet," playing "Eleanor Rigby" (an octet), commenting *curious!*" After a youth-politics digression, the program concludes that "the verdict on their music is in: a great deal of it is good."

Via such legitimizing discourse and "good music" radio efforts at youthful programming, the adult MOR increasingly welcomed Hot 100 hits. Across 1966–67, crossover hits appear more routinely and are tied to both over-twenty-five MOR acts and rock-pop acts who employ MOR-related production. From April 1967, a number of under-twenty-five acts achieve MOR and Hot 100 crossover. For example, Harpers Bizarre climbs both charts, peaking at number 8 on the EL chart and 13 on the Hot 100 on 8 April 1967 with their baroque-pop cover of Simon and Garfunkel's "The 59th Street Bridge Song (Feelin' Groovy)" (arranged by the Wrecking Crew's Leon Russell). On the Hot 100, Harpers Bizarre competes with the Turtles' "Happy Together" at number 1, the Mamas and Papas' "Dedicated to the One I Love" at 2, and the Beatles "Penny Lane" at 6—all in the baroque-pop vein. This hit leads the way for crossover hits with related production. By July 1970, when "Close" and "Make It" reside on both charts, the EL chart contains 25 percent of the Hot 100's top twenty.

Commercial Top 40 pop was an equal participant in soundmania, often via recombinatorial production that mined traits from other hits. Such models included influential groups who were critically seen to be more "authentic" despite their commercial success. In *Billboard*'s 1965 "advice by

[a] pop arranger," it is noted that "you have to be able to analyze new trends and develop new ideas [within those trends,] . . . continuously listening to Top 40 radio. When an arranger stops listening he stops working."[61] In 1969, when advising how to reach "Middle of the Road Listen[ers]," the magazine discusses a later "fractionalizing of the [radio] audience" and asks "how mod should your [format] sound be?" This article suggests a later MOR cleaving from soundmania that parallels an emergent "back to roots" movement in both the singer-songwriter vogue and soft rock. The new "soft" idioms nonetheless retained formerly innovative "sounds"—orchestral textures, harpsichords, opulent multitracked vocals, and certain guitar and keyboard sounds, for example. This retention of sounds from former hits echoes *Billboard*'s 1969 MOR programming advice to play a record "after it becomes a hit," thereby stressing the familiar. The same article notes that across the later soundmania period, MOR "listeners didn't leave Top 40 . . . [the] Top 40 left . . . the majority of the listeners."[62] This historical narrative trajectory, then, involves an explosion of innovative recordings, with commercial pop chasing production trends, and then a gradual pulling back to an MOR "softer" pop for the mainstream market while rock moved toward a harder place.

SUNSHINE POP AND BAROQUE POP, 1966–68

Central to the 1965–68 soundmania tributary streams that inform soft rock are California's sunshine pop, baroque pop, and commercial psychedelia. The musicians from Bread and the Carpenters had ties to these trends, with each ultimately refashioning baroque- and sunshine-pop textures under a 1970s MOR soft-rock aesthetic that expurgated late 1960s rock-pop eclecticism. The post-1990 subgenre categorizations of "sunshine pop" and "baroque pop" have foundations in 1960s and 1970s pop discourse, however tenuous. Period criticism suggests that the few references that speak of an L.A. "sunshine" rock or pop sound are British (like Laing's "sunshine rock" comment). By contrast, references to "baroque pop," "baroque rock," "Bach rock," etc., were common from mid-1966, particularly following the Left Banke's "Walk Away Renee." Subsequent discourse on 1960s baroque pop emerges in the 1990s to characterize influences on indie-rock acts like Belle and Sebastian, Elliott Smith, Sufjan Stevens, and others, often overlapping with "twee pop" in Great Britain.[63] While the use of baroque and sunshine pop as designations for 1960s production practice is problematic in light of tenuous historical grounding and consensus, following Keightley and Gendron, I find that these terms do capture shared traits within stylistic, historical, cultural, and geographical contexts. They are especially useful for articulating influence chains because, following Zak and Reynolds, pop recordings are understood and created in relation to other recordings.

AllMusic.com employs both baroque and sunshine pop as 1960s subgenres. They base their historical subgenre distinctions on subsequent reception and "the platforms on which the music is sold."[64] Despite elements of subjectivity, the website's descriptions do help to triangulate the usage of these terms. Each is said to relate to "chamber pop," a "subgenre of [post-1990] alternative/indie rock" that draws "heavily from the lush, orchestrated work" of 1960s baroque, sunshine, and Brill Building pop (citing Bacharach, Hazlewood, and the Beach Boys' Brian Wilson).[65] Chamber pop thus embodies retromania's recombinatorial relations to "*other* music, *earlier* music" via a "constellation" of "reference points and allusions."[66] Such referentiality mirrors both sunshine pop's and Brill pop's relations to traditional luxe pop, and the referentiality of baroque pop. For instance, *Melody Maker* describes Procol Harum's 1968 Bach-rock classic, "A Whiter Shade of Pale" (with a Bach-derived melody), as a "beautiful monster," a phrase that underscores baroque pop's recombinatorial aesthetic: the "monster" is built from scavenged parts sewn together into a new whole; its "pretty" orchestral textures are comparatively "beautiful" in the hard rock era.[67] Sunshine pop shares similar textures (e.g., harpsichords) but references to past musical practice (e.g., classicistic textures) are less obvious (the harpsichord is a hip keyboard sound rather than a baroque referent).

AllMusic describes sunshine pop as exuding 1960s California's smiley-face, pop-kitsch garishness via its "rich harmony vocals, lush orchestrations, and relentless good cheer." It further notes the idiom's light evocations of psychedelic pop (minus "mind expansion"), applications of "production innovations of the time," and its intersections with folk-pop, Brill Building pop, and "elaborate and melancholy baroque pop." AllMusic identifies sunshine pop centrally with the Turtles, the Association, the Mamas and the Papas, the Monkees, and *Pet Sounds*–era Beach Boys.[68]

Keightley's 2011 essay, "The Historical Consciousness of Sunshine Pop," is one of the few scholarly considerations of this subgenre.[69] Like the present chapter, he identifies a continuum from sunshine pop to soft rock across a 1965–72 framing. Keightley observes that this period was "not coincidentally the crucible of rock culture . . . thus propos[ing] the pop inside the rock" as industry "introduce[d] rock and psychedelic elements into 'softer' songs."[70] Keightley too frames sunshine pop via collector discourse, emphasizing that the most valued tracks now are the obscure "flops" amid the "proliferation of [commercial] soundalikes."[71] Chart-topping sunshine pop—by Harpers Bizarre, the Monkees, the Association, the 5th Dimension, and others— was emulated in these practices by both successful bands and second-tier acts who failed to chart. Keightley frames this as a "strange counterpoint to mainstream rock," an "alternative sixties" outlook on *unpopular* pop." He also sharply observes that, as a phrase, "sunshine pop" "slyly rewrites the genre 'light music.'"[72]

Obscure baroque pop has likewise been of interest in these collector discourses. With reference to influences from "the Left Banke, the Beach Boys, . . . Spector, and . . . Bacharach," Allmusic describes the subgenre as "a majestic orchestral sound far removed" from other period rock due to both its "dramatic intensity" and its infusion of "elements of classical music," and its "hallmarks" of "layered harmonies, strings, and horns."[73] What is missing is an articulation of this idiom's "baroque"/classicistic signifiers—whether a harpsichord or orchestral instruments, or classical-signifying harmonic, melodic, or contrapuntal features. Such elements are generally inventive topical colorings employed within pop production norms. Further, the "majestic orchestral sound" is in fact not "removed" from rock textures, but commingles with rock textures, sometimes in a sustained tension between two class-style opposites. Nonetheless, much of this music embraces a "soft," twee, or pretty textural quality in comparison to countercultural rock. Lastly, All-Music additionally notes overlaps between sunshine and baroque pop and cites the Beach Boys and Harpers Bizarre, where, for example, the latter's baroque-inflected "Feelin' Groovy" (1967) is sunshine-filled cheer with little "dramatic intensity" or "melancholy."

Mamas and Papas, "Monday, Monday" (1966)

Mid-1960s Mamas and the Papas hits provided key vocal-harmony and orchestral-pop textural influences to both of these subgenres. Their breakthrough hit "California Dreamin'," released December 1965, entered the Hot 100 in January and peaked at number 4 on 12 March. The group was signed to Dunhill by Lou Adler, who was first told by "Top 40 radio gatekeepers" that the song was "MOR shit" (it ultimately broke on "minor-league stations").[74] Their follow-up, "Monday, Monday," achieved their first number 1 hit in May 1966. Neither single intersects the MOR/EL chart. Both included arrangements by Gene Page (who arranged the Spector-produced Righteous Brothers' 1964 hit, "You've Lost That Loving Feeling," and later worked for Barry White) and backing by Wrecking Crew musicians, including Osborn, Blaine, and Knechtel.

Example 6.3 shows an excerpt from the chorus of "Monday, Monday." The group's vocal harmonies, arranged by John Philips, partly relate to the Greenwich Village folk scene, but Philips and "Mama" Cass Elliot both had

EX. 6.3. Mamas and Papas, "Monday Monday" (arr. Gene Page).

ties to vocal jazz and influences from the harmony vocals of the Four Fresh-man, the Hi-Lo's (both of which influenced the Beach Boys), and Lambert, Hendricks, and Ross.[75] While the latter group was tied to canonic jazz, the first two influences represent white mid-century MOR jazz-pop. Philips simplified these models and merged them with folk-pop textures. His bluesy lead vocal is foregrounded with minimal reverb ambience and a nasal, folksy delivery. Note the widely spaced, triad-based open voicings of the backing vocals, set in considerable reverb. In the MOR-pop context, this *was* an enriched vocal idiom—a "complex simplicity"—but that luxe interpreta-tion is enhanced by the orchestral backing. Observe the high-register octave strings and earlier harmony pads. Interstitial flourish-fills—here the violin run—accent sectional divisions. The track features "hip" sounds like harpsi-chord and fuzztone guitar. The former is not overtly "baroque," particularly in that Knechtel's busy contributions simply function as comping. The drums, percussion, and bass provide a beat-combo foundation. This hybrid sound is emulated in hits by the Association and the 5th Dimension, among other acts. While the track competes on the charts with the Beach Boys' "Sloop John B" single, the second from the *Pet Sounds* sessions (number 3 on 7 May under the number 1, "Monday, Monday"), it arrives before the mid-May 1966 release of that influential album. It is also without Beatlesque influences, and was released before *Revolver*, which marked the onset of soundmania.

· · ·

One crystallizing moment in defining baroque pop is found in producer Bob Stanley's 2007 CD boxed set, *Tea and Symphony: The English Baroque Sound, 1967–1974.*[76] The focus is again on sound-alike obscurities, not hits. In a related essay, "Baroque and a Soft Place," Stanley posits that catalysts for the UK vogue for "harpsichords and string quartets" were the Rolling Stones' April 1966 "Lady Jane," the Kinks' October 1966 "Too Much on My Mind," and the Beatles' August 1966 "Eleanor Rigby." Each helped lead pop away from hard blues rock and fuzztone guitars, but Stanley identifies the July 1966 "Walk Away Renee" by the New York–based, "anglophile" Left Banke—formed late 1965—as "the first bona fide baroque pop hit."[77] "Renee" marks the moment that baroque pop became a commercial trend. Gendron's preferred term, "baroque rock," is one of several phrasings that gained wide currency for rock-pop recordings employing harpsichords, string quartets, and so on. Gendron notes the trend's "small accreditory function" of "appending a high-prestige concept" onto low-prestige rock-pop.[78] Such attempts at aura transference are evoked in the many classical references in Left Banke promotional copy, even while the band was marketed as a teen pop group. Gendron's chief concern, however, is with accreditory efforts and rock's aspirational employments of classical topics.[79] He does not consider the repertory of commercial-pop emulations of these production innovations for profit and chart success. The latter is the topic here, and specifically the transition from soundmania, to baroque pop, to further tributary streams for 1970s AM Gold and soft rock. "Baroque *pop*" thus offers a distinction from "baroque *rock*," which better describes an *aspirational* soundmania and idioms that point toward progressive rock. Baroque pop held few "art" aspirations.

"Walk Away Renee" peaked at number 5 on 29 October 1966. The track foregrounds chamber strings, solo cello, motoristic harpsichord figurations, and alternating faux-UK-English lead vocals and duet vocal harmonies on the chorus, all backed by beat-combo drumming. The Left Banke's promotional copy displays a curious mixture of brow aspirations and personal information targeted at a preteen and teen fan base. The opening line of several PR releases—"There's one new New York rock group that strictly has decided to go for Baroque (if you'll excuse that pun!)"—echoes period industry efforts to popularize baroque-related recordings (e.g., the Swingle Singers' Bach-inflected jazz-pop releases).[80] Michael Brown, the group's teen-idol singer-songwriter and harpsichordist, describes "the Beatles, the Mamas and the Papas, and the Beach Boys" as favorite artists, commentary that underscores an influence chain.[81]

The Left Banke is said to have brought "a 'new sound' to beat music . . . [adding] a string quartet and a harpsichord" to create a "Ba-roque and roll sound" for "the 'mainstream' of today's teen tastes."[82] The copy continues:

> Perhaps the[ir] success . . . can be attributed to a growing sophistication . . . among contemporary teenagers. . . .
> . . . By their own admission [they are] a "long hair group" and that is strictly meant in every sense of the phrase . . . both in their tastes musically . . . and in hair fashions! All . . . the boys have long English-style cuts that perfectly accompanies their total "Mod" dress.
> Leading this ensemble is . . . Mike Brown . . . [who] digs all sorts of 18th century keyboard instruments.[83]

This "mod" look is apparent in the sartorial details of their first album's graphics, where they are indistinguishable from other mod-styled bands circa

1966, including the Monkees.[84] The press copy has significant commentary that invokes cosmopolitanism, but such inclinations are overt in the band's name, with its French reference and the precious spelling of "banke" with a superfluous "e."

Such copy indicates some expectation of the baroque gimmick resonating with a fan base, whether teen or young adult. Such aspirational pop rhetoric did apparently connect with teens, as seen, for example, in *Go* magazine, which had the "world's largest circulation of any teen weekly."[85] With its celebrity-focused photo essays on fashion and pop-idol love lives and marriages, *Go* was the type of US fan magazine that the new rock criticism hated. In its pages from 1966 to 1967, there is notable attention given to the Left Banke, a Wilson "genius" article, and coverage of the Association, the Walker Brothers, and Harpers Bizarre, among other baroque-pop acts, all from a teenage female-fan perspective, and without musical discussion. One article features English rock singer, Eric Burdon (of the Animals), complaining about baroque-inflected "pretty" pop. He describes the Beatles as catalysts, and juxtaposes their Liverpool-rocker early years with 1966–67, when they "unfortunately . . . got pretty." Burden argues that "pop today has reached the stage where it was a few years before the Beatles came in. . . . They're playing PRETTY music."[86] The Left Banke was indicative of this "pretty" trend.

Baroque pop's intersections with psychedelia peaked over 1967–68, as can be partly evidenced in the kaleidoscopic cover of the 1968 album, *The Left Banke Too*, which places the band overtly in a manor house and eighteenth-century garb with long coats, waistcoats, breeches, ruffled cravats, and leggings. *Crawdaddy* observes that the album holds some of the "best coordinated and assimilated electronic effects to be heard since 'Sgt. Pepper.'"[87] This post-*Pepper*, psychedelic-tinged extension of baroque pop is heard in "Dark Is the Bark," but the vocals further suggest the forthcoming tight harmonies of Crosby, Stills and Nash set alongside acoustic guitars, mandolins, harpsichord, electric guitars, oboes, jazz trumpet and brass, chamber strings, swinging drums, and psychedelic lyrics.

The commentary of critic Sandy Pearlman (later of the hard-rock band, Blue Öyster Cult) represents how baroque pop was heard in the counterculture. Pearlman observes that with "Renee," he was "struck by the far-too-sophisticated name of the group," adding that he "refused to listen . . . believ[ing] that this was just more fag-rock." Nonetheless, "the omnipresence of the big hit forced me to [change my mind]. . . . I realized this was a masterpiece."

The homophobic slur reflects Pearlman's aversion to twee-inclined pop, and indeed he contends that for the Left Banke, "the beautiful has become a stylistic goal." Their "self-consciously beautiful" songs are said to "have such a high density of real or Bizzaro pretty cliches," built from "the best cliches of Baroque, Romantic and 20th century music," he argues, "who could dare assert that they aren't nice?"[88] Pearlman's guilty-pleasure assessment of this "very agreeable" recombinant pop sits on the knife-edge of the emergent rock-versus-pop chasm, with the Left Banke positioned within commercial, derivative pop despite press-copy attempts to project rock authenticity.

In November 1966, Tom Nolan—who later wrote a major, positive cover story on the Carpenters for *RS*—contributed an extended *Los Angeles Times* story on the city's "Frenzied Frontier of Pop Music." Nolan contends that "the Stones, the Beatles, [and] the Beach Boys . . . have created in the New Music a melting-pot of musical styles, effects and elements which can be drawn upon . . . in any combination." The soundmania innovations of these groups are said to have been "sucked into the ever-widening mainstream."[89] Nolan's innovation-to-mainstream scenario maps well onto later discourse framing of the baroque-pop centrality of the Beach Boys, their May 1966 album, *Pet Sounds*, and specifically the track "God Only Knows."[90] The Wikipedia page for "baroque pop," a forum for commonly circulated opinions, provides a number of far-flung citations that point to *Pet Sounds* as a key influence, although the claim that the album "almost single-handedly created the idea of 'baroque pop'" is problematic.[91] I have not found 1966–67 *Pet Sounds* criticism or promotional copy referring to "baroque" traits. It is contended, though, that Wilson's *Pet Sounds*–era "pocket symphonies"—a phrase coined by publicist Derek Taylor (formerly with the Beatles)—centrally influenced "producers, engineers, and recording artists."[92] This assertion is supported in, for example, Paul McCartney's 1966 comments regarding the overall "musical invention" of the album, and "God Only Knows" as the best song ever written.[93]

The UK press took greater interest in the "musical inventions" of the album than commentators in the United States. By July 1966, *Melody Maker* was asking music industry figures if *Pet Sounds* was "the most progressive pop album ever," with English musicians weighing in.[94] There are passing comparisons to classical composers—Rimsky-Korsakov, Mozart, and Palestrina—that indicate accreditation discourse in parallel with the Wilson "pop genius" promotional campaign that Taylor introduced.[95] The album nonetheless is situated in a soundmania-influence trajectory between the Beatles and Beach

Boys in the competition for ever-more "progressive" pop experimentation. In the United States, the new-rock criticism of *Crawdaddy* largely displays an absence of Beach Boys attention until a three-part, extended-essay series on Wilson in April, May, and June 1968.[96] Indeed, in US rock criticism (*RS*, *Crawdaddy*, etc.), there is minimal attention to non-Beatles baroque pop over 1966–67, and critical discussion of the Beach Boys masterpiece subsided after the sonic revolutions of *Revolver* and *Sgt. Pepper*.

Beach Boys, "God Only Knows" (1966)

Pet Sounds and "God Only Knows" introduce a range of elements that were soon heard again in L.A.-produced baroque pop. While some critics heard Spector's influence in this music, Wilson directed his Wrecking Crew collaborators toward idiosyncratic music in the sessions for the album and "Good Vibrations." Like Spector, the backing tracks were recorded at an initial session, with vocals added later, but unlike Spector, *Pet Sounds* involves multi-track overdubbing.[97] The sessions included Campbell, Knechtel, Blaine, the later Campbell producer Al de Lory (on organ), and other studio musicians who were contracted for similar baroque-pop work in the coming years. With such connections in mind, it should be observed that while the *Pet Sounds*–era singles do not intersect the EL charts, their music was appropriated by EL artists. For example, 1964 saw the Capitol release of the Hollyridge Strings's *The Beach Boys Songbook: Romantic Instrumentals* (a companion to their *The Beatles Song Book*) and the EL maestro, Hugo Montenegro, recorded an amazing 1969 version of "Good Vibrations." A *Billboard* "Spotlight Singles" review noted that its "clever arrangement" enhanced Wilson's original "with Top 40 and Easy Listening appeal."[98]

Example 6.4 transcribes several bars from the contrapuntal coda (2:00–2:53) that closes "God Only Knows."[99] The passage includes elements heard earlier, including the French horn theme, the layered accordion/harpsichord/tack-piano comping, the reverb-heavy "clip clop" percussion (plastic bottle halves), and the sleigh bells, tambourine, electric bass, and drums. The track develops via a "majestic" buildup of sounds, but orchestral instruments do not always signify baroque/classicistic textures, as with the comping of the harpsichord or the whole-note string pads that add background color. These are unique Wilson-contrived textures operating as a sort of elevated pop. Nonetheless, these instruments do perform some classicistic gestures, as in the contrasting four-bar interlude (1:04–1:12)

EX. 6.4. Beach Boys, "God Only Knows" (comp., arr., and prod. Brian Wilson). A pirate track–stem set isolates "God Only Knows" into two stereo pairs of the isolated vocals and backing accompaniment, respectively. The example references orchestral tracks A and B, with lowercase roman type meaning that there is background presence of an instrument in that channel. In the album, there is little stereo separation.

involving stiff, unaccompanied flute-and-harpsichord set against militaristic snare-drum responses. Also, once the track's foundational, loping comping groove returns, the recording initiates a new vocal-counterpoint texture (1:13–1:27) squarely heard as a baroque-pop topic. Philip Lambert compares the texture to "a chorus of a Baroque oratorio or cantata." The track's closing is likewise described as a display of this "oratorio" vocal-counterpoint model, with the two lower voices being "strictly imitative, while Wilson's upper obbligato restates the French horn melody from the introduction."[100] Other *Pet Sounds* songs contain textures that might be potentially read as baroque-pop-related, but more often, the non-rock orchestral instruments— harpsichord, clarinets, woodwinds, strings, tympani—are employed in combined textures (apparently inspired by Spector) that involved "combining the sound of two instruments to create a third, brand-new sound" where it is impossible to discern individual components.[101]

. . .

Beyond the Left Banke and *Pet Sounds*, the February 1967 Beatles single, "Penny Lane," added a host of production tropes for baroque pop prior to the May release of *Sgt. Pepper*. The Turtles' "Happy Together," an L.A. baroque-pop confection, pushed "Penny Lane" from the top of the charts in March/April. Reportage on the Turtles comments on their goal of "bridg[ing] the gap existing between the musical tastes of adults and teens."[102] This gap-bridging agenda is a harbinger of EL and Hot 100 crossover. February releases also included Harpers Bizarre's "The 59th Street Bridge Song." This "soft" baroque-pop track marks an initial crossover to the EL chart. The single, arranged by Leon Russell and performed by Wrecking Crew colleagues, peaked on the Hot 100 at no. 13 on 8 April (with "Happy Together" at number 1, Mamas and Papas at 2, and "Penny Lane" at 6), while simultaneously hitting number 8 on the EL chart. The band's 1967 album, *Feeling Groovy*, built out this peppy, over-the-top pop sound with songs from Van Dyke Parks, Randy Newman, and Harry Nilsson, each of whom soon employed baroque-pop tropes in foundational albums for the L.A. singer-songwriter scene. Stylistic expansions of these baroque-pop templates also appeared in 1967. In April of that year L.A.'s Nitty Gritty Dirt Band released "Buy for Me the Rain," featuring harpsichord, baroque strings, and a quasi-folk arrangement and production by David Gates. (The band's second album, also 1967, notably includes Jackson Brown's "Shadow Dream Song" in full baroque-pop production.) In a similar direction linking baroque-pop, country-rock, and folkish Americana, the young Linda Ronstadt—soon central to the Troubadour singer-songwriter scene and soft rock—was then part of the folk trio the Stone Poneys, whose baroque-inflected, harpsichord-and-strings hit, "Different Drum" (by Mike Nesmith of the Monkees), rose to number 13 in January.

In Britain, by end of 1967, rock's flirtations with orchestral instruments, new technologies, and "classical" influences led to the Moody Blues hit, "Nights in White Satin," which combined the tape-sample orchestral sounds of the Mellotron keyboard, alongside the London Festival Orchestra. This hit and the Beatles' earlier "A Day in the Life" (*Sgt. Pepper*) presaged a range of 1968–70 rock-pop with self-consciously "symphonic" backings, usually for dramatic or filmic effect (and aspirational intentions).

Away from the singles charts, there were a host of 1967 L.A.-produced expansions on baroque-pop and proto-chamber pop, with nods to psychedelia, folk-rock, countrypolitan, and emerging singer-songwriter trends. Such intersections are heard, for example, on Love's *Forever Changes* (November), Tim Buckley's *Goodbye and Hello* (August), and the eclectic psychedelic-Americana debuts of Van Dyke Parks (*Song Cycle*, November), and the Beatles' L.A. sidekick, Nilsson (*Pandemonium Shadow Show*, December). Some bands explored this trend through single tracks, such as Buffalo Springfield's grandiose Neil Young feature single, "Expecting to Fly" (December), arranged by Nitzsche in a film score–like illustrative underscoring. In September, *Billboard* announced a "sophisticated and serious" pop vogue that encouraged "longer hours in the studio" in the pursuit of "artistic triumphs as well as commercial success."[103] The Beatles' influence is noted and there is emphasis on orchestral pop, including discussions of the Left Banke and the Beach Boys.

In 1968 these trends increased, albeit further off the charts. For example, the pop-defined Monkees turned "serious" via psychedelia, orchestral pop, and experimental film in a post-television film, *Head*, which included the Nitzsche-orchestrated, Wrecking Crew–performed "Porpoise Song" (October; barely a Top 100 single). The failed debut albums of Randy Newman (which featured broad-Americana eclecticism and rich orchestrations), James Taylor, and Joni Mitchell (the latter two soon moved to L.A.) arrived in 1968. Mitchell's non-orchestrated debut, *Song to a Seagull*, produced in L.A., is an outlier of the "return to roots" movement in the folk transition to the singer-songwriter trend.[104] Despite baroque-pop affectations (harpsichords, etc.), Taylor's debut was not so much Beatlesque as a foreshadowing of the folksy-bluesy sound of his breakthrough 1970 single, "Fire and Rain," overlaid with string-centered chamber backings. There is a singer-songwriter, orchestrated-confessional kinship with Britain's Nick Drake (*Five Leaves Left*, recorded 1968–69) and the 1968 L.A. albums of Newman and Nilsson (*Aerial Ballet*), and the somber chamber-music textures on releases by Leonard Cohen (*Songs of Leonard Cohen*, recorded in New York). Taylor's debut also presages some of the soft orchestral-pop textures of the Carpenters and Bread, and the orchestral build of Taylor's first version of "Carolina on My Mind" further points to Spector's heavy orchestration on the Beatles swan song, the 1970 "The Long and Winding Road." In New York across late 1968 and 1969, soft singer-songwriter aesthetics likewise mixed with Spector-esque orchestral melodrama in Simon and Garfunkel's sessions for *Bridge over Troubled Water*, which included the Wrecking Crew's Blaine, Osborn, and Knechtel (arranging and keyboards). Neil Young's January 1969 eponymous debut demonstrates a rock-centric shift in this over-production direction, mixing acoustic guitars, Black-gospel backing vocals, country-rock, skronking guitar solos, and Nitzsche's orchestrations. In the expansive orchestration of "The Old Laughing Lady" and the "String Quartet from Whisky Boot Hill" (with acoustic guitar, rough performance, and a closing dissonant harmony), the album presents a rock-pop counterpart to the cinematic stylistic juxtapositions heard in Ennio Morricone's pop production–influenced film soundtrack to *The Good, the Bad and the Ugly*—which topped the album charts in 1968 while a cover of the film's theme by Montenegro rose to number 2 on the Hot 100 chart.

In sum, over 1968, while youth culture's surface was dominated by hard rock and counterculture, these hybrid luxe trends reveal movement in another direction. The industry took notice. In August, *Billboard* reported that "forms of 'hyphenated-rock,' 'acid-rock,' 'psychedelic-rock,' 'hard-rock,' and the easy listening 'housewife-rock,' are being combined . . . to capture both teen and adult, AM and underground radio markets with a sound that is being labeled 'soft-rock.'"[105] The article observes that the "overall instrumental sound of these groups is soft," but "their lyrics still retain the attitude of today's 'hard-rock.'" This music "is easier for the adult's ear to accept while ingredients of underground airplay are still present: heavy lyrics, complex instrumentation, and youthful group attitude."[106] EL programmers contended that "rock groups are choosing sounds that lead to easy listening airplay," thereby offering a "transitional bridge" to "what is happening now." This soft, EL-friendly trend is said to include music of Cohen, who used chamber-pop backings, as well as Judy Collins, Buffy Sainte-Marie, and Ritchie Havens, who did not. All were foundations for the singer-songwriter trend. This new soft rock is said to provide "a vital function in making underground sounds more palatable to [pop-curious] older listeners." The article situates "this sound" in relation to roots in the Beatles' "Yesterday," and hits from Harpers Bizarre, Spanky and Our Gang, and the Fifth Dimension. The framing is clear: industry saw soft rock as an extension of sunshine and baroque pop.

Over 1966–69, the careers of David Gates, Rob Royer, and the Carpenters intersect with these trends in significant ways. As a studio songwriter, arranger, producer, or musician before the 1968 formation of Bread, Gates contributed a million-selling hit for the Monkees ("Saturday's Child," 1966), and worked for Spector, Wilson, Bobby Darin, Elvis Presley, Connie Stevens, Percy Faith, the Walker Brothers, Engelbert Humperdinck, Herman's Hermits, and the Nitty Gritty Dirt Band, among others. Two key developments of 1967 were, first, that Gates grew dissatisfied with working for other acts and became interested in signing as an artist; and second, he was engaged to work as producer/arranger with the Pleasure Fair, the aforementioned group that included Royer.[107] Gates greatly shaped the resultant 1967 eponymous album's grab-bag of flower-power, baroque-/sunshine-pop textures, including tight vocal harmonies reminiscent of the Mamas and Papas or the Association, motoristic baroque-ish harpsichord, (bad) faux-British accents emulating a music-hall crooner (with added disc-crackle noise), chamber woodwinds, strings, brass, harp, a cover of a Beatles tune, fuzztone guitar, and more.[108] The endeavor underscores the relevance of Zak's commentary concerning both the "symbolic attributes of performance styles" and "the rhetorical aspect[s] of timbre," and Reynolds's remarks on the long history of recombinant commercial pop. The debut albums of the Carpenters and the Pleasure Fair display clearly audible pop-chart aspirations via commercial soundalike production textures based on recombinant, synecdochal references to other near-contemporaneous sources. This recombinational soundalike approach was central to attracting audiences and building identities for these young artists.

In late 1966, the Carpenters made the acquaintance of bassist Joe Osborn, who had developed a small garage studio and record label. Osborn performs alongside Blaine and Knechtel on much of the music discussed in this chapter. The young siblings were offered open use of his studio, which included a four-track recorder and a Chamberlin Music Master keyboard (a Mellotron precursor), among other equipment. Osborn assisted on their demos, including a single release. The 1966 "Looking for Love" / "I'll Be Yours," reflects beat-oriented, girl-group idioms, including simple vocal harmonies and Richard's string arrangements for the Chamberlin. Their "Parting of Our Ways" demo reveals Beatlesque baroque-pop in its tack-piano with classicistic phrasing (harpsichord-like?) alongside Chamberlin flute obbligato.[109] The demos led to the founding of Spectrum, which they later described as a rock-oriented band.[110] That characterization suggests their rock-venue performance contexts, but their sound was more choral pop with syncopation, harmonies, time signatures, electric-piano comping, and drumming that blended West Coast jazz and L.A.'s jazzy commercial vocal pop (e.g., the Mamas and the Papas). A Spectrum member noted her embarrassment when the group opened for the hard-rock band Steppenwolf ("we thought we were going to get killed"), but the audience listened attentively.[111] As Spectrum struggled, the siblings developed further demos, applying Spectrum's tightly arranged vocal harmonies to overdubbings with their own two voices, thereby creating the characteristic Carpenters' sound that led Alpert to sign the band to A&M upon hearing their "Don't Be Afraid" demo.[112] Despite nods toward contemporary pop lyrics like "love is a groovy thing" alongside baroque harpsichord, Beatlesque faux-classical flourishes, and so on—the production also displays Karen's full, warm voice and the Carpenters' lush, jazz-indebted vocal harmonies. This transitional, recombinant sound colors their underperforming October 1969 debut, *Offering*, which Richard later described as "a product of its time, the sixties" with strong "'67, '68 influences."[113] Similarly, a 1975 interviewer noted to Richard that *Offering* "sounds like a lot of Sixties groups. Not exactly psychedelic, but sort of ambitious."[114]

1970: HEARING AM GOLD IN THE CARPENTERS AND BREAD

The AM Gold record series was the progeny of midcentury record-of-the-month clubs, as updated for off-prime-time cable television advertising. This later AM Gold repertory, however, only modestly intersects with 1960s middlebrow-adjacent culture, while "of-the-month" mail-order clubs were central to middlebrow discourse.[115] But this music is a microcosm for pop class and taste discourses in American popular music of the period. Andreas Huyssen has famously articulated twentieth-century Western culture's "Great Divide," the "powerful imaginary" opposition between high modernism and the commercial market. However, Huyssen notably observes that rather than being a static binary, in practice, "time and again," this "categorical separation" was violated.[116] The popular idea of an increasing schism—an imaginary binary—between rock and pop in this era, which was an idea fostered by the former's growing cultural legitimation across 1967–69, suggests a revised "great divide" in the context of popular music's marketplace, even though in practice such concerns for "serious" artistry versus commercialism were hardly clear-cut.

Two ads capture the AM Gold aesthetic. "Imagine owning all your favorite AM radio hits for *just* $12.99!" intones a smooth announcer over the soaring strings, down-home guitar, and plaintive vocals of both Dion intoning "have you seen my old friend John?" and Campbell's blue-collar ode, "Wichita Lineman."[117] This 1999 ad's music excerpts casually mix 1960s and 1970s pop. Nilsson's "Everybody's Talkin'" follows not long after, along with tracks in related MOR styles. A 2000 advertisement asks, "Remember when the songs made you smile? Now you can enjoy all your favorite songs again in one incredible collection!" as track titles from the Association, the Turtles, Harpers Bizarre, the Monkees, the Fifth Dimension, Spanky and Our Gang, and others scroll by. Both ads underscore the centrality of the trends discussed in this chapter to AM Gold, and the repertory and ad copy further conveys associations with the commonplace and everyday life, the sentimental, and the relatability of both rural and suburban life. The series includes fifty-plus "various artists" compilations, but only one CD was devoted exclusively to a single artist: the Carpenters. The group's hits appear throughout the series, but this 1993 solo spotlight underscores the primacy of this group to a core AM Gold aesthetic, if there is one.[118]

AM radio programming, as refined across the 1960s and 1970s, is central to this repertory. AM was an MOR tastemaker, guiding consumers toward sales consumption. While period commentary loosely essentializes Top 40 pop as forming a semi-unified aesthetic, AM Gold is nonetheless a nostalgic, retrospective associative categorization rather than a genre designation. AM Gold is defined by the crossover overlap between the demographics, artists, and hits of the Top 40 and MOR formats. Based on its advertising, media-outlet placement, and low-quality packaging, the compilation series seems to have targeted an audience somewhat down-market from the middle-class readership of *Time* magazine, a quintessentially lower-middle publication also from Time-Life. Following Mitchell Morris's characterization of the audience for a similar 1998 seventies-hits boxed-set compilation, *Have a Nice*

Decade: The '70s Pop Culture Box, the consumers for this nostalgia were likely in their "late thirties or perhaps forties" in the 1990s, as their pop interests were presumably formed as teens and preteens in the 1970s.[119] (This is in all probability true, but as 1960s *Billboard* radio trade discourse makes clear, even in its day, most of this music broadly targeted an MOR twenty-five-to-forty-nine age demographic.) However, whereas Morris's imagined boxed-set audience held potential for ironic or guilty-pleasure purchases, the AM Gold sales demographic likely bought this series with sincere appreciation. AM Gold has none of *Have a Nice Decade*'s ironic packaging buffer against the music's "'excesses' of style.[120]

MOR expanded to include a diversity of idioms and eras of music, a trend that continued under the category "adult contemporary" from 1979 forward.[121] Among later programming subformats was "gold-intensive," which Christina Baade describes as "80–90 percent oldies with a small playlist of current AC hits."[122] Here is the "gold" in "AM Gold," where hits keep on generating income well after their prime through seductive nostalgia and familiarity. The series titles that Time-Life chose—*Super Hits!* and *AM Gold*—speak volumes about the centrality of mainstream media and nostalgia to understanding the cultural fields, discourses, and audiences to which this music relates. There is an assumed inescapable ubiquity, and these are the mega "golden" hits (they possess pop centrality) and not the misses (obscurity).

Two ideal complementary examples for historically hearing the musical topics and quintessential textures of luxe AM Gold are found in Bread's "Make It with You" and the Carpenters' "Close to You." Considered together, these tracks illustrate how the trends discussed thus far intersect circa 1970 in the "complex simplicity" of nascent MOR soft-rock aesthetics. When "Close" topped the Hot 100, it was number 1 on the Top 40 Easy Listening chart for the exact same four weeks across 25 July to 15 August. It hit number 1 first, though, on the EL chart on 18 July. "Close" dropped to number 2 on the Hot 100 as Bread arrived at number 1. Bread's "Make It" was released by Elektra Records in June 1970. The record peaked as the Hot 100 number 1 on 22 August, while simultaneously attaining number 4 on the Top 40 Easy Listening Chart.

Bread, "Make It with You" (1970)

Table 4a presents an overview of the multitrack production to "Make It." This graphic sketches the textural combinations across the track, as

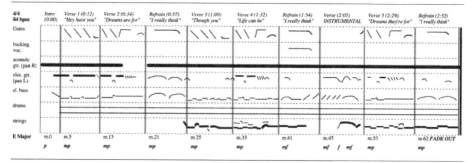

well as register placement and mix presence for individual parts, melodic contour and harmonic density in parts, and the arrangement form. The singer-songwriter framing is heard in the track opening with Gates and his guitar. Numerous critics had panned the group's first-album vocal harmonies as being derivative of CSNY, whose debut was released first and widely celebrated. Bread recalibrated after that reception. By summer 1970, this single fell directly at the forefront of the singer-songwriter trend led by Taylor's second album, *Sweet Baby James*, released February 1970, and its radio hit, "Fire and Rain." The latter track peaked at number 3 from 31 October to 14 November, *after* the arrival of Bread. Both epitomize the idiom's ethos of a sensitive male singer with an acoustic-guitar and folk-rock band backing.

The key texture of the guitar part, the Emaj7 to B7sus progression, is also heard in the passage in Example 6.5a. Gates describes these chords as the song's origin, noting how their voicings work "against some open tones, where you let the E strings ring." When he first struck the B7sus voicing, he happened to sing "I want to make it with you," before reacting, "God, that might be a little raunchy" because of its "sexual connotation." He then transformed it into a "mellow[ed] out" double entendre by "mak[ing] it more of a love story."[123]

Gates was concerned with how to capture a "gentle" sound. With full band, the song sounded "too hard." He rethought the multitrack building process, starting with the soft voice and acoustic guitar. From there, bass was added, then drums, then electric guitar, with each maintaining sensitivity to earlier layers. He then arranged and recorded the strings. This then-unorthodox, piecemeal approach was "the only way I could get it to be gentle enough."

EX. 6.5. Bread, "Make It with You" (comp., arr., prod. David Gates). Excerpts: (a) 1:54; and (b) 2:11.

This process is heard as the track unfolds and builds an emotional arc. In contrast to the Carpenters, the production here aligns with singer-songwriter simplicity, though Gates introduces some light complexity (e.g., the B7sus). The acoustic guitar strums in the right of the audio soundbox, while the clean electric guitar is on the left. The latter alternates between single-line responses to the vocals (both rock- and country-leaning), single chord accentuations, and a verse-melody based solo. The direct-to-mixer bass is unobtrusive, alternating between roots and fifths and arpeggiated lines like those in Example 6.5a. This is the one passage with Royer harmonizing, employing a higher-register, country-style harmony on thirds (accentuating the title lyric). The mellow-drama of Gates's strings elevates this track to prettified commercial pop via rich, closely voiced harmonic pads on triadic and seventh harmonies. Sometimes the pads change register, or the strings offer countermelodies for lyric accentuation. In the instrumental verse, however, the strings rise to foreground exchanges with the guitar solo. Example 6.5b shows one "serious" texture with polyphonic, contrary-motion writing during a motivic statement (restating the opening vocal trill). Note the dramatic phrase that ends the passage in a two-octave scoring which includes a sixteen-note descending motive harmonized in sixths. There is a sense of lovelorn passion bursting forth via the emotion-laden strings. These juxtaposed textures defined the popular Bread ballad sound.

Carpenters, "Close to You" (1970)

Table 4b presents a graphic overview of the production for "Close." The track was likely recorded onto sixteen-track tape. Richard's recordings of his arrangements likewise employed piecemeal development, with orchestral sweetening and vocal backgrounds added in subsequent sessions. The vocal-harmony layerings involved bounce-down transfers (i.e., combining two or more tracks into a third to free tracks for reuse). The complexity of the vocals and the spare areas of the "Close" arrangement led Richard to use a click track to steady tempo, but it still took forty-seven takes (not including overdubbing) to achieve the desired performance.[124]

The introduction (0:00–0:10) features Richard's right-hand piano shuffle based on simple triadic harmonies. As this unfolds, a vibraphone doubles the melodic top note. The first-verse (0:10–0:31) foregrounds Karen's warm solo vocal. The piano modestly expands to include a single-line bass. There is much commentary on the "intimacy" heard in Karen's recorded voice here, which

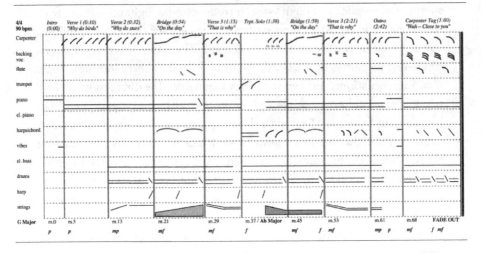

includes audible breaths and other soft but expressive laryngeal vocal textures that suggest emotive details. Karen, a contralto, was praised for her lower and mid registers, where she displayed careful control of dynamics and tonal colors through a strong, warm tone. She never belts, largely works from head-voice resonance, and selectively employs a fuller vocal-mechanism. Richard takes umbrage with arguments about her microphone technique, contending that "Karen had the intimacy built right into the sound of her voice."[125] That said, a near-field microphone richly captures a host of bodily and physical details, including breath, mouth resonance, vocal-formation subtleties, and laryngeal noises—details that Roland Barthes calls the "grain" of the voice. In verse 1, listen to Karen's expression of "suddenly appear" (0:12–0:13), with the slightly drawn-out, breathy "s" (with a pause after the "s" of "birds") and the second "p" in "ap-pear," which has a light, creaky laryngeal rasp. The colors of a glottal stop of "t" on "time" (0:16) and the dynamic pull-back are audible, as is the delicate expressive vibrato in her registral jump up to "near" (0:19). All of these qualities of grain are exposed in the mix to convey the intimate emotions of the protagonist, who is mapped onto the "wholesome" image of twenty-year-old Karen.

Verse 2 (0:32–0:53) pulls listeners further into the emotions of the voice as the arrangement builds (drums, bass, soft strings). The turn-around includes a vocal-dynamics expansion in Karen's lower register, which is set over a drum-tom fill and harp-sweep, before the arrangement pulls back and restarts the building process across the bridge (0:54–1:14).[126] This passage adds a light harpsichord, and the piano reenters alongside a muted cymbal. As seen in Table 4b, the strings expand in register, but they lie deeper in the mix beneath harp sweeps and flute interjections. Hear how these augmentations are sparing and painterly, adding elements selectively, consistently shifting textures, roles, density, and colors dropping out across the soundscape. After "eyes of blue" (1:12), everything drops away except two downward arpeggios from the piano and drum-tom fills.

The third verse (1:15–1:37) follows similar strategies before the expansions of the instrumental verse (1:38–1:58). The latter starts with a brassy, vocal-like trumpet solo (on the melody) backed by the rhythm section with plodding harpsichord comping. After another harp sweep, there is a modulation a half-step up. The backing strings reenter, and the melody for the second line of the verse is stated in unison with Karen on a wordless "ah" vocalese alongside a full, melodic piano harmonization. Though it is not jazzy (yet), the locked-hand, melodic approach of Richard's piano recalls the style of George Shearing (Richard's piano inspiration).[127] The strings accompany half of this statement, with a clipped countermelody of short harmonized interjections (built from piano-intro material) before giving way to a lush, low harmonic pad.

The subsequent second bridge statement is a near repeat of the first. In Example 6.6a, observe the piano part accompanying "eyes of blue," first in two high-register arpeggiated piano chords, followed by a full low- and mid-register dramatic closing chord with tremolo bass. This is a dramatic high point to emphasize "blue." The harp again provides two upward sweeps, on top of a ride-cymbal swell, downward drum-tom fills, and harmonized, backing vocals swelling on "eyes of blue." Here the vocals expand for the first time to three parts.

Verse 3 (2:21–2:41) closely follows verse 2 until a varied-repeat coda (2:42–2:59). A variation of the intro returns while Karen sings "close to you." The section pauses on an unresolved harmony before the joyful, vocal-harmony "wah!" of the coda unexpectedly bursts in. From 3:00, lush, ninth-based harmonies enter in an "out of left field" vocal coda (as Richard called it).[128] This is built from a jazzy vocalese "wah" and "close to you." Example 6.6b transcribes an excerpt. The whole involves two chords, A♭maj9 and D♭maj9, over a backing of piano, harpsichord, bass, drums, and flute.

This big-finish texture, "vocals stacking up," is a product of multitrack production. This sound became a trademark of the group, but it owes much to Richard's arranging inspirations both from postwar jazz arranging, with its

EX. 6.6. The Carpenters, "(They Long to Be) Close to You" (arr. and prod. Richard Carpenter). Excerpts: (a) 2:07; and (b) 3:10.

chord-tone substitutions and modern jazz voicings, as well as jazz-pop from the 1940s–1950s. The latter influences included Jud Conlon's Rhythmaires and the overdubbed/multitracked vocals of Les Paul and Mary Ford.[129] Richard describes his process as involving triple recordings of each of their voices, building up four-part harmonies, and pushing them "way up in the mix!"[130] This tag relies on four-way close voicings (notes arranged in the closest positions), often with chord extensions or "tension" notes (9, 11, and 13) being substituted for chord tones (1, 3, 5, 7). An example is the harmony on "close" (Example 6.6b), where the 9 (B♭) of A♭maj9 substitutes for the tonic below the 3/5/7 (C–E♭–G) of the harmony. These lush vocals add postwar jazz-luxe topics typically associated with big band textures.

EX. 6.6. (continued)

• • •

Each of these two tracks is a stylistic potpourri, or rather pop-purée—a smooth, creamy, sweet mixture of top-of-the-charts ingredients reassembled from inspirations across the late 1960s Top 40 charts. Such reworked, familiar pop elements were routinely commented upon in the bands' press receptions, particularly by rock-centric critics. A brief closing discussion of the rockist critical reception of the Carpenters and Bread will help to underscore the cultural wars that were implicated in the AM Gold aesthetics these two artists represent.

CONCLUSION(S): STRAIGHT FROM LA!
YOU'RE GONNA LOVE 'EM!

The *RS* writings of Lester Bangs on the Carpenters and Bread embody contradictions present in other male- and rock-centric criticism concerning the new soft rock. Despite his predilections for rougher-edged rock,

Bangs wrote numerous soft-rock reviews. His 1971 manifesto, "James Taylor Marked for Death," captures the existential stakes of the soft rock-onslaught. The essay, a "pube punk fantasy" about garage rock, rants against the "posturing and fake glamour" of soft-rock "superpersonalities."[131] Bangs remarks that his "spleen is reserved for Elton John, James Taylor, all the glory boys of I-Rock," a term he coined for music so "egocentric that you . . . actually stop hating the . . . poor bastard[s]" and want to kick their asses, "preferably off a high cliff."[132] For Bangs, the Troggs' "Wild Thing" was a recording of "godawful beauty" and "pure fuckin KLASS," but he admits "I'm a sucker for sentiment of the right kind" in pop.[133] The Carpenters and Bread were this "right kind" of guilty-pleasure pop, as seen in his 1969 review of Bread's first album, which is written in the cadences of 1960s advertisements:

> Hi kids! Here's another great group, made just like you like 'em! Straight from LA. . . . You're gonna love 'em! You've got to if you like the Beatles, Byrds, Bee Gees, Buffalo Springfield, . . . Van Dyke Parks, Randy Newman, or male clotheshorses with giant collars.
>
> Make no mistake, kids, this album is no synthetic bullshit. The[se] three boys . . . wrote all their own songs . . . played all their instruments, . . . and their lyrics have . . . simple eloquence. . . .
>
> . . . But you should hear the *music* . . . —the epitome of Taste. "A highly refined amalgam of the sweetest, most successful elements in both rock and country and western"—L. Bangs, *Rolling Stone*. . . . All you "over thirties" will love this album too. It never descends to grating noise and unspeakable vulgarities so many groups find necessary to get attention. . . . There will be some cynical critics who'll say that Bread's music is bland, . . . and even bubble-gummy. But we need not listen to those malcontents. . . . [Bangs then lists bands that Bread is said to have emulated.]
>
> Buy this album today. You're sure to get your money's worth: twelve highly polished numbers, just like a year's supply of hit singles! Catchy, bright, snappy, wholesome.[134]

The fence-sitting, meta nature of this review (where he fake-quotes himself as an authority!) drips with cynicism. Central are both the backhanded implications of the band being a "polished," industry-created "synthetic" "amalgam" of recombinant borrowings, and the "sweet" EL implications of the music being contrasted with the "grating noise" of hard rock.

Bangs's begrudging appreciation for Bread, despite their "*sans* hip status," is foregrounded in his 1971 review of their third album. This review retains themes about Bread's "crassly calculating process," but there is an appreciative twist: "They sound a little like the Beatles at their most saccharine, a bit like the insipid heart of CSN&Y, and a lot like . . . last year's most sentimentally pseudo-personal balladic trends. . . . In the wake of [such] used-up styles . . . they manage to be thoroughly appealing."[135] While "Make It" is recalled as being "limp," he observes that it is "always nice to have one wistful ballad" even if your reaction "vacillate[s] between irritation . . . and even liking its . . . contrivances in the same way that every hit of the Carpenters have had intruded . . . on your tastes. It was *nice*." Bangs closes with the faint praise: "It's hard to imagine going out of your way for [Bread], but they're nice to have around." Both the chart-topping sales and *Billboard*, among other sources, confirm that there was a major market for such "nice" music.

In January 1970, prior to the breakthrough of both "Close" and "Make It," *Billboard* suggested that "the Top 40 station and the easy listening radio station may eventually disappear if [the] music 'stealing' trend continues" between both formats. The problem was such that "in many markets today, the difference between the leading rock station and the leading easy listening station is only a matter of seven or eight records."[136] The article describes how Top 40 expanded to include an audience demographic of twenty-five- to thirty-five-year-olds, and how the twenty-five-to-forty-nine age-group market of MOR/EL had encroached upon the soft hit singles on the charts (while "avoid[ing] the bubblegum" and "hard rock records"). "Close" and Make It" epitomize each of these trends. *Billboard* further observes that older MOR/EL artists were covering current Top 40 hits in new styles that copy "everything that comes along." MOR programmers note that they "had to eliminate some . . . established artists like Peggy Lee and Frank Sinatra" because the music did not blend with "new material by the Fifth Dimension and the Blood, Sweat & Tears." Foreshadowing later adult-contemporary "gold" strategies, these 1970 programmers are said to be playing more rock-pop "oldies"—with one example being the 1967 (!) "Groovin'" by the Rascals—alongside current hits.[137] Adjacent to this article are others that note an FM station (once the platform for EL "beautiful music") shifting to album-oriented rock and hard rock, and a trend in "the soft sound of flat-top guitars," with groups "abandoning amplification" following the model of CSNY.[138] To quote the title of a full-page April 1970 *Wall Street Journal* article, what this all meant was that "Record Firms Spin to [the] Sweetest Music They Ever Heard—the

Sound of Money."[139] A core focus of the latter article is this money-making expanded MOR territory, which in fact is largely AM Gold. Six months later, this trend would dominate the airwaves with—to borrow from an *RS* review of the Carpenters—the "exceptionally sharp middle-of-the-road" hits of these two bands.[140]

SEVEN

Isaac Hayes and Hot Buttered (Orchestral) Soul, from Psychedelic to Progressive

THIS CHAPTER EXPLORES genre, hybridization, and industry questions around postwar intersections of jazz and symphonic soul. In the early 1970s, the word *progressive* was attached to a number of popular music idioms beyond progressive rock. For instance, across 1971–75, the term *progressive soul* was applied to various music in the wake of Isaac Hayes's 1969 album, *Hot Buttered Soul ("HBS")*.[1] Both this album and its progressive characterization illuminate important understandings of both late 1960s symphonic soul and the genre permeability of the period's *Billboard* jazz charts. Through progressive soul discourse across 1969 to 1974, and using Hayes as my foil, this chapter concerns "progressive" trends in Black popular music, and how critics, the Black middle-class press, and magazines like *Billboard* and *Down Beat* understood the intersections of soul, funk, rock, and jazz in this era. The larger whole opens a window on the continued development of luxe-pop aesthetics into African American popular music of the late 1960s and early 1970s, and how musical topics from jazz occupied an adjacent jazz-luxe aesthetic in parallel with more traditional orchestral luxe pop.

Central to this era of genre-flux and hybridization in popular music are questions of industry concerns for how to sell jazz as a genre, and the Black middle-class interest in the prestige of jazz. Consider the 12 December 1970 *Billboard* Best Selling Jazz LPs chart, where Hayes's just released album, *To Be Continued*, tops the chart, and where his 1969 *HBS* has moved down two slots to number 10 after seventy-four weeks on the chart, and his earlier 1970 *The Isaac Hayes Movement* has dropped from 2 to 8 after thirty-four weeks.[2] While the chart includes Miles Davis (number 4, *Bitches Brew*, and 5, *Miles Davis at Fillmore*) and John Coltrane (12, *The Best of John Coltrane*), jazz artists covering rock-pop tunes (e.g., Paul Desmond covering Simon and

Garfunkel), and sales-topping soul-jazz artists like Ramsey Lewis, organist Charles Earland, Quincy Jones, and Wes Montgomery, Hayes was not someone I expected to see here, and his albums seemed more curious than the chart presence of B.B. King or the spoken-word Last Poets. Just after this, Hayes dually won the National Association of Record Merchandisers best-selling male R&B vocals award *and* the "Best Selling Jazz Artist" award in March 1971.[3] His Oscar- and Grammy-winning soundtrack to the 1971 *Shaft* (MGM) won him the exact same NARM awards in 1972. Jazz institutions like *Down Beat* were likewise lax in their genre border controls, as seen in a 20 April 1971 extended interview of Hayes by *Down Beat* editor Dan Morgenstern. This article was complemented by a psychedelic, green cover image of Hayes alongside the magazine's new "Jazz-Blues-Rock" logo (only in its second month).[4] That said, while a handful of similar soul artists, such as Curtis Mayfield, briefly appear on *Billboard*'s jazz charts, Hayes oddly remains on the jazz charts from 19 July 1969 to 6 November 1971, with *Shaft* at number 1,[5] after which the jazz LP chart was dropped without explanation until early 1973. During this period, various US and UK critics would promote the idea of progressive soul, a tenuous genre construct with perceived jazz connections that was rarely mentioned after 1975. Nonetheless, so-called progressive soul artists, including Hayes, laid an important foundation for the luxe, jazz-indebted inflections of a range of 1970s sophisticated soul, including disco.

In chapter 1, I considered the accumulated cultural associations of Hayes's symphonic soul sound by way of Jay-Z's later sampling of Hayes's 1970 cover of Burt Bacharach's "The Look of Love." This was a Black-soul signification on the lounge jazz-pop of Bacharach and Dusty Springfield. I noted how the track's lush, "Vegas luxe" big-band brass, jazz flute, and easy-listening trumpet work, organ pads, wah-wah electric guitars, lush strings, French horns, and woodwinds connected with a dense fabric of associations. The present chapter will return to this track, alongside other examples, to parse the nuanced differences between progressive-, psychedelic-, and sophisti-soul, and to explore the cultural and musical foundations that these late 1960s and early 1970s luxe symphonic soul subgenres provided for the rise of disco.

This chapter and the next further consider the implications of lower-middle taste-public perspectives on classy cultural capital in this period's growing Black middle classes (however unstable in their economic security), and Black middle-class popular music market. The interests of this demographic are seen in the pages of *Jet* and *Ebony*, African American lifestyle magazines. Beyond considerable interview material from artists themselves, there is a relative paucity of Black critical voices in the US and UK popular-music press. By contrast, *Jet* and *Ebony* also included a significant amount of musical coverage, but typically this press focused on lifestyles rather than musical criticism. For the purposes of this book, however, such lifestyle and culture discourse is immensely valuable, although not all music contributors in these magazines were Black, or even American, as can be seen with the UK's Geoff Brown, who contributed to *Jet*. That said, there was one significant Black US critic writing about the new soul: Vernon Gibbs. Gibbs was based in New Jersey and metropolitan New York.[6] His views on "progressive soul" trends (he seems to have coined the term) are echoed by various artists and are partially taken up by other critics, especially in Great Britain. It is problematic, however, to hold Gibbs's voice as singularly representative for this new Black American middle class. This same music was of great interest to *Jet* and *Ebony*, but their focus was more commonly on the fabulous trappings of the success of these artists, especially their beautiful spouses and homes. Such coverage suggests an aura transference from lifestyle class-culture markers to extramusical attributes associated with the music itself and the images of artists.

The press and critical coverage of this new era of Black popular music is widely varied. Beyond the mainstream trade coverage of *Billboard* and *Cash Box*, the new rock criticism of magazines like *Rolling Stone* and *Creem* did, in fact, display some inclusivity with regard to select R&B, soul, funk, jazz-rock, and jazz coverage. While the British mainstream-pop magazines *Melody Maker* and *New Musical Express* included some Black American music coverage, the UK also fostered a "little magazine" tradition of smaller periodicals devoted exclusively to Black American pop. These publications were a curious mix of both the new "serious" rock-pop criticism and the older, collector-fan-discographer tradition of white British jazz-enthusiast writers (e.g., the *Jazz Journal, Jazz Monthly, Storyville*, etc.). In the 1970s, a similar group of white British fetishist collector-critics wrote for small-circulation periodicals like *Blues and Soul* and *Black Music*. These magazines catered to UK fans (white and Black) of American soul, funk, R&B, and disco, and they included US writers contributing both on-the-scene criticism and reportage. These two magazines included regular contributions from Gibbs, for example, who covered recordings, performances, and developments in Black soul and funk. While each started US editions circa 1972, it is doubtful that they had wide circulation among African American or white US fans, though one member of the Ohio Players noted that he "read [*Black Music*] back in the States, man."[7] In addition to the above, the jazz-press standard bearer, *Down Beat*, also took interest in the new early 1970s soul idioms, particularly music with jazz-leaning textures or jazz-trained musicians.

The critical oppositions of "authenticity" versus commercialism are widespread in this journalism. The music discussed across this chapter outlines developments that lead successively to the glitzy commercial height of 1970s luxe pop in disco. Barry White was positioned as an epicenter for the subsequent disco backlash, as critics routinely identified his music as epitomizing disco's overt commercialism and adherence to formula. White's music was first framed, however, via the discourse of "sophistisoul," an early to mid-1970s sound that emerged from "progressive," "symphonic," and "psychedelic" soul of the late 1960s and early 1970s. Sophistisoul denotes a range of sweet symphonic-soul trends following "progressive" Hayes (1969–71) and before string-laden disco emerged as a mass-culture phenomenon in 1974–75.

Similarities between the symphonic soul idioms of Hayes and White are of considerable interest in press coverage of the early to mid-1970s. As this discourse emerges, the praise of Hayes noticeably declines. This chapter focuses firstly on the *HBS/Shaft*-era reception of Hayes, just prior to the emergence of White. Here, Hayes's music is central to notions of progressive and psychedelic soul. Second, Hayes's symphonic soul will be contextualized via comparative discussions of Motown's influential psychedelic soul, particularly from the Temptations, circa 1969–70, and Thom Bell's early production work with the Delfonics (one foundation for the Philadelphia soul sound). These artists were in turn retrospectively called early progressive soul, and the latter group was further characterized as a primary sophistisoul tributary.

PROGRESSIVE OR PSYCHEDELIC SOUL?

In October 1969, the trade magazine *Variety* proclaimed, "R&B Goes 'Progressive' Soul."[8] This article announced that "Taking the cue from the new crop of rulebreaking [*sic*] rock musicians, such performers as Isaac Hayes and J. J. Jackson are attempting to revise and expand r&b music into a 'progressive' soul movement." The writer outlines the "rulebook" and "formula" set for soul and describes soul as having stagnated while rock musicians "matured" in their musicianship. By contrast, Hayes is said to have introduced a new progressive soul, in part through the extended track lengths and "abundant" improvisation heard on *Hot Buttered Soul*.

The article's mention of the lesser-known Jackson coincides with the release of his late 1969 album *The Greatest Little Soul Band in the Land*, which was advertised with the all-caps tag line "PROGRESSIVE SOUL" and the comment that "they sure got chops."[9] The *Billboard* author may have appropriated "progressive soul" from this ad, which coincides with the *Variety* article. Jackson, an African American R&B singer, songwriter, and arranger, was based in the UK. *Variety* describes his musicians as being "well-grounded in jazz and rock as well as soul," and his mixed-race band notably featured prominent UK jazz and jazz-rock musicians. In addition to extended tracks, another key facet of progressive soul was perceived to be its comparative increases in musicianship and instrumental mastery. Jazz literacy was a marker for such mastery, alongside improvisation. For example, *Variety* notes that "like Hayes, Jackson's band improvises freely over a soul structure and strives for new effects that would still be considered part of that idiom."[10] Similar jazz-leaning commentary is found in Hayes's critical reception from 1969 forward. With Jackson's music, these traits are apparent in the album's six-plus-minute tracks, its uses of hybrid textures invoking both sweet Motown and raw Stax soul idioms set against fuzztoned electric guitars (evoking contemporary rock), and both jazz-indebted solo improvisation (from the brass and reeds) and occasional four-part brass-reed horn arrangements. Examples of the jazz horn-section elements are heard in both "Tobacco Road" and "Tenement Hall," each of which includes borderline anarchic, jazz-boogie breakdowns (from 3:21 and 2:42, respectively).[11] Here, such passages echo hard-bop-informed, collective improvisation textures found in various bluesy Charles Mingus tracks (like his 1960 "Moanin'" on *Blues and Roots*). Both Jackson tracks also conclude with extended-harmony textures that invoke a simplified version of the "modernist" 1950s progressive jazz of Stan Kenton. For example, from both 3:14 and 5:03, "Tenement" has a dramatic written passage that features repeated alternations between low baritone-sax stabs and a dissonant, upper-register extended harmony in the reeds and brass (the texture also modulates up by a whole tone). Lastly, *Variety* further notes Jackson's additional "interest in lyrical content," which I assume is a nod to the socially progressive but clunky lyrics of 1969 numbers like "Tenement Hall" (which concerns Black, poor residents of a ghetto tenement).

From late 1969, there is an absence of press discourse on "progressive soul" until 1971–72, when the idea reemerges. Here, late 1960s music by Hayes,

Jackson, and others—some of whom were termed "psychedelic soul" in the 1960s (discussed below)—is identified as a key influence on new progressive music by the Ohio Players; Earth, Wind and Fire; Curtis Mayfield; Hayes; Kool and the Gang; Donny Hathaway; War; Mandrill; Funkadelic; and others. These artists—many of whom were later tied to mainstream disco—favored larger ensembles, with music ranging from horn-section funk to orchestral soul. The "progressive soul" characterization typically excluded a range of sweeter orchestral soul, including Philly soul, music that some of these critics called "sophistisoul" (also discussed later).

The elements identified in these sources are regularly mentioned in coverage of Hayes and his musicians circa 1969 and 1970. Such elements include a grounding in soul idioms but greater musical mastery, as evidenced through jazz training or foundations, solo improvisation, extended track and performance lengths, inspirations from idioms beyond soul, expanded instrumentation, increased harmonic and formal sophistication, and the embrace of rock guitar and more adventurous rock production.

Hayes was typically positioned as a progressive soul catalyst, and his September 1969 and November 1970 album releases, *Hot Buttered Soul* and *To Be Continued* respectively, are landmarks.[12] It was the July 1971 film release of *Shaft*, however, with its chart-topping "Theme from *Shaft*" (henceforth "Shaft") that most typified Hayes's sound in the popular imagination (the double album was released in August 1971, and the "Shaft" single in September). For some, the cross-media saturation of the soundtracks to the two top blaxploitation films, *Shaft* and the 1972 *Super Fly* (Warner Bros.), positioned the string-heavy orchestral soul of Hayes and Curtis Mayfield as being among the "top three artists in the progressive [s]oul field," as the UK critic, John Abbey, reported in early 1972.[13] The August 1973 review in *New Musical Express* (*NME*), a UK magazine, by Vernon Gibbs—the Black American critic mentioned above—of a Hayes Madison Square Garden performance underscores important artful-entertainment complexities in "progressive" soul's codes of sophistication. Gibbs notes that "with chains, shades, pink skintight leotards, capes, semi-nude dancing girls . . . and a 40-piece orchestra, Hayes . . . [is] the king of macho glitter soul and one of the most talented entertainers in the business." Gibbs adds both that Hayes "is the *only* Black superstar who can elicit . . . [such a tumultuous] response from a primarily black audience," and that he "is well equipped to put out on a *musical* level [and in] a context in which R&B can be judged as an instrumental music." Though "not nearly as refined as the most mediocre jazzman," Gibbs stresses that Hayes "is expanding R&B [alongside] younger groups like Funkadelic, The Ohio Players and many others who, under the influence of Sly [Stone], [Jimi] Hendrix and jazz, have started the new music that I call 'Progressive Soul.'"[14]

In a 1970 *Blues and Soul* "Psychedelic Soul" article that invokes "progressive soul," an unnamed UK critic, "BP," tries to tease apart late 1960s soul terminology. While curiously contending, "In the sixties progressive soul was the label attached to recordings by such artists as the Impressions, the O'Jays, . . . and . . . Jerry Butler," BP observes that the "smooth sounds and unusual harmonies of these 'earlier' performers are still present" in such music as "the brilliant Delfonics," a group who formed a cornerstone of the Philly soul idiom (discussed later). BP further observes that "today 'progressive' has a different meaning. From the [influence of the production innovations of the] Beatles a new branch of popular music has evolved—the Underground. Now perhaps for the first time the Negro music of North America [in 1970s soul music] is being seriously influenced by the white recording artists' styles."[15]

This presumed crossover of production influences and soundmania eclecticism is an associative key to the conceptions of both progressive and psychedelic soul. BP discusses Sly and the Family Stone as being especially representative of "psychedelic soul," a term he conflates with progressive soul. BP does not mention many musical specifics, but points to the "electronic sounds and feed-back guitar," "unusual voice patterns and fantastic off-key brass sound" of Sly Stone as being a major 1968–69 psychedelic soul originator. This characterization builds on views of late 1960s psychedelic art and music counterculture, and its associations with mind-expanding enlightenment. In music, this culture was manifest in lyrics, stage and fashion presentation, and soundmania-influenced studio experimentation and sonic expansion. For the foundations of psychedelic soul, BP further points to Motown tracks like "Cloud Nine" (1969) and "Psychedelic Shack" (1970) by the Temptations. After briefly noting other Motown psychedelic productions, BP observes that "now we have ever suave Marvin Gaye with progressive sounds." On the latter's evolution, the article (written before Gaye's 1971 "What's Going On?") adds that Gaye's musical development has been accompanied by lyrics focused on social issues, thereby connecting "progressive songs [that] suit the progressive style." BP further points to extended track-lengths as being a central difference between the more recent progressive trend and the earlier psychedelic idiom: "Six or seven of even four extended tracks is becoming the order of the day. Isaac Hayes . . . has an 18 minute version of 'By the Time I Get to Phoenix.'"

The reference to psychedelic "electronic sounds" includes both the contemporary keyboards and effects pedals that Stone used, as well as production elements. An example like the 1968 hit, "Dance to the Music"—which exhibits a striking aesthetic and production shift from contemporary R&B and soul—helpfully illustrates the eclecticism of psychedelic soul. Building on the funk foundations of James Brown (as heard from Brown's May 1967 hit, "Cold Sweat," forward), "Dance to the Music" exhibits the wide sonic palate of the Family Stone, which blends Black and white, male and female, and musicians with backgrounds spanning a range of genres. "Dance" exhibits four co-lead singers with vocal textures that wildly shift in their soulful approaches across a range of registers. These textural shifts include verbal interjections, and grooving, percussive, a cappella doo-wop. Textures continually shift every few bars and there is sharp panning of sources across the stereo separation. The production shifts from thick, full-band sonic accumulations to a string of two-part juxtapositions (such as rock guitar or fuzz-bass against drums) or a cappella voices. Guitarist Freddie Stone adds various rock-style contributions. Alongside the guitar's rambling, string-bending psychedelic solos (with a biting tone), the music includes Sly's gospel-tinged Hammond organ pads and fills, the fuzz-toned distorted bass of Larry Graham, and R&B trumpet/sax riffing with overtly jazzy solo sax fills that are often paired with rock guitar soloing. Lyrically, the song is sparsely built around the repeated title. This penchant for eclecticism and juxtaposition resembles aspects of the Jackson tracks discussed previously. The Family Stone, the Chamber Brothers, and the Norman Whitfield-produced Temptations reside at the top of most period references to psychedelic soul. With the Family Stone's emergence from the San Francisco Bay Area's rock scene, it is not surprising that critics described the eclectic, mixed-stylistic pop aesthetics noted above as "psychedelic."

The Temptations' own account of their psychedelic period points to expansions on the influence from Stone's group. Critics, including Lenny Kaye, heard Whitfield's "debt owed to Sly Stone" despite the "genius" and "patented perfection in his 1972 masterpiece of 'Papa Was a Rollin' Stone.'"[16] The Motown scholar Andy Flory points to the October 1968 release of "Cloud Nine" as the group's "departure into psychedelic soul."[17] In 2008, Otis Williams, the one active remaining founding member of the group, contended that he originally suggested to Whitfield that the Temptations "take some cues from Sly and the Family Stone's raucous psychedelic soul." Whitfield purportedly responded negatively ("that ain't nothin but a little passing fancy"). However, within several weeks, Whitfield presented the group with "Cloud Nine," his first adaptation of Stone's aesthetic.[18] Flory describes thirty-three "psychedelic soul records written and produced by Norman Whitfield for the Temptations" over 1968–73, with most being built on the template of "Cloud Nine." Flory remarks that tracks "after 1968 frequently ... were six minutes or longer," and often relied upon "song form[s] that used soul cinematically by fusing symphonic gestures with funk riffs and texts about inner city life."[19] The Temptations were thus viewed as near equal progenitors in their expansions on psychedelic soul's innovations, though the Family Stone were widely seen as the idiom's "heralded exponents and instigators."[20]

Whitfield's production contributions typically embraced soul traditions, synthesized contemporary inspirations, and innovated. For instance, Flory describes the 1966 Temptations/Whitfield hit, "Ain't Too Proud to Beg," as an example of "hybridity between soul and the Motown Sound." It exhibits "a Motown Beat, a typical Motown solo saxophone, a subtle [barely audible] string arrangement, and a strong independent bass line." But the track also employed "soul-oriented slang and vernacularisms, gruff lead vocals performed by [David] Ruffin, gospel-oriented backing vocals, brassy horn arrangements, and prominent bongos."[21] Such grab-bag juxtapositions led directly into Whitfield's eclectic psychedelic soul.

Despite the stylistic and textural similarities between Hayes's *HBS* and the Whitfield/Temptations psychedelic recordings, I have seen no criticism that calls the latter "progressive." Nonetheless, at least one UK critic describes the 1973, post-Temptations recordings of the Temptations' former lead singer, Eddie Kendricks (a 1970s solo star), as progressive soul.[22] Interestingly, despite their base at Motown, the Temptations' psychedelic recordings do not include strings until the April 1971 "Smiling Faces Sometimes." This track follows Hayes's July 1969 *HBS* and November 1970 *Continued*. The next Whitfield/Temptations recording to include strings was the June 1972 ballad, "Mother Nature," from the August 1972 album, *All Directions*, which includes strings on six of its eight tracks, including "Papa," which was released as a single in September. There were thus fifteen psychedelic tracks before Whitfield reintroduced strings within Temptations productions. (The July 1971 release of *Shaft* arrives in the fourteen months between the releases of "Smiling" and *All Directions*.) In some respects, the Hammond B3 organ on many of the earlier Temptations psychedelic recordings replaces the conventional presence of Motown strings. Many of the psychedelic Temptations recordings appear to be in dialogic exchange with contemporary soul (echoing and likely influencing period soul and progressive soul textures), as well as the message-music of Curtis Mayfield (both solo and with the Impressions).

HEARING THE MELTING POT IN PROGRESSIVE/PSYCHEDELIC SOUL

The aesthetics of orchestral progressive/psychedelic—or even "cinematic"—soul can be illustrated through a comparison of "Shaft" and "Papa Was a Rollin' Stone" ("Papa"). Both were recognized in their day as landmark recordings. "Shaft" won Best Engineered Recording and Best Instrumental Arrangement Grammys in 1972 (but lost in the Best Instrumental, Record of the Year, and Best R&B Performance Duo or Group categories). "Papa" won the 1973 Best R&B Instrumental Performance, Best R&B Song, and Best R&B Performance Duo or Group categories.

For all the commentary regarding the extended lengths of Hayes's recordings, little attention is paid to *how* these tracks work in terms of form and development. To be frank, there is little that is aspirationally "symphonic" in the extended arrangements of Hayes's orchestral soul. For example, in a manner akin to the reduced harmonic language of post–James Brown soul and funk, the 4'29" album version of "Shaft" is built from merely three chords. These harmonies back a multipart intro (80 mm.), five texted verses interspersed with two instrumental interludes (28 mm., with the interludes built on the verse background), an interlude built on intro materials (18 mm.), and a coda (11 mm. built on the primary two-chord intro materials). Despite this economy, as the Recording Academy recognized, the track displays rich, evocative details that hint at "progressive" and creative production choices, all while maintaining a smoldering groove.

Stax historian Rob Bowman notes that while the film soundtrack was recorded in Hollywood "at a three-track facility," for the album, Hayes "wanted to get a better sound than was possible in a movie studio and consequently recorded all the songs at Stax." Beyond presumably allowing access to eight-track technology, the process also gave him the opportunity "to stretch out some of the songs beyond the length of time they were allotted in the movie."[23] The film's director, Gordon Parks, initially tested Hayes with "raw footage of three scenes." These included the main title scene, to which Hayes supplied "Theme from *Shaft*." Bowman notes "cultural clashes" at the Hollywood session when an engineer requested sheet music, and Hayes responded "we don't write anything. We're just going to do it headwise."[24] Hayes and the rhythm section completed their work in a single day, with "the string and horn parts" being recorded the next day (and vocals added the day after that). While basic arrangement ideas were likely worked out—by Hayes, or Hayes with assistance—in advance of the sessions, sources indicate that much was worked out within that single-day session. This suggests that the arrangers had little time for transcribing Hayes's ideas, elaborating those materials into an orchestration, and copying parts. Of the fifteen tracks/cues on the soundtrack album, only seven have strings. "Shaft" alone employs a prominent use of countermelody, as opposed to the lush, backing harmonic-pad string textures that dominate the other six tracks. Thus, the arrangers' work was largely focused on the horn-section contributions, which are more richly scored than the strings and shift between R&B and big-band textures. The principal assistant to Hayes in co-arranging and transcription was the Detroit-based Johnny Allen, a pianist/arranger who had worked with Hayes since *HBS*, had arranged for Motown—one reason he was originally sought out—and played in Detroit jazz combos. The co-arranger for "Walk from Regio's" was the veteran jazz trombonist/arranger, J. J. Johnson.

A 1971 documentary on the making of *Shaft* includes sections of dialogue between Parks, Hayes, and the rhythm section in the studio.[25] The first passage concerns "Regio's," and the second concerns "Shaft." The documentary implies that these sequences were filmed at real moments in the creative process. These were seemingly shot during the Hollywood sound studio period, but Parks's "descriptions" of what he wants—and the band's reciprocation with fleshed-out performances—suggest that these sequences were staged after Hayes had shared his first ideas with Parks in the aforementioned "test." Parks explains to Hayes that "The sequence we saw . . . [with] Times Square, panned down off the skyscrapers along 42nd Street . . . and with Shaft [who] pops up out of the subway, that's when this should really come on [Hayes: *riiight* . . .] and carry him all the way through Times Square, right through to his first encounter with a newspaper man. And that should be a driving, savage beat . . . so that . . . [*pause, then fingersnap*] we're right with him all the time. [Hayes: *uh-huh*.] . . . What I heard you working on earlier seems great for that Shaft walk."

Cheo Hodari Coker, the African American creator of Netflix's *Shaft*-influenced series, *Luke Cage* (2016–18; Coker calls Cage the "sensitive Shaft"), points to the filmic connections that *Shaft* created between the music and the "walk" of its main character. Coker further comments on the film's later montage where Shaft walks around Harlem looking for an old friend (circa 27:28, backed by the Hayes-sung "Soulsville"). He contends that "that moment, of a black man walking with rhythm, is one of the staples of the blaxploitation hero." Parks recognized this too, commenting: "We need heroic fantasies about our people. We all need a little James Bond now and then." This commingling of a Black "James Bond" and the coolness of a "black man walking with rhythm" is centrally witnessed in the main title sequence.

The title sequence begins with ambient sounds from Times Square, then moves (following Parks's description) from the skyscraper-to-dirty-streets pan shot (a tradition dating back to the 1931 *Street Scene*) to the newspaper stand. After the marquee shots (which show street trash and film fare by Robert Redford alongside red-light adult films like *School for Sex*), and the establishment of sleazy 1970s Times Square, a bright red "Shaft" title card appears. The camera pans to John Shaft emerging from the subway, just as the opening hi-hat hook and the wah-wah guitar riff enter. (I will refer to the wah-wah effect pedal as simply "wah.") The montage must have been recut to sync various shots with the arrangement of the Hayes Hollywood score. Richard Roundtree's Shaft emanates self-assured cool, with a determined walk, purposefully negotiating the streets and everything he encounters (with occasionally amused facial expressions). Roundtree appears in a brown-and-beige ensemble of a tweed suit, turtleneck, and knee-length, dark-brown leather trench coat. Audiences see a suave, tall, handsome, muscular, driven man with dark-toned skin, a mid-length natural afro, and prominent 1970s "chevron" mustache. This is the epitome of 1970s Black-male masculinity and glamour. Indeed, the character is an embodiment of the image that Roundtree specialized in for *Jet* and *Ebony* advertisements, including Ballantine's whiskey, Duke hair products, Bull Beer, and so on. Though not overly synchronized, the walk is frequently near the tempo of the music, as the lyric intones about his "complicated," "bad mother—" character, about his job as "black private dick," his "sex machine" skills that "the chicks" "dig," his moral center as "the man who would risk his neck for his [Black] brother," and so forth. ("Can you dig it?") The character is dripping of male chauvinist, blaxploitation swagger which is deeply reinforced by the walk and the music.

Isaac Hayes, "Theme from Shaft" (1971)

At its 4'34" length, in the early 1970s, the album version of the track is not exactly an "extended" Hayes recording. And while it was edited down to a 3'15" single, 4.5 minutes is not uncommon for a single, though "Shaft" is longer than the three-minute pop-single archetype. Bowman observes that "Shaft" contains "an inordinate amount of hooks." He traces the hi-hat figure back to a drum break in Otis Redding's November 1966 "Try a Little Tenderness" (heard at 3:03).[26] Bowman contends that guitarist Charles "Skip" Pitts's wah riff predated the Redding borrowing.[27] This is unlikely, as Vox patented and introduced the wah in 1967, and in a documentary, Pitts comments that the wah riff was the result of "tuning up" and "riffing" in the studio. Hayes took note, and they built from that. The bassist James Alexander adds that they were told, "'Don't change anything, . . . stay right there,' and so for about an hour and a half he just played that little groove . . . over and over again." Alexander stresses that repetition was central to how Hayes developed music. With "Shaft," Hayes started the building process by adding elements: "Isaac just started [by] hitting *dohnghh* [on the piano]. . . . For about thirty minutes, he just played *dohnghh*. . . . Then . . . he started trying different variations of it," and building parts from there.[28] This account maps well onto the "development" strategies of the track, which evince its origins as an additive, jam-developed head arrangement. The wah hook is the bedrock from start to finish, with only slight shifts up or down to accommodate the Fmaj7, Em7, and G7 harmonies. (The hook—alongside the persistent hi-hat hook—plays a foundational funk-groove role similar to the repeating, two-bar popping bass line in Stone's "Thank You.") The post-rhythm-section overdubbing offered opportunities for building greater compositional qualities into this jam foundation. For example, while by no means a prominent connection, as Bowman notes, "to integrate the film's main theme with the rest of the soundtrack,"[29] Hayes derived the flute line of "Shaft" (1:00ff.) from "Bumpy's Lament" (0:00ff.), and a French horn countermelody (from 1:15ff.) from "Ellie's Love Theme" (0:31ff.).

In the 2'40" introduction, these additive processes build across four sections. This opens with two bars of the iconic hi-hat groove. Part B (0:04) is eleven bars long and based on the wah riff (built on octave Gs) set on top of the drum groove. Both hooks are seen in Example 7.1a. After three bars of guitar alone, the low piano octaves enter along with a unison bass (the *dohnghh*), which starts an important bass shift between F and E, with the

A. **1:31**

wah riff continuing. The first full texture arrives at section C (0:26). The low bass, with its lead-in riffs, provides a bedrock to the groove. Section C includes the flute's melodic lead over the Fmaj7-to-Em7 oscillation that underscores most of the track. Repeated five times, the section continually adds textures and countermelodies. These include a thin, high Hammond B3, crisp mid-range trumpet arpeggios, bleating low trombones, jazz-flute riffs, and a French horn countermelody. At the fifth iteration, the lush, high-register, parallel-octave strings enter (somewhat recalling the strings in John Barry's James Bond scores). Example 7.1b (from 1:31) shows these elements in dialogue. Following a sweeping string glissando, this maximal texture leads to part D, which opens to a bright, brassy G major (led again by a bass-riff groove)—the only shift away from Fmaj7–Em7. In the film, this shift accompanies the sudden "wake-up" of Shaft confronting a street hustler. The section's staccato brass riffing (studio 2:07; film 2:47) overlaps with Shaft's amused expression to the crazy encounters and people he sees as he moves up Broadway, and (like the crowds) the music textures gets ever thicker with bustling activity, high (strings) and low (funk).

EX. 7.1. Isaac Hayes, "Theme from Shaft," album version. Excerpts: (a) 1:31; (b) 2:15; and (c) 3:55. The following notation has been used with the guitar: + = closed wah-wah; o = open wah-wah; ø = half open/closed; X = non–fretted ghost note, finger touching string above indicated note; ∨ = upstroke: and ⊓ = downstroke.

Mitchell Morris writes of 1970s "black masculinity and the sound of wealth" via examples from "Shaft," "Papa," and Barry White, among others. With "Shaft," Morris observes, "Hayes creates a notably cinematic [air] . . . by establishing . . . an 'irregular,' desultory quality in his layering of motives and components of the groove." While he is correct about the "accretionary" qualities here, "desultory"—meaning unfocused? randomly occurring?— does not quite capture the inventive unfolding of the arrangement, which to my ears only involves modest "irregular" qualities (e.g., occasional 5/4 bars in section C). But in his discussion of the "lavish instrumental sound," which is said to doubly evoke "not only the exciting hubbub of the street but also the lush way of life of the title character," Morris suggests a firm ground for hearing "cinematic" traits in the mapping of certain associative qualities onto well-known luxe and cinematic musical topics from popular music and media (as discussed across this book).[30]

In "Shaft," there are five three-line verses, each four bars in length, backed by the familiar Fmaj7–Em7 progression. The verses involve call-and-response between Hayes and his female background singers (plus brass section responses), and involve a high-register sustained violin countermelody (in two variants), sometimes with countermelody material in the mid-low trombones. The vocals slightly vary melodic material and include a "rap"/spoken verse ("They say this cat Shaft," etc.) and a final crooned verse ("he's a complicated man," etc.). Morris aptly observes the "intense black sexuality . . . enacted" in the song, particularly in the "hypersexism" of the lyrics."[31]

Following the verses, there is a two-part interlude. Part A (3:36) shifts to G7 and a new accretionary process. This begins first with a major-key guitar-riff variation, then a countermelody riff in unison between lead guitar and bass, alongside drums and tambourine. Next enters a bluesy, single-line, mid-register piano riff. Following a two-beat ninth bar, the full registral spectrum is suddenly filled with the accented, Fmaj7 full-orchestral hits (3:56; see Example 7.1c), building on the tradition of postwar crime-jazz film underscoring with a brassy stinger, plus the wah scratch guitar. This starts a trading-two exchange (2+2+2+2) between the orchestral hits versus the contrasting, spare Em7 scratch-guitar/hi-hat. The coda then merges these materials into one texture. After a progression of Fmaj7–Em7–Fmaj7 hits on the first beat of every other bar, the final two-bar Em7 sequence inventively shifts the orchestral hits to every three beats (| x - - x | - - x - |). The final brass-free Fmaj7 cadence features lush, full strings and a great pulsating guitar (panning right to left) tape-echo chord fading over three full bars.

In contradistinction to the formal complexities of other luxe pop explored thus far, this Hayes arrangement is deeply tied to jam-derived, soul-funk groove-building following the models of Sly Stone and James Brown. The secondary-level, multitracking luxe-arrangement contributions, are notably innovative. These include shifting, accretionary orchestral, instrumental and vocal additions (with modest electronic effects), as well as likely cutting, editing and ordering at the mixing stage (as evidenced through album and single edits). The track is "progressive" in most senses outlined in progressive-soul discourse outside of solo instrumental improvisation. And it also evinces traits widely associated with psychedelic soul.

Temptations, "Papa Was a Rollin' Stone" (1972)

Like "Shaft," "Papa Was a Rollin' Stone" was released in two versions. Both are extended—the single edit is nearly seven minutes long, while the album version is 11′46″. The album's name, *All Directions*, captures its pan-soul strategy, with "Papa" being the psychedelic entry. Like "Shaft" and "Thank You," "Papa" is built on a repeating, foundational rhythm-section hook: a four-bar riff in the bass, often accompanied by a closed-hi-hat pattern of eighth notes accentuating each beat (wah guitar also interjects in a complementary rhythmic role). The track displays a relatively straightforward verse-chorus design. The single starts with a two-minute introduction (four minutes on the album) reminiscent of the accretionary process of "Shaft," and then the recording unfolds over three verses (all 16 mm.), three chorus statements (two 16 mm., and the last 8 mm.), two interludes (16 and 12 mm.), and a coda (16 mm.). "Papa" employs approximately the same instrumental palette as "Shaft"—a duo of electric guitars; drums, with emphasis on the hi-hat; electric keyboard; dry electric bass; brass, though only a single jazzy trumpet; and lush orchestral strings. Around this foundation are handclaps and, notably, an orchestral harp, a color that would soon adorn the productions of Barry White and disco. There are also studio enhancements, including stereo-spectrum placement, field movement of sonic elements, and depth placement within the mix (through both balance and varied reverb levels).

Flory notes the "juxtaposed musical elements of rock and pan-African culture" in Whitfield's psychedelic productions.[32] The rock textures of "Papa" include three guitar tracks of different tone and timbre panned left, right, and middle, with wah, fuzz , and delay effects (delays are also on the horns), and the chorus- and vibrato-laden electric piano (likely the relatively new Fender Rhodes). Pan–African American qualities are evidenced in traits from contemporary soul, funk, electric blues, and more. For example, the handclaps—on the second and fourth beats—evoke a cappella doo-wop, early R&B, or even field holler, ring shout, or rural gospel practice. Thus, the track displays a sonic palette that spans Black popular music, from the rural to youthful urban street idioms to middle-class adult pop to elevated qualities (lush strings, harp, and jazz trumpet). Flory observes that Whitfield's psychedelic tracks often use repeated, two- to four-bar bass-line patterns, and that many of these tracks "chang[e] chords very slowly and deemphasiz[e] harmonic progression." He adds that over Whitfield's arrangements, "rhythmic elements enter and exit in a modular fashion, in logical accordance with the four-measure riff cycle."[33] This modular practice is a cousin to the Hayes accretionary process. A variety of modules are seen in Example 7.2b, which shows the start of the bass riff alongside the hi-hat pattern, all at the front of the mix with a dry ambience. At the center foreground is the echo- and reverb-glazed trumpet. The brief, high-register, unison-octave string interjections

A.

B.

EX. 7.2. Temptations, "Papa Was a Rollin' Stone," single version. Excerpts: (a) 1:14; and (b) 0:25.

enhance the groove but are set in a reverb haze slightly back and right in the mix. The string figure marks the trumpet exit and the entry of handclaps and a harp glissando, both panned to the left. The Paul Riser–arranged strings have their own hook, a minor, two-bar, melodic arch played in high-register with shuttering tremolo. The more-common antecedent version is shown in Example 7.2a. In sum, Whitfield's psychedelic soul extends the earlier sonic and cultural eclecticism of the Family Stone model. These extensions include the "electronic sounds" of sonically manipulated electric guitars and keyboards, the wide palette of soulful Black vocal textures, funk-informed groove accumulations of modular sonic and textural materials, stylistic mixing across soul, jazz, rock, funk, and blues, etc.

The narrative of "Papa"—about an impoverished son's account of hearing about the wayward and philandering ways of his deceased father—may not have been typical soul message music, but the lyric carries a social commentary on a negative model of Black masculinity. Thus, this *is* progressive soul in a lyrical sense. This narrative—acted in first person with Greek Chorus responses—is cinematic in a manner akin to the antihero tales of contemporaneous blaxploitation films. There is a message *and* there is antihero glamorization in what Morris calls the "hedonism of the player lifestyle" and "macho [Black] toughness."[34] Within the blaxploitation film, the textures of psychedelic soul quickly become musical topics for the urban Black, working-class experience, forms of Black masculinity ranging from aspirational to streetwise, and self-empowerment of Black youth and Black power.

HEARING CINEMATIC SOUL FOR THE DANCE FLOOR

When hearing "Shaft" and "Papa" historically, it must also be recognized that both were popular dance floor tracks, as witnessed on *Soul Train* (discussed later). From this perspective, the pre-1974 Hayes and Whitfield modular-accretional arrangements, and their single and album edits, portend the extended disco-edit and -remix culture. The latter practice was pioneered by engineer-producer Tom Moulton and DJ/producer Walter Gibbons from 1974 forward. Particularly important are Moulton's landmark 1973 studio remix of B.T. Express's "Do It Til You're Satisfied" (extending 3′31″ to 5′52″), his 1974 pioneering of the twelve-inch commercial single with Al Downing's "I'll Be Holding On," and his introduction of the disco breakdown in his 1974 remix of Don Downing's "Dream World."[35] The resonances with the Hayes and Whitfield accretional processes are readily heard in the ninety-second breakdown (the stripping away of most instruments) in "Dream World" (from 2:40), which sets a disco-edit template through its liberal use of echo and reverb, as all the tonal instruments drop out to reveal the percussive, groove core (bongos and kick). From there,

Moulton slowly brings in, combines, and recombines select modular elements into ever thicker textures. All these elements, including the use of studio effects, mix depth, and use of stereo field, are foreshadowed in the procedures of "Shaft" and "Papa."

The production continuum from Hayes and Whitfield to the producer-engineer-driven remix is only a short distance, particularly as all these recordings are centrally tied to the functional-music environment of the emerging discotheques in New York and elsewhere. The disco edit is a process that values and builds contrasts following (or leading to) repeated musical climaxes, frequently even combining with upward modulations for further excitement. In reference to the disco "formula" and the music's interest in the "overlay of sounds," pioneering 1970s disco journalists Vince Aletti and Michael Gomes argue in 1978 that soul music did not end when disco culture emerged. They refer to Marvin Gaye's 1971 "What's Going On?" as the first disco record and "Papa" as being the first of this sort of new production practice that discotheque DJs played and that you could "dance to."[36] They further point to Philly soul's Kenny Gamble and Leon Huff as being among the most influential producers for this tradition. Thus, despite purists decrying the death of soul with the arrival of disco, from a dance-culture, insider perspective, a continuum was recognized from psychedelic-, to progressive-, to sophisti-soul (discussed below), to disco.

Then there is the matter of audiences hearing this music as "cinematic." Flory does this, as does Morris, who describes a "near-cinematic collage" in the track.[37] He comments on Whitfield using "soul cinematically" through "symphonic gestures . . . funk riffs and texts about inner city."[38] This resonates with post-2000 anachronistic characterizations of yet another supposed subgenre, "cinematic soul." An Apple Music "Cinematic Soul" playlist, for example, describes music that is "dripping with pleading vocals and strings, . . . sticky soul and R&B joints . . . perfect for scoring that crucial scene or just strutting around the house. And . . . action!"[39] (The playlist includes Hayes's "Look," White's "You're the First," Bobby Womack, Gaye, and other music up to recent Adele.) Note the potential for internalized, personal soundtracks—a detail that ties in with Barry White (see chapter 8). The Temptations' Wikipedia page describes the group as having gone through a 1968–73 psychedelic and cinematic soul period, followed by a "funk to disco to contemporary adult" progression. Echoing Flory, the page contends that the Temptations' psychedelic music "gave way to 'cinematic soul'" via "lengthy recordings featuring detailed orchestration, extended instrumental introductions and bridging passages," as well as "lyrics about the . . . inner cities of black America," and other "heavy" influences from the music of Hayes and Mayfield.[40] While cinematic soul is not a historically supported subgenre, the connection of 1970s blaxploitation film underscoring to a distinct, Hayes- and *Shaft*-influenced orchestral soul with progressive soul associations is a fact. Moreover, Stax cofounder, Al Bell retrospectively discussed his production vision for *HBS* both in cinematic terms and in terms of the relation of this production to the Motown Sound.[41]

The above discussion suggests a mode of cinematic listening that relates to topical details of instrumentation and timbral textures, melodic gestures, uses of rhythm, production qualities, and narrative unfolding. Simon Frith postulates that a mode of cinematic listening to popular music is "an effect of years of going to the cinema, [and] it does not depend on specific cinematic images." He argues that "film music's emotional and cultural codes . . . are free-floating, they inform *all* our music listening." Frith points to a circular cultural-literacy process in which "Hollywood taught us how to hear musical signs . . . even as it drew upon our commonsense readings of sound settings" and the "everyday semantic connotations" accumulated from Western music history. In turn, "listeners take musical meaning *from* films" through "which we've learned what emotions and cultures and stories sound like."[42] Michael Long has similarly theorized about cinematic listening to specific types of popular music, with particular emphasis on music that relates to his conception of the classical register. This topical area again centrally concerns Hollywood "movie music." The sound of midcentury luxe pop had considerable overlap with movie music from the 1950s and 1960s crime jazz underscoring forward—on radio, film, and television, with lush combinations of strings, woodwinds, and harps combined with big-band jazz-pop textures. This branch of film scoring richly expanded classical Hollywood's movie-music practices. Following the late 1960s shift to pop-compilation underscoring, especially after *The Graduate* (Embassy, 1967) and *Easy Rider* (Columbia, 1969), as well as pop-indebted hybrid soundtracks like Ennio Morricone's underscoring for *The Good, the Bad, and the Ugly* (Constantin Film, 1966), audiences were led further toward hearing popular music "cinematically" if textural and topical qualities encouraged such narrative-based listening. Frith also points to Philip Tagg's studies of listening in relation to the film music of *The Virginian* (Paramount, 1946), where Tagg found that many people listen "narratively" to instrumental music rather than "emotionally."[43] Such tendencies are only enhanced by music that invokes music textures that are familiar to the cinematic experience.

"Shaft" and "Papa" also emerge during the initial boom in pop-compilation underscoring. Writer Geoffrey O'Brien posits that blaxploitation films—an idiom built on the bedrock of Hayes's *Shaft* soundworld—"scarcely existed as anything but vehicles for soundtracks." That these luxe-soul soundtracks stood in opposition to the low-budget acting and productions of these films reinforces this claim. O'Brien sees this relation as a "triumph of movie music, [where] the sounds [were] permitted to take over completely . . . in a world where the same music is on the screen and on the street, on the radio and on the turntable and coming out of the car window and echoing from the fire escape. A private soundtrack becomes the public soundtrack."[44] Here is the private experience of "soundtracking" in everyday musical consumption. O'Brien calls it a "manipulative listening, where the listener forces the music to serve . . . an extraneous [personal] narrative. . . . Any recording . . . can become the music for an imaginary movie."[45] Long too contends that cinematic listening is a "process of simultaneous audiation and envisioning," especially to the hybrids of classical and vernacular musics.[46] Such hybrids of movie music and popular music, particularly popular music widely heard "in the streets," are precisely the cinematic nature of "Shaft" and "Papa."

The choreography of musical elements in "Shaft" to individual montage shots further reinforced the cinematic potential of textures that already expanded on earlier jazz-pop-related film underscoring. One need look no further than the Quincy Jones–led underscoring of television's *Mod Squad* (ABC, 1968–73) to hear cinematic jazz-pop underscoring sounds passing from generation to generation on the way to Hayes. The show included a Black scoring collective that included Jones—a jazz- and pop-production genius who led the Count Basie band in Las Vegas for the Rat Pack—elder saxophone legend Benny Carter, and trombonist J. J. Johnson, among others. Jones not only advised Hayes on film scoring, he brought Johnson, Tom McIntosh, and other young, Black, jazz-trained musicians, into the Hollywood studios for film music work. In *Mod Squad*'s soundtracks, you hear blaring Vegas- and crime-jazz brass and reeds, electric bass, fuzz and wah guitars, whining transistor organs, jazz flute, and other textures that connect jazz-pop film-music practice from 1950s–60s Henry Mancini, to 1960s James Bond films, to funk-infused 1970s blaxploitation, among other markers on this crime-jazz continuum. In the shadow of this practice, both "Shaft" and "Papa" are pregnant with cinematic—and private soundtracking—potential in a circular, pop-consumption/production relation. Even without an accompanying film, the long instrumental introductions of these tracks announce a cinematic narrative mode in the manners that main-title film music announces the codes of cinematic genre and that a company fanfare announces the medium of "cinema" and movie music.

Writing in 1970, one UK, soul-focused writer characterizes the 1967–69 psychedelic soul of groups like the Temptations as a "melting pot" of production innovations.[47] While Hayes is not mentioned, as implied in chapter 1 and above here, this aesthetic amply applies to Hayes albums of the period. The Stax house band, Booker T & the MGs, released the album *Melting Pot* in 1971 amid the label's flood of Hayes releases. Hayes's longtime colleague, Booker T, saw his own Stax album—with an 8'15" jam-based title track whose grooving, shifting textures echo the Hayes extended jam textures—as symbolic of their music's "progress."[48] As such, this characterization seems ideal for discussing Hayes's early 1970s Stax albums. With Hayes, this progressing-soul, melting-pot aesthetic ties into the music's incorporations of both Motown strings and jazz-leaning qualities, as well as the long, static-harmony, extended-jam textures it shares with both psychedelic- and jazz-rock music of the early 1970s. One UK critic comments in 1972 that the *Shaft* soundtrack album "has a totally different feel" from earlier Hayes because it reveals significant connections to the "jazz-rock field with strong electric-piano work and having an affinity with recent recordings by Herbie Hancock ('Fat Albert Rotunda' for instance) and other jazzmen."[49] This comment is insightful, as there are affinities between the jam-oriented rhythm tracks of the *Shaft* soundtrack and Hancock's 1969 *Fat Albert Rotunda* album. The latter similarly had its origins in media underscoring—in this case a 1969 NBC television special that later gave birth to Bill Cosby's 1970s animated Fat Albert series.[50] The latter album marks Hancock's first foray into post–Sly Stone soul and funk, marking a transition from 1960s soul jazz to what becomes hybrid jazz-rock. In the special, the music likewise underscored Black, urban street life. These convergences illustrate the two-way influences between progressive soul and period jazz. Indeed, Hayes commented that with "Cafe Regio's" (the B-side to the "Shaft" 45 rpm single), which diegetically underscored a film scene at said cafe (as jukebox music), he specifically modeled the track on popular jukebox records from jazz guitarist Wes Montgomery.[51] What these associations further reveal is the operation of a jazz-luxe register within luxe soul.

Neither *Ebony* nor *Jet* adopted the term "progressive soul," but their coverage of this music was extensive. Their pride in the achievements of these Black artists was immense, and their commentary highlighted the sophisticated qualities of the music and purported ties it had to Black jazz heritage. For these magazines, the Black music that carried the clearest elevated and respected cultural position was jazz, as seen in their routine coverage of jazz's leading figures and elders.

The trope of jazz in progressive soul criticism notably intersects with discourse on youth and musical training, and this element partly traces to Gibbs. His influence is especially strong in the UK, where the New Jersey–based writer often found work contributing to music publications. The overlaps and differences between Gibbs and his UK critical peers are partly evinced in discourse about youth being central to progressive soul. In 1975, for example, as disco was becoming a mass movement, the London writer Tony Cummings describes the Ohio Players as "the summation, the logical high-point, of the evolvement of a new kind of black music, a music sometimes called street funk or black rock or progressive soul but a music whose most consistent characteristic is youth—music played by eclectic black musicians who've swopped [*sic*] 'roots' for brilliantly executed immediacy." Cummings identifies the origins of this music in late-1960s creative Black musicians like "Jimi Hendrix and Sly Stone [who] began to absorb influences, instrumentations and musical direction from the eclectic world of white "progressive rock." By 1970, [soul had become] *more tightly played* than any previous kind of R&B [and with] compulsive, complex rhythms made itself THE music of black American youth."[52]

Gibbs, by contrast, argued that progressive soul was defined by *youth who kept an eye to Black cultural values from the past*, particularly to jazz, both stylistically and in terms of professional image. In this, he echoes the Black press, but Gibbs notes that this generation had a superior "ability to mix jazz influences with the Memphis [soul] sense of easy abandon."[53]

Gibbs's characterization of a balance of street cred and musical mastery— whether cross-cultural or Black, whether rock or jazz derived—was central to the accounts of other writers. These writings also foreground the vital role of funk groove. Gibbs's poetic description of Kool and the Gang captures the balance of attributes he employed to articulate the traits of progressive soul—in terms of its Blackness, contemporaneity, attitude, and heritage, as well as its sustained juxtaposition of street and sophistication. The group is said to have

> that easy ride, . . . that cool energy. Got that diddley daddy chenka chenk guitar . . . [and] sharp horns riding rat-at-at at a bounce, got that strut. Got the snappy groove. It got Kool with a badass bass. . . . Got that city sense, easy grace like the streets.
>
> Kool got the beat. . . . No one sits down when Kool's around. Got such laughter, like happy party times. . . . Makes you glad you BLACK again. . . .
>
> Kool & The Gang got the message; the message of John Coltrane and Charlie Parker. Got the primordial wail, stretched back and laid out. Got the sweaty groove, midnight at the Five Spot, laid back and curling. Got the tension, got the flow, got the fire that was blazing up from those times. Got the screech and the holler, got the distance. Got the urge of black genius rebelling against confinement, got the creative simmer, got the go. Got the passion.[54]

Kool and the Gang ("Kool") is ideal for discussing the jazz-meets-funk-and-soul discourse of progressive soul, as well as its boundaries. Both this group and Earth, Wind and Fire ("EWF") received significant attention for their training in—and passion for—jazz. Here, Gibbs foregrounds Kool's roots in jazz: "They started as musicians primarily influenced by the jazz legacy, and as teenagers attempted to play it. Commercial considerations dictated otherwise." The musicians themselves reinforce such status-invoking, jazz-heritage associations, as for instance saxophonist Ronald Bell, who told Gibbs that "'my greatest influence was John Coltrane. . . . It was like a call. . . . He was like a God. . . . Once I understood what 'A Love Supreme' was, that was it, that was the call right there." This reverent acknowledgment was not just talk, however, as demonstrated in the 9′30″ jazz-rock instrumental "Wild and Peaceful" from their 1973 commercial-breakthrough album of the same name. Gibbs piles on the hyperbole in his praise of Bell, citing his "stunner" soloing stamina through circular breathing and the "showstopper" solo on this track. Gibbs likewise points to the group's youth and their need to woodshed to achieve the skill-level of their jazz idols. He clarifies that the group maintains this jazz adherence even while "their music continues to grow, and even the renditions of the bump and boogie favourites like 'Hollywood Swinging,' 'Funky Stuff' and 'Jungle Boogie,' contain the kind of smouldering jazz solos that have their precedents in . . . funky jazz . . . from Eddie Harris, The Crusaders and King Curtis, to Willis Jackson."[55] While "Wild and Peaceful" evokes the latter jazz, which leans toward 1970s, pop-friendly fusion jazz, the chart-topping singles mentioned are what led the band up the charts and onto discotheque dance floors.

Kool and the Gang, *"Jungle Boogie" (1973)*

"Jungle Boogie" illustrates the intersection of Kool and the Gang and progressive soul aesthetics outside jazz-luxe orchestration additions. When the band started out as the Jazziacs led by bassist/vocalist Robert "Kool" Bell, they comprised of a rhythm section (bass, drums, keys, guitar) and a horn section of two multi-instrumentalist reed players and a trumpet player (each also contributes vocals). The latter are central to the progressive qualities of the group. Like Hayes, Kool developed material through jam-centered head arrangements built up through accretive, groove-oriented elements. Gibbs observes that their sound "is built around the rhythmic patterns of the guitar, which usually serves as a basis for a song . . . with a catchy little riff around which the rest of the band builds. The formula has worked well . . . [for] some of their best disco smashes."[56] Example 7.3 shows transcriptions from "Jungle Boogie." The group's Stone-influenced funk is apparent in the rhythm-section groove. The

EX. 7.3. Kool and the Gang, "Jungle Boogie." Excerpts: (a) 0:16; and (b) 0:33.

music is grounded by the rock-leaning drums with accented eighth-note back-beat accentuations by the closed hi-hat and snare on beats 2 and 4, alongside groove-inducing, bass-drum sixteenth notes that lean into beats 1 and 3. The rhythm section builds on single-line, two-note, grooving oscillations of the scratch rhythm guitar, whose shifting patterns propulsively fill in the groove around each beat, rising above the texture through a nasal wah-pedal setting. The funk-aligned clavinet simultaneously participates in jazz topics when it joins the multi-octave unisons of the horns and Kool's bass for a beat-defying (through held notes), jazz-informed, melodic line that pushes and pulls against the groove foundations. This material starts in the clavinet and bass at the end of Example 7.3a, which leads to the horn section rising to a peak at 0:33 in Example 7.3b. In addition to the brief solos, such jazz-informed material—centrally from the horns—is surely part of the "progressive" qualities Gibbs adored. The horn-section parts also deploy groove-focused riffs, as seen in sixteenth-note arpeggios of Example 7.3. In an era of rising disco-production sheen, these elements were likely heard as jazz-informed elevations of R&B horn-section riffing (hence "progressive"). Lastly, the group-chant funk vocals

EX. 7.3. (continued)

of the Family Stone are seen here in terms of textures and the repetitive, minimal, party-oriented lyric. The 1970s live performances found on YouTube adhere to the arrangements and do not open for improvisational showcases.

• • •

Numerous critics echo Gibbs's interests in Kool & the Gang, as well as War, Mandrill, Funkadelic, Ohio Players, and EWF, among other Black soul-funk musicians who represented "progress" in this jazz-informed, sophisticated but youth-based sense. The 1970s jazz-rock-enhanced horn work of EWF, Kool, and peers circa 1973 is not reflected in earlier Hayes horn-ensemble work. The latter derived from big-band models via Hollywood, Las Vegas, and jazz-ensemble scoring, albeit without horn-focused soloing. "Progress" with Hayes, though, is still a matter of Black, urban modernity status through markers of jazz-indebted arranging sophistication, technological sophistication, and enriched production textures, with and without strings, a harp, or a flute.

In the soul-to-jazz and jazz-to-soul influence chains within the Hancock and Hayes generation of Black musicians (each born in the early 1940s) who were at their career peaks in the early 1970s, such cross-genre debts are not hidden appropriations. This was seen in Hayes's account of his sound amalgamation, discussed in chapter 1, where he noted his indebtedness to Motown, Bacharach, midcentury crooners, and the funk of Stone and other psychedelic sources. In the progression from funk and psychedelic soul to mid-1970s disco, with much of this music being the foundation of Black, commercial dance music, these cross-genre, melting-pot interactions involve perpetual readjustments of discrete ingredients, ultimately increasing the proportions of sweetness and sophistication, while subduing harder-edged funk and overt jazz elements. *HBS* is a marker in the rise of such tendencies, alongside Philly soul, and each helps to reset the new pulse of 1970s soul as it transformed into mainstream disco. Further, *HBS* and the *Shaft* soundtrack were central to defining the luxe, hybrid properties of disco in tandem with the sophistisoul models from Barry White to Philly soul. The latter was defined by producers Gamble and Huff, the founders of Philadelphia International Records, and the arrangements of producer/arranger Thom Bell. White stands between these two models. The social roles of this music, alongside the progressive soul bands mentioned above, are seen in the dance-music playlists of the Black television show, *Soul Train*, which began its broadcasts in 1971. YouTube is rich with show excerpts that underscore this point. Examples include dancers grooving to both "Theme" and "Papa" (with the Temptations performing in amazing pink tuxedos).[57] There are also a multitude of excerpts related to the *Soul Train* dancers getting down to *Shaft*'s blaxploitation film-score, hit-single progeny.

Soul Train is one of many period dance floor contexts where progressive and psychedelic soul met sweeter sophistisoul, which carried many similar traits and formed the most direct foundation for disco as a style. This music—in reference to White's Love Unlimited Orchestra, MFSB (the in-house luxe studio orchestra of Philadelphia International), and Van McCoy—is "not so much urban music but urbane music," as the disco chronicler Peter Shapiro notes.[58] *Soul Train*'s 1973 third season change in theme songs signals a seismic shift in Black pop away from Stax-influenced soul toward a new center in sweet sophistisoul. The show dropped the 1971 King Curtis and the Rimshots specially recorded, show-theme track ("Hot Potatoes") for the Gamble and Huff "TSOP (The Sound of Philadelphia)." Specifically created for *Soul Train*, the latter was performed by MFSB ("Mother Father Sister Brother," which alludes to a family-wide enterprise) and a vocal trio, the Three Degrees. Aletti reports for *Rolling Stone* that between its 1973 premiere on *Soul Train* and its February 1974 single release of this track, MFSB became "stars in their own right, ready to follow up Barry White's . . . 'Love's Theme' to the Number One spot with their new breed big-band sound."[59] As Shapiro notes, each epitomized the new sophistisoul.

MFSB was comprised of the core studio musicians that Gamble and Huff routinely employed. At the 1978 height of disco, *Billboard* described the latest release of the renamed Gamble-Huff Orchestra as going "through its sophistisoul paces, offering smooth rhythms, mellow horn work and cooing femme vocals, with just an occasional hint of fire" and "worthwhile MOR and jazz moments."[60] This characterization captures the MFSB sound, studio sheen and polish—particularly their lack of progressive, jazz-leaning or funk-inclined fire—that typified the Black-MOR centricity of sophistisoul. While period press suggests that *sophistisoul* was not a widely used term, it was common. A 1975 *Black Music* (UK) extended issue feature on Barry White, notably connects White and the Hayes "Black Moses" era to contemporary sophistisoul: "In '73 while the 'Black Moses' album was offering its pretentious outpourings to a sophistisoul audience, a single . . . "I'm Going to Love You Just a Little More Baby" . . . smashed quickly to the top of the charts. Its recordist was a then unknown . . . Barry White. The album . . . was soon certified gold . . . but was condemned by critics for being derivative of the billowing sophistisoul of Black Moses."[61] Beyond the sophistisoul reframing of Hayes, the reference to his 1971–73 fall from grace from hard-hitting innovator to increasingly MOR-focused softer soul is notable. Some critics saw this music aligning with period soft-rock trends, as heard in *Black Moses*, a 1971 album that features extended covers of the Carpenters' (and Bacharach's) "Close to You," a Gamble-Huff tune, Curtis Mayfield, and the Jackson Five.[62]

Sophistisoul is employed as a glamour- and class-inclined characterization of this shift from adventurous, orchestral progressive and psychedelic soul to commercialized and regularized, dance-oriented sweet MOR soul. This music has been characterized both as proto-disco, circa 1972 to early 1974, as well as a disco subgenre (following Shapiro). Sophistisoul first topped the charts with three central hits in 1973–74: the Gamble-Huff written/produced "Love Train" for the O'Jays, backed by MFSB, hit number 1 on 24 March 1973; the Unlimited Love Orchestra's "Love's Theme" hit number 1 on 9 February 1974; and "TSOP" achieved number 1 on 20 April 1974. By December 1974, recycling of the "disco formula" was well underway, as Carl Douglas's "Kung Fu Fighting" topped the charts on 7 December 1974. Douglas's hit was produced and arranged by the Indian-born, London-based Biddu, who applied his MFSB- and Barry White–influenced production to a range of instrumental hits.

In August 1975, Aletti explained the "disco craze" to *Rolling Stone* readers in a special disco issue with a glossy extended essay on Barry White that concludes by asking "What must it feel like to be the first disposable King of Muzak?"[63] (Is there a non-disposable Muzak king?) This comment captures a backlash (largely white) against disco and sophistisoul as soulless commercial luxe pop formula evocative of 101 Strings–style, MOR easy-listening instrumentals or elevator-enhancing corporate Muzak.[64] This taste-based reception reversal—from a positive, "progressive" characterization to negative critical reception—between two related, immensely popular Black pop idioms is central to this chapter, but will be further explored with Barry White in chapter 8. This reception shift—from elevated to culturally degraded luxe pop—occurs in the shift from sophistisoul to mainstream disco, as this music reached a wider, and whiter, audience. (The *Rolling Stone* disco issue also includes two illustrated pages—with *white* dancers—on how to do the Hustle and Bump.)

Aletti's article describes disco through a framing that references bestringed, luxe, commercial polish, but (as a proponent) in a *positive* light. The article explores disco "madness" as a reaction to 1975's bleak socioeconomic climate, positing disco's glamour and excess in relation to "These Mean Recession Streets" (a partial reference to Martin Scorsese's 1973 film, *Mean Streets*). He explains to the magazine's largely white readership: "Though the new disco music evolved from the hard dance records of the Sixties—primarily Motown and James Brown—the direction has been away from the basic, hard-edged brassy style and toward a sound that is more complex, polished and sweet. If one style dominates now, it's the Philadelphia Sound, which is rich and elegant, highly sophisticated but full of punch. The Philadelphia producers are the masters at using strings energetically, to boost as well as soften the arrangements, and . . . [they] perfected the glossy sound."[65] Aletti recognizes that "much new 'disco music' is merely a replay of several set formulas, established for or by Barry White, George McCrae and Gloria Gaynor." He further adds that "White's sound is heavy on the strings, light on the vocals, with an emphasis on pillow talk."[66] Aletti additionally chronicles the rise of the disco DJ and the art of the disco mix, and the mainstreaming of discotheques in parallel with the popular 1975 hit, "The Hustle" (number 1 on 26 July) by Van McCoy and the Soul Symphony (openly modeled after White). That year also saw emergent international artists, the rise of Eurodisco, and disco-crossover jazz-pop artists (Grover Washington, Herbie Mann, etc.), among other trends. Aletti also cryptically alludes to the possibility of a day when "the disco scene eventually self-destruct[s]," because of the rising recycling of "disco clichés" and problematic "music biz definitions of 'disco.'"[67]

MFSB, "TSOP" (1973)

With this 1973 disco-mainstreaming of sophistisoul in mind, it is useful to consider "TSOP" in relation to Aletti's production commentary. Gamble and Huff productions are exemplary models of period sixteen-track recording practice. Example 7.4 presents two excerpts from "TSOP," from the opening, and from 0:59. The beating heart of the Philadelphia sound is in the drums, percussion, and bass parts. The cornerstone is the groove established by drummer Earl Young. As Philly soul chronicler John Jackson notes, Young's "steadily thumping four-on-the-floor bass drum and telltale hiss of an open hi-hat joining each beat brought him acclaim as an originator of the disco groove."[68] MFSB guitarist T. J. Tindall called Young "a very simple drummer [whose] whole thing was just [playing] right in the middle of the groove [not behind or ahead of the beat]. . . . Earl was

A.

EX. 7.4. MFSB, "TSOP (The Sound of Philadelphia)." Excerpts: (a) 0:00; and (b) 0:59.

right in the middle, almost like a machine."[69] Example 7.4a shows a typical Young groove, with a characteristic propulsive hi-hat hiss created via offbeat eighth-note accentuations from striking the open hi-hat cymbal. The bass drum is squarely on beats 1 and 3, with groove propulsion via a sixteenth grace note just before beat 3, and the crack of snare hits on backbeats 2 and 4. The obligatory Latin conga part involves a busy, one-bar complementary pattern, accentuating backbeats 2 and 4. While largely reinforcing tonic notes on beats 1 and 3, the bass part also involves groove-enhancing walking elements that move between these roots and excite weak-beat areas of the groove. To this foundation is added the obligatory wah rhythm guitar with scratching over beats 2 and 3. Keyboards offer simple whole-note harmonies, likely just one-handed triads, alongside swell-based harmonic turnaround accentuations from the Hammond organ. In these passages, the strings are

B.

0:59

EX. 7.4. (continued)

given lead material, presenting themes in call-and-response with the horns. The strings typically exhibit upper-mid-register, two- and three-part harmonized, monophonic writing in triads. They are often written as melodic, vocal-type lines rather than accent-based disco-string flourishes. The strings even act as vocal stand-ins when the Three Degrees (backing singers) are absent. The unverbalized words here are "soul train, soul train," later heard from the Three Degrees. The brass interjections (monophonic unisons or triadic-/seventh-based harmonies), backed by a reed section buried in the mix, stand at the forefront during these responses.

•   •   •

Rolling Stone's Dave Marsh noted that this track represents "what these ingredients sounded like in the [original] test tube"; six months later, the industry "convert[ed] the beat and strings into a rigid formula called disco."[70] Beyond the impact of "TSOP" as the "codification of disco" in its "swirling strings, orchestrated heavy beat, and whispered female backing," Jackson additionally notes that this formula is dependent upon elaborate sixteen-track production, an "incessant" 150-beats per minute, "sinuous Latin dance rhythms," and lush orchestrations "mindful of the Big Band era of the 1940s."[71] Here too is the jazz-luxe register. This big-band-plus-strings framework is readily seen in videos of MFSB in tuxedoes with glittery sequins. Their presentation echoes the Unlimited Love Orchestra, but again Hayes was a forebear. Hayes's orchestral soul idiom overflowed with similar soul luxe-showbiz inclinations, and Gibbs was quite positive in his reading of this showbiz excess. *Jet* and *Ebony* concurred in this assessment.

All this is useful in situating Hayes's early 1970s progressive-to-sophistisoul reception and his fall from praise as an innovator to being characterized—by *white* critics—as an MOR showbiz act lost in a sea of commercial disco excess. Hayes was "credited (or accused) of fostering a large slice of the movement."[72] This 1975 comment, by the UK's Cliff White, a soul purist, is framed via both the onslaught of the "disco trade" and Hayes's stylistic similarities to Barry White, MFSB, and Van McCoy, among others. While Cliff White complains about disco's omnipresence as "party wallpaper," he recognizes that "there's good and bad in them there orchestral soul records," and that much of this material is commendable as "music by black arrangers who are trying to appeal to as wide an audience as possible by using the full range of orchestral technique at their disposal to create records that are, hopefully, emotionally satisfying, attractive to listen to, good to dance to, without destroying all traces of traditional black roots."[73] Such a perspective is representative of both the ideals of the jazz legacy and new performance arenas for jazz-trained musicians in showbiz, soul, funk, and disco.

CONCLUSION: ISAAC HAYES IN RELATION
TO 1970S POP HYBRIDITY

Ebony often described Hayes's music in comparison to jazz. This occurs, for example, when they note that the "'boss' track, 'By the Time I Get to Phoenix,' had run more than 18 minutes," adding "only the late jazz great John

Coltrane had claimed the right to take *that* long with one song. . . . Hayes hadn't even sung or played during most of the 18 minutes. He'd just struck a basic chord on the organ, sustained it against a rhythm background and gone into a soliloquy."[74] With Hayes's "Look of Love," chapter 1 discussed how Hayes's early 1970s sound ideal as heard in "Look of Love" could be understood within the history of luxe pop—past, contemporary, and future. Hayes ideally demonstrates the intersections of historical listening, absorption, and recombination. This is central to the jazz-luxe register, which can be illustrated via a deeper examination of the intersections of Hayes and *Billboard*'s jazz, R&B, and soul popularity charts.

While the postwar period saw the decline of the big band as a commercial force, hi-fi-era reinventions of swing-indebted music were a regular presence on 1950s recording popularity charts. As mid-1950s rock-pop instigated the era's hi-fi/lo-fi schism between youth and adult markets, jazz-trained talent found studio employment as musicians, arrangers, and producers in various hi-fi pop music trends. These developments are central to the postwar jazz-luxe register. Such jazz-indebted music of the 1950s to 1970s spans popular entertainment—from film to television to Vegas supper club glitz, and so on—but also 1950s/1960s orchestral R&B and soul, and 1970s funk horns, symphonic soul, and disco, among other trends. These out-of-sight contributions of jazz musicians to pop shaped the sound of postwar popular music, particularly Black idioms (hence invoking "out of sight" both literally and as a reference to a 1970s slang phrase for hipness and/or excellence).

When examining *Billboard* and *Down Beat* for evidence of music-industry framing of post-1960 jazz, several interesting trends stand out with the album releases of Hayes. While jazz-rock trends have received scholarly attention over the last two decades, 1960s/1970s soul jazz idioms—and the era's rock, soul, and rock/pop parallels to such jazz-meets-pop hybridizations—remain under-researched. In jazz studies, this situation reflects what Catherine Parsonage terms the "unpopular problem" of the "popularity of jazz."[75] Here, she refers to the scholarly oversight of the popular-culture legacy of jazz. The porous stylistic boundaries of jazz in the late 1960s and 1970s are especially problematic. For example, Daniel Goldmark has written of the problems of genre and jazz-label image branding and stylistic eclecticism in Atlantic Records' 1967–74 jazz album releases.[76] The early 1970s curiosities centered on Hayes and jazz culture that I stated previously—that is, Hayes's presence on the *Billboard* jazz charts, his winning of jazz-artist awards, and Hayes's *Down Beat* coverage—are illustrative. These examples illuminate how the industry tracked and marketed "jazz" in that period. I have noted David Brackett's study of genre instability in *Billboard*'s early 1960s R&B charts.[77] The late 1960s and early 1970s mark a parallel moment where jazz was (to paraphrase Brackett) "losing its identity" despite its role as a racially defining, elevated Black music idiom. *Billboard*'s jazz LP charts no longer consistently referred to recordings that others—core jazz fans, then or now—readily recognized as jazz. Both the legibility of genre and the question of how the magazine tracked sales are of paramount importance to understanding the Venn-like overlapping genre boundaries here. Hayes's curious presence on the jazz charts from July 1969 to November 1971 is useful for dissecting *Billboard* magazine's relationship to jazz and what specifically *Billboard*—the recording industry's primary organ—understood to be jazz or of interest to consumers inclined to jazz in this era.

Citational topics from traditional jazz-pop—like the citationality of the style(s), timbres, phraseology, harmony, grooves, and arranging of the core jazz tradition—have long been employed in a range of music, often with overtones to glamorous entertainment. This is the sound of showbiz "jazz," or Hollywood, Broadway, or Vegas luxe pop, and it intersects with easy listening, areas of MOR, and so on. As noted in earlier chapters, jazz and "jazz" share much and differ in important ways, but both can involve *the same* pools of musicians working different gigs. Hayes and Gibbs both noted that Hayes's symphonic soul had connections to earlier conventions and invocations of both jazz and Vegas/showbiz "jazz." This framing of genre instability is helpful for understanding both the genre-identity problems of the 1969–73 *Billboard* jazz charts and postwar precedents.[78] So, the question remains: Why did *Billboard* and the National Association of Recording Merchandisers (NARM, now called the Music Business Association) see Hayes as chart-topping jazz? And what did Hayes mean to these jazz-inclined editors and critics?

This era overlaps with the rise of jazz-rock, especially early electric Miles Davis, Charles Lloyd, and other jazz-centered artists who merged jazz with R&B, funk, and rock. These trends are reflected on the jazz charts. When the *Billboard* jazz charts return in January 1973, Davis's *On the Corner* was number 3, just after Curtis Mayfield's *Superfly* and Chicago's *Chicago V*.[79] The charts were still mixed, with Miles, Pharoah Sanders, and John and Alice Coltrane set alongside soul and soul jazz and spots of rock and pop. By February, soul, funk, and rock-pop are gone from the jazz charts, never to return, thus implying an accounting shift in jazz recording sales and popularity.[80]

The 1971–73 absence of the *Billboard* jazz charts echo the 1963–65 absence of the *Billboard* R&B chart, but by late 1968 *soul* had become the "de facto term for black popular music."[81] These developments set the stage for the identity confusion of the Hayes-jazz-chart era. Granted, there is a continuum from 1960s soul and funk to jazz engagements with these styles, but most soul was seen to lie at a pop-culture distance from improvisation-based jazz-rock, at least until Herbie Hancock's 1973 *Headhunters*.

From the late 1950s to 1967, jazz is only sporadically tracked in *Billboard*. In March 1967, "special survey" jazz LP charts were introduced.[82] These charts show minimal crossover from the "Rhythm and Blues" chart. Despite this latter outdated categorization, from 1968, the magazine paired these charts with a "Soul Sauce" column. By then, "soul" was associated both with Black pop and soul jazz. Indeed, the "Best-Selling Jazz LP's" column is a sub-section of the "Rhythm & Blues" subsection, set beside the R&B LP charts, and opposite the R&B singles chart and "Soul Sauce" column.

Despite musical dialogue between jazz- and Black-pop trends, *Billboard*'s first critical reference to jazz in relation to both "soul" and "funk" was likely a 1960 review of organist Les McCann.[83] Also, in 1961 the magazine, possibly following the lead of Riverside's influential 1960 promotion of saxophonist Cannonball Adderley, refers to a Blue Note single as a "good side for the soul jazz fans."[84] Jazz magazines like *Down Beat* were slow to discuss soul jazz as a style until circa 1962, starting with the article "Soul Jazz and the Need for Roots."[85] Though it had little to do with soul jazz, just before these press adoptions of this term, there was a mini-trend of "jazz soul" albums, including *The Jazz Soul of Oscar Peterson* from 1959 and *The Jazz Soul of Little Stevie* from 1962, the debut of Stevie Wonder (which covers the soul-jazz landmark, "Moanin'"). The latter follows the 1961 Ray Charles *Genius + Soul = Jazz* LP, with arrangements by Quincy Jones and Charles on soulful Hammond organ. (The connection of these two albums is seen in Wonder's 1962 *Tribute to Uncle Ray*.) Wonder's *Jazz Soul* arrived just as Booker T.'s "Green Onions" rose to number 3 on the Top 100 and R&B charts. *Billboard* though calls "Onions" a "danceable blues tune for teens," a characterization likely tied to the "wailing guitar work" and heavy drums, not the organ of Booker T.[86] The latter is stylistically not that far from the bluesy organ of Charles or even Jimmy Smith, whose albums appear on the R&B charts. "Onions" illustrates the proximity of some 1960s R&B instrumentals to early jazz-meets-soul idioms, and Wonder's *Jazz Soul* (e.g., "Fingertips") is not far from Quincy Jones's 1962 "Soul Bossa Nova," with its big-band sound, jazz flute, and bossa nova beat. These jazz-pop-meets-soul confluences reveal many period genre overlaps in Black pop, but even to early 1968, the jazz charts show few intrusions of Motown- or Stax-influenced soul, even with a release like *Genius* that foregrounded jazz-trained musicians and marketing.

Fabian Holt notes that "the jazz economy took a steep dive in the 1960s and reached a low ... around 1972."[87] Nevertheless, *Billboard* began tracking jazz again in March 1967. The instability of jazz can be seen throughout industry press. In May 1968, *Billboard* announced "Jazz Skipping New Beat as 'Poppouri.'" Here, jazz producer Joel Dorn claims "jazz has become so broad ... it is ... difficult to pigeonhole," and he notes the "overlap of ... album[s] on the pop and jazz charts."[88] A 1967 *Variety* article by Leonard Feather cites Quincy Jones as saying, "In the jazz magazines nowadays ... they seem to be writing about everything but Jazz," and Feather himself laments that "the charts seem to include everything but jazz." Writing just prior to the return of *Billboard*'s jazz charts, Feather notes that on pop charts he can only find "the names of 10 artists who, by ... [any] stretch of the imagination, could be identified with jazz." Feather identifies albums of Jimmy Smith, Wes Montgomery, and Lee Morgan as "genuine jazz with only minor compromises" to the "soul or rock 'n' roll trends." He suggests a distanced jazz debt in music by Paul Butterfield, Ray Charles, and Lou Rawls, and the bottom of the barrel on his jazz-debt list includes the "pop group sound" of Doc Severinsen, "the rhythm and blues bag" of Ramsey Lewis, the "bossa nova, showmanship" of Sergio Mendes, and Count Basie's covers of Beatles songs. Feather observes that jazz can only succeed in the marketplace "by deviating from pure jazz" through "Tijuana Brass imitations, rock tunes, and the like."[89]

Down Beat demonstrates jazz press adjustments to the new jazz economy. In a June 1967 editorial, Morgenstern announced that the magazine was expanding to cover "the musically valid aspects of ... rock."[90] Privately, Morgenstern noted to me that the magazine "was forced to open its pages [to rock] due to pressure from advertisers. ... We managed to finesse it, and eventually it ... vanished. ... But then the soul thing came along, which unlike rock was ... a black phenomenon, also seen, from a jazz perspective, as a trend that ought to increase interest in the real thing among [a] younger black audience."[91]

While this agenda in promoting jazz heritage at its market nadir is not typical of *Billboard*, similar concerns appear there. In 1972, *Billboard* featured both "Jazz Scene" (29 April) and "Soul Emergence" (29 January) special issues. The latter proclaimed—with testimonial from Jones and Adderley—that "Jazz Is Soul's 'Cousin' and the two have a swinging relationship."[92] In the 1972 "Jazz Scene" issue, Dorn describes his Atlantic releases—from Roland Kirk to soul artists like Donny Hathaway—as simply "adult black music," a description that captures this market.[93] The lead article concerns a "new wave of enthusiasm" of "youth respond[ing] to . . . contemporary rhythms" mixed with jazz, with new players "coming out of acid rock" and others "coming from the ghetto."[94] The article concerns producers' views on jazz-rock, but the contributions of Black, urban popular culture are relevant here. Despite white producers talking about the "ghetto," 1972 was saturated with Black-produced film and pop images of the "ghetto." In the Black Power era, as Hayes topped jazz and R&B charts, the "ghetto" was not an entirely negative construction in Black pop culture. Lastly, there is the article "Looking for Freshness on a Pop Date? Hire a Jazz Sideman."[95] This trend of jazz musicians lending their talent to pop production is highly relevant to *all* of the music discussed in this chapter. For example, Hayes's work on the *Shaft* soundtrack included major assistance by both jazz arrangers and jazz-trained studio musicians. These connections, what Aaron Johnson has called "the university of jazz,"[96] illustrate that in 1972 these stylistic cousins lived and worked in the same swinging neighborhood.

In the 1968 jazz "Poppouri" issue, such crossovers are entirely an LP phenomenon. This may imply certain socioeconomic and age demographics. But on the best-selling R&B LP chart, anomalies like *The Good, the Bad, and the Ugly* soundtrack stand alongside choice 1968 soul, a Wes Montgomery cover of the Beatles, and soul-jazz brethren like Jimmy Smith, Eddie Harris, Ramsey Lewis, and the Soulful Strings.[97] Jack McDuff and Booker T. are side by side, and joined by Hendrix, Vanilla Fudge, and comedians. The R&B charts thus reflect general sales in stores catering to African Americans. Jazz sales are not easily reduced to one demographic, though. Beyond pop tune covers, the first pop penetration onto *Billboard* jazz charts appears to be Burt Bacharach's *Reach Out* in January 1968. By May, this LP was joined by Aretha Franklin, Lalo Schifrin's *Mission Impossible* soundtrack, and Ray Charles.[98] While Davis's *Nefertiti* and albums by Gerald Wilson, Buddy Rich, and Don Ellis anchor a core jazz tradition, other entries include soul jazz (e.g., Smith, Montgomery, and Herbie Mann), and the Soulful Strings, which bridged jazz-pop, adult pop, and easy listening.

The sound of late-1960s jazz-pop is heard in Bacharach's bossa-meets-Tijuana-Brass arrangement of "The Look of Love" on *Reach Out*.[99] Despite its distance from *Nefertiti*, "Look" reflects other jazz-chart sounds with its

Hammond organ and citations of Lou Donaldson's R&B-infused "Alligator Boogaloo" sax, the bossa of Mendes, and so on. What is missing are Mann-style jazz flute and Montgomery-style guitar; Bacharach instead favors crisp Tijuana Brass horn textures. Much of the jazz-pop I have noted on this 1968 chart crossed over to the pop LPs charts. Not *Reach Out* though, an album that likely involved Herb Alpert's Tijuana Brass musicians. Conversely, Alpert's releases top the LP and Easy Listening charts but do not enter the jazz charts, nor does *Reach Out* appear on the Easy Listening chart.

There is a postwar easy-listening-meets-jazz kinship between *Reach Out* and *Groovin' with the Soulful Strings*. *Groovin'* enters the jazz charts in early 1968.[100] The album's cross-market conception is heard in its covers of Davis's "All Blues," the Young Rascals' "Groovin'," Bacharach's "Alfie," and an original, "Burning Spear." The album is all over the jazz-chart-read-as-adult-contemporary-pop map. There is Miles, rock-pop, jazz-with-strings, adult pop from films, tunes from Mann and the Beatles, and funk-infused world-grooves, all with jazz solos, especially flute, sax, guitar, and Hammond. Like "Look," it stylistically references almost every album on the May 1968 jazz chart. If this were released as soul and appeared just two years later, it would be seen as "progressive." Like these later recombinatorial trends, the Cadet label's A&R director, Esmond Edwards, reimagined and remixed stylistic elements from earlier models—in this case, 1950s jazz-with-strings and mood music trends—and repackaged the whole for a contemporary market. Similar to the later mixed-background and mixed generation musicians assembled for Hayes, Edwards's ensemble includes Chicago jazz and soul staff musicians for the Chess and Cadet labels alongside studio orchestra musicians.

So, is this just a matter of the industry "wishing" jazz to be conceived in a certain way or a case of white record men not "getting" Black music? Again, it is more complicated than such essentializations of Black culture. Based on the easy-listening concept, liner notes, and redheaded album-cover model, one might assume that the Soulful Strings' Edwards was a white A&R executive. He was in fact a noted Black producer and photographer tied to Prestige and Verve. There was cross-racial, adult-music appeal on the consumption *and* production sides of this soul-meets-jazz-meets-pop territory. As seen in the jazz discussions in the pages of *Jet* and *Ebony* in this era, this perspective proves insightful for understanding the elements of glamour and sophistication that some Black audiences, and critics in general, appreciated in the jazz-indebted textures of progressive soul, sophistisoul, and early disco.

Edwards—and Jones—illustrate the era's expanding executive opportunities for Black creative talent. The blaxploitation film genre was prominent here and it opened doors to Black directors, actors, and musicians. This opportunity and success, in parallel with the immense sales of similarly scored chart hits, allowed numerous Black artists to add expanded orchestration, including strings and big-band backings, thanks to increased budgets that allowed premium production treatments. This industry support conveyed a recognition of artistic and/or industry prestige—somewhat like the top-of-the-line, 1972, gold-plated, luxury El Dorado (with white fur lining) that Cadillac gave Hayes to honor the success of *HBS*. And by 1973–74, such luxe recording productions became a genre norm as the disco tsunami moved ever closer to mainstream. Such instrumental pop-and-soul releases on *Billboard*'s jazz charts resonate with Hayes, whose penchant for Bacharach tunes, soulful strings, and jazz-flute overlap with many MOR, adult-contemporary peers. But this still does not explain the dominance of Hayes on the jazz charts.

As Frith notes, the music industry has never been "clear or consistent" in its "genre maps," which "change according to who they're for."[101] Is this merely a matter of soul-meets-jazz-as-Black-adult-music on the jazz chart? I am not so sure, but without documentation on chart tabulation, it is impossible to know the factors in these sales assessments. Frith notes that "one would . . . get a strange notion of pop . . . history" from the Grammy awards and *Billboard* charts, which he astutely says "give one a good sense of how the . . . music industry would like to see the market."[102]

Morgenstern observed that in this era jazz was "a convenient label for music hard to categorize, and . . . an industry synonym for black." This comment maps onto *Billboard* discussions of Hayes representing a new "progressive" and "adult" soul, which is not far from my soul-meets-jazz-as-Black-adult-music characterization. Morgenstern notes, however, that, as "for the *Billboard* so-called jazz charts, [*Down Beat*] never took them seriously. . . . The charts [were] about as reliable as pre-election poll results."[103]

Hayes's *Shaft* score—which included many soulful, jazzy instrumental tracks—was an influential cornerstone with its jazz-pop flute and vibraphone, soulful strings, both Tijuana-style staccato brass and Quincy-like big-band textures, wah guitar, Hammond, and so on. Jazz citations were central to this sound, courtesy of top-tier (often Black) jazz arrangers and musicians benefitting from the university of jazz, like other period soul and funk. *Billboard*'s coverage of the soul-to-jazz continuum includes commentary from label execs, producers, and musicians who repeatedly characterize Black music as an overlapping family of genres, and who remark that genre labels are inherently too reductive with regard to the "swinging relationships" among these musical cousins. This outlook is echoed in the Black press. For example, in an issue with a cover photo and interview of Hayes, *Ebony* introduced its first annual "Black Music Poll." After noting negative connotations to the word *jazz* and the hope for an "evolve[d]" new word, the magazine remarks that "black music transcends categories" due to "striking similarities running through gospel, jazz, blues and rhythm and blues." While noting difficulties in the "correct [genre] placement" of various "multitalented" musicians, they ask: "Where does one form of black music begin and the other end?"[104] It is from this historical-cultural perspective that Hayes's jazz-chart presence makes some sense in the genre turmoil of the day. Here, the university of jazz—meaning jazz-culture contributions to pop—stands as a rich popular-music territory that lies just outside the broad, porous genre boundaries of the core jazz tradition. Though *Billboard*'s 1968–73 jazz charts muddy genre history maps, and while I hesitate to call Hayes jazz, this music is clearly both deep in the groove of this era's jazz-inflected, "progressive" and "adult" soul music and undeniably indebted to the university of jazz.

As seen in the 1973 Gibbs review of Hayes at Madison Square Garden, commercial or entertainment leanings were not necessarily a negative in delimiting progressive soul. Gibbs favorably describes the entertainment routines of Hayes ("the king of macho glitter soul") that played with the inherent class expectations an audience might have in seeing a soul artist fronting an orchestra. The positive showbiz elements Gibbs describes are in fact important parts of Black entertainment heritage. For example, Gibbs further describes Hayes's "warm luxurious voice" as having "traces of other dark voiced crooners especially Billy Eckstine, Brook Benton and Arthur Prysock."[105] Here, Gibbs references three major Black jazz-pop stars of mid-century who were often characterized as being "sepia" versions of Sinatra and the Rat Pack.

Apparently, the balance between the right amounts of progress, groove, and entertainment was difficult to maintain. The turn from progressive soul and early sophistisoul to the mass appeal of soul- and funk-infused disco, with its increasing reliance on production sheen and formula, led most progressive proponents to delimit commercial boundaries for the idea of progressive soul. Despite the centrality of Gamble and Huff to the rise of disco commercialization, the artist who centrally marks the shift from positive musical and cultural progress to negative critical disparagement for perceived commercial formulation is Barry White, who—to some—became the disposable king of Black Muzak. This criticism arises precisely at the same time that White had achieved immense popularity with all segments of the disco audience, but especially among the Black middle-class readership of *Jet* and *Ebony. Jet*, for example, features White on six cover stories across the 1970s, more than any other musical artist outside the Jackson Five. Hayes too receives extensive lengthy coverage, and—following the lead of mainstream music press—the two are routinely referenced as being in a "battle for the top," to echo the cover story of one 1978 *Jet* issue.[106]

Gibbs's emphasis on the "maturity" and artfulness of jazz echoes the jazz characterizations of Black middle-class magazines like *Jet*. In 1977, the latter proclaimed "Jazz Giants Help Turn Black Music Classical" as a means to underscore that the jazz canon had created music of artistic parity with the European concert music. Similar class hierarchies in Black music can be seen in *Ebony*, as, for example, in the October 1973 issue—with "Isaac Hayes: New Wife, New Career, New Image" as the cover story—that announced the "First Annual Ebony Black Music Poll." Despite the intention to "encompass the total black experience in music," the poll places jazz as the first and most-often-mentioned genre. It elevates jazz by giving the genre the only two musician images on the first poll page, and places jazz at the forefront with two full pages of twenty-three jazz nomination categories, some with up to fifty-six potential candidates.[107] The other genre categories include R&B-Pop for two-thirds of a page, blues for a half page, and gospel for a single column. Classical receives no mention. The only advertisement amid the poll is two-thirds of a page for Gordon's London Gin. The ad features a fashionably clad, Black, early-thirties couple reclining on the floor in playful spirits. There are LP covers lying about. The pair drink gin and tonics amid mentions of England and the world. The ad implies affinities between these elements and an adult, cosmopolitan, urbane, aspirational lifestyle—that is, precisely the lifestyle that mainstream jazz occupied in early 1970s Madison Avenue marketing. Such class-culture elevation is likewise seen in *Jet*'s unprecedented 13 June 1974 issue devoted to Duke Ellington's death. This includes fifty-six pages of coverage of his "royal" legacy. No other African American is honored in such a fashion in either magazine. By contrast, classical music is rarely mentioned in the pages of *Jet* and *Ebony*, even though references to the genre (like White's orchestral extravaganzas) were present in Black culture and popular culture.

The pages of both magazines resonate with the industry commentary that characterized Black music as an overlapping family of genres with dialogue among the family's subgenre cousins. It is from such perspectives and the reception of soul-funk-jazz hybrid idioms as "mature" or "adult" Black middle-class music that Hayes's jazz-chart presence and progressive soul must be understood. What remains curious is that while White was routinely claimed by critics to have modeled his sound and persona after Hayes, he is rarely afforded the music-critic accolades that Hayes was across 1969–71. Quite to the contrary. In opposition to this negative discourse, underground dance-music insiders (e.g., Aletti) and the Black press greatly appreciated White, and his music did receive an immense amount of music-press coverage. Nonetheless, much of this coverage was often written in an amused and entertaining manner about the Unlimited Love Orchestra spectacle (aural and visual) despite a generally limited critical love.

EIGHT

From Sophistisoul to Disco

BARRY WHITE AND THE
FALL OF LUXE POP

THE DECADE OF THE 1970S represents the high-water mark of luxe-pop practice in North America and Europe. Beyond the increased pop-charts presence of MOR and orchestral soul idioms, the overwhelming center of these trends was mainstream disco. As one of the most disparaged and beloved pop idioms of the twentieth century, disco embodied notable shifts in American notions of entertainment glamour and sophistication—as well as middlebrow-adjacent impulses—in relation to music, materialism, fashion, and media. Moreover, with the late 1970s arrival of string synthesizers, there was a relative taste devaluation in the cultural currency of string-section sounds. This was particularly true as the "disco sucks!" countermovement gained ground. By the late 1970s, punk spat at the decadent kitsch of disco, and then New Wave and the New Romantics (UK) embraced the electronic string pads of new technology rather than employ real strings.

Chapter 7 charted various idioms that coalesced into the disco sound across 1973. Disco—as a culture and idiom—evolved into an omnivorous cultural juggernaut by 1975. *Rolling Stone*'s aforementioned 1975 disco special issue was a thirteen-page overview that included an extended insider account by Vince Aletti, four pages on dance, a detailed account of the technology and environment of disco, a celebratory account of gay disco culture, a two-page overview of disco artists, and writer/critic John Lombardi's two-page artist overview, "Barry White: The Billy Jack of Disco."[1]

Discourse around disco was predominantly focused on the music's excesses, overt commercialism, and materialist culture. As Richard Dyer wrote in 1979: "Much of the hostility to disco stems from the equation of it with capitalism. Both in how it is produced and in what it expresses, disco is held to be irredeemably capitalistic."[2] Dyer captures the sentiments of many who held an ironic appreciative distance to the genre, with both reservations and guilty-pleasure attraction to the culture's materialist excess. Speaking of the "scale of money squandered on" disco and the music's "tacky sumptuousness" in his 1979 essay, "In Defense of Disco," Dyer observes that the idiom "is a riot of consumerism, dazzling in its technology . . . , overwhelming in its scale (banks of violins, massed choirs, the limitless . . . percussion instruments), lavishly gaudy in the mirrors and tat of discotheques, the glitter and denim flash of its costumes." This article frames 1970s discourse on a new gay international consciousness within arguments that sought to consider disco "seriously."

The luxe, consumerist expressions of disco are central to this chapter, alongside the ironic distancing around the music's glitzy sumptuousness. Like Dyer, I aim to consider this discourse "seriously," including the fascinating mixture of flamboyant hyperbole and kitsch entertainment. More specifically, the chapter articulates ways in which associations of glitz and glamour, middlebrow-adjacency, aspirational materialism, and entertainment, lead to the "excesses" of disco which mark a culmination of the entertainment aesthetics traced across this book.

Barry White and his Unlimited Love Orchestra were omnipresent across mid- to late 1970s popular culture. Period opinions and associations concerning White and his music can be illustrated through Lombardi's account of White for *Rolling Stone* (*RS*). This article is far from flattering and includes no commentary from White himself or his representatives. Something of Lombardi's *RS*-colleague Hunter S. Thompson's "gonzo," first-person participatory journalism style—and its satirical tone, personal perspectives, exaggeration, wit, and biting social criticism—can be found in this article. This is to White's detriment, but a self-amused style permeates White discourse, with many critics expressing a reserved appreciation for White's music, oversize personality, and entrepreneurial showbiz wherewithal from an ironic distance. Lombardi's guilty-pleasure account of his experience of the Love Unlimited Orchestra ("LUO") spectacle embodies this distance as he revels in the cross-class, -race, -sexual, -fashion, and -cultural collisions inherent in White's performance, the orchestra, their audience, and his own participation.

Lombardi describes a 1975 performance by White, his female vocal trio, Love Unlimited, and the orchestra, in Tarrytown, New York (north of the Bronx). The article provides a wealth of references to disco scenes, tribes, and clubs, and paints a rich picture of the trappings of a Barry White theater performance, including commentary on the expensive "Maestro Barry White" concert programs. Lombardi notes the orchestral impression: "41 pieces, the musicians dressed in black tie and tails, the balding conductor in a white kimono . . . playing a song that sounds like 'Love's Theme.'" (The latter is a jab at what Lombardi describes as the interchangeability of White's repertoire.) On the star's entrance, he observes: "The violins tremble. The French horns bleat. And the biggest man I've ever seen enters. . . . He doesn't have to do anything. The crowd begins sighing. . . . He's at least 6'3", probably 300 pounds . . . Barry White!" The fashion juxtaposition against the largely white orchestra is given particular attention: "He has on an orange velvet suit. And orange silk shirt with a collar so big an ordinary man could use it as a hang glider. . . . Barry has on orange patent leather loafers. Diamond rings to make [author and one-time pimp] Iceberg Slim and Ringo Starr weep. . . . Everyone is going completely crazy, party-partying and banging on the seats."[3]

The greatest impact of the entrance is from White's "*basso profundo* . . . hitting buttons in the audience." Lombardi's companion, Trude Heller (owner of a famous Greenwich Village lesbian cabaret) observed, "The voice without the image is the thing. . . . The first time I heard him, I was relaxing in bed . . . , we were smoking, relaxing after the battle [sex], and this . . . *voice* . . . big, strong, but lush—*uncoils*, you know?" The phallic snake analogy underscores the sexuality and seduction of the musical experience, but Lombardi and his sources argue for the safe nature of this sex symbol's seduction:

> The thing about Barry White's music—lush, romantic, biracial, bisexual—is that it operates out of a reassuring frame. . . . It is so broad based it reaches all the disco dancers and disco listeners—black, gay, straight, adult, etc. A lot of the other stuff . . . is so raunchy it appeals to the hard-core party-partyers but leaves others out, and this makes the radio and record company types nervous. It's so unpredictable. . . . Nobody could predict the rise of the [mainstream] discos [though] . . . and then—Hollywood!—a Spanish Harlem rose growing right out of the cracks in the sidewalk where the Peppermint Lounge died.[4]

Lombardi references here both the 1960 "Spanish Harlem," a luxe-pop hit that bridges Leiber and Stoller and Phil Spector, and the Peppermint Lounge, an epicenter of the Twist dance craze and an early employer of the Ronettes, whose campy sexual image was formed in that venue. While this earlier luxe pop was seen as innovative, and while White has "got all those strings, all that orchestration," Lombardi emphasizes a contrary, non-luxuriant impression of White as being "predictable as prime-time television."

Lombardi's ironic appreciation is reinforced by commentary from the promoter, Howard Stein, who opines that White offers his audiences

> easy emotion, no challenges. He brings romanticism back. . . . He appeals to women on a kind of "love for one woman" basis. Despite all of our liberation talk, women still like the idea of fidelity. . . .
>
> He also erases the difference between black and white. . . . He replaced Isaac Hayes because Hayes came on like the Black Moses. [But h]e still has something of the old James Brown funkiness, which is . . . exclusively black. Barry just keeps talking about love, brotherhood, morality and also . . . old-fashioned material values. They call it "progressive soul." Barry's accessible to everyone.[5]

Stein's musico-cultural framing of White is broad, spanning Black and white rock, pop, and "progressive soul," the dethroning of Hayes, the politics of Black sexuality, multiculturalism, universal "love" amid hedonistic commercialism, the sexual revolution, and changing ideals of glamour. Each of these contexts is central to the *positive values* that White's fans, past and present, have found in the luxe-pop disco that he helped birth.

As seen across this book, the US tradition of entertainment glitz—meaning, again, the American showbiz aesthetic that embraces flashy, superficial extravagance and flamboyance, as well as garishness, gaudiness, and pretentiousness—is central to the discourse of luxe pop. It is especially central to anti-disco discourse. This criticism began with, and was sustained at, White, a pivotal figure for the critics of disco's excess and formulaic nature. A study of his music captures a vital disco essence—musically, culturally, aesthetically, and performatively. In the reception of White, this sound is initially placed in the broader context of early and mid-1970s "sophistisoul," which emerged before disco became a genre and in relation to progressive, symphonic, and psychedelic soul.

Central to the concerns of this chapter are the accusations against sophistisoul (White, MFSB, etc.)—and, in turn, disco—of being formulaic in production and arrangement, but also the shifting valuative reception and the relation of critical assessments to musical and production details. Such commentary underscores again the relevance of David Brackett's theorizing of the interrelations between genre-defining, musico-topical features and overlaps of both citationality and iterability between individual tracks and other recordings. As seen with earlier luxe pop, recombinant style topics (Rebecca Leydon) and/or musemes (Philip Tagg) and the referential universe of record production practice (Albin Zak) all play important roles in both how this music was intended to communicate and how it was received by musicians, audiences, and critics.

There are several iterative and recombinant topical references that the music of White was regularly received within. First, press routinely—positively and negatively—discussed White's music in relation to the progressive soul of Hayes. Circa 1973–74, just as disco was breaking into the mainstream, White was regularly characterized as being at the forefront of sophistisoul, alongside the Philly soul architects Kenneth Gamble, Leon Huff, and Thom Bell. Over 1974–75, when disco became a mass phenomenon, White's music was reframed in terms of the overt, trend-chasing commercialism of artists like Van McCoy, whose astronomical success with 1975's "The Hustle" made disco known throughout the Western world. Lastly, in spite of his immense success, White's music was more often derided as being regressive and evidence of a Black Muzak or Black easy-listening idiom.

Each of these referential areas will be explored, using White as a means to consider the fall from grace of luxe-pop idioms. As articulated in the afterword, across the late 1970s and early 1980s, the discourse and reception of luxuriant production went from being seen as an elevated marker of glamour, cosmopolitanism, and sophistication to a derided sign of commercialism, kitsch, and datedness. This shift away from luxe-pop production was stimulated by both the backlash against the cultural, musical, and showbiz excesses—and racial and sexual politics—of disco and new technologies that offered budgetary and work-flow reductions as well as an expanded modern sonic palette. This chapter is chiefly concerned with the mixed and curiously shifting reception of music that went from being perceived as "progressive" (positive, forward-looking) to being characterized as Black Muzak (with negative, regressive implications).

THE CRITICS INTERPRET BARRY WHITE

The mixed coverage of White can be seen in the UK- and US-circulated magazine, *Black Music*, which published "The Barry White Story" in July 1975. This folio included a six-page cover story that provides an extensive mid-1970s consideration of White, including a page-plus mini essay on "The Sound," before moving to "The Story," "The Image," "The Man" (an extended interview conducted at an "opulent" London hotel by a female writer), "The Show," and "The Records" (his discography). In this coverage, the sound of White's music is a synecdoche of both the disco formula and the constellation of culture, race, class, and glamour associations of disco. Tony Cummings's essay on "The Sound" captures key themes from the musico-cultural DNA of the White formula—that is, the record-production code (formulaic elements) that carries the musical-genus instructions for sophistisoul disco. Cummings opens by noting: "Symphonic soul . . . sophisti-soul . . . orchestral soul . . . black muzak. Everyone seems to coin a different name for the music of Barry White."[6] A meandering introduction frames "the sound" in relation to soul history, a trajectory that both constructs symphonic-soul "authenticity" and acknowledges the criticisms of detractors. The 1969 arrival of Hayes forms a cornerstone within an outline of the "controversy" that painted early 1970s Hayes as an ideal of "progress," and characterized White "as a sinister threat to the continuing evolvement of black music."[7]

The article is a resource-rich means to explore the citational genealogy and sociocultural associations of White's music. The cultural distance of the UK author may be a reason for the close attention to this discourse, as the UK collector-critic-aficionado community might have been more singularly preoccupied with issues of authenticity around soul than white American counterparts or the Black audience for this music. Cummings connects White's music back to a "root . . . almost as old as 'soul music' itself. For it was in 1959—when Jerry Lieber and Mike Stoller first conceived of . . . large symphonic orchestrations behind the Drifters' 'There Goes My Baby' and came up with a whole new philosophy in rhythm and blues production—that the sound was born."[8]

The early 1960s are described as the "beat concerto era" of soul, when "a dozen more producers were utilising violins, violas, french horns and harps in accompaniment behind black singers with gospel-derived vocal styles." While Phil Spector's productions are said to have been targeted at a "purely popular audience," and this intent is juxtaposed against something described as "Uptown R&B" (marketed to a Black audience?), Cummings argues that "the techniques of an orchestral–R&B fusion were first evolved in . . . New York." Mid-1960s soul is described as a continuation of this "classical soul" while diversifying "into several directions," including "the layered, rhythmic, tambourine-driven soul of Detroit, and the rootier, raunchier, brass-dominated soul of Memphis." In mid-1960s, New York–region productions, Cummings finds sophistisoul roots with Black producers like Luther Dixon, Van McCoy, and early Bell, as well as the white Burt Bacharach. Oddly,

Motown is not noted in this context. Mentions of Dionne Warwick and the Delfonics set up a defining moment:

> In 1969, a Memphis songwriter/producer took symphonic instrumentation (utilising . . . the Memphis Symphony Orchestra) and added two new elements, namely a rhythm section emphasizing instruments (particularly the wah wah guitars) borrowed from the eclectic Sly Stone "black rock" movement, and also spoken monologues which often carried as much lyrical impact as the songs. . . .
>
> . . . Isaac Hayes . . . crystalized all the previous developments . . . of using complex, lush orchestrations in . . . "soul" music. But because Hayes' music was SO lush, . . . some rock critics took it as the final affront to the artistic integrity of soul.

Where other critics saw a foundation for progressive soul, Cummings finds legitimacy for the White sound. He specifically situates Hayes's music within the "controversy" around sophistisoul productions. He observes that while the detractors first derided the "beat concertos" as being flawed by bringing "gospel-based R&B singers . . . to a white audience with little or no aesthetic considerations," the productions of Black producers—Dixon, Bell, McCoy, and Hayes—are said to undermine such racial essentialization of Black musical tastes. Cummings suggests that critics of sophistisoul then "redefined" their critique "to run roughly along the lines that Hayes was basically a frustrated middle-of-the-roader with disgustingly middle-class tastes and aspirations . . . who had taken to banks of violins and an increasingly 'romantic' musical approach to appeal to those blacks who wanted a taste of something 'respectable' and those whites who wanted a hint of soul without having to face the reality." In sum, the "immense sales success" of Hayes was met with "purist" critics who, according to Cummings, "maintained that all Hayes had succeeded in becoming was the first purveyor of Black Muzak." Cummings further defines Muzak as being "universally recognized as any kind of music which SOUNDED like it should be insidiously oozing from the speakers of a supermarket, laundrette, or hotel lobby. . . . [Muzak is] devoid of any memorable quality [because it is] being PLAYED TO BE IGNORED, intended simply to rest in the subconscious in soothing vapidity." Cummings locates the pivotal shift from innovation to Muzak in the "pretentious outpourings" of Hayes's 1973 *Black Moses* album, where "following the same instrumentation (lashings of strings et al.) the bald-headed maestro was fast becoming almost as boring . . . as [easy-listening artists] James Last, Bert Kaempfert and other middle-of-the-road heroes, releasing too many similar-sounding albums with production-line frequency."

On similarities between White and Hayes, Cummings observes that both "used layer upon layer of strings counterbalanced by electrofunk rhythm tracks," and both "used moody, extended monologues" and "sang and rapped in a throaty, resonant voice with more 'presence' than note-holding ability." In contrasting the two, he points to White's adherence to original music as opposed to Hayes's penchant for covers of "classy" MOR pop. Whereas Hayes employed "standard strutting funk grooves," White's "rhythm wizards displayed endless rhythmic nuances with . . . spurts of wah wah and crisply zipping cymbals."[9] On artist image, Cummings contends that while "Hayes's music and raps" were "self-important and pseudo-significant, locked in mumblingly dull worldliness," White "came across as . . . a sensuous, understanding but virile lover."[10] Lastly, though acknowledging that detractors found both artists shirked their responsibility to "'progress' (. . . to stylistically change)" in favor of "formula," Cummings argues that each was working firmly within a Black-pop tradition of "finding an individualistic style and only superficially deviating from it." Further defense for "classical soul"/sophistisoul is brought in from Bell, who is quoted saying "The black American today has a new level of awareness. He wants music that is sophisticated, complex even, but still has links to [everyday] reality. . . . Large string sections aren't selling out soul, . . . they're just giving it a new voice with which to speak."

Cummings's account represents a middle ground between the press and both public proponents and critical detractors to White and Hayes. He embraces both, standing for a multivalent taste perspective that I suspect was not uncommon with much of the luxe-pop music discussed across this book, as well as White and Hayes specifically. There is a resistance to kitsch and excess, while at the same time there is a guilty pleasure in embracing the glamour, spectacle, and sensory lushness.

White's rise to fame represents a shift from the sophistisoul of Hayes, Curtis Mayfield, and Marvin Gaye, top-tier early 1970s Black artists whose lush multitracked arrangements could be performed live, toward the mid-1970s DJ-and-record-centric dance culture that became disco. The latter context is where White first found a toehold on success. But the former context—live performance—remained vital to his income and image, thus suggesting production associations that crossed the live with the virtual in the public and critical mindset in a way that other disco artists without live-performance acts lacked. Just as the discotheque boom began to be tracked in the press in late 1974, White's music, such as "You're the First, the Last, My Everything" (henceforth "You're the First"), became central to the wall-to-wall aural shag carpeting of 1970s American discotheques.[11] White's most important early contribution was LUO's November 1973 single, "Love's Theme," which was released both on Love Unlimited's July 1973 album, *Under the Influence of . . .* and the January 1974 LUO album, *Rhapsody in White*. White as a solo artist emerged in the 1973–1974 recordings of "Can't Get Enough of Your Love, Babe" (hereafter "Can't Get") and "You're the First," released in August 1974 on the album *Can't Get Enough*.

As mainstream disco madness hit, much of the coattail commercial music was quickly derided by detractors, including progressive-soul, soul-purist, and rock proponents. White was doubly framed as an architect of the disco formula and as an artist who directly built his sound and image off of earlier Hayes. In the perceived shift from "progressive" to *regressive* (as Black Muzak, MOR, or easy listening), the trends outlined here illustrate an unstable reception of intertwined music whose success precariously balanced mass appeal and sales with—to echo critic Vernon Gibbs's criticism of Earth, Wind, and Fire moving from progressive to commercial—both gilded commercial allure and production gloss, and the finesse of inventive, eclectic productions and jazz-indebted instrumentalists who redefined and polished soul and funk.[12] Press descriptions frame White's orchestral excess as juxtaposed mixed-class, -race, -style, and -genre topics. These frictions are encapsulated in the tensions between the strings, the disco-era soul-funk-Latin rhythm section, and baroque-pop overtones (e.g., the harpsichord). Other readings were mixed in as well. For instance, critic Joe Nick Patoski opines that his "love of old movies" is the source of "much of the melodramatic [orchestral] effects of the White sound."[13] This filmic reading of the White extravaganza echoes interviews with the artist that emphasize his love of classical Hollywood cinema. He was likewise quoted often on plans to contribute music to, or act in, film productions. While the scoring of his music has little to do with the score idioms of his favorite films (e.g., music by Max Steiner, Alfred Newman, or Bernard Herrmann), the sonic stereotypes of Hollywood-style instrumentation do resonate with long-standing musical and visual glamour codes, and with such glamour codes in Black popular culture (and mass culture) in the 1970s. These codes are certainly activated by the LUO.

The LUO was a main part of White's live-performance draw. An entourage photographer reported "that teenage white girls tell [me] they come for the orchestra. 'They say they just like all that rich music.'"[14] The orchestra was popularly spotlighted in an instrumental medley introduction—similar to a main-title cue for a film?—and Patoski notes the conductor's observation that here often "The French horns get a rousing ovation."[15]

Less-enthusiastic critics echoed the sentiments of the UK's Bob Fisher, who, in 1974, argues that White's music is "decidedly middle-class, Black music, without any associated connotations."[16] This comment is made via observations of how White "took over" Hayes's territory *without* the hyper-masculine, racially charged, Black-power connotations. There are derogatory implications here against MOR, middle-class, cross-racial, homogenized popular culture. Such commentary implies that the big, orchestral production adds economic and filmic glamour without the distasteful, class-exclusive baggage of highbrow classical music. Part of this perception may tie into the juxtaposed musical topics as well as the functionality of the music for dance and personal soundtracking. All three areas are highlighted in American writer Harvey Kubernik's observation that "White's live attack is highlighted by lush strings, a wah-wah guitar and a throbbing percussion section. Perfect background music for sexual endeavors and the discotheques."[17]

The cocreator in White's sophistisoul was arranger Gene Page, who was five years older than White. Page has been mentioned across chapters 5 and 6, and he is an important "degree of separation" between generations of luxe-pop practice. Page became something of a mentor to White well before their LUO work. The two met in 1963 at a session for the L.A. duo, Bob and Earl, when they recorded the R&B hit, "Harlem Shuffle."[18] Page and White are credited as co-arrangers. As White could not write/read music notation, this was also the beginning of Page's functioning as what White calls his "unofficial transcriber." White describes Page as "one of the most educated black men in music."[19] Initially, Page had dreams to become a concert pianist (with studies at Brooklyn Conservatory of Music), but he turned to arranging, and by the early 1960s, he was an arranger for Frank Sinatra's Reprise Records.[20] He did do some Rat Pack arranging, such as his 1965 Reprise album work for Dean Martin.[21] His breakthrough, though, was as a stand-in for Jack Nitzsche on Spector's production for the 1964 Righteous Brothers hit, "You've Lost That Lovin' Feelin'." Along luxe-pop lineage, he worked with the Drifters, the Mamas and the Papas, Glen Campbell, Motown's Holland-Dozier-Holland, and others. In 1972, he was contacted by White for help on the debut single of the Love Unlimited trio. From there, according to his obituary, he "became an indispensable right-hand man, listening intently to White's ideas and directions, writing out charts . . . and helping him fashion his unique, symphonic soul sound."[22] He is quoted as saying that "Barry dictated, demonstrated, hummed out the parts. It was highly unorthodox, and it was also brilliant." And the two are said to have created "what some sexologists still define as a 'Barry boom'" in the 1970s population, with the "rhapsodic strings" arranged by Page being central to these "pillow-talk recordings." In his work for artists like Elton John, Natalie Cole, Aretha Franklin, the Four Tops, Lionel Ritchie, Whitney Houston, and others across the 1970s and 1980s, Page encapsulates a microcosm of luxe-pop practice.

Disco-era press on White and Page notes the shift from live-ensemble performances in the studio to the fragmentary modern multitrack process. Such concerns are painted neutrally, but press circa 1974–75 also includes an increasingly negative reception to the anonymity of the studio musician, the absence of musicians in the "performance" of recordings in discotheques, and the commercially calculated construction of the music. For instance, the UK critic Geoff Brown notes his frustration with not being able to find "the full facts concerning the more crucial instrumental contributions" on a White LP beyond the roles of White and Page.[23] Brown observes that

> One of the cornerstones of White's music is the guitar. . . . [But w]ho gets the credit? . . . Who is responsible? White wrote the songs and co-arranged, yet such is the style of MOR soul (suitable for funky Sainsburys [grocery stores] and hip hotel lounges) that it remains the guitarist's interpretations, I'd say, which gives life to the bones of White's ideas.
>
> Ah, reply Barry's defenders, but the chemistry . . . comes about by the interpretation of instrumentalists he's picked because they possess certain qualities. He identified the ingredients, he put them together, he blended them.[24]

Brown further notes there is nothing on this White album that "you have not heard before," adding "the songs have different titles but that . . . seems merely a token gesture." Likewise, part of Lombardi's cynical argument against White is that "he's interchangeable, like his music."[25] This string of commentary underscores white critical anxiety about the mixed stylistic levels in White's "formula," and rockist perceptions of the commonalities of commercial Black dance music.

In 1977, *Jet* published a surprisingly detailed general-public account of record production practice entitled "Big Barry White Mixes His Music for Lovers Only."[26] The title appears to refer to the 1952 Jackie Gleason *Music for Lovers Only* mood-music album discussed in chapter 4. This presumed reference to mood music and the connection of big-band-plus-strings production to a glamorous, imagined "player's" lifestyle is significant. Such themes tie into White's imagery on album covers and elsewhere, and *Jet*'s frequent coverage of his self-made-man success and glamorous lifestyle, among other topics.

The "Lover's Only" feature describes the artist as a musical and technological maestro. This characterization is illustrated through a photo spread of White conducting his orchestra and conducting engineers and musicians from behind the mixing board. The article tells readers that "White whips up his secret recipes in the control room of a recording studio. The main ingredients are music and love."[27] White typically worked in one of several Glendale, California, studios with engineer Frank Kejmar. White too refers to their production methods through analogies to formula. On Kejmar's postproduction multitrack mixing ("modulat[ing] every separate sound on the track"), White notes,

> "It's just like when he's working on a beautiful recipe for a salad. . . . He takes all kinds of ingredients. . . .
> "Bring them cellos in. . . ." Kejmar flips a switch, and the music swells to a crescendo. "Yes, Lord! now the strings. . . ." [. . . A] cascade of violins pour from the huge speakers. "Have mercy!" . . . And as the spool of tape unwinds, he stirs and blends the sounds into a pulsating entity.

Despite this reference to a "beautiful recipe," *Jet*'s coverage on White undercuts the negative associations of "formula" with an elevated, creative aura of his role as a "composer" and "conductor," alongside references to craftsmanship, and the smarts of a self-made businessman.

Throughout the article, White describes his process as a quest to achieve taken-to-church, near-spiritual epiphanies and his sense that his audiences will achieve similar experiences through the proxy of the recordings. This elusive spiritual ingredient is characterized by White as "love"—and, more specifically, romantic or sexual love—and he describes this element through gendered stereotypes, mass commercial intent, and production and instrumentation:

What I do with music is to put you in the mood for love. . . . I have to say to myself "what instruments put people in the mood?" Do you use a lot of horns and no strings? A lot of strings and no horns? Just rhythm? Just violins? My combination is [that] you need a little of all of it. . . .

. . . Women love strings, women love light instruments. . . . Now, there are women who love horns, but the majority . . . love violins; they're very sensitive to them. Men love horns. They're masculine, they're rich. . . . Horns represent the macho man. The rhythm—guitars, bass, drums and piano—that's the bed where you're gonna make love. . . .

. . . The horns—French horns, trombones, trumpets, flutes, saxophones— that's the man. Cellos, violas, violins, harp—that's the woman. Now you've got to put them together, because now they're really gonna make love! . . . They have to blend, to come together so that when the ear hears them, it automatically pleases you. . . . That puts you in the mood.[28]

Here, the opulent instrumentation "formula" that White employed— elements that inspired much negative (mostly white) commentary—was seen *positively* by the artist and the Black middle-class press as markers of artistic and business success. Central elements were further preconceived as a mood-music soundtrack for love making, with White's voice and the mixed-instrumentation being characterized as a surrogate for the dialogue and emotions of both partners. This commercial and artistic image was calculated. In a 1974 *Jet* article, White noted,

I did research from 1968 to 1970 on the industry, very closely watched it. I saw Motown fading out. I saw Gamble and Huff fading in. I saw Thom Bell come in. This is everyday studying, . . . being around a record player and a tape recorder constantly all day, just listening. You play it at different speeds, you listen to it at different hours of the day or night, you learn a lot of things.

. . . And when I put my concept together, we came with Love Unlimited's first album . . . a million seller . . . masterpiece. And I came again with Barry White['s solo albums]. I hit. I came again with [the LUO's] *Rhapsody In White*. . . . It's nothing but homework. [I] took care of my homework."[29]

The implications are that White followed the symphonic-soul multitrack practices developed at Motown and by Gamble, Huff, and Bell, among others. Under these practices, a foundational rhythm track is rehearsed, developed, and recorded first, followed by later tracking sessions for the orchestral sweetening, as well as further overdubbing for additional rhythm section and percussion contributions. From at least mid-1974 forward, based on master-tape evidence, White and Kejmar were working with two-inch, twenty-four-track technology.[30] In considering the formula, recipe, or DNA of the White sound, it is useful to dwell on both musical and technological creative practice, as technological choices were musical, and musical results are mediated by the technology in ways that build on both traditional pop and studio practices discussed across this book. And in articulating White's "recipe," it is further helpful to consider both his work in the studio, and in live contexts.

The development of a typical 1970s White multitrack arguably resembles the evidence of what was employed for "Can't Get" and "You're the First," or "Let the Music Play." The latter was released in early 1976, just after the arrival of mainstream disco following Donna Summer's "Love to Love You, Baby," among other contributors, but before the arrival of the December 1977 release of the juggernaut film, *Saturday Night Fever* (Paramount). "Let the Music Play" finds White adapting his earlier, proto-disco, sophistisoul sound to the crystalizing traits of disco as a genre.

While White claimed in 1974 that "Everybody thinks I'm either from Detroit, New York, or Philadelphia" (i.e., the key sophistisoul centers), he felt that his hometown of Los Angeles was central to his sound.[31] Like with Spector and the Beach Boys, White found L.A.'s studio musicians to be central to creating his music. He similarly relied on many of the same musicians from recording to recording. As implied, in source after source—albums, interviews, press, concert programs, and performance video footage—White's musicians remain largely anonymous. The albums simply credit White, the Love Unlimited vocal trio, and Page. That said, sources indicate that at various times he employed saxophonists Ernie Watts and Kenny Gorelick (later Kenny G), bassist Nathan East, and guitarists David T. Walker, Lee Ritenour, Melvin Ragin (a.k.a. Wah Wah Watson), Emmett North Jr., and Don Peake. He notes in a 1974 interview that "a lot of [musicians] in the string section they change," but points out that "we got the greatest horns and string sections . . . in Los Angeles because of the movies. . . . They get experience that no string players or horn players get exposed to elsewhere." On his rhythm section, he states: "I use four guitars, a bass, drums, myself, I play piano, harpsichord, electric piano. I do mostly all the over-dubbing, sometimes I play drums on my sessions. . . . Hey, we get down man. They don't go out on the road with me. The reason for that is number one, it would be too expensive. . . . A lot of producers in Los Angeles know who my musicians are and they use them all together, but they cannot get that [LUO] sound, they cannot get it to save your life."[32] On the difference between studio and live performances, White notes that "I use the same amount of musicians, maybe there's overdubbed instruments that I don't play in concerts live that I do in the studio but basically the sound is the same."[33]

THE LOVE UNLIMITED SOUND AND "HOW A DISCO RECORD IS MADE"

White's multitracks typically involve two vocal takes by White, and a similar two-take approach with Love Unlimited if female background vocals are included. These parts usually occupy the top tracks on the tapes, followed by the foundational rhythm section work. The latter includes configurations of the following:

- 3–4 tracks devoted to three guitars in distinct, interlocking parts, often with different instruments and effects (reverb, wah-wah, delay, slight distortion, etc.) and some variable sound spaces (e.g., direct-input, room space, and amplifier miking), and possibly also a "composite" guitar track;
- direct-input electric bass;
- a track devoted to hi-hat and snare; or two tracks, one with isolated snare, the other with hi-hat (and snare bleed);
- a kick-drum track;
- later recordings include a track for the toms; and
- one keyboard, often either piano or harpsichord played by White himself, recorded on two tracks for two-position/two-mic mixing options.

The orchestral sweetening sessions typically involve four strings tracks, with both high and low divisions doubly miked. The ensemble performed together, apparently with headphone monitoring for recording isolation. Individual tracks are devoted to the harp, French horn section, and woodwind section (combinations of solo flute, oboe, English horn, clarinets), each of which have playback-monitor bleed, suggesting either isolated overdubbing or an isolation room. Additional percussion tracks (for cowbell, congas, etc.) were also part of secondary production sessions. Lastly, White added further keyboard work—typically two tracks for another piano or harpsichord—to complement the foundational rhythm-section recordings. Small variations exist, of course, such as an added fourth guitar and "disco horns" track on the 1976 "Let the Music" multitrack. Despite the latter detail, this 1973–76 studio work overall avoids big-band (or jazz orchestra) instrumentation of saxophones, trumpets, and trombones. However, period video of the orchestra in performance shows prominent brass-and-reed ensemble additions, and these sections are readily heard doubling parts present in the studio recordings.

Evidence in 1970s live performance videos (on YouTube), as well as press coverage, suggests that White employed a live orchestra of forty to forty-five musicians, including flute, oboe/English horn, two or three French horns, harp, harpsichord, piano, electric bass, three guitars, a small percussion section (congas, glockenspiel, vibes, tympany, etc.), and one or two kit drummers. This list totals twelve to thirteen players outside the string ensemble. Studio and show-band strings typically have sixteen or twenty players, with twenty being a balance of twelve violins, four violas, four cellos (and no double basses for the disco orchestra because of the rhythm section). Based on the multitracks, I suspect that White employed a three-part division of violins 1 and 2, and the cellos. Additionally, the ensemble included White, the three female vocalists, and his conductor (an important visual element), along with White conducting. With White's multitracks, there is little punched-in overdubbing or bounce-down combinations of audio sources in tracks, but such editing does exist. Various recordings also include ambient sounds, following earlier models like Marvin Gaye's "What's Going On?" (e.g., the rain and street-life sounds in Love Unlimited's first hit, "Walkin' in the Rain with the One I Love," 1972). These elements are like cinematic staging, providing environmental ambience and social-dramatic context.

The Strings

The center of the LUO entertainment spectacle lies with the strings. The section is foregrounded in critical reception (with commentary like "got all those strings, all that orchestration," "lashings of strings," "layer upon layer of strings," etc.). One useful way to articulate the role of strings in both Barry White's music and 1970s disco "formula" is to consider this music in relation to present-day emulations of the disco production model. The digital sample and loop market is a context where string-focused arrangers provide track-ready audio for producers and DJs. One such collection is the "Disco House Sessions" loop pack by the UK company Loopmasters. Such loop libraries are targeted at producers who seek to emulate, as the website notes, the "classic 1970s sound" used in disco, house, "club," and the music of the Salsoul label. The collection is said to replicate "the classic sound and essence of disco . . .

before the avalanche of . . . manufactured disco-pop that followed," promising that it "takes you back . . . , recreating the sounds and flavours from seminal party places such as the Paradise Garage and Studio 54, where classic DJ's like Larry Levan would play . . . classics that . . . top[ped] the charts."[34] Such descriptions point to pre–*Saturday Night Fever* music that emerged first in discotheques, including Barry White. Another Loopmasters source is the Organic Loops "Disco Strings" pack produced by Pete Whitfield, a UK-based multi-string instrumentalist, arranger, and recordist.[35] The collection ranges "from soaring melodies to rhythmical stabs, heart wrenching to uplifting," with "tempos ranging from 106–130 beats per minute."[36] Whitfield outlines the core disco-string arranging principles in a "how-to" video.[37] The video, which starts with a shot of a Barry White release in a montage of famous disco album covers, tells viewers "what [strings] do [in disco] and how they do it." Whitfield remarks that "strings in disco have a bit of a reputation for being flamboyantly emotional." He then breaks down their applications to "runs, riffs, melodies, counter melodies, pads, textures and effects." Such distinctions are helpful for articulating the practices employed by White and Page with LUO, and the relation of that music to mainstream disco. Like White/Page, Whitfield's loop library uses the aforementioned three-part division. Outside of his countermelody example, nearly all of Whitfield's arrangement examples—like in the loop library—are homophonic sectional writing (with all parts moving in synchronized rhythmic motion) except for ornamental fill and run material in the high-register strings.

Whitfield explains that "runs are the drum fills of strings—they go up, they come down. They can be measured, or just a rush of notes. A run can pull the dynamic or intensity of an arrangement from one level to another, use a continuous scale, or stagger the movement." He provides audio and score examples for each case. As fills, like drum fills, runs are typically placed at the ends of sectional phrases, "pulling" you into the next phrase. Runs are widely used by White and Page. Examples 8.1 and 8.2 offer several examples, the most famous of which is seen in the glitzy two-bar run-flourish for violins and flute that instigates "Love's Theme" (8.1a). The run sets up the third-bar D-major key establishment of the track through a scalar A5–A4 octave-doubling, then working a thirty-second-note sequential pattern stepwise up a Mixolydian/dominant scale (with the exception of a final sequence shift from C to C♯) up to an A6–A5 doubling. The latter, held for two bars, acts as an ethereal high mark on the fifth of the tonic chord, which complements the arrival of the low tonic-note D octave in the cellos. This outer-register framing is like a stage curtain parting, leading listeners to focus on the material in between. In the middle, the violas and cellos play a harmonized, grooving riff that moves from the suspension of an A-major dominant to the resolution of a tonic D major. This is answered by a restatement of the riff in the next bar by a clean electric guitar, which first stabs a high-octave D dyad with a downward glissando at the end of the previous bar. Mitchell Morris observes that these two bars are "the moment the groove begins to materialize," "establish[ing] a primary unit of organization (2 + 2 bars)."[38] Morris remarks that the "classicizing musical figuration" of this flourish recollects "an endless series of similar gestures in cinematic music," evoking memories of "the overture to a film by RKO Pictures or 20th Century Fox." While this flourish sets the listener's expectations for a sweet soul track, it also propels the music forward in a manner that invites dancers to the dance floor. What is heard in this track, to echo Peter Shapiro's characterizations of Gamble-and-Huff sophistisoul, is a soul shift from urban music to *urbane* music.[39] Both Morris and Shapiro identify the sophistisoul sound as a musical symbol of Black capitalism, and Morris specifically describes White's music as the "sound of wealth."[40] While "Love's Theme" dominated both the soul/R&B and Hot 100 charts, it also spent several weeks at the top of *Billboard*'s Easy Listening chart across early 1974. Thus, urbane commercial pop maps on to other MOR associations ranging from smooth, suave, and polite to bland—that is, Black Muzak.

Example 8.1b shows an extended passage from the string underscoring for the 1974 "Can't Get Enough," which displays the lush string-run sweeps and swoops that quickly became standard in disco. As Whitfield implies, such textures function similar to forward-propelling drum fills that mark sectional divisions and escalate intensity. These are also central to Whitfield's characterization of disco strings as "flamboyantly emotional." Shapiro's discussion of "Love's Theme" concerns how DJs in New York's Fire Island gay discotheque scene championed the track "months before it was played on the radio, making it 'the first "disco" record to become a #1 hit.'"[41] Shapiro describes it as "the perfect disco record" in its "unabashed celebration of 'beauty' and its lushness and its complete willingness to go over the top in . . . its strings." He finds the record's "groove" to be "somehow at once the least funky thing" while being "redolent of sex" and "utter lasciviousness." This hallmark of a "flamboyantly emotional," or queered, sensibility with kitsch sexual overtones of "lushness" is announced in these extravagant string runs and flourishes. Michael Long points particularly to such "take-off" gestures in disco introductions—a tradition influenced by this track. Long also

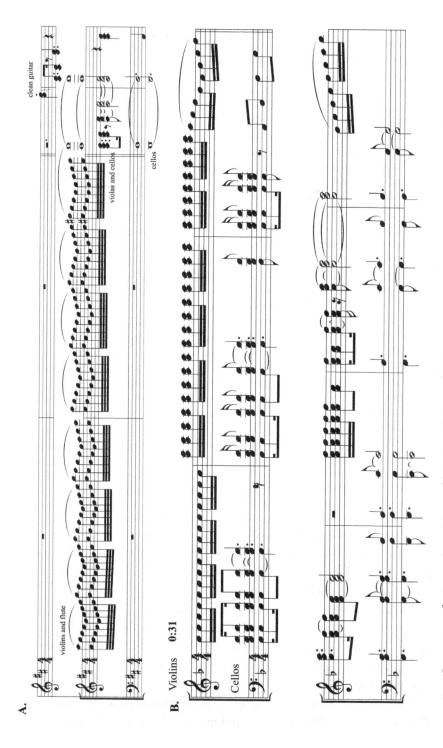

EX. 8.1. Comparison of string section writing in: (a) The Love Unlimited Orchestra, "Love's Theme," excerpt from 0:00; and (b) Barry White and the Love Unlimited Orchestra, "Can't Get Enough of Your Love, Babe," excerpt from 0:16.

EX. 8.2. Barry White and the Love Unlimited Orchestra, "You're the First, the Last, My Everything." (Timings are from the 1974 album release of this track.)

frames this as part of disco's "registers of the gay vernacular." Like Morris, he suggests a "pop-cinematic model" for the song orchestration, pointing to similarities with Percy Faith's easy-listening, string-centric scorings of film-music themes in the manner of Muzak.[42] What these descriptions do is place the music within the audience reception of various white audience segments, straight or queer. That said, in relation to the Hayes/"jazz"/Soulful Strings questions of the previous chapter, and below in terms of Black middle-class celebrity culture, there are justifications for mapping MOR entertainment glitz, glamour, and middlebrow adjacency onto the aspirational consumerism of the Black middle class.

Whitfield observes that disco string "riffs" are "typically repetitive, partial melodies, providing rhythmic drive and maybe a bit of a hook," and that

EX. 8.3. Barry White and the Love Unlimited Orchestra, "You're the First, the Last, My Everything." Excerpts: (a) 1:26; and (b) 1:52. (Timings are from the 1974 album release of this track.)

"in disco, . . . syncopated, and chromatic movement is common." He offers an example (at 1:35 in the video) that is remarkably close to the opening strings in "You're the First." In this latter track's introduction, the pizzicato, three-part strings leap over a fifth in a horn-call-like gesture that shifts in beat accentuation over two bars. This happens in parallel with low piano, building up to a three-octave texture with a final orchestral heightening of flute and French horns. A varied repeat then ends with a two-beat neighbor-note response figure (repeated) that has the function of a "fill" string run (underscored by White's black-and-white-key, hand-slap, downward piano glissandi). Example 8.3b shows the horn and flute parts from an interlude that reemploys the riffs from this introduction.

Example 8.1b shows an internal-scoring riff in the cellos of "Can't Get Enough" (see second stave). The cellos present a common use of a static harmonic voicing as a rhythmic riff. Harmonically, it is a pad; rhythmically, the riff propels the music forward with the repeated violins' sixteenth notes on C4, then jumping an octave to a C5-A4 dyad before giving way to a dipping sixteenth-note run (with an upward cello counterpoint run). This leads into a harmonized string statement of thematic material (soon tied to the lyric "My darling, I"). Here, the strings offer dual-function scoring, with the octave-jump violin move adding flamboyant intensity.

Whitfield emphasizes the melodic functions of strings in disco, noting that they "are enormously versatile, so melodies can be sweet and simple, or agile, fragmented, and ever changing." They also shift from melody to countermelody "when it's responding to another featured line." While such details "will probably be less complex," he adds that "high, soaring countermelodies are very common." Example 8.2, from "First," shows an exemplary White/Page swooping strings countermelody. Lushly scored as a monophonic, harmonized melodic line over three octaves, the countermelody ebbs and flows in wave-like response behind the "calls" of the vocal melody. There are plenty of held, pad-like notes, as well as note accentuations that involve additional grace notes or upward-sweeping glissandi to highlight vocal delivery. This can be seen in the sweep that leads into the high-tessitura E5 of "my guiding star" (performed with vocal stress and strain).

Whitfield observes that the use of strings as harmonic pads "provide[s] some glue in an arrangement," by employing a "simple, legato texture, while other busy stuff goes on." He cautions that "a pad shouldn't draw attention to itself, but stay clear behind the featured lines." These practices have a long history in dance-band background arranging, whether strings, reeds, or both. Such pads were seen in bars 3–4 of "Love's Theme," as well as the first seven bars of "Can't Get Enough" (in Example 8.1b), which combine legato harmonic support with an unobtrusive countermelody in the top line of the homophonic strings. Above the latter, White rumbles a bedroom rap about making sweet love, with the guitar and strings adding small responsorial interjections above the groove laid down by the closed hi-hat. Various motivic materials first appear in the arrangement here.

Whitfield also notes that disco strings "have a bag full of interesting effects to play with. . . . There are pull-downs, tremolo, trills, slides. Articulations make a big difference too." While there is little use of trills, Examples 8.1–8.3 offer a variety of these arranging ornaments, such as the rapid-iteration tremolo in the violins in 8.1b (from "Can't Get Enough"), as well as the grace-note slurs and glissandi in 8.2 and the shifting accents of the foregrounded strings that perform in unison with the flute and horn transcribed in Example 8.3b (both from "First").

In this sea of orchestral spectacle, White and Page further add topical colors from concert music, chiefly flute, oboe and English horn, and French horns. As in Example 8.3b (from "First"), these instruments are commonly scored for brief melody and countermelody fragments, and as color augmentations for string lines. By contrast, the harpsichord (a layover from psychedelic soul) was typically overdubbed by White after the initial rhythm section session. His piano work is strictly on-the-beat, rhythmic chordal comping supplemented by root-based, or minimally walking, bass lines. The whole sits largely in the bass-clef register. In the octave above this, on the offbeat second quarter note, he adds the harpsichord's held, arpeggio-phrased, one-octave triad voicings with brief grace notes.

There are luxe-pop elements here that share a pop lineage with the materials discussed in the last chapters, dating back through progressive soul, to baroque pop, to Brill Building pop, to Lieber and Stoller and Spector (and then further back). The dramatic excess of the textures just described—their over-the-top nature—also suggest elements of Long's classical register or classicistic musical figurations. While these elements offer an instrumental spectacle that in part evokes orchestral spectacle (whether cinematic or concert-music), it is the *massing* spectacle—whether virtual (recorded) or live performance—that listeners locate this spectacle in. Despite the classical-associative ghost, what an audience indulges in is luxe orchestral glitz and glamour. Patoski's 1975 account of a White performance captures this orchestral glitz perfectly:

> Sid Garris co-manages White and conducts the Orchestra on the road. A pipe smoking gray haired gentleman. . . . "You know," he says, "a lot of these young people at the concerts have never heard or seen a French horn. They cheer almost as loud as for Barry when they hear it. We don't talk down to them like a classical symphony, but play what they relate to. It's like a jewelry store. When they show the finest diamond, it's not with all the other rings in the display window. It's all alone on some nice black velvet. Barry's funk is the velvet."[43]

Patoski adds: "His music is pretty, almost syrupy and, easy to grasp, with soaring strings that reach a crescendo as predictable as the sunrise. The words are simple and sweet, a . . . clichéd Romanticism, babe. . . . It is Stravinsky with snap, Mantovani you can move to. The clincher is of course the half rap, half baritone soul shout that has too often triggered the perfunctory Son of Isaac comparisons."[44]

Stravinsky might be a bit too far, but Patoski captures the reception of White's sophistisoul as spectacular glitzy, urbane easy listening. For some, this is a positive spin on the cultural-decline nightmares of Dwight Macdonald about "breaking down . . . barriers of class, tradition, and taste, dissolving all cultural distinctions," "scrambl[ing] everything together," and refusing "to discriminate against or between anything."[45] The postwar American boom in spectacular, glitzy musical entertainments—luxe pop, the scores of widescreen Cinerama films and television, Las Vegas casino and nightclub floorshows, etc.—echo this early 1960s critique about cultural homogenization, whether such manifestations were aspirational middlebrow, middlebrow-adjacent, or glitz. The connection of the White/Page sound to the music of Hollywood showbiz is unmistakable across the 1970s and 1980s, with numerous soundtrack emulations. As Patoski notes already in 1975, "Love's Theme" set "an international standard heard on commercials, news shows, movie themes, on television, on black grit soul radio and bland MOR Easy Listening stations alike."[46] And White and LUO further hold a long list of film and television credits from 1974 to present.[47] Often these hits act out the sexual and romantic fantasies of (typically white) characters, just as White promoted the social function of his music.

The Voice

Beyond its soul-meets-Mantovani qualities, this music's luxe kitsch—meaning a matter of questionable taste due to excessive garishness and sentimentality, but potentially appreciated in an ironic way—also depends upon the Voice and White's particular lyrics and bedroom vocal raps. As seen in Example 8.2, White's two vocal tracks reveal subtle improvised variations between them. The final mix involves a composite that shifts between both tracks and combinations that harmonize with each other. (The bedroom-inclined guttural groans and breaths that many critics comment on are complemented by other aural-physical multitrack artifacts—the heaviness of a large man breathing, for example—that suggest not all of White's aural-physicality was suitable for enhancing his passionate image.) Responding to the "controversy" of the White versus Hayes "sound-alike" criticism, White "growled" that "Isaac Hayes has a baritone voice. I have a *bass* baritone voice. That puts me a whole octave lower than him."[48]

The sensuality of the Voice is central to much press. In 1974, one reviewer notes, "It's likely that his biggest percentage of fans come from girls between 18 and 30. It's that voice . . . [that] gets them, that low sensual growl and those crawling lyrics."[49] Lombardi also asked straight, white male fans "what they liked about Barry and received replies like this: 'I just listen to his voice.'"[50] On the difference between disco-era, sophistisoul White, and earlier crooner models, Lombardi observes: "The man has a very effective voice, and were he to sing more—hold notes, sustain lines, build his songs—he might succeed *as a singer* in the non-rock, MOR territory he's staked out. Barry White could very well be a kind of ballsy, soulful Nat 'King' Cole. But he doesn't sing. He keeps threatening to sing. You feel he's on the verge of singing."[51] What writers describe as White's "mumbling" raps and singing actually enhanced the sexual innuendo. One writer notes, for instance, that "as he growled and murmured in distinctive basso profundo, the scenes of [female] adulation grew."[52] This voice is said to lie "exactly half way between the . . . crooner and the aggressive stud," feeding into "the subconscious needs and hopes of a mass female audience."[53] But discourse also emphasizes White's *non-threatening* sexuality—through his self-image as a spiritual-sexual guru, his happily married family man image, or his heavy-set physicality as a sex symbol. Robert Christgau, for instance, commented that "the man's commonness is as monumental as his girth, and that's no insult," and that "it took real creative will to shape *Reader's Digest* virtues and that face and body into a sex symbol."[54]

The Rhythm Section

In White's productions, the rhythm section tracks—including percussion and guitar overdubs—infuse the whole with residual elements from progressive soul. As some proponents argue, despite the lavish exterior, the "percussively powerful" rhythm section "makes nonsense of all those 'Black Muzak' jibes."[55] Example 8.2, from "You're the First," illustrates this practice. The drums emphasize the disco four-on-the-floor beat, but by way of intermediate ghost notes on the "and" of each beat. This eighth-note pulse creates a sense of urgency. The bass drum emphasizes 1 and 4, while snare cracks emphasize backbeats 2 and 4. An open high-hat turns the bar-long groove around on the "and" of 4. The drums are predominantly isolated, but with guitars 1 and 2 bleeding in through the snare and hi-hat tracks. As expected with a dance track, the drum part is basically a straight repeat of this pattern with occasional accenting such as the ensemble unison emphasis that underscores White's passionate final syllables on the "one-and" beat closing "That's what YOU ARE!" Following the stop-time break (1:27ff.), the drummer opens the next verse with simple snare and splash cymbal interjections before returning to the basic groove. In sum, the drums firmly maintain the basic groove as "a seething rhythmic torrent with a zipping bubbling backbeat."[56]

The remaining rhythm-section instruments on "You're the First" were the three guitars, electric bass, and White's piano. The guitar parts nicely layer with complementary functions. The third guitar track, the foundation, is likely a humbucker guitar (Gibson?) set to neck pickup (a mellower sound), using direct-input or a close-miked amp, with clean tone and dry signal. This player comps the harmonic changes, but often avoids roots by emphasizing 3-5-7 chord tones, building a core groove. This is enhanced often through a ghost note on the "and" of beat 4. The second guitar track is brighter, and likely a single-coil guitar (Fender?) using the bridge (lead) pickup for a bright tone. This tone heightens the guitar's accentuated stabbing chords, which use a full, dry signal. This is tightly interlocked with the first part, which often stabs dyads. The first guitar track is effect focused, and likely uses the then-brand-new Roland Space Echo tape unit (Roland RE-201, introduced 1974). The echo reiteration is tightly synchronized with the track tempo. Underneath, the active, syncopated bass part propels the groove. It is notably more complicated than the heavy-handed piano comping (by White). While the piano bangs away at the beat and harmony, the bass is not always within harmony on a given beat, arriving on roots sometimes ahead of the down-beat. The color of the bass, with its crisp pick attack, is direct-to-board and flat sounding (as in Motown practice). The live-bleed audio artifacts on the piano tracks and one of the snare tracks suggest that there was another bass line (largely root based) altogether in the original session. Either this earlier performance was strictly for the first tracking session, played live in the room, or the original bass track was wiped in favor of the later, more-active, groove-focused bass line (likely recorded at same session).

Brass and Reeds

The above account suggests that very little jazz/jazz-luxe legacy from pro-gressive soul is part of White's sophistisoul. As noted, though, in mid-1970s performances, a brass/reeds section, however small, can be seen. It seems that the onstage practices of the LUO were informed more by the entertainment models seen across this book (e.g., show bands, variety-model big bands) than highbrow philharmonic orchestras, even though that latter discourse is invoked (as it was in prior luxe-pop history). Nonetheless, the identifiable White rhythm-section players largely come from R&B, soul, funk, and gospel backgrounds. These areas are also White's developmental milieu. These sidemen—top studio musicians—were expected to subdue virtuosity in favor of the greater commercial whole (to echo the aforementioned critique by Gibbs about Earth, Wind and Fire). Similarly, through production reliance on brevity and familiarity (again paraphrasing Gibbs), White chose to abandon much from the jazz legacy that progressive soul foregrounded. While such choices moved some critics to hear "safe" "Black Muzak" in these string-heavy productions, such characterizations are too reductive, as the White ensemble often had progressive groups like the Ohio Players as their opening act.[57]

The Process

White's development process resonates closely with period descriptions of disco production practice. In 1978, CBS News broadcast an investigative report, "Disco," on their news program, *60 Minutes*. The reason for this unprecedented news-program attention to disco is the bottom line: money. The pursuit of money—commercialism—is central to the critiques against "formula" and the perceived downward slide of White's music away from "progressive" ideals toward "Muzak." Money is a repeated motif throughout the CBS segment, which underscores the unparalleled financial success of disco five months after the release of *Saturday Night Fever*. Act two of the report is a five-minute edutainment montage of "how a disco record is made." This first segment focuses on the producer/singer-songwriter Peter Brown and the singer Betty Wright in their studio session for the 1978 hit, "Dance with Me." The segment explains multitrack recording, highlighting the artificiality behind "the illusion that most of us [have] . . . that a large group of musicians and singers gathers in a studio to record a song." Despite noting that most modern pop is based on multitrack production, the emphasis on artificiality—in the context of emphases on superficiality in disco culture— winkingly imply to the mass audience that it is not "real" music, but banal, factory-assembled product built entirely to generate money off of a mass trend.

The "business" implications of the mass-culture-meets-class-culture dichotomy in the LUO's promotion are observed in the music of the news segment. After remarking that "for disco to be a disco, you need a very heavy bass [drum] beat," the host, Dan Rather, explains that "the bass drum and other percussion have already been recorded [and] so have the strings, believe it or not, of the New York Philharmonic, . . . all done on other occasions." Viewers see a guitarist add his chord-stab overdub, while the popping bass is heard as part of the completed tracks. As a pianist noodles through variations on a riff for overdubbing, Rather again underscores business—the label, T. K. Records, is said to have "seven and one-half million dollars in gross disco sales a year." This framing implies that the incessant beat and the irresistibly sweet strings are primary selling points, so much so that such a classy institution as the New York Phil would moonlight on background session work. (The single's label makes no reference to this connection; likely, the association is merely string players who have performed with the organization.[58]) The segment also highlights various Svengali- (or Spector-?) type traits that White as a producer also routinely foregrounds in his press coverage. With the "Dance with Me" track, while providing clunky explanations of how "Peter directed" the sessions, Brown is just seen casually grooving in the background, occasionally pointing his finger or shouting "you got it!" The Wright overdubs are a highlight. They jump from the first-layer "gotta keep on making me high" to her second and third grooving harmonies being built up, thereby—again—underscoring the simple, repetitive, groove-focused nature of disco production. This gives the impression, as is stated at the segment's end, that this process is simply "easy money." White's detractors similarly emphasize production polish as a means to easy-money commercialism.

Rather tells his audience that a multitrack session is "only the first step" in making a hit. The segment then turns to a session with the producer-arranger John Ferrara, founder of the label Discomania, who observes that the "job at this stage [of developing his track, "Mi amore,"] is mixing twenty-four tracks . . . into a finished product that will defy you to keep from moving to the dance floor." We learn that he has "invited disc jockeys from prominent New York clubs to listen and advise" and that "mixing is a particularly . . . laborious process . . . almost like composing on the spot." He is heard instructing the engineer to drop "everything out," and bring up the bass drum, adding, "This is going to be our focal point, everything is going to be based around the bass drum, right? . . . Get it as hot and pulsating as we can." (Would any disco producer have to say this in 1978?) As parts come in, and DJ and producer exchanges ensue, all start grooving in mixing room—then the segment segues to an ecstatic floor full of polyester-clad dancers, a disco ball, and lights at a disco called New York, New York.

Recall the 1977 *Jet* magazine overview of White's production practice. I noted how production and instrumentation mapped onto what he described as his "beautiful recipe for a salad," or dance floor hit, with his gendered stereotypes of how the balance of instrumentation and mix allowed his music to achieve cross-gender, cross-race, cross-sexuality mass-commercial success. This cliché of a hit recipe is central to White's discourse. In a 1975 *Black Music* article, Cummings notes the same disco-formula ingredients in White that Rather describes with general disco production. Cummings suggests that in White's recordings "the momentum is positively unstoppable. White's special trick is his ability to set the richest, lushest string[s] . . . against an incredibly hard and loud percussion track," which includes the "spurting guitar licks and the relentless snapping drums."[59] Here are White's gendered-instrumentation tensions. This formula equally carries urbane/street, Black/white/Latino, high-middle/low, glitz-glamour/cool, nouveaux-riche/aspirational, straight/queer sustained tensions that are central to disco's core democratic cultural ethos. Such readings of White's music (and he encouraged this) are seen in Lombardi's *Rolling Stone* story, where White's industry impact is said to bridge "party-partying" at the discos, radio saturation, exponential sales, MOR aesthetics, and the "lush, romantic, biracial, bisexual" qualities that fueled the "disco sucks!" movement of 1979.

GLAMOUR AND LIFESTYLES
OF THE RICH AND FAMOUS

In building a multivalent cultural reading of sophistisoul-disco through White, insights can also be gleaned from relevant celebrity coverage in *Jet* and *Ebony*. A typical cover story can be seen in a 28 June 1973 *Jet* article that offered "A Visit with Isaac Hayes and His Bride." The photos and captions say much about interests in Hayes as a social figure—we are shown the couple "relaxing in their Memphis home," where "the handsome pair sunbathe in [their] pool," "outfitted in sporting attire." They are shown leaning "on their gold-plated Cadillac which cost more than $26,000," and readers are told that "a chauffeur-driven limousine, a [Lincoln Continental] Mark IV and two Jaguars complete their collection of automobiles." Another photo depicts "the Black composer serenad[ing] his wife . . . before trying to match wits with her in a game of chess." Outside of shots of Hayes in dashiki robes (symbolizing an affiliation with Black empowerment), each photo also features the attractive couple in glamorous 1970s Black fashion "relaxing" at home. In text and image, Hayes is presented as a powerful businessman with "a cluster of gold and platinum records, Grammy Awards, plaques and citations." Sewing all this together is a portrait of the couple as upright, model, moral citizens with a healthy relationship (both sexual and as friends and life partners who would "like two children")—even despite mentions of Hayes's ex-wife and huge alimony payments. When not massaging her husband (two photos), Mignon (his wife), described as one of Memphis's "privileged few," it is reported, "divides her time between tennis, horseback riding and skydiving." Her "marble-sized diamond ring and . . . jewelry that Hayes has showered his new bride with are indication enough of his love."[60] The article is followed by an advertisement for the double-album *Isaac Hayes Live at the Sahara Tahoe*, with the "Black Moses" image of bare-chested Hayes in his classic gold-chain vest.

The 22 August 1974 *Jet* cover story, "Barry White Raps about His New Wife, New Life," again foregrounds the luxe-upgrade trophy wife and life of an upstanding model of Black manhood, monogamy, and citizenry. This amply illustrated, nine-page story highlights the same economically aspirational, classy-lifestyle clichés as the Hayes article. The couple is shown "surveying" their one-acre Sherman Oaks "suburban" home with "swimming pool in the back yard." They plan to "remodel and add a golf putting green, volleyball court and . . . a complete recording studio." He is described as "big, brainy and Black: Texas-born, California-reared and worldly-wise." His rags-to-riches story is recounted at length, with detail on his youthful decision to turn from an impoverished life of crime and street gangs to become a self-invented, self-educated businessman. The article underscores that since White "walked away from his precarious past, he has made a positive and prosperous future," listing his work as a "successful composer, arranger and producer," the owner of record and production companies, a film music composer, and a celebrated audio engineer and "developer" of hit acts, as well as his achievement of "the sales of $16 million records last year." The article frames this success via his "establishment"-grounded moral life, marriage, and monogamy as opposed to "today's permissive society, characterized by . . . experimentation with . . . open marriage, homosexual marriage, communal marriage and shacking up." White admits "I am old-fashioned—that's my brand." Married fourth of July in Las Vegas to Glodean (a member of Love Unlimited), White grounds his union in 1970s pop philosophy as a "musical marriage [that] leads to spiritual, physical union." The magazine places great value on his role as a welcoming father to her children alongside his own previous four children. We see full images of their "spacious and handsomely decorated living room," which is said to be "a real conversation piece for guests." Their "spacious master bathroom" is also of interest. We see images of the talented children, White conducting business, White in the happy role as father, and so on. He is described as a "buddha," meaning both physically and spiritually, particularly as his life philosophy is meant to "inspire their children." We further see Glodean posing with her toy poodle beside his Mark IV (with the plate "MO-SOUL"), and hear of White's philanthropy plans for a "boys town" for troubled youth (which he accomplished) that includes a horse ranch (one of his hobbies) and recording studio.[61]

Morris's study on 1970s "black masculinity and the sound of wealth" articulates insights into "instrumental glitz," "black Masculinity trans- formed" and "black capitalism and the business of black music," among other themes for much of the music and culture discussed here.[62] The pres- ent chapter adds a complementary, historically and analytically documented reception study of both these luxe musical sounds (the formula) and Black middle-class, celebrity-focused aspirational values in the 1970s. The above accounts of two of the many *Jet* and *Ebony* lifestyle, glamour, and moral- model articles on White and Hayes underscore the abundant social under- currents in the *positive* Black middle-class reception of these artists. What is observed is a Black journalistic equivalent to the 1980s aspirational, voyeu- ristic television show, *Lifestyles of the Rich and Famous*. The theme music for this show—with its disco beat, Latin bongos and deep funky bass, lush string theme, dual wah-plus-scratch-rhythm guitars, enriched horn-section responses, and English horn countermelody—is a direct commercial distil- lation of "TSOP" and "Love's Theme." The white film composer-arranger Bill Conti (also composer of the 1976 *Rocky* film score) wrote this music for a 1979 film. With *Lifestyles*, the main-title cue fades in about halfway into the track during a brassy bridge that leads to an all-out scoring of a third cho- rus statement. A voiceover describes the show's "unchallenged authority on wealth, prestige, and success," and its focus on "the stars of show business and big business" and how "life's winners live, love, and spend their fortune." The voice promises to show viewers "their dazzling world of luxury on privileged tours of the[ir] fantasy palaces." You see shots of a beautiful, classy lady on the hood of a Rolls Royce, bedazzling jewelry, tropical homes with lavish pools, a gold setting for a banquet, a luxury speedboat, champagne, and so on, all before the entry of the posh British tones of host Robin Leach. Here is the beating, enviable heart of the celebrity lifestyle culture that luxe pop came to underscore in the postwar years. Such excess was central to the backlash against disco and the shift away from luxe production textures.

Period writings amply emphasize that, like much of the music discussed in this book, a core production value in White's music—recorded or live—is its orchestral excess. The centrality of this *luxe-excess entertainment aesthetic* is captured in a 1975 *Melody Maker* announcement for performances of the "Barry White Extravaganza." This was an abbreviated tour due to the "high costs involved" in bringing White's "15-strong entourage—including his Spiritual Adviser!," Love Unlimited, and a "45-piece orchestra."[63] The idea of a *production extravaganza*—whether on stage and in recording—is key to this promotion. Live, the ensemble was augmented by an impressive number of "musicians dressed in black tie and tails" with "balding [white] conductor in a white kimono." *Melody Maker* describes the theatrics in alignment with commentary cited above—here, the entrance of the voice is said to be enhanced by violins that "tremble" and horns that "bleat." Size matters. This "big" luxe image has been observed throughout this chapter, but descriptions of two presentation images can help to concretize this. The first is the LUO's 1974 appearance on *The Midnight Special* (NBC) performing "Can't Get Enough."[64] In the opening of the performance, the camera regularly pans across the expansive orchestra, with its hyperactive kimono-clad conductor and musicians in subdued black-and-white, suit-and-tie dress. The whole is framed by immense overhead orange neon lights spelling out the artist's name, and an elegant, stage-front white grand piano available for maestro White. The heart of the spectacle though is White, who appears in a Vegas-meets-boudoir, bedazzled, pink-orange smoking jacket, with gold sequined overlays, immense lapels, and paisley sparkling rhinestone patterns. This is coupled with a pink turtleneck and red-polyester leisure pants. In combination with his multiple sparkling rings, chunky gold watchband, significant physical presence, and his straightened, slicked-back signature mid-1970s coiffure (Lombardi describes this as a "grown out Gertrude Stein hairdo falling in giant swoops"),[65] he suggests a Black, glamour-inclined masculinity that meets Hugh Hefner and Liberace midway. His press photos and filmed performances display numerous variations on this.

The midcentury-masculine/queered-kitsch pairing in this image was likely intentional and was perceived in different ways by his mixed audience. White further told *Jet* that "his music reflects the two sides of what manhood ought to be: 'The power side—I am very domineering in business and music,' which manifests itself in the rhythm of his music; [and] 'the sensitive side of me are the strings.'"[66] Lombardi attempted to explain the queered appeal: "Among gays . . . Barry works in two ways, too. Sophisticated types . . . appreciate his campiness. His stuff is funny without meaning to be." White "also provides gays with a 'romantic' hetero image that is so grotesque it's easy to ridicule, even though the ridicule may be unconscious—Barry is a *caricature* romantic hero."[67] From a hetero, white perspective, Cummings argues both that "White is the 1975 embodiment of a popular music tradition of singing sex/romance super-heroes which began with Sinatra and continued through Presley and Jagger," and that unlike the "slightly menacing figure of Isaac Hayes, the rotund figure of Barry White represents no real sexual threat . . . to the women, or to their men. . . . Maybe that's why White superseded Hayes."[68] Such commentary reflects 1970s sexuality prejudices against plus-sized individuals, but this perceived desexing of 1970s Black filmic hypermasculinity was part of white critical perspectives, as when one critic comments that White's "dress . . . is more slick Vegas styled than pimp flash."[69] But the same critic saw a *classy glamour* such that "you'd think it was either Sinatra or Elvis from the women in heat jammed against the stage. Cigarette in hand, White is debonair as if he was in a dim lit cabaret instead of a hockey rink."[70] This is the White in the *Midnight Special*.

White was further complemented by Love Unlimited, who appeared in fashionable, glamorous evening wear, with sparkling glitter and prominent afros. Part of the gendered and sexual juxtapositions of White and the vocal trio, can be seen in the cover to the LUO's first album, *Rhapsody in White*, a title that juxtaposes the artists who gave the world "Love's Theme" against their luxe-pop progenitor, George Gershwin's rhapsody. Note the contextual updating however on this album image (Figure 8.1): White, the trio, and an even more svelte Black model pose in sun-dappled, upscale West Coast architectural modernism by the reflecting pools at the Mark Taper Forum of the Los Angeles Music Center (the 1967 L.A. response to Lincoln Center). While those in the know would make this site connection, I suspect that the modern architectural framing might be seen as a generic modern, travertine-toned cultural temple (similar to Lincoln Center and the Metropolitan Opera), replete with female muses, against a background easily recognized as L.A. Such a reading conveys volumes about the supposed wealth and taste of White at the center of the image, foregrounding Black masculinity. With White's streetwise tan leather suit jacket, brown slacks, and tan Italian loafers, alongside the Hollywood-glamorous, white-clad ladies posing behind (like a Black reinvention of statuesque Ziegfeld girls), the image demands to be read as

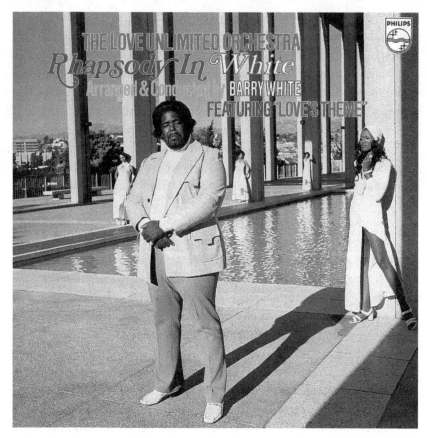

FIG. 8.1. Cover of the Love Unlimited Orchestra, *Rhapsody in White*, 1973.

simultaneously streetwise and upscale, an L.A. analogue to John Shaft, who commands attention in high-class (not necessarily high-culture) environs.

The juxtapositions—of race, sexuality, socioeconomic and cultural class, and era—echo Lombardi's characterization of White as the "Billy Jack of Disco." This backhanded compliment references the low-budget, woodenly acted independent film *Billy Jack*, a box office failure in its 1972 release, but a hit when rereleased in 1973. The film tells the story of a "peace-loving" ex-Vietnam vet. The *New York Times* calls it a "a low-budget fusion of counterculture piety and martial-arts violence that . . . became a prototype for independent filmmaking."[71] The comparison of White and the film functions on several levels. Firstly, as the rerelease of *Billy Jack* "caused Hollywood to rethink its approach to releasing films," White's emergence as a star via the influence of discos rather than radio foreshadowed significant music-industry changes in 1974. Second, Lombardi's analogy underscores the lack of music-critic love for White amid his near-universal audience appeal. The *Times* notes the film's original "tepid reviews" based in part upon its genre mish-mash "amalgam" of film "archetypes." As observed, White was routinely criticized for his supposed reliance on derivative formulas based on amalgam materials from better models. *Billy Jack*'s moral message and caricature protagonist likewise might be perceived as pop-culture parallels to White's caricatured image as a sex symbol and a purveyor of universal love. Lastly, while White unexpectedly conquered the mid-1970s music industry in near tandem with the film's underdog success, the broadly wrought kitsch of both White's extravaganza show and his media image, fashion-sense, and packaging may have resonated with over-the-top, but generically middle-of-the-road aspects of *Billy Jack*. Nonetheless, both meant a great deal to many, many people.

The aspirational framing of White's coverage in *Jet* and *Ebony* reflects real-world socioeconomic politics in Black middle-class culture. For instance, in March 1973, a Waldorf-Astoria Hotel Bankers convention speech from *Jet* publisher John H. Johnson was quoted at length as an editorial. Johnson argues against the damage he sees in a Black "politics of poverty," and underscores that the "greatest fight today is for the greater participation in the economic abundance" of the USA, adding that "many blacks...in the central city are middle class people with no desire to move to the suburbs."[72] The juxtaposition of such editorial commentary alongside these magazines' aspirational interests in White illustrates the importance of the middle-class politics of Black respectability, which are central to the *Rhapsody in White* cover and nearly every facet of White's presentation. This is a matter of respectability on the terms of 1970s Black American culture and values, and it reflects a particular class-culture-race filtering that results from White having risen above his impoverished, Black Los Angeles origins in the pre–civil rights era to join the city's glamorous celebrity classes in the post–civil rights 1970s.

CONCLUSION: THE POLITICS OF RESPECTABILITY,
EXCELLENCE, AND EXTRAVAGANZA

A 2018 Coachella festival extravaganza by the pop queen, Beyoncé, prompted a *New York Times* opinion piece by Myles Johnson on the potential "end of respectability politics." Johnson articulates the long "oppression" of the "performance of respectability," by which he means "the policing of black people's behavior and appearance to better appeal to white people." He defines this as a negotiation strategy where "parts" of Black culture that are "underappreciated, disrespected or misunderstood by white people" have often been tempered for "majority-white audience[s]" to make "it easier to forget cultural differences."[73]

The purported smoothing of the rough edges of Black funk and soul in the music of Hayes and White via MOR- and Muzak-indebted lush orchestrations certainly could be read in terms of this Black performance of respectability. Such a perceived tempering of Blackness might be described as allowing White to achieve his immense and diverse audience. This interpretation harkens back to earlier iterations of Black respectability politics represented by artists from Motown to Nat King Cole to Black jazz orchestras that adopted strings, and so on. But I sense this reading is but one side of an interpretive coin, with the other side of the coin being a recognition that these artists and large sections of their Black audiences were fully appreciative of this luxe, Black, MOR music—that its artfulness and craft represented to them areas of "Black excellence." The latter is also a phrase from current race discourse. This resonates with 1970s "Black is beautiful" and "Black power" (and empowerment) movements. "Black excellence" fits well both with capturing how White was portrayed in *Jet* and *Ebony* in the 1970s, and for how disco-funk peers like Earth, Wind, and Fire ("EWF") are celebrated by Black media writers today. For example, in *Los Angeles Times* coverage of EWF Day in the city, critic Michael Wood expounds on the "essential optimism" of the group's "sophisticated" 1970s songs, "which carried ideas of what's now called black excellence into the pop mainstream." There is emphasis on the musical, cultural, and fashion codes of sophistication as well as "excellence" in career achievement. Such markers are further balanced with cultural optimism and pride that is centrally intended for Black audiences while at the same time speaking more broadly across racial, regional and international audience lines. Wood holds up bandleader Maurice White's comment that EWF is "following in the same tradition as John Coltrane or Miles Davis or Duke Ellington—or James Baldwin." To Wood, such figures represent key purveyors of a Black excellence lineage that carried an important racial uplift message. Such models demonstrate cultural respectability, and the art and artfulness of Black culture and thought without overtly "policing . . . black people's behavior and appearance to better appeal to white people." There are likely roots to this outlook in Barry White's career and reception in the

1970s—not from the perspective of the class-focused cynicism of certain critics, but from the appreciative commentary cited from fans noted above.

The main artists in chapters 7 and 8—Hayes (b. 1942), White (b. 1944), and Kenneth Gamble (b. 1943) and Leon Huff (b. 1942)—all represent postwar success stories of impoverished Black youth rising to prominent wealth and career success in the years just following the 1968 Civil Rights Act. Their achievements mark them each as beneficiaries of economic, social, and cultural uplift following the Great Migration and rapid race and prosperity changes in postwar America. As Morris suggests, their lush orchestral sounds can certainly be interpreted as signification codes for Black wealth and success, even if such plush textures likewise spoke to the luxe, aspirational lifestyle associations of disco culture, regardless of race. In this sense, the luxe excess of Hayes and White's LUO sound codes of Black glamour. Through its symphonic-soul lineage, this music is multiply tied to glorified street images (blaxploitaion), Black empowerment (positive messages), Black street glamour (album covers), and reclamation of white cultural signifiers (e.g., rock guitar, sophisticated studio production, symphonic conducting, or covers of white MOR pop). There is, of course, a middlebrow element to the desire to show class markers via symphonic signification, but these musical codes are less indebted to highbrow philharmonic orchestras than to glamorous entertainment-spectacle models from television show bands and nightclub stages from Las Vegas to New York. As illustrated in Isabel Wilkerson's 2010 oral-history, *The Warmth of Other Suns*, African Americans only gradually were accepted as patrons in such venues after midcentury.[74] Equal participation in this glamorous milieu was an important social-achievement marker for the new, postwar Black middle classes.[75] *Jet* and *Ebony*'s coverage of White and the LUO underscore his achievements in crossing this cultural barrier.

The *sound* of White evokes a range of strong images for his audiences. Beyond the arguments made thus far, White further encouraged audiences to adopt the lush sexuality-centered musical and lyrical content of his music as a soundtrack proxy for personal romantic relationships. In the aforementioned article, "Big Barry White Mixes His Music for Lovers Only," he explains,

> What Barry White does is help you think of things to say.... When you hear me rappin' on a record, that's when the man has got his lady.... He don't have to do nuthin'. He can let me do it for him. He can just be gettin' her prepared.... You dig what I'm sayin'?
> "It works for the ladies, too. There are men who don't know how to talk to women, they don't know how to express themselves.... So what she'll do is

make believe . . . while they're actually makin' love to a man (they've told me) "that's what my man is sayin' to me . . . right now!"[76]

A reviewer (from England) likewise understood the LUO's instrumentals as an opportunity to act out the Barry White love-god persona. Describing the "great fun" of this, and in an act of cross-racial appropriation and dated dialect Black-voice imitation, the reviewer wrote in 1977 that "You can huff and puff, grunt and growl along to them, be the real Big Husky Hunk in the comfort of your own warm parlour. A complete hoot. . . . Pull yourself up . . . wait for the wah-wah guitar to go 'chickity-wah, chikkity-woo,' let out a four-bar guttoral [sic] sigh, end with a sudden grunt . . . and then, in your best dirty-old-man rasp say 'Neeeeagh, baby. You sho' nuff do it to me—can I do it to you,' or something along those lines."[77] White encouraged such fantasies, which spoke to his own cultural community and white—even white English—fans. Yes, there are elements of parody with serious racial issues, but there is a genuine appreciation in such commentary on White and the orchestra. This sort of reception is akin to the 1970s guilty-pleasure appreciation discourse discussed chapter 6 in relation to soft rock. As this book has illustrated, luxe pop has long occupied such a guilty-pleasure position as a soundtrack to American fantasies of glamour and seduction, whether of aspirational wealth or romance.

AFTERWORD

Barry White's music, image and reception richly illustrate the class, culture, race, entertainment, fashion, lifestyle, and spectacle themes that accreted and changed in luxe-pop practice across more than half a century. Chapter 8 is thus a companion bookend to chapter 1, which outlines ways in which this classy, luxe-pop tradition has continued to be relevant to, and reinvented in, more recent American pop. The transition from the late 1970s disco mainstream to the 1980s, however, marks a major cultural rejection of areas of this legacy.

The orchestral and chamber textures of disco, symphonic soul and R&B, as well as MOR, soft rock, and singer-songwriter trends were not exclusive in the 1970s rock-pop ecosystem, as the era witnessed a range of related orchestral-pop production practices. Though this era's progressive rock presented itself at an "art rock" distance from commercial pop, there were also more commercial-minded luxe-rock expressions. By the mid- to late 1970s, some chart-topping rock had taken on self-conscious qualities of theatricality, bombast, irony, and camp, expressing new types of high-low glamour in fashion presentation and sonic combinations. While partly evoking the theatrical glamour of Hollywood-style artifice and spectacle, glam rock artists such as T. Rex and the early David Bowie (each UK)—both of whose albums include orchestral-backed tracks—also exploited gender-bending, decadence, and random cultural collisions in their self-consciously bohemian, pop-culture aesthetic vision. Such trends were further combined with the neo-Beatlesque, often classicized/classicistic pop of the Electric Light Orchestra, or in Queen's merging of British Music Hall, early hard rock, theatrical camp, and "epic" arrangements that avoided orchestral instrumentation but nonetheless borrowed heavily from quasi-elevated choral and operatic textures for comparatively design-intensive arrangements. Among US artists, such developments can be seen in select tracks by Lou Reed (produced by David Bowie), for example. Each of these trends in mainstream Anglo-American 1970s rock and pop further illustrate the role that modern studio production and technology played in adaptations of the luxe-pop aesthetic in the decade following the Beatles. Nonetheless, the epitome of 1970s luxe-pop excess was disco, and that genre faced the greatest commercial and cultural backlash.

Peter Shapiro's history of disco points to the near-riot of the infamous 12 July 1979 Disco Demolition Night at Comiskey baseball park in Chicago as "'the shot heard round the world' in the antidisco campaign.[1] He aptly characterizes this backlash as being "emblematic of the politics of resentment of the white everyman that would enable the 1980s conservative revolution."[2] Shapiro traces these conservative, homophobic, racist, white undercurrents across the 1970s. He comments that this era "finally escalated into a full-fledged culture war when Reverend Jerry Falwell founded the Moral Majority in 1979" in near tandem with the anti-homosexuality campaign of "'pro-God, pro-family' former beauty queen and orange juice shill Anita Bryant."[3] Such conservativism followed American job losses, oil crises, humiliation on the international stage (e.g., the 1979 Tehran hostage crisis), urban blackouts, declining currency, and the economic collapse of New York, among other events that shook the foundations of a middle-class, white, suburban security and postwar prosperity. For many white rock enthusiasts and white cultural conservatives, disco represented a nontraditional, non-masculine flamboyance, and an excessively liberal racial and sexual inclusiveness, particularly in light of its roots in Black, Latino, and gay urban cultures.

Disco's omnipresence and rampant commercialism was such that the *New York Times* published a glossy February 1979 exposé, "Merchandising Disco for the Masses: DI$CO." The report describes "an industry estimated to generate $4 billion annually, making it as big as network television," and predicts "soon, franchised discos will be fixtures in suburban shopping malls coast to coast."[4] As Shapiro notes, this outrageous commercial success was based on entertainment excess in a period of shifting American cultural mores. This tension led to disco's mainstream collapse across 1979–82. Shapiro documents the ways in which disco and its original subculture community went back underground and transformed into international dance music. In some contexts it merged with punk, while at the same time the latter genre reinvigorated the bloated 1970s rock tradition, emerging as a commercial force with non-luxe new-wave and synth-driven British New Romantic artists, who entered the charts in the early 1980s. Likewise, the latter years of disco paralleled and intersected with early hip-hop, which broke through commercially with the 1979 Top-40 hit, "Rapper's Delight," by the Sugar Hill Gang. The latter is built from a re-performance of the groove from Chic's 1979 hit, "Good Times," which Shapiro calls disco's "last hurrah."[5] "Rapper's Delight" notably cuts the strings of the original—the very texture that made the group glamorously "chic" in luxe sonic coding.

As Shapiro observes, "With its mincing campness, airbrushed superficiality, limp rhythms, flaccid guitars, fey strings, and overproduced sterility, disco seemed emblematic of America's dwindling power. The high falsettos of disco stars like the Bee Gees and Sylvester sounded the death knell for the virility of the American male. Disco came from New York, 'Sodom on the Hudson,' the home of both . . . knee-jerk liberals and . . . 'Northeast liberal media elite.'[6] As seen in this book's final chapters, the white-conservative anti-disco backlash was manifest as a *musical* and *stylistic* war within the long-embattled territories of class, taste, sexuality, gender, and (supposed) moral character. The fall of disco due to this backlash had a profound impact on the presence of luxe-pop production practice on the Hot 100 charts. Even so, orchestral pop's "luxury" production practices were also economically *expensive*. This quality was part of their attraction for many artists, of course, as a large production budget for an orchestra signified industry respect and power, and so this considerable economic factor likewise contributed to shifts away from luxe production at the end of the disco era.

As disco broke through the commercial mainstream in 1974 with artists like White, however, producers and artists were introduced to the technology of the ARP Solina String Ensemble, which was marketed 1974–81. This is heard, for example, in the Bee Gees 1975 hit, "Nights on Broadway," where the Solina both ably substitutes for a string section and adds certain synthetic qualities in areas that point to the future replacement of analogue strings in favor of synthesized string pads. The move of dance music toward synthesis was prominently foreshadowed in Donna Summer's 1977 hit "I Feel Love" (produced and written by Giorgio Moroder and Pete Belloite), but by this time, synthesized string pads were already regularly used to enhance or replace analogue strings in pop production. A telling turning point toward the non-luxe string pads of many 1980s hits is in the 1980 Hall and Oates cover of the Righteous Brothers' "You've Lost That Loving Feeling," which owed much to the Spector-produced original but replaced the luxe original strings with a Solina. The ability to play string-like pads with polyphonic synthesizers started circa 1978 with the Sequential Circuits Prophet-5, but the commercial breakthrough came with the affordable Yamaha DX7 (from 1983) with preset string sounds that helped define much 1980s production—all decidedly non-luxe in intent.

Early sampling technologies such as the Mellotron from the UK likely led to other changes in the cultural associations of electronic-produced string sounds. The Mellotron, first marketed in 1963, was a UK electro-mechanical keyboard based on the far less successful 1950s Chamberlin keyboard from the United States. Each reproduced prerecorded instrument sounds via magnetic tape technology. The Mellotron impacted rock, especially progressive rock, from the 1970s. With this instrument-sampling technology, *actual* string (and other orchestral) sounds are heard. Surely some of the class associations of these orchestral instruments were carried over sonically, as in the Beatles' 1967 "Strawberry Fields Forever" (with Mellotron flutes), the Moody Blues' 1967 "Nights in White Satin," or Led Zeppelin's 1975 "Kashmir" (both using Mellotron strings). However, the technology had its mechanical and sonic limitations such that it also imparted a sense of otherness (often valued) that distinctly offset its "canned" sounds from recordings of live performers. In practical use, some groups like the Moody Blues notably complemented the Mellotron with live orchestras. Regardless, rock and pop later routinely substituted live string/orchestral instruments with their digital simulacra via early digital sampling, starting with the immensely expensive Fairlight CMI (from 1979), and the market-friendly samplers that appeared by the later 1980s. However, as with synthesized strings, the connection to real-world luxe performance connotations and practice oftentimes was secondary to new sonic possibilities and budgetary concerns.

Such trends led to the temporary decline of luxe production in the pop charts across the early 1980s, with an increasing absence of traditional orchestration on Hot 100 hit singles in favor of new technologies. Based on the charts, the nadir of an absence of traditional luxe-pop production appears to be circa 1984. Nonetheless, synthesized modernity and analogue luxe coexist through this period, as in the production of Whitney Houston's 1985 hit, "The Greatest Love of All," which is rife with both DX-7-like synth textures and soaring strings—all lushly performed live with orchestra (where the real strings were even more prominent) at the 1987 Grammy Awards. At this event, Houston's backing orchestra is almost unseen in the shadows, a point which underscores that from the mid-1980s such pop glamour was often freed from orchestral-visual signifiers in media contexts like this. And, more importantly, rock-pop glamour thrived well outside of such traditional orchestral signifiers. Nonetheless, from the early 1980s—with pop hits like "Endless Love" (by Lionel Ritchie and Diana Ross, 1981)—luxe-orchestration practice, centrally with strings, survived in the milieu of big, MOR pop-ballad and mid-tempo production, which remained relevant well into the 1990s (and beyond). For instance, in 1995, a period where the *Billboard* Hot Singles chart was increasingly oriented toward hip-hop and R&B idioms, five of the Top 10 singles of the year are this sort of mid-tempo or ballad production and include strings and orchestral instrument textures, whether real or sampled. These include Coolio's "Gangsta's Paradise," TLC's "Creep," Seal's "Kiss from a Rose," Boyz II Men's "On Bended Knee," and Madonna's "Take a Bow." What is noticeable, however, is that more often than not these orchestral textures are merely employed as conventional urbane instrumental colors within mainstream popular music. There is a lack of *conspicuous*—or foregrounded—symphonization and little obvious invocation of the luxe topics of traditional showbiz glitz, glorification, or classy sophistication, despite updated, contemporary qualities of entertainment glamour. "Gangsta's Paradise," however, notably points to the mid-1990s emergence of hip-hop uses of cinematic strings.

The 1980s also witnessed the rise of Great American Songbook discourse, beginning in part through Linda Ronstadt's three Nelson Riddle–arranged albums of pre-rock traditional-pop standards (starting 1983). The market for these hit albums was largely the mainstream adult demographic that often guides Grammy nominations and the conservative tastes of the Recording Academy members. Indeed, as implied by the Whitney Houston example above, from the 1980s, event shows like the Grammy and Oscar broadcasts have reliably dressed up post-1980 pop in traditional showbiz glitz, melodramatic orchestral pathos, and glamorous orchestral arrangements that invoke luxe cultural codes, at least within the same ballad and mid-tempo production areas discussed. Prime contrasting examples of such luxe showbiz presentations are seen in the 1998 Oscars' live performance of the melodramatic, mainstream-pop bombast of Celine Dion singing "My Heart Goes On" (used famously in *Titanic*, Paramount 1997) in front of a white-tuxedoed orchestra on a misted stage, and the indie-rock singer-songwriter Elliott Smith—brilliant but visibly uneasy and outside his cultural comfort zone—presenting a lushly orchestrated rendition of his "Miss Misery" (from the soundtrack to *Good Will Hunting*, Miramax, 1997).[7]

The legacy of pre-1980 orchestral pop also manifest itself in interesting ways beyond MOR pop across the late 1980s to the 2000s. Traditional rock-history narratives position the late 1970s New York and London punk rock and synth- and guitar-leaning new wave scenes (and their inherent aggressive spirit and DIY aesthetic) in part as a reaction to the excesses and sophistication of mainstream 1970s rock, pop, and disco production. In such narratives, punks found this latter music to be overly ostentatious, sentimental, and/or unnecessarily technical (in a musical sense) or technological (in a studio production sense). That said, as early as "Smithers-Jones," a 1979 track by the British punk band The Jam, post-punk, alternative, and indie rock artists increasingly found interest in adapting luxe-pop idioms to rock subgenre offshoots. This was particularly the case from the 1990s forward. For example, while Smith's aforementioned 1997 "Miss Misery" was not originally a luxe/chamber-pop track, at the time of his Grammy appearance, Smith was in the midst of recording his fourth album, *XO*, released in August 1998, which marks his first embrace of chamber pop production. The album includes orchestral textures from a string octet, horn players, and Jon Brion's Chamberlin contributions. A variety of UK indie acts, such as Tindersticks (e.g., *Tindersticks [I]*, 1993) and Belle and Sebastian (*If You're Feeling Sinister*, 1996), were active with similar textures, but bigger US alternative rock acts like R.E.M. (e.g., *Automatic for the People*, 1992) and the Smashing Pumpkins ("Tonight Tonight," *Mellon Collie and the Infinite Sadness*, 1995) had higher profile embraces of chamber/orchestral pop production earlier in the 1990s (alongside similar tracks by major mid-1990s Britpop acts like Blur, the Verve, Paul Weller, etc.). The US and UK indie chamber pop vogue took flight in the 2000s, notably after a 1999 VW Cabriolet advertisement with Nick Drake's non-luxe "Pink Moon" (from 1972) unexpectedly sparked indie-rock interest in the lush baroque pop of this previously obscure UK singer-songwriter. Much of this post-1990 music connects to retromania interests in 1960s and 1970s rock-pop, and invokes a range of topical extensions from this pre-1980 luxe-pop legacy.

As this suggests, post-1980, rock and indie-rock subcultures embraced orchestral pop textures in various ways that built off of earlier luxe textures and modes of intention. Chamber pop idioms and cinematic symphonic melodrama were of particular interest within indie and alternative rock, as well as hard rock and metal. Within the latter, there are certainly 1980s and 1990s orchestral-backed examples of heavy-metal ballads, including, for instance, Ozzy Osbourne's 1983 single, "So Tired" (from *Bark at the Moon*). The promotional music video notably sets Osbourne onstage in a decaying luxe music hall, with the orchestra in the pit covered in dense cobwebs (a commentary on the state of orchestral-pop production circa 1983?). While heavy metal and hard rock include select artists with orchestral pretensions dating as far back as 1970s Deep Purple and Ritchie Blackmore (both UK), by the 1990s, metal artists such as Osbourne, the Scorpions, and Motörhead (all European), among others, employed dramatic strings on individual tracks (typically ballads). These efforts though do not involve more expansive efforts in building new orchestral group sounds or in spectacular orchestral events. In many ways, this trend extends mainstream rock album practices from the 1970s and early 1980s for ballad tracks, where proven successful bands were afforded orchestration budgets for one or two tracks on their sophomore albums forward (e.g., two tracks from Foreigner's 1978 *Double Vision*, their second album, include strings). Many of the later hard rock and metal productions seem to reverse the mid-1980s adoptions of synthesized/sampled strings (common in 1980s pop metal and hair metal), and the simple string-pad sounds of these metal ballads often sound closer to analogue versions of synthesized/sampled strings than to earlier luxe-pop string writing. Further outside both mainstream metal and the classy/glitzy showbiz tropes of traditional luxe pop, the late 1980s and 1990s also saw the emergence of melodramatic "symphonic metal" as a small subgenre, with roots in bands like Celtic Frost (Switzerland), Therion (Sweden), and Believer (US).

Following the MTV "Unplugged" specials of Maria Carey (aired 29 April 1992), k. d. lang (28 March 1993), and Rod Stewart (5 May 1993), a host of artists—from R&B, hip-hop, pop, and rock—would perform live on the show, and outside the show in "unplugged" special events, with strings and other orchestral backings.[8] While Nirvana's *Unplugged* use of a single cello was relatively lost in the mix, the visual of the venerated grunge band, dressed in shabby thrift-store chic, with a cellist, amid candles, floral arrangements, and flowing plush red and blue curtains (see, for example, "Where Did You Sleep Last Night?"; the show was aired 14 December 1993) began a long tradition for indie rock unplugged performances. From the mid-1990s, this intersected with increasing indie retromania for baroque and chamber pop, as noted previously.

Hard rock artists too embraced the unplugged performance event format, as seen with Jimmy Page and Robert Plant's 1994 "Unledded" MTV special, *No Quarter*, which reunited the Led Zeppelin front men with full orchestra and band. In the context of MTV, this hard-rock event likely benefitted from the massively popular 1991 Guns n' Roses video, "November Rain," in which the band's epic, 9'16" ballad with synth string pads was visually mimed by a full orchestra. In one of its tableaus, the video expands on a 1980s hair-metal performance-focused music-video tradition by placing Guns n' Roses in a deluxe movie palace theater as part of a "live" concert, with the band set in front of the dramatically lit, tuxedoed orchestra and Axl Rose set as the singer-soloist on a grand piano. The textures of the "November Rain" "strings" themselves harken back to the Mellotron strings and horns on Led Zeppelin's 1975 "Kashmir" (from *Physical Graffiti*). In the 1994 "Unledded" performance, the Mellotron was replaced by real strings. Such high-profile metal-meets-orchestra examples brought a resurgence of orchestral mergings with hard rock and metal, and by the 2000s, indie rock followed suit. Such "special" events include heavy metal bands with symphony orchestra, like Metallica with the San Francisco Symphony Orchestra in 2000 (*S&M*, or "Symphony and Metallica"), or Kiss with the Melbourne Symphony Orchestra in 2003, occasions that were documented in lavishly packaged CD and DVD releases. On a slightly less pretentious level, post-2000, various symphonic pops series—like those offered by the Los Angeles Philharmonic (at the Hollywood Bowl), the Brooklyn Philharmonic, and the Boston Pops—instituted regular summer appearances backing contemporary indie rock bands such as the chamber-pop bands The Decemberists and Belle and Sebastian (Scotland); the indie rock bands Bright Eyes, Grizzly Bear, Death Cab for Cutie, and the Ben Folds Five; as well as the French ambient pop duo Air and the alternative country-rock band the Cowboy Junkies. Similarly, trip-hop/electronica artists (Portishead, Goldfrapp, etc.) and—returning full-circle to the focus of chapter 1—hip-hop acts (Kanye West, Jay-Z, and P-Diddy) began to hire sizable string sections for performances and recordings. From the hip-hop perspective, these trends do in fact have loose but important connecting threads.

There are examples of ghetto-life rap with string textures prior to Jay-Z's 2006 *Reasonable Doubt*, including, for instance, the aforementioned 1995 "Gangsta's Paradise" by Coolio (which samples Stevie Wonder). And there are mid-1990s gangsta rap precedents for Jay-Z's "Can I Live" in "Warning" (1993) by Jay-Z's friend the Notorious B.I.G., and in 2Pac's "Me Against the World" (1995). But while these releases borrow from Hayes's 1969 luxe cover of Bacharach's "Walk On By," and while both tracks evoke thug-life narratives (B.I.G.'s is an homage to *Scarface*), each samples rhythm-section funk rather than symphonic soul. However, the 2001 "Jay-Z Unplugged" performance for MTV was particularly impactful in the hip-hop community, albeit on a less luxe scale than was afforded several years later.[9] This studio show included Mary J. Blige, the Roots, a string quartet, and guest jazz flutist. While its "chamber" soul arrangements and rich blue staging suggest inspirations for the later spectacle, this event was performed in street clothes and a nightclub-type setting. Nevertheless, as the live-band arrangements enhanced the 1970s soul, funk, and jazz sample-based beats of the original tracks, there are clear personnel and aesthetic ties—musically and performatively—between Jay-Z's Radio City event and this "Unplugged" date.

In 1996, for Jay-Z or Gotti, the inspiration for the *Reasonable Doubt* luxe-soul samples might have come from Portishead—the string passage resembles their "Glory Box" on the album *Dummy*, which adapts a sample from Hayes's "Ike's Rap II" (*Black Moses*, 1971).[10] *Dummy* is also notable for how Portishead painstakingly performed and recorded material to vinyl and tape, then degraded these media for "vintage" audio crackle and hiss before sampling, mixing, and scratching manipulation. The album illustrates a progressive side of retromania, much in the way that Jay-Z "reimagines" Hayes for the hip-hop era.[11] The ethereal string-section figure in "Glory Box"—like Jay-Z's Hayes sample—offers a quintessential, post-1990 "cinematic" pop scoring trope.[12] Reynolds notably comments on the "'cinematic' prism" of such recent pop-retromania as Lana Del Rey's early videos with their lush, 1960s-leaning orchestral pop.[13] Such aural-visual "cinematic" aspirations emerged at least a decade earlier, though, with both Portishead and Jay-Z in the mid-1990s.

While Simon Reynolds's "retromania" characterization primarily concerns pop music of the 2000s, he admits that such trends have always been central to rock-pop production. Indeed, the roots of post-2000 mixtures are readily seen in the influences of bands like The Jam and the Ramones, who proudly displayed their love of the music of the Beatles, Motown, and other 1960s sources. Such fan-based musical eclecticism is also typified in the post–new wave career of Elvis Costello, who has mined classic pop and luxe-pop models, from the countrypolitan idiom to Burt Bacharach's lounge pop. Similarly, this artist-as-fan retromania is also seen in the luxe influences of some of the 1980s and 1990s music just discussed.

Among the interesting post-2000 manifestations of orchestral/chamber rock-pop in the era of retromania are the releases of two millennial, Brooklyn-centered music communities. One, the Dap-Kings—a revivalist band focused on accurately re-creating 1960s and 1970s soul and funk—was an epicenter of retromania, with one notable manifestation being their work on the Spector-influenced, Mark Ronson productions for Amy Winehouse (e.g., "Black to Black," 2006). Another of the borough's communities fostered new, potentially "nobrow" rock-pop and "indie classical" aesthetics.[14] Both are illustrated through 2000s indie rock, where chamber-pop artists such as Sufjan Stevens, The National, Grizzly Bear, the Dirty Projectors, Antony and the Johnsons, and My Brightest Diamond, among others, further collaborated with the Brooklyn Philharmonic and the Brooklyn Academy of Music on multimedia events and stage and concert works. Much of this combined indie-rock aesthetics with post-minimalism (influenced by Steve Reich and Philip Glass, the latter of whom also arranged for rock-pop artists; Glass's celebrated former protege, Nico Muhly, provided many orchestrations for his Brooklyn peers). This music is certainly connected in loose ways to the discourses of luxe pop outlined in this book, but the core *classy* entertainment milieu and the *glitz* of pre-1980 luxe pop is notably absent. Also greatly changed are the cultural brow politics. Such a shift away from traditional classy- or glitzy-entertainment discourse characterizes much—but by no means all—post-1980 orchestral pop. This shift parallels changes in American mainstream entertainment and consumption discourse, however.

The disco histories of both Shapiro and Anthony Haden-Guest both point to the media coverage of Studio 54 as a harbinger of "celebrity culture," which emerged in the 1980s.[15] In this era, key areas of change in class politics align with this shift in both aspirational culture and cultural codes and values in displays of glamour and wealth. These changes hold implications for luxe pop. As noted, sociologist Juliet Schor and documentarian Lauren Greenfield see celebrity culture and its consumer-culture impact as an outgrowth of postwar modern media and promotional practices, the cultural elevation of celebrity, the expanded middle class, the luxury goods industry, and the changing practices of conspicuous consumption. They note a two-way economic class influence, where working- and middle-class consumers aspire toward celebrity-influenced affluence markers, while at the same time, many high-economic-class youth consumers seek consumer luxury goods that emulate the hip or cool cultural cachet of "street" culture. In tandem, many upper-class adults seek to identify with everyman "normcore" fashion. (Normcore fashion—unpretentious, normal-looking clothing—signals a rejection of luxury consumption, even if such goods can be haute couture.) Schor argues, as observed, that social structures across the 1950s through 1970s were horizontal—that is, "with people comparing themselves to and following consumption patterns of others of similar economic status." By contrast, "beginning in the 1980s, social comparison began to reorganize with a vertical pattern." Greenfield and Schor identify the influence of 1980s "television programming [which] shifted in the direction of portraying more lavish lifestyles," arriving in the post-2000s with "millions" viewing the "outsized lifestyles" of celebrities and dreaming of achieving such glamour in their own lives. Schor characterizes this "aspirational gap" as "the distance between what people want and think they need to keep up, and what they earn." This has led to a mainstream culture engrossed in the "performance of wealth."[16] These trends map in interesting ways onto the pop-music history just outlined.

Orchestral pop textures, luxe or otherwise, continue to have present-day relevance, but I sense there are different aspirational discourses in play than the lower-middlebrow or middlebrow-adjacent modes discussed across this book. The post-1980 decline in luxe pop has much to do with modes and discourses of "street" or "authentic" popular-music hipness, fashion, and cool that do not intersect with luxe-production sonic markers. This is true even while sometimes fashion "bling"—haute couture, diamonds, luxury cars, etc.—still builds on "high" aspirational consumption among the new-money wealth of pop-culture celebrity. Some of this complexity is discussed with regard to orchestra-augmented hip-hop in chapter 1, but each of chapters 5–8 suggest shifts leading toward post-1980 celebrity culture. Nonetheless, post-1980 contexts where live orchestral musicians have continued to be employed in popular music—at events like Jay-Z at Radio City, the Brooklyn Philharmonic indie rock concerts, or television music spectacles—involve a dialogue, retromania or otherwise, with the residual discourse and topical associations of glamorous or classy luxe pop.

In the symphonic jazz age, the 1928 song "Crazy Rhythm" (by Irving Caesar, Joseph Meyer, and Paul Whiteman's bandleader competitor, Roger Wolfe Kahn) offers the lines: "They say that when a high-brow meets a low-brow, walking along Broadway, / Soon the high-brow, he has no brow, ain't it a shame, and you're to blame." For more than a century, pop culture has routinely found both amusement and concern in the discourses of the "brows," with all sorts of colorful slang—and musical slang—permutations that skewer cultural-hierarchy pretensions. As the song suggests, thanks to slumming highbrows cavorting with supposed lowbrows, there may have been a potential "nobrow" danger in this discourse from early on. (And, as the song says, "you're to blame.") Or maybe the problem is a pop-culture interest in fashion-forward musical spectacles, as this verse also implies. Nobrow was not a broadly circulated term until after 2000, and by the 1930s these high-meets-low culture collisions were subsumed under the idea of "middlebrow." This book documents a long history of middlebrow, classy pop which reached its zenith—and momentary demise—in the late 1970s.

In his 1983 book, *Class*, cultural historian Paul Fussell offers another extension of American sociology's class studies. While still engaging with the culture-class brow literature discussed across *Hearing Luxe Pop*, Fussell's updated list of nine class-hierarchy tiers involves a shift toward economic class. His four-part, proletarian middle stratum takes on a Marxist air. At the outset, however, he stresses that "it's not riches alone that define these classes." He quotes one "working man" as saying "it can't be money ... because nobody ever knows that about you for sure." Fussell adds that "style and taste and awareness are as important as money."[17] Building on Russell Lynes's comments about the "taste and knowledge and perceptiveness that determine class," Fussell contends that it is the ways in which people attain and employ money, especially in modes that "simulate identity," that is most significant.[18] Paired with both his post-1980 emphasis on "style and taste and awareness," Fussell points toward the economic- and celebrity-aspirational distinctions I have described across this book, both as middlebrow-adjacent culture and via my account of Greenfield's post-1990 "generation wealth." The latter is "a social milieu" defined by "celebrity accelerants" in which "consumer presentation is all that counts for identity, status, and a basic sense of self."[19] While this theorization and its documentation map well onto understandings of post-1980 mainstream culture, they also suggest a neutralization or devaluation of traditional brow discourse in this more recent era. However, post-1990, writers have recalibrated earlier brow discourse into theories of "nobrow" and "omnivore" cultures.

The term *nobrow* appears to have been coined in the 2000 book, *Nobrow: The Culture of Marketing/The Marketing of Culture*, by the *New Yorker* journalist John

Seabrook, who used the term to discuss the transformation of his employer from an arbiter of elite culture and taste to a cultural brand. Seabrook describes good taste and signifiers of cultural class having disappeared across the 1990s. In their place, a market "hierarchy of hotness" was governed by branding, introducing a new classless culture, a sort of "ground zero, the exact midpoint at which culture and marketing converge."[20] Seabrook characterizes nobrow as both an amorphous fusing of the brows, high and low, with mainstream and avant-garde, brand marketing, hype, and cultural values all converging into a classless homogeneity. In 2005, contrary to other authors, Peter Swirski argued that nobrow culture—meaning for him, the simultaneous targeting of both high and low taste—can be traced to the early twentieth century.[21] This anachronistic application is a fault in Swirski's argument, as brow discourse was central to interwar and postwar culture, a period when middlebrow framed such high-low juxtapositions. In a response to Seabrook, Lawrence Levine argued that the middlebrow still exists, but he also added that supposed nobrow trends of mixing, crossing, and juxtaposing taste and class cultures are akin to—and a return to—a sort of cultural fluidity that he identified with nineteenth-century culture, where people moved more easily between genre and taste boundaries under a cultural-pluralist mindset.[22] Seabrook argues that such fluidity has become a status marker (this resonates with omnivore theory, discussed later). But as Levine has demonstrated, this fluidity was always valued in the United States, despite the brow rhetoric.[23] Levine suggests we are in a "period of transition" where "the barriers between kinds of culture are becoming more permeable," where Americans are more "culturally ... ambidextrous," and where "we don't have to stay within the confines of [hierarchical] places people label us."[24] This argument implies that cultural fluidity has allowed for mutable identities that both consume and creatively mix, cross, reference, and juxtapose tastes against a backdrop of still-present class-hierarchy taste paradigms or "socially constructed boxes." I believe these arguments hold implications for understanding post-1990 chamber and orchestral pop.

In the blogosphere, "nobrow" is linked to postmodernism. Jonathan Kramer has usefully listed a range of presumed traits of postmodern music, including anti-elitist claims, a lack of respect for boundaries between procedures of the past and present, challenges to "barriers between 'high' and 'low' styles," a questioning of the "exclusivity of elitist and populist values," an embrace of "pluralism and eclecticism," and so forth. Kramer insists that postmodern music "is, on some level ... , ironic."[25] If nobrow music exists, this idea of postmodern irony may be an important boundary line, though obviously there are questions of habitus, subjectivity, generation, literacy, and so on involved in such distinctions. Where one hears nobrow, others may hear postmodernism or middlebrowism.

Beyond retromania, areas of post-2000 chamber pop operates in a somewhat different manner from middlebrow and classy middlebrow-adjacent luxe pop. This can be heard, for example, in the aforementioned music from the Brooklyn indie-rock community of the 2000s that included musicians who hold dual conservatory and vernacular/rock-pop backgrounds, and who have chosen to pursue careers in rock-pop idioms as performers, writers, and arrangers (e.g., Bryce Dessner from The National is one such musician). While much of this community's efforts resist easy categorization along the postmodern-nobrow continuum, little of this music relates to midcentury middlebrowism. An example can be found in the 2000s music of Sufjan Stevens, a key social and musical "hub" of these artists. In an MTV interview that was part of the promotion of his 2005 *Illinoise* album, Stevens suggested that his sound defied easy genre labeling: "I think [my music is] sort of like high art meets low art. It's folk music but with sort of the sophistication of, like, the symphony orchestra kind of clashing together. . . . So you're not quite sure if, like—is this good music? . . . Or is this just silly. . . . I kind of like that tension . . . of my performances sounding like sixth-grade band."[26] With his ironic but sincere stage presentations (which have included Stevens in angel wings alongside band, orchestra, hula hoopers, and cheerleaders), Stevens has carved out a non-retro sound that nevertheless functions via recombinant uses of earlier music topics. These juxtapositions work in a stylistically polyamorous manner that weaves together banjo folk, singer-songwriter sincerity, twee pop, occasional bursts of distortion-leaning rock, electronica, postminimalism, chamber pop, and the unvarnished beauty of amateur music.

Stevens offers a quintessential case of a wherever-you-want-to-file-it performer operating at a postmodern-nobrow pop border aptly characterized as "omnivore" culture. David Blake has studied how the inclusive musical tastes and intellectual proclivities—and elite higher education backgrounds—of the Dirty Projectors and Vampire Weekend (both post-2000 Brooklyn indie bands) embody "omnivore" taste paradigms.[27] He relies in part on Richard Peterson and Roger Kern, who describe an emergent, elite "omnivore" culture in their 1996 essay, "Changing Highbrow Taste: From Snob to Omnivore." Peterson and Kern document how pop consumption tastes among "high-status persons" have shifted from "snobbish exclusion" to "eclectic" and "omnivorous appropriation."[28] "Omnivorous taste" does not imply "liking everything *indiscriminately*," rather the term "signifies an *openness* to appreciating everything." This has in turn given rise to new ways of evoking cultural status through omnivorous stylistic and referential juxtapositions.

In sum, many post-2000 pop-music invocations of luxe pop still give rise to associations of elevated status, whether via retromania, modern-entertainment spectacle codes enacted as generation-wealth musical bling, postmodern/nobrow pluralism, eclecticism, or irony (where status is a sign of cultural command, literacy and wit), or status gained via the eclectic display of omnivore taste. In the internet era, the popular-culture past is ever-present in our media consumption universe of Hollywood films, television and digital video streaming (YouTube, Netflix, etc.), Spotify and other near-bottomless audio streaming, the ubiquitous and incessant soundtracks of our retail and commercial surroundings, and so on. Here, both recycled and evolving cultural associations from pre-1970 luxe pop still thrive. Most consumers of American media—both nationally and internationally—possess a degree of literacy with this rich field of luxe-pop associations, even if the world they live in is profoundly changed from the eras that gave rise to this earlier music. As seen with Jay-Z and the Hustler Symphony Orchestra, these associative connections between contemporary orchestral pop and luxe pop's many pre-1970s classy, glamorous, sophisticated themes will likely exist in perpetuity as long as examples from this media remain well known, valued, and in wide circulation.

NOTES

As the notes provide extensive documentation on sources, a bibliography has not been included in this book. Several choices in the citational practices should be noted, however. Discography information is provided for only select sources discussed at length. Discography information for commonly available recordings mentioned only briefly can be found through AllMusic.com or Discogs.com, and the recordings can be heard via sources such as Spotify and YouTube. Detailed bibliographic information for popularity charts in *Billboard* is only provided for charts that are discussed at length. The necessary source information (date and chart name) is provided to guide readers toward locating the sources either through the digitally scanned issues that are available through the Proquest Entertainment Industry Magazine Archive, or via Top40Weekly.com, which provides truncated *Billboard* charts from 1955 to present.

INTRODUCTION: FROM PAUL WHITEMAN, TO BARRY WHITE, MAN

1. See the "Researcher Database" on "Middlebrow: An Interdisciplinary Transatlantic Research Network," https://www.middlebrow-network.com, as well as the site's bibliography and "Defining the Middlebrow" pages. See also Christopher Chowrimootoo, and Kate Guthrie, "Music and the Middlebrow," 2019, http://www.musicandthemiddlebrow.org (accessed 25 November 2019). Both Chowrimootoo and Guthrie have notable contributions to this literature and have been central to fostering a musicology community devoted to this subject. See, for example, Kate Guthrie, *Music and Middlebrow Culture in Modern Britain* (Oakland: University of California Press, 2021), Christopher Chowrimooto, *Middlebrow Modernism: Britten's Operas and the Great Divide* (Oakland: University of California Press, 2018), and "Colloquy: Musicology and the Middlebrow," *Journal of the American Musicological Society* 73, no. 2 (2020).

2. Albin Zak, *The Poetics of Rock: Cutting Tracks, Making Records* (Berkeley: University of California Press, 2001); Simon Zagorski-Thomas, *The Musicology of Record Production* (Cambridge: Cambridge University Press, 2014).

3. See, especially, chapter 3 in Zagorski-Thomas, *Musicology*.

4. Ibid., 37.

5. Ibid., 33.

6. Ibid.

7. Jann Pasler, "Material Culture and Postmodern Positivism: Rethinking the 'Popular' in Late-Nineteenth-Century French Music," in *Historical Musicology: Sources, Methods, Interpretations*, ed. Stephen Crist and Robert Marvin (Rochester, NY: University of Rochester Press, 2004).

8. Pierre Bourdieu, *Distinction: A Social Critique of the Judgement of Taste*, trans. Richard Nice (Cambridge, MA: Harvard University Press, 1984; orig. 1979), 170.

9. Herbert J. Gans, *Popular Culture and High Culture: An Analysis and Evaluations of Taste*, revised/updated ed. (New York: Basic Books, 1999).

10. Thomas Hine, *Populuxe* (New York: Alfred A. Knopf, 1986).

CHAPTER I. HEARING LUXE POP

1. Jon Pareles, "Street Smarts Meets Old-Fashioned Showbiz," *New York Times*, 20 July 2013, Arts, http://www.nytimes.com/2013/07/21/arts/music/street-smarts-meets-old-fashioned-showbiz.html (accessed 22 July 2013).

2. See Josiah Howard, *Blaxploitation Cinema* (Goldalming, UK: FAB Press, 2008), and *Can You Dig It? The Music and Politics of Black Action Films, 1968–75*, Soul Jazz Records SJRCD214, 2009, two compact disc box set.

3. Simon Reynolds, *Retromania* (New York: Faber and Faber, 2011), xx.

4. Ibid., xxiii.

5. Robert S. Hatten, *Interpreting Musical Gestures, Topics, and Tropes: Mozart, Beethoven, Schubert* (Bloomington: Indiana University Press, 2004), 2.

6. Philip Tagg, *Music's Meanings: A Modern Musicology for Non-Musos* (Larchmont, NY: Mass Media Music Scholars' Press, 2012), 306.

7. A promo video can be found at "daKAH Hip Hop Orchestra Promo, Starring Double G (Filmed by Mike Marshall)," 2009, https://www.youtube.com/watch?v=VaChsKO6ksU (accessed 28 May 2020).

8. Amy Spencer, "A Fashionable Life: Kanye West and Alexis Phifer," *Harper's Bazaar*, August 2007, http://www.harpersbazaar.com/print-this/fashionable-life-west-0807 (accessed 23 July 2013).

9. See "Wired Strings," Wired Strings, 2014, http://wiredstrings.com (accessed 11 December 2014), and John Rockwell, "Barry White Sings at the Music Hall," *New York Times*, 13 February 1976, 19.

10. Jay-Z, *MTV Unplugged: Jay-Z*, Roc-A-Fella 586617, 2001, compact disc.

11. Paul Croughton, liner notes to Kanye West, *Late Orchestration*, Island Def Jam 985317-5, 2006.

12. Kanye West, *Late Registration*, Roc-A-Fella B0004813-02, 2005, compact disc.

13. Jake Brown, *Kanye West in the Studio: Beats Down! Money Up! The Studio Years (2000–2006)*, Kindle ed. (New York: Colossus, 2006).

14. Austin Scaggs, "Kanye West: A Genius in Praise of Himself," *Rolling Stone*, 20 September 2007, http://www.rollingstone.com/music/news/kanye-west-a-genius-in-praise-of-himself-20070920?page=3 (accessed 1 December 2014), and Portishead, *Dummy*, Go! Discs 828553, 1994, compact disc.

15. Jon Burlingame, *The Music of James Bond* (New York: Oxford University Press, 2012), 96.

16. "Interview" on Kanye West, *Late Orchestration* (Island Def Jam, 2006), 985317-5.

17. This is the subtitle to Reynolds, *Retromania*.

18. Mark Beaumont, *Jay-Z: The King of America* (London: Omnibus Press, 2012), 5.

19. Ibid., 8. See also Adam Park, "Jay-Z: The World's Biggest Rap Star Reveals All!," *Clash*, 2009, http://www.clashmusic.com/feature/jay-z-interview (accessed 16 November 2015).

20. Park, "Jay-Z," 63.

21. Jay-Z, *Jay-Z: Reasonable Doubt*, Classic Albums EV30230-9, 2007, DVD.

22. Ibid.

23. Jay-Z, *Decoded* (New York: Virgin, 2011), 106, 107n6.

24. Jay-Z, *Jay-Z: Reasonable Doubt*.

25. Ibid.

26. The timings reference the 11'12". version of the track on Isaac Hayes, . . . *To Be Continued*, Stax 9020453860, 2002, compact disc.

27. I have no documentation on where I found these tracks online circa 2008.

28. "Coca Cola Stage Side: Coca Cola Presents Jay-Z's Tenth Anniversary of *Reasonable Doubt*," 2006, http://www.youtube.com/watch?v=WnYxZ0wyG-M (accessed 16 January 2020).

29. Rebecca Leydon, "Recombinant Style Topics: The Past and Future of Sampling," in *Sounding Out Pop*, ed. Mark Spicer, and John Covach (Ann Arbor: University of Michigan Press, 2013), 201, 209–10.

30. Albin Zak, "No-Fi: Crafting a Language of Music in 1950s Pop," in *The Art of Record Production: An Introductory Reader for a New Academic Field*, ed. Simon Frith, and Simon Zagorski-Thomas (London: Ashgate, 2013), 43.

31. Arthur Lange, *Arranging for the Modern Dance Orchestra* (New York: Arthur Lange, 1926).

32. "The Drifters: There Goes My Baby," *Billboard*, 4 May 1959, 59.

33. Jerry Leiber, Mike Stoller, and David Ritz, *Hound Dog: The Leiber and Stoller Autobiography*, Kindle ed. (New York: Simon and Schuster, 2009), location 1883.

34. Ibid., location 1860.

35. Jack Nitzsche, "Interview," interview by Karel Beer, MP3 file, broadcast 16 January 1982, 1981.

36. Ben E. King, "Spanish Harlem," Atco 45-6185, 1960, 45 rpm.

37. Leiber, *Hound Dog*, location 1860.

38. Ibid., location 2007.

39. See Gil Kaufman, "Obituary: Composer Stan Applebaum Dies at 96," *Billboard*, 28 February 2019, https://www.billboard.com/articles/news/obituary /8500517/stan-applebaum-composer-dead-obituary (accessed 16 January 2020), "Arranger, Composer and Conductor Stanley Applebaum Donates His Archive," New York Public Library, 2018, https://www.infodocket.com/2018/12/13/music -the-new-york-public-library-for-the-performing-arts-acquires-stanley-applebaums -collection/ (accessed 26 June 2019), and "Stan Applebaum," Discogs.com, https:// www.discogs.com/artist/366888-Stan-Applebaum (accessed 26 June 2019).

40. Mark Burford, "Sam Cooke as Pop Album Artist: A Reinvention in Three Songs," *Journal of the American Musicological Society* 65 (Spring 2012): 118.

41. See Keir Keightley, "Long Play: Adult-Oriented Popular Music and the Temporal Logics of the Post-War Sound Recording Industry," *Media, Culture, and Society* 26 (2004): 375–91.

42. Burford, "Sam Cooke," 116. Burford expands here upon Keir Keightley, "Music for Middlebrows: Defining the Easy Listening Era, 1946–1966," *American Music* 26 (Fall 2008): 309–35.

43. Burford, "Sam Cooke," 118.

44. Ibid., 117.

45. Ibid., 118.

46. Leiber, *Hound Dog*, location 2063.

47. Mitchell Morris, *The Persistence of Sentiment: Display and Feeling in Popular Music of the 1970s* (Berkeley: University of California Press, 2013), 44.

48. Andrew Flory, email communication, 23 December 2014. For an in-depth study of the crossover aesthetics discussed here, see Andrew Flory, *I Hear a Symphony: Motown and Cross-Over R&B* (Ann Arbor: University of Michigan Press, 2017).

49. Robert Fink, "Goal Directed Soul? Analyzing Rhythmic Teleology in African American Popular Music," *Journal of the American Musicological Society* (Spring 2011), and Andrew Flory, "Motown and the Black Middle Class" (paper presented at the Experience Music Project Conference, Los Angeles, February 2011).

50. Ibid. The photo is reproduced in Berry Gordy, *To Be Loved* (New York: Warner, 1994).

51. Morris, *Persistence*, chap. 2.

52. Ibid., 242.

53. See, for instance, Morris's uses of this term in Morris, *Persistence*, 53 and 56.

54. Gordy, *To Be Loved*, 202.

55. See "Artist Biography: Dick Jacobs," AllMusic.com, 2019, http://www .allmusic.com/artist/dick-jacobs-mn0000211224/biography (accessed 24 June 2019) and "Dick Jacobs: Biography," IMDB.com, 2019, http://www.imdb.com /name/nm1103404/bio (accessed 25 June 2019).

56. Gordy, *To Be Loved*, 96.

57. Ibid., 127.

58. The score was provided in 2008 by the American Society of Music Arrangers and Composers, Van Nuys, CA.

59. Richard Buskin, "Classic Tracks: Marvin Gaye 'What's Going On?,'" *Sound on Sound*, July 2011, http://www.soundonsound.com/sos/jul11/articles/classic -tracks-0711.htm (accessed 21 December 2014).

60. Ibid.

61. Ibid.

62. Tom Bennett, "Arranging Music for Radio," in *Music in Radio Broadcasting*, ed. Gilbert Chase (New York: McGraw-Hill, 1946).

63. Ibid., 81–82.

64. Nelson Riddle, *Arranged by Nelson Riddle*, ed. Jeff Sultanof (New York: Alfred Music, 1985), 124.

65. Gordy, *To Be Loved*, 127.

66. Isaac Hayes, *Hot Buttered Soul*, Enterprise ENS-1001, 1969, LP.

67. Don Heckman, "Rapping with 'Black Moses,'" *New York Times*, 23 April 1972, Arts and Leisure, D23. Promotional copy manual (ca. 1996–1998), 2–3, from the "Isaac Hayes" clippings file of the Institute of Jazz Studies, John Cotton Dana Library, Rutgers, The State University of New Jersey, Newark, NJ.

68. Dan Morgenstern, "Isaac Hayes: His Own Story," *Down Beat*, 29 April 1971.

69. "Isaac Hayes: A Brief History," news release, Ted Kurland Associates, n.d.

70. Morgenstern, "Isaac Hayes."

71. "Isaac Hayes," Ted Kurland Associates, 2.

72. Morgenstern, "Isaac Hayes," n.p.

73. See especially "The Look of Love" on Isaac Hayes, *Isaac Hayes: The Black Moses of Soul* (Good Times, 2004), 05-81756.

74. Phyl Garland, "Isaac Hayes: Hot Buttered Soul," *Ebony*, March 1970, 83.

75. "Isaac Hayes," Ted Kurland Associates, 3.

76. Sinatra's most celebrated live Vegas recording, the 1966 *Sinatra at the Sands*, paired the singer with the hard-swinging Basie band and musical director Quincy Jones. See Frank Sinatra, *Sinatra at the Sands*, Reprise Records 2FS1019, 1966, double LP.

77. Morgenstern, "Isaac Hayes."

78. Garland, "Isaac Hayes," 83.

79. See the back-cover "Hotter than Bond, Cooler than Bullitt" blurb on Ernest Tidyman, *Shaft* (New York: Macmillan, 1971). The comparison circulates the blogosphere.

80. Leonard Ratner, *Classic Music: Expressions, Form, and Style* (New York: Schirmer, 1980), 9. Also Hatten, *Interpreting*.

81. See Leydon, "Recombinant."

82. See ibid., and Tagg, *Music's Meanings*.

83. Tagg, *Music's Meanings*, 107.

84. Michael Long, *Beautiful Monsters: Imagining the Classic in Musical Media* (Berkeley: University of California Press, 2008), 12.

85. Ibid., 26.

86. Ibid., 27.

87. Morris, *Persistence*, 55–56.

88. Rockwell, "Barry White Sings at the Music Hall," 20.

89. Long, *Beautiful Monsters*, 39. See also Robert Fink, "The Story of ORCH5, or, the Classical Ghost in the Hip Hop Machine," *Popular Music* 24 (2005): 339–56.

90. Mark Katz, *Capturing Sound: How Technology Has Changed Music* (Berkeley: University of California Press, 2004), 156.

91. Albin Zak, *The Poetics of Rock: Cutting Tracks, Making Records* (Berkeley: University of California Press, 2001), 64.

92. Ibid.

93. Ibid., 62.

94. Ibid., 48.

95. Diana Taylor, *The Archive and the Repertoire: Performing Cultural Memory in the Americas* (Durham, NC: Duke University Press, 2003), 94.

96. Ibid., 102.

97. See the related semiotic issues that Robert Fink outlined in his discussion of corporate "production music" in Fink, "The Story of ORCH5."

98. The original ad in the series, with Sinatra's "Come Fly with Me," was released in October 2008. See "Diddy/Sinatra Ciroc Commercial," 2008, https://www.youtube.com/watch?v=fF3G7vdM2UI (accessed 16 January 2020).

99. Dwight Macdonald, "Masscult and Midcult, Part 2," *Partisan Review*, 1960, 593.

CHAPTER 2. THE (SYMPHONIC) JAZZ AGE

1. The Roxyettes are billed as The Russell Makert Girls.

2. Harry E. Modisette, "Universal's King of Jazz Triumph," *Hollywood Daily Screen World*, 26 March 1930.

3. See Elijah Wald, *How the Beatles Destroyed Rock 'n' Roll: An Alternative History of American Popular Music* (New York: Oxford University Press, 2009); as well as John Howland, "Between the Muses and the Masses: Symphonic Jazz, 'Glorified' Entertainment, and the Rise of the American Musical Middlebrow, 1920–1944" (PhD diss., Stanford University, 2002); *Ellington Uptown: Duke Ellington, James P. Johnson, and the Birth of Concert Jazz* (Ann Arbor: University of Michigan Press, 2009); Joshua Berrett, *Louis Armstrong and Paul Whiteman: Two Kings of Jazz* (New Haven, CT: Yale University Press, 2004); Don Rayno, *Paul Whiteman: Pioneer in American Music, 1890–1930*, vol. 1 (Lanham, MD: Scarecrow); *Paul Whiteman: Pioneer in American Music, 1930–1967*, vol. 2 (Metuchen, NJ: Scarecrow, 2013); and the Whiteman discussions in Ryan Bañagale, *Arranging Gershwin: Rhapsody in Blue and the Creation of an American Icon* (New York: Oxford University Press, 2014), and Jeffrey Magee, *The Uncrowned King of Swing: Fletcher Henderson and Big Band Jazz* (Oxford: Oxford University Press, 2005).

4. Robert S. Hatten, *Interpreting Musical Gestures, Topics, and Tropes: Mozart, Beethoven, Schubert* (Bloomington: Indiana University Press, 2004), 2.

5. See, for example, Kay Shelemay, "Musical Communities: Rethinking the Collective in Music," *Journal of the American Musicological Society* 64 (2011): 349–90; Georgina Born, *Rationalizing Culture: IRCAM, Boulez, and the Institutionalization of the Musical Avant-Garde* (Berkeley: University of California Press, 1995); and Adam Krims, *Music and Urban Geography* (New York: Routledge, 2007).

6. Diana Taylor, *The Archive and the Repertoire: Performing Cultural Memory in the Americas* (Durham, NC: Duke University Press, 2003), 104.

7. Ibid., 94.

8. Ibid., 86.

9. Winthrop Sargeant, *Jazz: Hot and Hybrid* (New York: E.P. Dutton, 1938/ 1946), 231–32.

10. Howland, *Ellington Uptown*, 145–47.

11. Henry Jenkins, *What Made Pistachio Nuts? Early Sound Comedy and the Vaudeville Aesthetic* (New York: Columbia University Press, 1992).

12. Ibid., 63 (emphasis added).

13. See Howland, *Ellington Uptown*, 83–87.

14. Jenkins, *What Made*, 61.

15. Ibid., 79.

16. This paraphrases the 1922 Victor Records promotional catalog copy for the 1923 Whiteman recording of *I'll Build a Stairway to Paradise*. This text is quoted in Charles Edward Smith's liner notes to Paul Whiteman, *Paul Whiteman*, RCA Victor LPV-555, n.d., LP.

17. Jenkins, *What Made*, 68.

18. Ibid., 69.

19. Ibid., 69–70.

20. "Paramount (Paul Whiteman's 'Rainbow Rhapsody' Unit)," *Variety*, 4 April 1928, n.p.

21. "At the Paramount," *Journal*, 30 March 1928, n.p.

22. See Gavin Jones, *Strange Talk: The Politics of Dialect Literature in Gilded Age America* (Berkeley: University of California Press, 1999).

23. Jenkins, *What Made*, 70–71.

24. Ibid., 71.

25. Olin Downes, "A Concert of Jazz," *New York Times*, 13 February 1924, n.p.

26. Olin Downes, "Whiteman's Jazz," 8 October 1928, 27.

27. Ibid.

28. Ibid., emphasis added. Also see Howland, *Ellington Uptown*, 154–57.

29. "The Jazz Problem: Opinions of Prominent Men and Musicians," *The Etude Music Magazine*, August 1924, full special issue.

30. Winthrop Sargeant, "In Defense of the High-Brow," *Life*, 1949, 102.

31. See Sargeant, *Jazz*, 221–34.

32. Paul Whiteman, "The Japanese Sandman/Whispering," Victor 18690, 1920, 78 rpm.

33. Russell Sanjek, *From Print to Plastic: Publishing and Promoting America's Popular Music, 1900–1980* (Brooklyn: Institute for Studies in American Music and Brooklyn College, 1983), 13.

34. Henry Osgood, *So This Is Jazz* (New York: Little, Brown, 1926), 100.

35. See "F. C. Coppicus Presents Paul Whiteman and His Greater Concert Orchestra in Their Second Transcontinental Concert Tour, Season 1925–1926," news release, 1925; "F. C. Coppicus Presents Paul Whiteman and His Greater Concert Orchestra in Their Third Transcontinental Concert Tour, Season 1928–1929," news release, 1928; and "F. C. Coppicus Presents Paul Whiteman and His Orchestra of Twenty-Five in Their First Transcontinental Concert Tour, Season 1924–25," news release, 1924. From the Paul Whiteman Collection ("Whiteman Collection") of Williams College, Williams, MA.

36. See Rayno, *Paul Whiteman*, vol. 1; and Thomas DeLong, *Pops: Paul Whiteman, King of Jazz* (Piscataway, NJ: New Century Publishers, 1983).

37. See Howland, *Ellington Uptown*.

38. This "Lady Jazz" reference was conveyed in Abbe Niles, "Lady Jazz in the Vestibule," *New Republic*, 23 December 1925, 138–39; and Osgood, *So This*, 204, which was the quotation source.

39. Osgood, *So This*, 131.

40. Isham Jones, "American Dance Music Is Not Jazz," *The Etude*, 24 August 1924, 526.

41. "Not Jazz Band, Whiteman Says of Famous Orchestra at the Coliseum Tonight," *Musical Leader*, 19 November 1925, n.p.

42. Paul Whiteman and Mary Margaret McBride, *Jazz* (New York: J. H. Sears, 1926). On the Modern American Music concert-works, see Howland, *Between the Muses*.

43. Lance Bowling, "Arthur Lange: A Biographical Sketch," *The Cue Sheet*, December 1990, 12.

44. Lance Bowling, "Arthur Lange on 'Dardanella,'" *The Cue Sheet*, December 1990, 130–31.

45. Selvin's Novelty Orchestra, "Dardanella," Victor 18633, 1919, 78 rpm. See Tim Gracyk, *Popular American Recording Pioneers: 1895–1925* (New York: Routledge, 2000), 285. Lance Bowling suggests this recording sold 6.5 million copies. Bowling, "Biographical Sketch," 129. This figure probably derives from a trade article in Lange's estate. This number seems exaggerated. Whiteman's 1920 "Whispering"/"Japanese Sandman" was celebrated for having sold 2.5 million copies, and his 1923 "Three O'Clock in the Morning" reportedly sold 3.5 million copies. James Lincoln Collier, "Jazz," in *The New Grove Dictionary of Jazz* (New York: St. Martin's Press, 1994), 587.

46. Bowling, "Arthur Lange on 'Dardanella,'" 130.

47. "Melody Mart," *Billboard*, 22 April 1925, 22.

48. Arthur Lange, *Arranging for the Modern Dance Orchestra* (New York: Arthur Lange, 1926).

49. Whiteman, *Jazz*, 219–20.

50. Lange, *Arranging*, 214.

51. Ibid., 82.

52. Ibid., 188–89. See also Whiteman, *Jazz*, 191–216 and 198–99.

53. Lange, *Arranging*, 87 and 90.

54. Ibid., 178–79.

55. Ibid., 207.

56. See Sargeant, *Jazz*, 231–32.

57. Ibid., 263.

58. Tom Bennett, "Arranging Music for Radio," in *Music in Radio Broadcasting*, ed. Gilbert Chase (New York: McGraw-Hill, 1946), 77–79.

59. Ibid., 86.

60. Ferde Grofé, "Carve Out Your Own Career," *Etude*, July 1938, 426.

61. Osgood, *So This Is Jazz*, viii.

62. Ibid., 110.

63. Osgood, *So This Is Jazz*, 110.

64. Robert W. Snyder, *The Voice of the City: Vaudeville and Popular Culture in New York* (Chicago: Ivan R. Dee, 1989), 125.

65. This arrangement is part of the Whiteman Collection.

66. Lange, *Arranging*, 212.

67. See Howland, *Ellington Uptown*, especially pp. 151–57.

68. Though this chord type is infrequent in symphonic jazz and novelty ragtime, the jazz-practice "sus4" chord is anachronistic for this configuration.

69. See Martin Marks, *Music and the Silent Film: Contexts and Case Studies, 1895–1924* (New York: Oxford University Press, 1997).

70. Linda Mizejewski, *Ziegfeld Girl: Image and Icon in Culture and Cinema* (Durham, NC: Duke University Press, 1999).

71. Ibid., 11.

72. Ibid., 6.

73. Ibid.

74. Emphasis added. Abel Green, "Paul Whiteman's Concert," *Variety*, 10 October 1928, 53.

75. Lloyd Whitesell, *Wonderful Design: Glamour in the Hollywood Musical* (New York: Oxford University Press, 2018), 10.

76. Ibid., 37, 40.

77. Ann Douglas, *Terrible Honesty: Mongrel Manhattan in the 1920s* (New York: Farrar, Strauss and Giroux, 1995), 4.

78. See H. L. Mencken, *The American Language: An Inquiry into the Development of English in the United States*, 3rd ed. (New York: Alfred A. Knopf, 1923), 30, 33–34, 398–99, 402–3, for examples of "novel Americanisms."

79. Ibid., 30–34.

80. See Dwight Macdonald, "Masscult and Midcult, Part 1," *Partisan Review*, 1960, 203–33.

81. See, for example, Clement Greenberg, "Avant Garde and Kitsch," *Partisan Review*, Fall 1939, 34–49, Macdonald, "Masscult and Midcult, Part 1," and Dwight Macdonald, "Masscult and Midcult, Part 2," *Partisan Review*, 1960, 589–631.

82. Joan Shelley Rubin, *The Making of Middlebrow Culture* (Chapel Hill: University of North Carolina Press, 1992).

83. See Van Wyck Brooks, "America's Coming of Age," in *Van Wyck Brooks: The Early Years, a Selection from His Works, 1908–1921*, ed. Claire Sprague (New York: Harper Torchbooks, 1968), 79–158.

84. Ibid., xviii.

85. There is one rather problematic moment of Black presence in the film: in "A Bench in the Park," Whiteman hams it up with a pickaninny girl sitting in his lap.

86. See Magee, *Uncrowned King*, Jeffrey Magee, *Irving Berlin's American Musical Theater* (New York: Oxford University Press, 2012), John Wriggle, *Blue Rhythm Fantasy: Big Band Jazz Arranging in the Swing Era* (Urbana: University of Illinois Press, 2016), David Ake, "Jazz Historiography and the Problem of Louis Jordan," in *Jazz/Not Jazz: The Music and Its Boundaries* (Berkeley: University of California Press, 2012), 42–61, and Howland, *Ellington Uptown*..

87. Scott DeVeaux, from the abstract to Scott DeVeaux, "Core and Boundaries" (Leeds International Jazz Conference, Leeds, UK, 11 March 2005).

88. Idwal Jones, "Whiteman Dispenses Gay Music," *San Francisco Examiner*, 18 October 1926, n.p.

CHAPTER 3. JAZZ WITH STRINGS

1. Joseph Horowitz, *Understanding Toscanini: How He Became an American Culture-God and Helped Create a New Audience for Old Music* (New York: Knopf, 1987), 7.

2. Dwight Macdonald, "Masscult and Midcult, Part 2," *Partisan Review*, 27, Fall 1960, 628.

3. John F. Szwed, *Jazz 101: A Complete Guide to Learning and Loving Jazz* (New York: Hyperion, 2000), 6–10.

4. Otto Cesana, "Cesana Analyzes Use of Strings in Dance Bands," *Metronome*, 1942, 39.

5. The Dorsey Brothers Concert Orchestra ensemble can be heard in the nine-minute "Was It a Dream," parts 1 and 2, Okeh 41083, 78 rpm.

6. Artie Shaw, *The Trouble with Cinderella: An Outline of Identity* (Santa Barbara, CA: Fithian, 1992), 291.

7. Recordings can be heard on *Aircheck #1: The 1930s*, Aircheck Records (Vancouver, BC) no number, n.d., LP.

8. Shaw, *The Trouble*, 293–94. See Howland, *Ellington Uptown*, 150–57.

9. "Blues," on *Aircheck #1*.

10. Paul Grein, *Capitol Records: Fiftieth Anniversary, 1942–1992* (Hollywood: Capitol Records, 1992), 58.

11. Artie Shaw, "Good Enough Ain't Good Enough," liner notes to Artie Shaw, *Artie Shaw, Self-Portrait*, Bluebird RCA 63808, 2001, CD box set.

12. Tommy Dorsey and His Orchestra, "Blues in the Night," 1942; reissued on Tommy Dorsey, *The Sentimental Gentleman of Swing: Centennial Edition*, Bluebird 711672, 2005, compact disc box set.

13. A photograph is in Stanley Dance, *The World of Earl Hines* (New York: Charles Scribner, 1977), 96–97.

14. Barry Ulanov, "The Fatha!," *Metronome*, February 1945, 19.

15. Will Friedwald, *Sinatra! The Song Is You: A Singer's Art* (New York: Da Capo, 1997), 79.

16. Nelson Riddle, *Arranged by Nelson Riddle*, ed. Jeff Sultanof (New York: Alfred Music, 1985), 169.

17. Tommy Dorsey, "On the Sunny Side of the Street," 1944; reissued on Dorsey, *Sentimental Gentleman*.

18. "The Sy Oliver Story, Part 1," 1974, http://www.jazzprofessional.com /interviews/SyOliver_1.htm (accessed 25 June 2019).

19. John Rockwell, "6-LP Set, 'The Voice,' Samples Sinatra Years on Columbia," *New York Times*, 23 November 1986, H25 and 27.

20. Frank Sinatra, "I'm Walking Behind You," Capitol, 1953; reissued on Frank Sinatra, *The Complete Capitol Singles Collection*, Capitol 38089, 1996, compact disc box set.

21. Paul Weston quoted in Joseph Lanza, *Elevator Music: A Surreal History of Muzak, Easy-Listening, and Other Moodsong* (London: Quartet Books, 1994), 72.

22. Paul Weston, "You Go to My Head," Paul Weston, *Music for Dreaming*, Capitol BD9, 1945, 78 rpm album; reissued on Paul Weston, and His Orchestra, *Music for Dreaming/Music for Memories/Songs without Words*, Vocalion (Austria) CDUS 3023, 2002, compact disc. The orchestration was made available to me by Tim Weston, Weston's son.

23. *The Jazz Scene*, Verve 314521661-1, 1994, compact disc box set (orig. Clef Records 10413, 1950, 78 rpm vinylite box set).

24. "*Down Beat* Critics Poll Archive," http://www.downbeat.com/default.asp ?sect=cpollindex (accessed 14 January 2011).

25. Michael Levin, "Calls 'Jazz Scene' Most Remarkable Album Ever," *Down Beat*, January 1950, 14.

26. From page 3 of the concert program to Stan Kenton, "Stan Kenton and His Orchestra, Innovations in Modern Music for 1950," news release, 1950.

27. Stan Kenton and His Orchestra, "Lonesome Road," *Innovations in Modern Music*, Capitol P-189, 1950, 10″ LP; reissued on Stan Kenton, *The Innovations Orchestra*, Capitol 59965, 1997, compact disc.

28. "The Jazz Beat," 28 May 1949, n.p.

29. Charlie Parker, "Just Friends," *Charlie Parker with Strings*, Mercury/Clef MGC-501, 1949, 10″ LP; reissued on Charlie Parker, *Charlie Parker with Strings: The Master Takes*, Verve 314523448, 1995, compact disc. Source for sales ranking are Joe Goldberg's liner notes for this album.

30. Charlie Parker quoted in Nat Hentoff, "Counterpoint," in *The Charlie Parker Companion: Six Decades of Commentary*, ed. Carl Woideck (New York: Schirmer, 1998), 80.

31. Norman Granz, interview by Elliot Meadow, 27 February 1987. Transcript provided Tad Hershorn, Institute of Jazz Studies, Dana Library, Rutgers University Newark.

32. Norman Granz, liner notes to Parker, *Charlie Parker with Strings: The Master Takes.*

33. Borrowed from Scott DeVeaux, "Core and Boundaries" (Leeds International Jazz Conference, Leeds, UK, 11 March 2005).

34. See *"Down Beat* Critics Poll Archive."

35. For a complementary discussion, see David Brackett, *Categorizing Sound: Genre and Twentieth-Century Popular Music* (Oakland: University of California Press, 2016).

36. See ibid. and Russell Sanjek, *From Print to Plastic: Publishing and Promoting America's Popular Music, 1900–1980* (New York: Institute for Studies in American Music, 1983).

37. Charles Hamm, "Towards a New Reading of Gershwin," in *The Gershwin Style: New Looks at the Music of George Gershwin*, ed. Wayne Schneider (New York: Oxford University Press, 1999), 5–6.

38. "Pop Record Reviews," *Billboard*, 27 January 1945, 64.

39. See Bill Simon, "Categories of Jazz Disks," *Billboard*, 23 April 1955, 14, 22, 24, Is Horowitz, "Jazz Disks, Paced by LP, Hit Cool 55% Jump in Hot Year," *Billboard*, 1, 13, "Editorial: The Jazz Renaissance," *Billboard*, 13, and "Buying, Selling, Programming Jazz Records, Tunes, and Talent," *Billboard*, 23 April 1955, 13–24.

40. National Endowment for the Arts, *Jazz Masters, 1982–2011* (Washington, DC: National Endowment for the Arts, 2011), 47.

41. Both LPs appear in "Review Spotlight On," *Billboard*, 2 June 1956, 22.

42. National Academy of Recording Arts and Sciences, *52nd OEP Category Description Guide* (National Academy of Recording Arts and Sciences, 2010), 2, http://www2.grammy.com/PDFs/Recording_Academy/52guide.pdf (accessed 14 January 2011).

43. "Vinyl vixen" is borrowed from Benjamin Darling, *Vixens of Vinyl: The Alluring Ladies of Vintage Album Covers* (San Francisco: Chronicle Books, 2001). See also "Music to Make Your Eyeballs Pop: Jacket Art Hath Pulchritude to Soothe the Savage Breast," *Playboy*, July 1958, 31–33.

44. Gary Giddins, liner notes to Charlie Parker, *Bird with Strings: Live at the Apollo, Carnegie Hall, and Birdland*, TriStar Music 80913, 1994, compact disc (orig. Columbia Records, 1977, LP).

CHAPTER 4. DEFINING POPULUXE

1. By "democratizing," I mean both the popularization of the classical music canon "for the masses" and the creation of new, broadly accessible concert works, including "pops" repertoire.

2. See Lloyd Whitesell, *Wonderful Design: Glamour in the Hollywood Musical* (New York: Oxford University Press, 2018).

3. See Dwight Macdonald, "Masscult and Midcult, Part 1," *Partisan Review*, 27, Spring 1960, 203–33, "Masscult and Midcult, Part 2," *Partisan Review*, 27, Fall 1960, 589–631, and *Masscult and Midcult: Essays Against the American Grain*, ed. John Summers (New York: New York Review of Books Classics, 2011; repr., 2011).

4. Dwight Macdonald, "The Bright Young Men in the Arts," *Esquire*, September 1958, 39.

5. David Riesman, "Listening to Popular Music," in *Mass Culture: The Popular Arts in America*, ed. Bernard Rosenberg, and David Manning White (Glencoe, IL: Free Press, 1957), 414.

6. This middlebrow studies territory involves two-way cultural traffic, with middle-class aspirations/pretensions upward toward some facet of higher-brow cultural capital, and with highbrow-associated efforts (or compromises) leaning toward achieving some sort of popularity with the middle classes. The brow activity in either case concerned acts that were interpreted as aspirational incursions across the boundaries of higher *cultural* status, with highbrow being the hierarchically dominant means of measure. The wealth of activities that transpired on these paths have dominated middlebrow studies. This focus began with the Joan Shelly Rubin's 1992 *The Making of Middlebrow Culture* (Chapel Hill: University of North Carolina Press). This has also dominated studies in the Middlebrow Research Network and the research in the Music and the Middlebrow circle. See the citations noted in this book's introduction, endnote 1. This is all immensely valuable brow-studies work. However, the present argument for considering "middlebrow-adjacent" aspirations in "classy" entertainment contends that brow studies can benefit from attention to *both* the culture-aspirational paths just outlined, and lower-middle socioeconomic- and glamour-aspirational culture.

7. Russell Lynes, "Highbrow, Lowbrow, Middlebrow," *Harper's*, February 1949, 28, and 25–28 passim.

8. "High-Brow, Low-Brow, Middle-Brow," *Life*, 11 April 1949, 99–102.

9. André Kostelanetz, "Middle-Brow Recordings," *Liberty*, September 1947, 85.

10. Keir Keightley, "Music for Middlebrows: Defining the Easy Listening Era, 1946–1966," *American Music* 26, no. 3 (Fall 2008): 318.

11. Ibid., 309.

12. Hal Halperin, "Cocktail Lounges Now Big Business," *Variety*, 5 January 1944; and Abel Green, "Terrific N.Y. Nitery Biz Now So Consistent It's Become a Cliche," *Variety*, 5 January 1944.

13. Thomas Hine, *Populuxe* (New York: Alfred A. Knopf, 1986), 6.

14. Ibid., 11.

15. "It's No Longer Free Lunch; 'Cocktail Lounge' Is Classier," *Variety*, 7 January 1942, 183.

16. Halperin, "Cocktail Lounges Now Big Business," 207, and Green, "Terrific N.Y. Nitery Biz."

17. "N.Y. Copa Dates Como," *Variety*, 9 June 1943, 41.

18. Abel Green, "World War II Spending Responsible for Creating the Night-club Habit," *Variety*, 9 January 1946, 271.

19. George Phair, "Sinatra Slays the Girls, Bores the Boys in Pop-Symph Concert at H'wood Bowl," *Variety*, 18 August 1943, 3, 14.

20. "Swoon-Croon on the Wane," *Variety*, 17 July 1946, 1, 23.

21. Glenn Pullen, "Symphonic Music with Dinner May Set New Vogue," *Variety*, 22 October 1947, passim 1, 61.

22. See "Frank De Vol," Wikipedia, 2019, https://en.wikipedia.org/wiki/Frank _De_Vol (accessed 18 April 2019).

23. See Albin Zak, *I Don't Sound Like Nobody: Remaking Music in 1950s America* (Ann Arbor: University of Michigan Press, 2010). Also see James Bayless, "Innovations in Studio Design and Construction in the Capitol Tower Recording Studios," *Journal of Audio Engineering Society* 5, no. 2 (April 1957): 71–76.

24. Tom Perchard, "Mid-century Modern Jazz: Music and Design in the Post-war Home," *Popular Music* 36 (2016): 57.

25. Stephen Gundle, *Glamour: A History* (London: Oxford University Press, 2008), chapter 6.

26. Ibid., 231, 232.

27. Whitesell, *Wonderful*.

28. Ibid., 10, 37, 40.

29. "The Billboard Picks: Nature Boy," *Billboard*, 3 April 1948, 28; "Record Reviews: The King Cole Trio," *Billboard*, 27 August 1949, 34.

30. "The Billboard Picks: Land of Love," *Billboard*, 27 August 1949, 34, and "Record Reviews: Nat 'King' Cole," *Billboard*, 17 September 1949, 33.

31. The harmony from which the arranger was working was A7sus (A-D-E-G), and the string sweep is A5–G5–E5–D5–A4–G4.

32. "Cole Breaks Up Trio for Sole Billing," *Billboard*, 1 September 1951, 18.

33. Tom Bennett, "Arranging Music for Radio," in *Music in Radio Broadcasting*, ed. Gilbert Chase (New York: McGraw-Hill, 1946), 79 and 86 passim.

34. "Jazzbo" is colloquial postwar American slang that refers to a passionate but self-consciously cool or hip insider (fan, devotee, aficionado, or musician) of jazz culture. The discourses of midcentury jazz hipness are central here. On the latter, see Phil Ford, *Dig: Sound and Music in Hip Culture* (New York: Oxford University Press, 2013), passim.

35. Peter Levinson, *September in the Rain: The Life of Nelson Riddle* (New York: Billboard Books, 2001), 71–72 passim.

36. Quoted in Levinson, *September*, 93.

37. Ibid., 97.

38. "Cab Calloway's 'Hepster Dictionary,' a 1939 Glossary of the Lingo (the 'Jive') of the Harlem Renaissance," 2015, http://www.openculture.com/2015/01 /cab-calloways-hepster-dictionary.html (accessed 10 July 2019). A similar glossary is in Mezz Mezzrow, *Really the Blues* (New York: Random House, 1946).

39. Norman Mailer, "The White Negro: Superficial Reflections on the Hipster," *Dissent*, Fall 1957, https://www.dissentmagazine.org/online_articles/the-white-negro-fall-1957 (accessed 10 July 2019).

40. Keightley, "Music for Middlebrows," 317. On "beautiful music," also see Joseph Lanza, *Elevator Music: A Surreal History of Muzak®, Easy-Listening, and Other Moodsong®*, revised/expanded ed. (Ann Arbor: University of Michigan Press, 2004).

41. Ford, *Dig*, 5. Also see Thomas Frank, *The Conquest of Cool: Business Culture, Counterculture, and the Rise of Hip Consumerism* (Chicago: University of Chicago Press, 1997).

42. Levinson, *September*, 112.

43. Will Friedwald, *Sinatra! The Song Is You: A Singer's Art* (New York: Da Capo, 1997), 223.

44. Grein, *Capitol*, copyright page.

45. Stephen Holden, "Frank Sinatra at His Peak," in Grein, *Capitol*, 58.

46. Levinson, *September*, 75.

47. Holden, "Frank Sinatra at His Peak," 59.

48. Ibid., 58.

49. Ibid., 59.

50. Ibid.

51. See Andrew Berish, *Lonesome Roads and Streets of Dreams: Place, Mobility, and Race in Jazz of the 1930s and '40s* (Chicago: University of Chicago Press, 2012), 214–17.

52. Allison McCracken, "'God's Gift to Us Girls': Crooning, Gender, and the Re-creation of American Popular Song, 1928–1933," *American Music* 17, no. 4 (Winter 1999): 372.

53. Ibid., 368.

54. Ibid., 389.

55. John Rockwell, "6-LP Set, 'The Voice,' Samples Sinatra Years on Columbia," *New York Times*, 23 November 1986, H25.

56. "Swooner-Crooner: Satellites Sigh and Scream as Singing Sensation Sinatra Solos with Symphony," *Life*, 23 August 1943, 127.

57. "Paul Weston," Wikipedia, 2019, https://en.wikipedia.org/wiki/Paul_Weston (accessed 11 July 2019).

58. See Friedwald, *Sinatra*, passim.

59. Alan W. Livingston, "Giant Market of Adults Should Be Disk Target," *Variety*, 30 July 1952, 39.

60. Les Baxter, *Le Sacre du Sauvage*, Capitol T-288, 1951, LP.

61. Grein, *Capitol*, 66.

62. James Bacon, *How Sweet It Is: The Story of Jackie Gleason* (New York: St. Martin's, 1985), 119.

63. Untitled clipping dated 1948–50 from the "Gleason, Jackie" clippings file at the Institute of Jazz Studies, Dana Library, Rutgers University Newark.

64. See Benjamin Darling, *Vixens of Vinyl: The Alluring Ladies of Vintage Album Covers* (San Francisco: Chronicle Books, 2001).

65. Harold Lawrence, "What You Will: 'Music For' Disks Give Anything You Want," *New York Times*, 21 November 1954, XX9.

66. "Music to Make Your Eyeballs Pop: Jacket Art Hath Pulchritude to Soothe the Savage Breast," *Playboy*, July 1958, 31–33.

67. Hugh Hefner, "Editorial," *Playboy*, December 1953, 3.

68. Robert George Reisner, "Personality: Sinatra," *Playboy*, November 1958, 63.

69. This summary of Ehrenreich is taken from Reed Johnson, "Playboy at 50: A Man's Notes," *Los Angeles Times*, 28 November 2003, E-1. Johnson is referring to Barbara Ehrenreich, *The Hearts of Men: American Dreams and the Flight from Commitment*, Kindle reprint ed. (Garden City, NJ: Anchor Press, 1983).

70. Ehrenreich, *Hearts*, loc. 912.

71. Johnson, "Playboy," E-1.

72. Macdonald, "Masscult and Midcult," Part 1, 213.

73. Bosley Crowther, "Screen: 'Tender Trap,'" *New York Times*, 11 November 1955, 29.

74. Alexander's work is cited in the opening film credits. On Riddle's contribution, see Levinson, *September*, 121.

75. See the numerous connections one fan site outlines between Fleming (a Sinatra fan), the Bond character, and Sinatra at "A Salute to Sinatra," MI6: The Home of James Bond 007, https://www.mi6-hq.com/sections/articles/history-james-bond-and-frank-sinatra?id=04388 (accessed 13 July 2019). Also see the Sinatra index entries in Jon Burlingame, *The Music of James Bond* (New York: Oxford University Press, 2012).

76. I am indebted here to a discussion with Phil Ford about Sinatra and midcentury hipness.

77. Robert Legare, "Meeting at the Summit: Sinatra and His Buddies Bust 'Em Up in Vegas," *Playboy*, June 1960, 32.

78. "Letters to the Editors: High-Brow, Low-Brow," *Life*, 2 May 1949, see 8, 10, 12, here 10.

79. Herbert J. Gans, *Popular Culture and High Culture: An Analysis and Evaluation of Taste*, revised/updated ed. (New York: Basic Books, 1999), 10.

80. "Album and LP Record Reviews," *Billboard*, 18 February 1950, 40.

81. Gans, *Popular Culture*, 110.

82. Macdonald, "Masscult and Midcult, Part 2," 592–93.

CHAPTER 5. PHIL SPECTOR
AND THE LOWER MIDDLEBROW

1. Louis Menand, "Browbeaten: Dwight Macdonald's War on Midcult," *New Yorker*, 5 September 2011, http://www.newyorker.com/magazine/2011/09/05/browbeaten (accessed 18 April 2017).

2. National Endowment for the Humanities, "Tom Wolfe," 2006, https://www.neh.gov/about/awards/jefferson-lecture/tom-wolfe-biography (accessed 20 July 2019).

3. "Contemporary Thinkers: Tom Wolfe," Contemporarythinkers.org, 2019, https://contemporarythinkers.org/tom-wolfe/ (accessed 20 July 2019).

4. National Endowment, "Tom Wolfe."

5. See the reprints of these essays in Tom Wolfe, *Kandy-Kolored Tangerine-Flake Streamline Baby* (New York: Farrar, Straus and Giroux, 1965).

6. Mick Brown, *Tearing Down the Wall of Sound: The Rise and Fall of Phil Spector* (London: Bloomsbury, 2007), 3.

7. "Singles Reviews: The Crystals," *Billboard*, 3 August 1963, 18.

8. Maureen Cleave, "Disc Date," *Evening Standard* (UK), 24 January 1964, 6.

9. "Jack Nitzsche: Music Above All," *Record World*, 14 August 1965, http://www.martinruk.net/JackNitzsche/magazines.htm (accessed 29 May 2017).

10. Dwight Macdonald, "Masscult and Midcult, Part 2," *Partisan Review*, 27, Fall 1960, 615n7.

11. André Kostelanetz and the Robin Hood Dell Orchestra, *Music of Tchaikovsky*, Columbia Records ML 4151, 1950, LP, and André Kostelanetz, "Middle-Brow Recordings," *Liberty*, September 1947, 85.

12. Herbert J. Gans, *Popular Culture and High Culture: An Analysis and Evaluation of Taste*, revised/updated ed. (New York: Basic Books, 1999), 110.

13. Cleave, "Disc Date," 6.

14. Wolfe, *Kandy*, 104–5.

15. Ibid., 107.

16. Ibid., 98.

17. Ibid., 98–99.

18. Two sources list the episode as no. 699 with a broadcast date of 23 August 1964. See Archival Television Audio Inc., "'Open End' (a database search)," 2019, https://www.atvaudio.com/ata_search.php?keywords=OPEN+END+WITH+DAVID+SUSSKIND (accessed 8 August 2019), "The David Susskind Show (1958–1987): Episode List, 1964," IMDB.com, 2019, https://www.imdb.com/title/tt0369146/episodes?year=1964 (accessed 18 August 2019), and "The David Susskind Show," Wikipedia, 2019, https://en.wikipedia.org/wiki/The_David_Susskind_Show (accessed 8 August 2019).

19. Wolfe, *Kandy*, 97–98.

20. See "*David Susskind Show*."

21. See Scott DeVeaux, "Constructing the Jazz Tradition: Jazz Historiography," *Black American Literature Forum* 25 (1991): 525–60, and Bernard Gendron, *Between Montmartre and the Mudd Club: Popular Music and the Avant-Garde* (Chicago: University of Chicago Press, 2002).

22. "*Open End* to Discuss Pop Sound," *Billboard*, 23 December 1963, 8.

23. Wolfe, *Kandy*, 103.

24. Ibid., 105–6.

25. Ibid., 100.

26. The Spector literature is conflicting with regard to the date information for the Gold Star sessions to "Be My Baby," Philles 116, and "Then He Kissed Me," Philles 115, in July 1963. Based on evidence in reliable sources as well as the Nitzsche manuscript charts, my sense is that these tracks were arranged and recorded in very close proximity, with "Baby" being arranged and recorded first. See Phil Spector, *Back to Mono (1958–1969)*, ABKCO 7118-2, 1991, CD boxed set liner note booklet, 21, 24; Brown, *Tearing Down*, 142; and Phil Spector, *Phil Spector in the Studio, 1962–66: Gold Star Sessions*, vols. 1–5, ROIO/Bigozine2.com 2011, five compact disc set (private release bootleg recordings).

27. Jerry Leiber, Mike Stoller, and David Ritz, *Hound Dog: The Leiber and Stoller Autobiography*, Kindle ed. (New York: Simon and Schuster, 2009), 201.

28. Jack Nitzsche, "BBC Radio Oxford Interview," interview by Karel Beer, MP3 file, broadcast 16 January 1982.

29. Leiber, *Hound Dog*, location 2061.

30. Binia Tymieniecka, dir., *Da Doo Run Run: Story of Phil Spector* (Onchan, Isle of Man: Charly Films, 2009), DVD.

31. Richard Buskin, "Classic Tracks: The Ronettes 'Be My Baby,'" *Sound on Sound*, April 2007, http://www.soundonsound.com/sos/apr07/articles/classic tracks_0407.htm?print=yes (accessed 19 May 2017).

32. See ibid.

33. See ibid.

34. Buskin, "Classic Tracks: The Ronettes."

35. Tymieniecka, *Da Doo*.

36. Phil Spector, *The Phil Spector Sessions*, Seven Stories [no number], 2000, four compact disc box set.

37. Richard Williams, "Music: The Producer," *The Guardian*, 5 February 2003, https://www.theguardian.com/music/2003/feb/05/artsfeatures.popandrock (accessed 18 April 2017).

38. The session charts I have for the *Lonely Surfer* album were provided by Martin Roberts. Roberts received the charts from Steve Tordoff. The 31 May 1963 chart lists "Song for a Summer Night" (the B side) and "It's My Party" (never issued) first in pen, and "Lonely Surfer" in a light pencil, suggesting possibly that it was not originally planned for the session.

39. Brown states that the "Baby" session was held on 29 July. Brown, *Tearing Down*, 142. This is in close proximity to the "Kissed Me" session, which likely occurred afterward. See previous note.

40. "Album Reviews: Billboard Spotlight Picks, Pop Spotlight, *The Lonely Surfer*," *Billboard*, 28 September 1963, 28.

41. "Album Reviews: Pop Picks, *The Lonely Surfer*," *Cash Box*, 5 October 1963, 18.

42. Much of this information derives from Richie Unterberger, "Jimmy Bowen Biography," http://www.allmusic.com/artist/jimmy-bowen-mn0000354600 /biography (accessed 31 May 2017).

43. Marty Cooper, email communication, 28 May 2017.

44. I have not found this specific recording to verify details of the reworking, but an online copy of the B side of the same record—"La Macarena (The Bull Fight Song)"—reveals (as one might expect) a twangy, reverb-heavy surf-rock. See https://www.youtube.com/watch?v=6wxGrrM6BbY (accessed 31 May 2017). Various details from Martin Roberts, John Blair, and Stephen McParland, "Del Ray and The Roamers—Lonely Highway—Capella 101," 2007, http://www.spectropop.com/JackNitzsche/pastrotw6.htm (accessed 31 May 2017).

45. Kristian St. Clair, private email correspondance with the author, 16 May 2017. There are musical similarities, but on 28 September 1963, that track enters the *Cash Box* Top 100 chart (number 94), just as "Lonely Surfer" peaked in the weeks before at number 37 and had come down to 63. It seems the influence was the other way around, since "Surfer" was out first.

46. Mark Ribowsky, *He's a Rebel: Phil Spector, Rock and Roll's Legendary Producer*, 2nd ed. (New York: Da Capo Press, 2006), 290.

47. See Buskin, "Classic Tracks: The Ronettes."

48. Nitzsche, "BBC Radio."

49. Ibid.

50. See Buskin, "Classic Tracks: The Ronettes."

51. On this aesthetic, see Albin Zak, "No-Fi: Crafting a Language of Music in 1950s Pop," in *The Art of Record Production: An Introductory Reader for a New Academic Field*, ed. Simon Frith and Simon Zagorski-Thomas (London: Ashgate, 2013), 43–56.

52. Nitzsche, "BBC Radio."

53. See "Phil Spector Recording at Gold Star Studio," YouTube, 2019, https://www.youtube.com/watch?v=CJakW1Efmj8 (accessed 20 December 2019). This clip, from an unknown television broadcast, is widely circulated.

54. As based on the outtakes and Buskin, "Classic Tracks: The Ronettes."

55. "Singles Reviews: The Ronettes," *Billboard*, 17 August 1963, 32. Also see "Record Reviews, Pick of the Week, Newcomers, 'Be My Baby'," *Cash Box*, 17 August 1963, 10.

56. Liner note booklet, p. 21, Spector, *Back to Mono*.

57. David Brackett, *Categorizing Sound: Genre and Twentieth-Century Popular Music* (Oakland: University of California Press, 2016), 241.

58. Ray Coleman, "Britain's a Gas, Say Ronettes," *Melody Maker*, 11 January 1964, n.p.

59. Ibid.

60. Ronnie Spector, *Be My Baby* (London: MacMillan, 1990), 52.

61. Ibid., 1.

62. Ibid., 21.

63. Ibid., 1.

64. Ibid., 11, 10.

65. Ibid., 1.

66. Ibid., 13.

67. Ibid., 22.

68. Ibid., 26–27.

69. Ibid., 27.

70. Ibid., 31.

71. Ibid., 34–35.

72. Ibid., 36. The quote from Ronnie specifically concerns teenage Estelle, but reflects press 1963–1964 comments about Estelle's fashion tastes and contributions.

73. Ibid., 49.

74. Ibid., 41.

75. Ibid., 57.

76. Ibid.

77. Ibid., 59.

78. See "The Ronettes—Be My Baby [American Bandstand 1963]," https:// www.youtube.com/watch?v=rKWwyiHIm2o (accessed 11 June 2020).

79. "The Exotic Look [advertisement]," *Ebony*, 1966, 194.

80. Ibid.

81. Bobbie Barbee, "Rocking the Ronettes Towards Fame: Two Sisters and a First Cousin," *Jet*, 22 September 1966, 60–61.

82. Spector, *Be My Baby*, 93–94.

83. Coleman, "Britain's a Gas," n.p.

84. June Harris, "The Ronettes," *Disc*, 9 November 1963, n.p.

85. See "Murray The K—It's What's Happening, Baby," Wikipedia, 2017, https://en.wikipedia.org/wiki/Murray_The_K_–_It's_What's_Happening,_Baby (accessed 16 January 2020). Their excerpt can be seen at "The Ronettes—Be My Baby (1964)," YouTube, 2018, https://www.youtube.com/watch?v=B8wjMwgAwzQ (accessed 16 January 2020).

86. Noted in Gans, *Popular Culture*, xvi, with reference to Herbert J. Gans, "Popular Culture in America," in *Social Problems: A Modern Approach*, ed. Howard S. Becker (New York: Wiley, 1966), 549–620.

87. See Russell Lynes, "Highbrow, Lowbrow, Middlebrow," *Harper's*, February 1949, 12–28, and Russell Lynes, *The Tastemakers* (New York: Harper and Brothers, 1955).

88. Gans, *Popular Culture*, 110, 111.

89. Ibid., 110.

90. Russell Lynes, *Snobs: A Guidebook to Your Friends, Your Enemies, Your Colleagues and Yourself* (New York: Harper, 1950).

91. Gans, *Popular Culture*, 143.

92. Ibid., xi.

93. Ibid., xvi. Gans received his MA in sociology under David Riesman. See Herbert J. Gans, Nathan Glazer, Joseph Gusfield, and Christopher Jencks, eds., *On the Making of Americans: Essays in Honor of David Riesman* (Philadelphia: University of Pennsylvania Press, 1979).

94. See Richard Peterson and Roger Kern, "Changing Highbrow Taste: From Snob to Omnivore," *American Sociological Review* 61 (1996): 900–907 and

Richard Peterson, and Albert Simkus, "How Musical Tastes Mark Occupational Status Groups," in *Cultivating Differences: Symbolic Boundaries and the Making of Inequality*, ed. Michele Lamont and Marcel Fournier (Chicago: University of Chicago Press, 1992), 152–69.

95. Gans, *Popular Culture*, 212n12.

96. Ibid., 12.

97. Ibid., 7, 95.

98. Ibid., xv.

99. Ibid., 94, 96–97.

100. Ibid., 95.

101. Ibid., 10.

102. Ibid., 9–10.

103. Ibid., 19. Gans cites critiques of Bourdieu's cultural capital theory by Michele Lamont, Annette Lareau, Bonnie Erickson, and David Halle, see 213n21 and 214n23.

104. Ibid., 213n21.

105. Ibid., 137.

106. Arthur Bronson, "Longhair Outgrosses Baseball," *Variety*, 4 January 1956, 467.

107. "Singles Reviews: Darlene Love," *Billboard*, 5 October 1963, 12.

108. Stephen Gundle, *Glamour: A History* (London: Oxford University Press, 2008), 172.

109. Ibid.

110. Juliet Schor in Lauren Greenfield and Juliet Schor, *Generation Wealth* (London: Phaidon, 2017), 6.

111. Ibid., 7.

112. Ibid., 10.

113. Gundle, *Glamour*, 183–84.

114. Jann Wenner, "The *Rolling Stone* Interview: Phil Spector," *Rolling Stone*, 1 November 1969, 23.

115. Neil Postman, *Amusing Ourselves to Death: Public Discourse in the Age of Show Business*, 3rd ed. (London: Penguin, 2006), 92–93, 98.

116. Ibid., 98.

117. Ibid., 86–87.

118. Ibid., 11, 10.

119. Ibid., 86.

CHAPTER 6. MINING AM (WHITE) GOLD

1. Anne-Lise François, "'These Boots Were Made for Walkin': Fashion as 'Compulsive Artifice,'" in *The Seventies: The Age of Glitter in Popular Culture*, ed. Shelton Waldrep (New York: Routledge, 2000), 155, and passim, 155–57.

2. See Mike Callahan, David Edwards, and Patrice Eyries, "Time-Life Album Discography, Part 22: Super Hits/AM Gold Series," 2008, http://www.bsnpubs

.com/warner/time-life/22superhits-amgold/22superhits-amgold.html (accessed 15 November 2019); "AM Gold," Discogs.com, 2019, https://www.discogs.com/label/328190-AM-Gold?sort=year&sort_order=&limit=500&genre=All (accessed 15 November 2019); and "Time Life Music," Discogs.com, 2019, https://www.discogs.com/label/43337-Time-Life-Music (accessed 15 November 2019).

3. Bernard Gendron, *Between Montmartre and the Mudd Club: Popular Music and the Avant-Garde* (Chicago: University of Chicago Press, 2002), 161.

4. Ibid., 213.

5. Ben Fong-Torres, "Bread: Crosby, Stills, and Crumbs," *Rolling Stone*, 27 May 1971.

6. Tom Smucker, "The Carpenters: Forbidden Fruit," in *Yesterday Once More: The Carpenters Reader*, ed. Randy Schmidt (Chicago: Chicago Review Press, 2012), 38.

7. Albin Zak, *The Poetics of Rock: Cutting Tracks, Making Records* (Berkeley: University of California Press, 2001), 52.

8. See, for example, Barney Hoskyns, *Hotel California: Singer-Songwriters and Cocaine Cowboys in the LA Canyons, 1967–1976* (London: Harper Perennial, 2006).

9. Ibid., 37.

10. Ibid., 139.

11. Comments by group member Leslie Johnston and musician and audience member Randy Sparks, in Randy Schmidt, *Little Girl Blue: The Life of Karen Carpenter*, e-book ed. (Chicago: Chicago Review Press, 2010), passim, loc. 814 and 842. See also Spectrum's demos that were released on the Carpenters, *Carpenters: The Essential Collection, 1965–1997*, A&M 069493416-2 2002, four compact disc box set.

12. Schmidt, *Little Girl*, passim, loc. 806–25.

13. Bill Gavin, "Programming Newsletters: Middle-ists Have Their Problems," *Billboard*, 6 March 1965, 46.

14. Bill Gavin, "Middle-of-Road Stop, Go Signs," *Billboard*, 20 February 1965, 45.

15. Gavin, "Programming," 46.

16. Ibid.; and see Gavin, "Middle-of-Road," 45.

17. Eric Weisbard, *Top 40 Democracy: The Rival Mainstreams of American Music*, ebook ed. (Chicago: University of Chicago Press, 2014), loc. 2188.

18. See, for instance, Ulf Lindberg, Gestur Gudmundsson, Morten Michelsen, and Hans Weisethaunet, *Rock Criticism from the Beginning: Amusers, Bruisers, and Cool-Headed Cruisers* (New York: Peter Lang, 2005).

19. Dave Laing, "Bread: Gates' Philosophical Process," *Sounds*, 1975, http://www.rocksbackpages.com/Library/Article/bread-gates-philosophical-process (accessed 19 September 2019).

20. Frank Lieberman, "The Carpenters: Soft Rock and 14 Gold Records," *Saturday Evening Post* 1974 in Schmidt, *Yesterday Once*, 71–76.

21. Ben Hoyle, "Richard Carpenter: 'The Cultural Impact of the Carpenters Would Make a Great Doctoral Thesis,'" *Guardian*, 6 December 2018, https://www.thetimes.co.uk/article/richard-carpenter-the-cultural-impact-of-the-carpenters-would-make-a-great-doctoral-thesis-qzkvvbxcz (accessed 20 September 2019).

22. Paul Williams, "[Cover and Introduction]," *Crawdaddy*, 7 February 1966, 1.

23. Jann Wenner, "A Letter from the Editor," *Rolling Stone*, 9 November 1967, 2.

24. Tom Nolan, "Up from Downey," *Rolling Stone*, 4 July 1974, 60–68.

25. See Lester Bangs, *Psychotic Reactions and Carburator Dung*, ed. Greil Marcus (New York: Vintage Books, 1987).

26. Lester Bangs, "Carpenters: *Now and Then*," *Let It Rock*, November 1973, https://www.rocksbackpages.com/Library/Article/carpenters-inow-and-theni (accessed 14 March 2017).

27. Keir Keightley, "Music for Middlebrows: Defining the Easy Listening Era, 1946–1966," *American Music* 26 (Fall 2008): 309.

28. "Billboard Music Week: Programming Guide," *Billboard*, 6 November 1961, 35.

29. See Keightley, "Music for Middlebrows," 320, 323.

30. "Top 40 Easy Listening," *Billboard*, 5 June 1965, 4.

31. "Cash Box Record Reviews: Pick of the Week," *Cash Box*, 18 July 1964, 12.

32. Enoch Light, and His Orchestra, *Great Themes from Hit Films in Dimension 3*, Command RS871SD 1964, LP.

33. George Martin and His Orchestra, *Music from the Film "A Hard Day's Night,"* Parlophone GEP8930 1964, 7-inch EP.

34. Joseph Lanza, *Elevator Music: A Surreal History of Muzak®, Easy-Listening, and Other Moodsong®*, revised/expanded ed. (Ann Arbor: University of Michigan Press, 2004), chapter 13, and 206.

35. Ibid., 196.

36. Kevin Ryan, and Brian Kehew, *Recording the Beatles: The Studio Equipment and Techniques Used to Create Their Classic Albums* (Curvebender, 2006), 395.

37. Robert Hilburn, "Popular Records: Variety Is the Name of the Game," *Los Angeles Times*, 27 July 1969, 43.

38. Leonard Feather, "Mrs. Alpert's Son: The Unpushy Tycoon," *Los Angeles Times*, 2 June 1968, 32.

39. Pete Johnson, "One More Shift for the Animals," *Los Angeles Times*, 13 May 1968, Part IV, 23.

40. Danny Davis, *Danny Davis and the Nashville Strings Play Instrumental Versions of the Herman's Hermits Songbook*, MGM E4309, 1965, LP, and Floyd Cramer, *Floyd Cramer Plays the Monkees*, RCA-Victor LCM-3811, 1967, LP.

41. John Grissem Jr., "California White Man's Shit Kickin' Blues," *Rolling Stone*, 28 June 1969, 22.

42. "KIEV Radio 870," *Los Angeles Times*, 28 July 1967, 6.

43. Bill Williams, "Davis: Music Involved Yet Simple," *Billboard*, 1968, 78.

44. Ibid.

45. Gary Graff, "Like a Rhinestone Cowboy: Glen Campbell Soldiers on through Alzheimer's Disease," *News-Herald* (Southgate, MI), 6 May 2012, http://www.thenewsherald.com/news/like-a-rhinestone-cowboy-glen-campbell-soldiers-on-through-alzheimer/article_7803f56a-b683-55d4-81bc-f9f8a2494780.html (accessed 10 October 2019).

46. See AllMusic.com, "Glen Campbell: Credits," 2019, https://www.allmusic.com/artist/glen-campbell-mn0000664378/credits (accessed 10 October 2019).

47. Grissem, "California White," 19.

48. Kent Hartman, *The Wrecking Crew: The Inside Story of Rock and Roll's Best-Kept Secret* (New York: Thomas Dunne, 2012), 179–81.

49. Ibid., 183–84.

50. Robert Hilburn, "Glen Campbell Gives a Boost to Country Music Success," *Los Angeles Times*, 29 Decemebr 1968, 25.

51. Robert Hilburn, "Las Vegas Review: Campbell in Resort Debut," *Los Angeles Times*, 21 May 1970, Part N, 16.

52. Ryan and Kehew, *Recording*, 401.

53. Gendron, *Between Montmartre*, 180.

54. Ryan and Kehew, *Recording*, 387.

55. Nick Jones, "Soundmania!," *Melody Maker*, 28 May 1966, 3. "Sound" was a significant trope in rock-pop press of the day.

56. Gendron, *Between Montmartre*, 179. See, for example, "Hear That Big Sound," *Life*, 21 May 1965, 83–91, 97–98.

57. Jan Butler, "Clash of Timbres: Recording Authenticity in the California Rock Scene, 1966–1968," in *The Relentless Pursuit of Tone: Timbre in Popular Music*, ed. Robert Fink, Melinda Latour, and Zachary Wallmark (New York: Oxford University Press, 2018).

58. "Rock Groups Lead Search for New Instrument Sounds," *Billboard*, 24 June 1967, 59.

59. Ray Brack, "NAMM: New Musical Sound," *Billboard*, 8 July 1967, 1. Also see Ron Schlachter, "NAMM Show Focuses on the Latest Sounds," *Billboard*, 6 June 1968, 60; National Music Centre, "Baldwin Electric Harpsichord," National Music Centre (Canada), 2002, http://collections.nmc.ca/objects/205/baldwin-electric-harpsichord?ctx=cedc754f-cd3e-4924-980f-7da04725a0e2&idx=8 (accessed 16 October 2019); and "Harpsichord Added to Portable Keyboard Lineup," *Billboard*, 8 July 1967, 16.

60. CBS, "Inside Pop: The Rock Revolution," CBS (dir. David Oppenheim), 1967, https://www.youtube.com/watch?v=afU76JJcquI (accessed 17 January 2020).

61. "Classic Advice by Pop Arranger," *Billboard*, 6 March 1965, 4.

62. "Radio Programming Forum: How Mod Should Your Sound Be?," *Billboard*, 12 July 1969, 37.

63. See "Pop/Rock 'Alternative/Indie Rock' Twee Pop," 2019, https://www.allmusic.com/style/twee-pop-ma0000012201 (accessed 15 November 2019) and Marc Spitz, *Twee: The Gentle Revolution in Music, Books, Television, Fashion, and Film*, ebook ed. (New York: Harper Collins, 2014).

64. Ernie Smith, "The Story of AllMusic, the Internet's Largest, Most Influential Music Database," *Vice*, 2016, https://www.vice.com/en_us/article/53djj8/the-story-of-allmusic-the-internets-largest-most-influential-music-database (accessed 22 October 2019).

65. AllMusic.com, "Chamber Pop," 2019, https://www.allmusic.com/style/chamber-pop-ma0000012300/artists (accessed 21 October 2019).

66. Simon Reynolds, *Retromania* (New York: Faber and Faber, 2011), xxiii and xx.

67. Michael Long, *Beautiful Monsters: Imagining the Classic in Musical Media* (Berkeley: University of California Press, 2008), 129–30.

68. AllMusic.com, "Sunshine Pop," AllMusic.com, 2019, https://www.allmusic .com/style/sunshine-pop-ma0000012028/artists (accessed 22 October 2019).

69. Keightley, "Historical Consciousness of Sunshine Pop," *Journal of Popular Music Studies* 23, no.3 (2011): 343–61.

70. Ibid., 345.

71. Ibid. Keightley identifies a core repertory in Andrew Sandoval, producer, *Come to the Sunshine: Soft Pop Nuggets from the WEA Vaults*, Rhino Handmade 0349778182, 2004, compact disc box set.

72. Keightley, "Historical Consciousness," 346, 347.

73. AllMusic.com, "Baroque Pop," AllMusic.com, 2019, https://www.allmusic .com/style/baroque-pop-ma0000012101 (accessed 22 October 2019).

74. Hartman, *Wrecking Crew*, 126.

75. Matthew Greenwald, *Go Where You Wanna Go: The Oral History of the Mamas and Papas*, ebook ed. (New York: Cooper Square, 2002), loc. 164, 243, and see chapter 1, passim.

76. Bob Stanley, prod., *Tea and Symphony: The English Baroque Sound 1967–1974*, Castle Music (UK) CMQCD1541, 2007, compact disc box set.

77. Bob Stanley, "Baroque and a Soft Place," *Guardian*, 21 September 2007, https://www.theguardian.com/music/2007/sep/21/popandrock1 (accessed 5 November 2019).

78. Gendron, *Between Montmartre*, 174, 343n59.

79. Also see Janell Duxbury, *Rockin' the Classics and Classicizing the Rock* (Westport, CN: Greenwood Press, 1985); and Sara Gulgas, *Looking Forward to the Past: Baroque Rock's Postmodern Nostalgia and the Politics of Memory* (PhD diss. University of Pittsburgh, 2017). I disagree with the framing of baroque pop expressed in Gulgas. One problem lies in her coinage, "baroque bubblegum," to distinguish commercial recombinatorial pop from counterculture rock. Her use of "bubblegum" does not accord with period or rock-historiography uses of the term, nor the demographics of these hits. Moreover, there is no evidence that such pop was a self-conscious "counter-reaction to increasingly complex classical suites" of progressive rock (ibid., 211).

80. Publicity Dept., Smash Records, "The Left Banke: Walking Away with 'Renee,'" news release, 1966; and Philips, advertisement, "The Swingle Singers, Going Baroque: Swinging the Hits of Handel, Vivaldi, J.S. Bach, K. Ph. E. Bach, W. F. Bach," *Cash Box*, 18 July 1964, 27.

81. Publicity Dept., Smash Records, "There's No Let-Up for the Left Banke," news release, 1966.

82. Publicity Dept., Smash Records, "The Left Banke: Walking Away with 'Renee,'" 1, 2.

83. Ibid., 2.

84. Left Banke, *The Left Banke*, Smash Records 67088, 1967, LP.

85. Comments here are taken from the pages of *Go* magazine as held in the Michael Ochs Collection from the Rock and Roll Hall of Fame and Museum. Unfortunately, I did not fully document citations.

86. "Eric [Burden] Knocks 'Pretty' Pop," *Go*, 3 March 1967, 5.

87. "The Left Banke Is Still with Us," *Crawdaddy*, 1968, 50.

88. Sandy Pearlman, "The Left Banke: Walk Away Renee," *Crawdaddy*, 1968, 38 and 39 passim.

89. Tom Nolan, "The Frenzied Frontier of Pop Music," *Los Angeles Times West Magazine*, 27 November 1966, 39.

90. See, for example, BBC Radio 4, "Baroque 'n' Roll: 10 Things You Might Not Know about 'God Only Knows,'" BBC Radio 4 Soul Music, BBC Radio 4, 2018, https://www.bbc.co.uk/programmes/articles/5g8BKqgQj9ymqPfZQy9SblD /baroque-n-roll-10-things-you-might-not-know-about-god-only-knows (accessed 5 November 2019). See relevant accounts of baroque pop influences in Gendron, *Between Montmartre*, 172–73 and Gulgas, *Looking Forward*, 23–26.

91. "Baroque Pop," Wikipedia, 2019, https://en.wikipedia.org/wiki/Baroque _pop (accessed 6 November 2019), citing Benjamin Smith, "The Album May Be Dead, but the Beach Boys' Classic '*Pet Sounds*' Lives On in New Documentary," *Decider*, 2017, https://decider.com/2017/04/07/the-beach-boys-making-pet-sounds -showtime-documentary/ (accessed 6 November 2019). The claim is problematic because of the album's comparatively poor commercial performance, because baroque pop discourse does not emerge around the album or its singles, and because the one single with baroque-pop aesthetics, "God Only Knows," had middling US chart success (topping at number 39, but a top-five hit in England). See David Leaf, liner notes to Beach Boys, *Pet Sounds*, EMI 09463-69940-2-4, 2006, CD boxed set.

92. Leaf, liner notes, 14.

93. Beach Boys, *Pet Sounds*, liner note booklet, n.p.

94. "The Beach Boys: Verdict on *Pet Sounds*," *Melody Maker*, 30 July 1966, https://www.rocksbackpages.com/Library/Article/the-beach-boys-verdict-on-ipet -soundsi (accessed 6 November 2019).

95. Taylor's role in this publicity campaign are noted in Nick Kent, *The Dark Stuff: Selected Writings on Rock Music* (New York: Hachette, 2009), 27; and Mike Love, *Good Vibrations: My Life as a Beach Boy* (New York: Penguin, 2016), 146.

96. Though see the appreciation for Wilson's innovations evidenced in Jim Dele-hant, "Rock History: The Fall of the Vocal Groups," *Crawdaddy*, January 1967, 22.

97. Production details noted in Leaf, liner notes, 20. Separate instrumental and vocal tracks can be heard on Beach Boys, *The Pet Sounds Sessions*, Capitol C2724383766222, 1997, compact disc.

98. "Spotlight Singles: Hugo Montenegro, His Orchestra and Chorus, 'Good Vibrations.'" *Billboard*, 11 January 1969, 58.

99. There is a collection of *Pet Sounds* pirate track stems that has been widely traded on internet torrent sites. (Audio track "stems" typically include multiple isolated tracks submixed together into a single audio file. Stems are derived from a

multitrack master recording. They reduce a large multitrack to a more manageable remix package of a smaller number of submix stems.) The stem set for "God Only Knows" isolates two stereo-spectrum pairs of the vocals and backing accompaniment, respectively. There is some relation between the pirate track-stem set discussed in the example 6.4 caption and the stereo separation of *Pet Sounds* tracks on the 1968 Beach Boys instrumental album, *Stack-o-Tracks*, though certain mix details are further buried in the latter and elements like the clip-clop track are placed in the center on the stem set. See Beach Boys, *Stack-o-Tracks*, Capitol DKAO-2893, 1968, LP. The main difference between the stereo-spectrum vocal tracks (labeled tracks 1 and 2) of the pirate stem set is that the high voice is more foregrounded in the second track. Also, with the instrumental tracks, two electric basses seem to be used. In the first four bars of the excerpt in Example 6.4, for example, one bass is in the background reverb of the right channel, but at the tutti fifth bar, a foregrounded clean bass bursts forth.

100. Philip Lambert, "Brian Wilson's *Pet Sounds*," *Twentieth-Century Music* 5 (2008): 123, 128–29.

101. Leaf, liner notes, 10.

102. "Turtles Reach Turning Point," *Go*, 9 June 1967, 6.

103. Claude Hall, "Long Session Required for 'Serious' Pop," *Billboard*, 2 September 1967, 1.

104. See Gendron, *Between Montmartre*, 210–15; and Butler, "Clash of Timbres," 294.

105. Mike Gross, "Rock for All Reasons Steals Stations Play," *Billboard*, 31 August 1968, 1.

106. Ibid., 1, 4.

107. Fong-Torres, "Bread."

108. Information from David Gates, "Off the Record Interview with David Gates, 1986-10-05," interview by Joe Smith, 10 May 1986, https://hdl.loc.gov/loc .mbrsrs/mbrsjoesmith.1835679 (accessed 20 September 2019), Tim Hallinan, "In the Beginning (1)," 2011, http://www.timothyhallinan.com/blog/?p=4546#more -4546 (accessed 3 October 2019 2019); and "Pleasure Fair, The," Wikipedia.com, 2019, https://en.wikipedia.org/wiki/The_Pleasure_Fair (accessed 3 October 2019). The album (The Pleasure Fair, *The Pleasure Fair*, UNI 73009, 1967, LP) can be heard at "The Pleasure Fair - The Pleasure Fair (1967) (US, Baroque Pop, Sunshine Pop, Soft Rock, Pop Rock)," YouTube.com, https://www.youtube.com/watch?v=IJItVT _Ik0g (accessed 3 October 2019).

109. The single and demo are on Carpenters, *The Essential Collection, 1965– 1997*, A&M/Universal 4934162, 2002, four compact disc box set.

110. See "Interview (Your Navy Presents)," on ibid.

111. Schmidt, *Little Girl*, loc. 842.

112. The demo of the track is on Carpenters, *Essential Collection*.

113. Richard Carpenter, "Off the Record Interview with Richard Carpenter, [1986–1988?]-05-16," 16 May 1986–88, https://www.loc.gov/item/jsmith000204/ (accessed 7 March 2019).

114. "The Carpenters: An Interview," *A&M Compendium*, 1975 in Schmidt, *Yesterday Once*, 126.

115. See, especially, Joan Shelley Rubin, *The Making of Middlebrow Culture* (Chapel Hill: University of North Carolina Press, 1992).

116. This later articulation by Huyssen is cited in Robert Scholes, "Exploring the Great Divide: High and Low, Left and Right," *Narrative* 11 (2003): 245. The idea is centrally explored in Andreas Huyssen, *After the Great Divide: Modernism, Mass Culture, Postmodernism* (Bloomington: Indiana University Press, 1988).

117. Time-Life, "1999—Ad for 'AM Gold' CDs & Cassettes," YouTube, 1999, https://www.youtube.com/watch?v=yn1sy5nR1fM (accessed 17 January 2020).

118. AllMusic characterizes this repertory as "AM Pop." See AllMusic.com, "AM Pop," 2019, https://www.allmusic.com/subgenre/am-pop-ma0000012000 /artists (accessed 15 February 2019).

119. Mitchell Morris, *The Persistence of Sentiment: Display and Feeling in Popular Music of the 1970s* (Berkeley: University of California Press, 2013), 4ff. See the introduction.

120. Ibid.

121. Another relevant but anachronistic term is "adult contemporary," which *Billboard* changed its EL chart to on 7 April 1979. See Christina Baade, "Adult Contemporary," in *Continuum Encyclopedia of Popular Music of the World* (London: Continuum, 2012).

122. Ibid., 10.

123. This quotation and others here derive from Gates, "Off the Record."

124. Richard Carpenter, "Carpenters Fans Ask . . . Richard Answers," richard andkarencarpenter.com, 2004, https://www.richardandkarencarpenter.com/fans _ask_Archive-All.htm (accessed 8 September 2019).

125. Ibid.

126. See Robert Toft, "Hits and Misses: Crafting a Pop Single for the Top-40 Market in the 1960s," in *Pop Music and Easy Listening*, ed. Stan Hawkins (Farnham, UK: Ashgate, 2011), 149, 151; Robert Toft, *Hits and Misses: Crafting Top 40 Singles, 1963–1971* (New York: Continuum, 2011), chap. 7; and Carpenter, "Carpenters Fans."

127. Carpenter, "Carpenters Fans."

128. Ibid.

129. While the Rhythmaires gained fame backing Bing Crosby with far less jazz-indebted harmonies, they did have more adventurous late-1950s jazz-based album work, like the *Sax Gone Latin* album of saxophonist George Auld, where the group sounds akin to Lambert, Hendricks and Ross. Georgie Auld, *Sax Gone Latin*, Capitol T1045, 1958, LP.

130. Carpenter, "Carpenters Fans"; Richard Niles, *The Invisible Artist: Arrangers in Popular Music, 1950–2000*, ebook ed. (Niles Smiles Music, 2014). Niles's chapter is based on a 2002 interview with Carpenter.

131. Bangs, *Psychotic*, 59, 70.

132. Ibid., 71.

133. Ibid., 63, 62.

134. Lester Bangs, "*Bread*, Bread," *Rolling Stone*, 6 September 1969, 29 (accessed 6 October 2019).

135. Lester Bangs, "*Manna*, Bread," *Rolling Stone*, 13 May 1971, 46

136. Claude Hall, "'Stealing' Ties Top 40, MOR Radio in Unhappy Wedlock," *Billboard*, 31 January 1970, 1.

137. Ibid.

138. Ron Tepper, "Electronic Music Jolted," *Billboard*, 31 January 1970, 1.

139. Scott Schmedel, "Record Firms Spin to Sweetest Music They Ever Heard—the Sound of Money," *Billboard*, 23 May 1970, 49.

140. Jon Landau, "Carpenters," *Rolling Stone*, 24 June 1971, 43.

CHAPTER 7. ISAAC HAYES AND HOT BUTTERED (ORCHESTRAL) SOUL

1. Isaac Hayes, *Hot Buttered Soul*, Enterprise ENS-1001, 1969, LP.

2. "Best Selling Jazz LP's," *Billboard*, 12 December 1970, 44.

3. "Diamond Surprises: Warwick, Melanie, Taylor, Hayes Win," *Billboard*, 13 March 1971, 15.

4. Dan Morgenstern, "Isaac Hayes: His Own Story," *Down Beat*, 29 April 1971, cover, 14–15, 31.

5. Isaac Hayes, *Shaft*, Enterprise ENS-2-5002, 1971, LP.

6. African American author Greg Tate has noted Gibbs's pioneering role as a Black music critic. See Elizabeth Jordannah, "An Interview with Author Greg Tate," *New York Amsterdam News*, 18 August 2016, http://amsterdamnews.com/news /2016/aug/18/interview-author-greg-tate/?page=2 (accessed 16 January 2020).

7. Tony Cummings, "The Funk Masters #1: The Ohio Players," *Black Music*, April 1975, https://www.rocksbackpages.com/Library/Article/the-funk-masters-1 -the-ohio-players (accessed 16 January 2020).

8. "R&B Goes 'Progressive' Soul," *Variety*, 29 October 1969, 57.

9. "They Ain't Pretty, but They Sure Got Chops," *Rolling Stone*, 18 October 1969, 15.

10. "R&B Goes 'Progressive.'"

11. See "J J Jacskon [*sic*] Tenement Hall," https://www.youtube.com/watch?v= DOeIWqwmQDg, and "J.J. Jackson—Tobacco Road," https://www.youtube.com /watch?v=azbjcaw80O8 (both accessed 28 August 2018).

12. Isaac Hayes, . . . *To Be Continued*, Enterprise ENS-1014, 1971, LP.

13. John Abbey, "Curtis Mayfield," *Blues and Soul*, 4 February 1972, https:// www.rocksbackpages.com/Library/Article/curtis-mayfield-4?pfv=True (accessed 16 January 2020).

14. Vernon Gibbs, "Isaac Hayes: Madison Square Garden, New York NY," *New Musical Express*, 18 August 1973, https://www.rocksbackpages.com/Library/Article /isaac-hayes-madison-square-garden-new-york-ny (accessed 16 January 2020).

15. BP, "Psychedelic Soul," *Blues and Soul*, 2–14 July 1970, 14.

16. Lenny Kaye and David Dalton, "Four on the Floor: The Motown Sound," *Rock 100*, 1977, https://www.rocksbackpages.com/Library/Article/four-on-the-floor-the-motown-sound (accessed 16 January 2020).

17. Andrew Flory, *I Hear a Symphony: Motown and Crossover R&B* (Ann Arbor: University of Michigan Press, 2017), 94.

18. Dorian Lynskey, "The Temptations: The Band That Took Motown Higher," *The Guardian*, 31 October 2008, https://www.rocksbackpages.com/Library/Article/the-temptations-the-band-that-took-motown-higher (accessed 16 January 2020).

19. Flory, *I Hear*, 95, 96.

20. David Nathan, "Sly & The Family Stone: Lyceum Ballroom, London," *Blues and Soul*, October 1970, https://www.rocksbackpages.com/Library/Article/sly--the-family-stone-lyceum-ballroom-london (accessed 16 January 2020).

21. Flory, *I Hear*, 94.

22. David Nathan, "Eddie Kendricks: Holding On," *Blues and Soul*, February 1973, https://www.rocksbackpages.com/Library/Article/eddie-kendricks-holding-on (accessed 16 January 2020).

23. Rob Bowman, *Soulsville, U.S.A.: The Story of Stax Records* (New York: Schirmer, 1997), 229.

24. Ibid., 230.

25. Hugh Robertson, director, *Soul in Cinema: Filming Shaft on Location* (Byron Production, 1971).

26. Bowman, *Soulsville*, 231.

27. Ibid.

28. WNYC, *American Icons: Shaft*.

29. Bowman, *Soulsville*, 231.

30. Mitchell Morris, *The Persistence of Sentiment: Display and Feeling in Popular Music of the 1970s* (Berkeley: University of California Press, 2013), 49.

31. Ibid., 51, 50.

32. Flory, *I Hear*, 96.

33. Ibid., 96–97.

34. Morris, *Persistence*, 51, 52.

35. B.T. Express, "Do It Til You're Satisfied," Scepter SCE-12395, 1974, 45 rpm; Al Downing, "I'll Be Holding On," Chess CH-2158, 1974, 12-inch single, 33⅓ rpm; and Don Downing, "Dream World," Scepter SCE 12397, 1974, 45 rpm. See Peter Shapiro, *Turn the Beat Around: The Secret History of Disco* (London: Faber and Faber, 2005), 32–45.

36. Vince Aletti, *The Disco Files 1973–78: New York's Underground, Week by Week* (London: DJhistory.com, 2009), 32, 36.

37. Morris, *Persistence*, 52.

38. Flory, *I Hear*, 96.

39. "Cinematic Soul: Apple Music R&B, Apple Music Preview," Apple Music, 2018, https://itunes.apple.com/us/playlist/cinematic-soul/pl.ddad0bbf06b34b21b907900449a9d626 (accessed 7 August 2018).

40. "The Temptations," Wikipedia, 2018, https://en.wikipedia.org/wiki/The_Temptations (accessed 7 August 2018).

41. Bowman, *Soulsville*, 183.

42. Simon Frith, *Performing Rites: On the Value of Popular Music* (Cambridge, MA: Harvard University Press, 1999; repr., 3rd ed.), 122.

43. Ibid., 122, 101, 301n7. Frith references unpublished work by Philip Tagg.

44. Geoffrey O'Brien, "Interrupted Symphony: A Recollection of Movie Music from Max Steiner to Marvin Gaye," in *This Is Pop*, ed. Eric Weisbard (Seattle: Experience Music Project, 2004), 101.

45. Ibid., 102.

46. Michael Long, *Beautiful Monsters: Imagining the Classic in Musical Media* (Berkeley: University of California Press, 2008), 7.

47. Dave Godin, "The Dave Godin Column Investigates Today's Influence on Soul," *Blues and Soul*, 13–26 March 1970.

48. Bowman, *Soulsville*, 218.

49. Roger St. Pierre, "Isaac Hayes and the Platinum Pirates," *Record Collector*, January 1972, https://www.rocksbackpages.com/Library/Article/isaac-hayes-and-the-platinum-pirates (accessed 8 August 2018).

50. A clip from the special can be seen at "Rare Hey, Hey, Hey, It's Fat Albert (1969) footage," Pokemario99, 2017, https://www.youtube.com/watch?v=-kyb7-Hw0BE (accessed 8 August 2018).

51. Bowman, *Soulsville*, 230.

52. Cummings, "Funk Masters." The "eclectic world of white 'progressive rock'" phrasing of this last quotation references broader rock trends, including psychedelia, rather than progressive rock/art rock.

53. Vernon Gibbs, "Kool & The Gang: Street Gang," *Black Music*, February 1974, Kool and the Gang/1974/Vernon Gibbs/Black Music/Kool & The Gang: Street Gang/22/11/2017 11:39:22/http://www.rocksbackpages.com/Library/Article/kool--the-gang-street-gang (accessed 16 January 2020).

54. Ibid.

55. Vernon Gibbs, "If You Don't Believe Sly's Sinking," *New Musical Express*, 8 February 1975, https://www.rocksbackpages.com/Library/Article/if-you-dont-believe-slys-sinking (accessed 16 January 2020).

56. Gibbs, "Kool."

57. See "Soul Train Dancers: Theme from Shaft—Isaac Hayes," YouTube, 2018, https://www.youtube.com/watch?v=l2Sl7FKpMkY (accessed 24 August 2018), and "Temptations—Papa Was a Rollin Stone (1972)," YouTube, 2018, https://www.youtube.com/watch?v=FyBRTZbDi7g (accessed 24 August 2018). Also see "List of Soul Train episodes," Wikipedia, 2018, https://en.wikipedia.org/wiki/List_of_Soul_Train_episodes#Season_1_(1971–72)] (accessed 24 August 2018).

58. Shapiro, *Turn the Beat*, 142.

59. Vince Aletti, "Singles: 'TSOP': MFSB Plays Together," *Rolling Stone*, 25 April 1974, 26.

60. "Billboard's Recommended LPs, Soul: MFSB, the Gamble-Huff Orchestra," *Billboard*, 14 October 1978, 78.

61. Tony Cummings, "The Barry White Story," *Black Music*, July 1975, 6.

62. Isaac Hayes, *Black Moses*, Enterprise EN 52-5003, 1971, LP.

63. John Lombardi, "Barry White: The Billy Jack of Disco," *Rolling Stone*, 28 August 1975, 54.

64. See Joseph Lanza, *Elevator Music: A Surreal History of Muzak®, Easy-Listening, and Other Moodsong®*, revised/expanded ed. (Ann Arbor: University of Michigan Press, 2004).

65. Vince Aletti, "Madness . . . Churns Its Way Down These Mean Recession Streets," *Rolling Stone*, 28 August 1975, 43.

66. Ibid., 50.

67. Ibid.

68. John Jackson, *A House on Fire: The Rise and Fall of Philadelphia Soul* (New York: Oxford University Press, 2004), 153.

69. Ibid.

70. Ibid., 154.

71. Ibid.

72. Cliff White, "Orchestral Soul: So When Was the Last Time You Saw a Black Cello Player?," *New Musical Express*, 13 September 1975, https://www.rocksbackpages.com/Library/Article/orchestral-soul-so-when-was-the-last-time-you-saw-a-black-cello-player (accessed 16 January 2020).

73. Ibid.

74. Phyl Garland, "Isaac Hayes: Hot Buttered Soul," *Ebony*, March 1970, 84.

75. Catherine Parsonage, "The Popularity of Jazz, an Unpopular Problem," *The Source* (2004): 60–80.

76. Daniel Goldmark, "Slightly Left of Center," in *Jazz/Not Jazz.*, ed. David Ake, Charles Hiroshi Garrett, and Daniel Goldmark (Berkeley: University of California Press, 2012), 148–70.

77. See chapter 7 in David Brackett, *Categorizing Sound: Genre and Twentieth-Century Popular Music* (Berkeley: University of California Press, 2016).

78. For a more detailed account, see John Howland, "On *Billboard*, Isaac Hayes, and the 'Swinging Relationship' between Jazz and Its Popular Music Cousins, 1950–1973," in *The Routledge Companion to Jazz Studies*, ed. Nicholas Gebhardt, Nichole Rustin-Paschal, and Tony Whyton (London: Routledge, 2018), 105–16, from which the present chapter partly draws.

79. "Best Selling Jazz LP's," *Billboard*, 13 January 1973, 54.

80. "Best Selling Jazz LP's," *Billboard*, 24 January 1973, 48.

81. Brackett, *Categorizing Sound*, 271 and chapter 7.

82. "Best Selling Jazz LP's," *Billboard*, 18 March 1967, 28.

83. "Les McCann Ltd. Plays the Truth," *Billboard*, 9 May 1960, 41.

84. "Leo Parker," *Billboard*, 13 November 1961, 46.

85. Don Heckman, "Soul Jazz and the Need for Roots," *Down Beat*, March 1962, 5–7.

86. "Booker T. & the MG's," *Billboard*, 21 July 1962, 31.

87. Fabian Holt, *Genre in Popular Music* (Chicago: Chicago University Press, 2007), 86–87.

88. Mike Gross, "Jazz Skipping New Beat as 'Poppouri,'" *Billboard*, 11 May 1968, 1.

89. Leonard Feather, "How to Succeed in Jazz without Really Swinging," *Variety*, 4 January 1967, 170.

90. Dan Morgenstern, "A Message to Our Readers," *Down Beat*, 29 June 1967, 13.

91. Dan Morgenstern, email correspondence, 21 October 2012.

92. Eliot Tiegal, "Jazz Is Soul's 'Cousin' and the Two Have a Swinging Relationship," *Billboard*, 29 January 1972, 34.

93. Eliot Tiegal, "'Extended Energy' Jazz Energizes New Wave of Enthusiasm," *Billboard*, 29 April 1972, 14.

94. Ibid., 13.

95. "Looking for Freshness on a Pop Date? Hire a Jazz Sideman," *Billboard*, 29 April 1972, 24.

96. Aaron Johnson, "The University of Jazz" (unpublished essay), 2006.

97. "Best Selling Rhythm & Blues LP's," *Billboard*, 11 May 1968, 28.

98. "Best Selling Jazz LP's," *Billboard*, 11 May 1968, 44.

99. Burt Bacharach, *Reach Out*, A&M SP4131, 1967, LP.

100. The Soulful Strings, *Groovin' with the Soulful Strings*, Cadet LPS-796, 1967, LP.

101. Frith, *Performing Rites*, 77.

102. Ibid., 78.

103. Morgenstern, private correspondence.

104. "First Annual *Ebony* Black Music Poll," *Ebony*, October 1973, 143.

105. Gibbs, "Isaac Hayes."

106. Geoff Brown, "Hayes vs. White in Battle for the Top," *Jet*, 14 December 1978, 73–75.

107. "First Annual *Ebony* Black Music Poll."

CHAPTER 8. FROM SOPHISTISOUL TO DISCO

1. See Vince Aletti, "Madness . . . Churns Its Way Down These Mean Recession Streets," *Rolling Stone*, 28 August 1975, 43, 50, and John Lombardi, "Barry White: The Billy Jack of Disco," *Rolling Stone*, 28 August 1975, 53–54 (the folio articles run pp. 43–64).

2. Richard Dyer, "In Defence of Disco," *Gay Left*, Summer 1979, 23, http://gayleft1970s.org/issues/issue08.asp (accessed 21 September 2018).

3. Lombardi, "Barry White," 53.

4. Ibid., 54.

5. Ibid.

6. Tony Cummings, "The Barry White Story," *Black Music*, July 1975, 6.

7. Ibid., 7.

8. All of the following three paragraphs of quoted material are from ibid., 6.

9. Ibid., 6–7.

10. Ibid., 7.

11. See Vince Aletti, *The Disco Files 1973–78: New York's Underground, Week by Week* (London: DJhistory.com, 2009).

12. Vernon Gibbs, "War: *War Live* (United Artists UALA193-J2); Earth Wind & Fire: *Open Our Eyes* (Columbia KC 32712)," *Crawdaddy!*, July 1974, https://www.rocksbackpages.com/Library/Article/war-iwar-livei-united-artists-uala193-j2-earth-wind--fire-iopen-our-eyesi-columbia-kc-32712 (accessed 16 January 2020).

13. Joe Nick Patoski, "Barry White: Limitless Love, The Maestro's Message," *Zoo World*, 2 January 1975, http://www.rocksbackpages.com/Library/Article/barry-white-limitless-love- -the-maestros-message (accessed 17 January 2020).

14. Lombardi, "Barry White," 54.

15. Patoski, "Barry White."

16. Bob Fisher, "Barry White—Can't Get Enough," *New Musical Express*, 16 November 1974, https://www.rocksbackpages.com/Library/Article/barry-white---cant-get-enough-?pfv=True (accessed 17 January 2020).

17. Harvey Kubernik, "Too Much Love!," *Melody Maker*, 12 April 1975, 17.

18. Bob and Earl, "Harlem Shuffle," Mar Records 104, 1963, 45 rpm.

19. Barry White and Marc Eliot, *Barry White: Love Unlimited, Insights on Life and Love* (New York: Broadway Books, 1999), 60.

20. Derived from Pierre Perrone, "Obituary: Gene Page," *Independent* (UK), 21 September 1998, https://www.independent.co.uk/arts-entertainment/obituary-gene-page-1199645.html#r3z-addoor (accessed 18 September 2018).

21. Dean Martin, *Songs from "The Silencers,"* Reprise R-6211, LP, 1965.

22. Perrone, "Obituary: Gene Page."

23. Geoff Brown, "It's the Same Old Story," *Melody Maker*, 12 April 1975, 16.

24. Ibid.

25. Lombardi, "Barry White," 54.

26. Bob Lucas, "Big Barry White Mixes His Music for Lovers Only," *Jet*, 22 December 1977, 30–33, 46.

27. Ibid., 30.

28. Ibid., 33–34.

29. Richard Robinson, "Barry White: Nobody in the World Sounds Like Me," *Hit Parader*, August 1974, 44–45.

30. Many thanks to Harry Weinger, vice president, A&R, Universal Music Group, for generously allowing me archival research time with the White multitracks in 2015.

31. Robinson, "Barry White," 45.

32. Ibid.

33. Ibid.

34. Loopmasters, "Disco House Strings," 2018, https://www.loopmasters.com/product/details/21/Disco_House_Sessions (accessed 9 February 2018).

35. See Pete Whitfield's website for his work credits and biography, https://realstrings.wordpress.com/credits/ (accessed 9 February 2018).

36. The Organic Loops, "Disco Strings," 2010, https://www.loopmasters.com/products/485-Disco-Strings (accessed 9 February 2018).

37. Pete Whitfield, "Disco Strings," 2010, https://www.youtube.com/watch?v=Bzmgl8wifDI (accessed 9 February 2018).

38. Mitchell Morris, *The Persistence of Sentiment: Display and Feeling in Popular Music of the 1970s* (Berkeley: University of California Press, 2013), 38.

39. Peter Shapiro, *Turn the Beat Around: The Secret History of Disco* (London: Faber and Faber, 2005), 142.

40. See chapter 2, Morris, *Persistence*.

41. Shapiro, *Turn the Beat*, 67.

42. Michael Long, *Beautiful Monsters: Imagining the Classic in Musical Media* (Berkeley: University of California Press, 2008), 64.

43. Patoski, "Barry White."

44. Ibid.

45. Dwight Macdonald, "Masscult and Midcult, Part 1," *Partisan Review*, 27, Spring 1960, 212.

46. Patoski, "Barry White."

47. See Barry White's IMDB.com media credits at https://www.imdb.com/name/nm0924489/?ref_=fn_al_nm_1 (accessed 14 September 2018).

48. Geoff Brown, "Hayes vs. White in Battle for the Top," *Jet*, 14 December 1978, 74.

49. Fisher, "Barry White."

50. Lombardi, "Barry White," 54.

51. Ibid.

52. Cummings, "Barry White," 9.

53. Ibid., 8.

54. Robert Christgau, "Barry White: Consumer Guide Reviews," 2017, http://www.robertchristgau.com/get_album.php?id=8111 (accessed 24 November 2017).

55. Said in relation to White's 1975 single "I'll Do for You Anything You Want Me To." "Singles: Sophistisoul," *Black Soul*, July 1975, n.p.

56. Cummings, "Barry White."

57. See, for instance, Patoski, "Barry White."

58. Peter Brown, "Dance with Me," T. K. Records STKR 6027, 1977, 45 rpm. I have not been able to view the liner notes to confirm a connection to the New York Philharmonic.

59. Cummings, "Barry White," 10.

60. William Earl Berry, "A Visit with Isaac Hayes and His Bride," *Jet*, 28 June 1973, passim.

61. "Barry White Raps about His New Wife, New Life," *Jet*, 22 August 1974, passim.

62. Morris, *Persistence*, chapter 2.

63. "Barry White Dates," *Melody Maker*, 12 April 1975.

64. See "The Midnight Special 1974 Barry White Live," *The Midnight Special*, 1974, https://www.youtube.com/watch?v=FpJ38yclVWc (accessed 9 June 2020). Numerous clips from this broadcast can be found on YouTube.

65. Lombardi, "Barry White," 54.

66. "Barry White Talks about Music, Sex, Love, Marriage, Hobbies," *Jet*, 21 June 1979, 54.

67. Lombardi, "Barry White," 54.

68. Cummings, "Barry White," 8.

69. Patoski, "Barry White."

70. Ibid.

71. Paul Vitello, "Tom Laughlin, 82, Star of '*Billy Jack*' Movie Series, Dies," *New York Times*, 17 December 2013, http://www.nytimes.com/2013/12/17/movies/tom -laughlin-82-star-of-billy-jack-movie-series-dies.html (accessed 17 January 2020).

72. "*Jet* Publisher Says Blacks 'Must Abandon Politics of Poverty, Philosophy of Despair,'" *Jet*, March 1973, 16.

73. Miles Johnson, "Beyoncé and the End of Respectability Politics," *New York Times*, 16 April 2018, https://www.nytimes.com/2018/04/16/opinion/beyonce -coachella-blackness.html (accessed 18 November 2019).

74. Isabel Wilkerson, *The Warmth of Other Suns: The Epic Story of America's Great Migration* (New York: Random House, 2010), passim. See Dr. Robert Foster's commentary.

75. On the relation of the new postwar Black middleclass to the pursuit of the American Dream, see Burt Landry, *The New Black Middleclass* (Berkeley: University of California Press, 1987). On the Black middleclass, disco, and the politics of crossover, see Shapiro, *Turn the Beat*, 150–7.

76. Lucas, "Big Barry," 32.

77. G.B., "Barry White: Byronic Man," *Melody Maker*, 1 January 1977, 15.

AFTERWORD

1. Peter Shapiro, *Turn the Beat Around: The Secret History of Disco* (London: Faber and Faber, 2005), 235.

2. Ibid., 236.

3. Ibid.

4. Jesse Kornbluth, "Merchandising Disco for the Masses: DI$CO," *New York Times Magazine*, 18 February 1979, 18. Also see Shapiro, *Turn the Beat*; and Alice Echols, *Hot Stuff: Disco and the Remaking of American Culture* (New York: W. W. Norton, 2010).

5. Shapiro, *Turn the Beat*, 247.

6. Ibid., 237.

7. See Carl Wilson's discussion of this juxtaposition in chapter 1 of his *Let's Talk about Love: A Journey to the End of Taste* (New York: Continuum, 2007).

8. See *MTV Unplugged*, first ed., ed. Sarah Malarkey (New York: MTV, 1995), 173ff.

9. Jay-Z, *MTV Unplugged: Jay-Z*, Roc-A-Fella 586617, 2001, compact disc.

10. See R. J. Wheaton, *Dummy* (London: Continuum, 2011), 207. Isaac Hayes, *Black Moses*, Enterprise EN 52-5003, 1971, LP.

11. Wheaton, *Dummy*, 85.

12. Ibid., 84.

13. Simon Reynolds, "Retro Active," *Spin*, April 2012, http://reynoldsretro.blogspot.se/2013/06/normal-0-false-false-false-en-us-x-none.html (accessed 18 December 2014).

14. The "nobrow" characterization appears in a number of reviews of these bands in the early 2010s. This term is discussed at greater length later in this afterword. "Indie classical" is a common epithet for a range of post-2000 new music (classical) scenes that operate under similar D.I.Y. aesthetics to indie rock. It is a phrase commonly tied to Nico Muhly's multinational creative circles.

15. Shapiro, *Turn the Beat*, 211, and Anthony Haden-Guest, *The Last Party: Studio 54, Disco, and the Culture of the Night* (New York: William Morrow, 1997), 50.

16. All quotes from Juliet Schor, "Foreword," in Lauren Greenfield and Juliet Schor, *Generation Wealth* (London: Phaidon, 2017), 7.

17. Paul Fussell, *Class: A Painfully Accurate Guide through the American Status System* (New York: Ballatine, 1983), 16.

18. Ibid., 19.

19. Schor, "Foreword," 7.

20. John Seabrook, *Nobrow: The Culture of Marketing/The Marketing of Culture* (New York: Knopf, 2000), 28, 213.

21. Peter Swirski, *From Nobrow to Lowbrow* (Montreal: McGill-Queen's University, 2005).

22. "Highbrow, Lowbrow, or Nobrow?," podcast, *Talk of the Nation*, radio broadcast, https://www.npr.org/templates/story/story.php?storyId=1067846&t=1574419234238 (accessed 22 November 1999).

23. Ibid. Also see Lawrence Levine, *Highbrow/Lowbrow: The Emergence of Cultural Hierarchy* (Cambridge, MA: Harvard University Press, 1988).

24. "Highbrow, Lowbrow, or Nobrow?," podcast.

25. Jonathan Kramer, "Postmodern Concepts of Musical Time," *Indiana Theory Review* 17 (fall 1996): 21–22.

26. "Interview with Sufjan Stevens," *MTV News*, http://www.youtube.com/watch?v=0Hxhc_77neQ (accessed 16 January 2020).

27. See chapter 5 in David Blake, *"Bildung" Culture: Elite Popular Music and the American University, 1960–2010* (Stonybrook University, PhD diss., 2014).

28. Richard Peterson, and Roger Kern, "Changing Highbrow Taste: From Snob to Omnivore," *American Sociological Review* 61 (1996): 900–907. Also see Richard Peterson, and Albert Simkus, "How Musical Tastes Mark Occupational Status Groups," in *Cultivating Differences: Symbolic Boundaries and the Making of Inequality*, ed. Michele Lamont and Marcel Fournier (Chicago: University of Chicago Press, 1992).

INDEX

93–94; "sepia Sinatra" tradition, 22, 38, 119, 278, 305, 316; Stan Applebaum and, 26. *See also* Rat Pack, Reprise Records

Smith, Elliott, 210, 323

Snyder, Robert, 68

soft rock, 8, 187–236 (chapter 6), 319; contributory streams of, 189, 193–94, 193–94*fig.*

Songs for Swingin' Lovers, 94, 130–32, 132*ex.*

Songs for Young Lovers, 130, 132

"Song of the Dawn," 80. See also *King of Jazz*

sophistisoul, 240, 265–67, 285–91, 298. *See also* White, Barry

Soulful Strings, 275, 276, 300

Soul Symphony, 16, 267

Soul Train, 255, 264–65

Soxx, Bob B., and the Blue Jeans. *See* "Zip-A-Dee-Doo-Dah"

"Spanish Harlem," 25, 160, 283

Spanky and Our Gang, 196, 223, 225

Spector, Phil, 148–86 (chapter 5), 218, 286; fashion, lifestyle, and, 156–57, 180, 183–84; in relation to Motown, 24, 159, 200; on *Open End*, 157–58; pre-Wall of Sound career and life, 25, 153; Thomas Wolfe on, 149–50, 156–59. *See also* "Be My Baby"; Crystals; Gold Star Studios; Ronettes; teenage symphonies; "Then He Kissed Me"; Wall of Sound; "Zip-A-Dee-Doo-Dah"

Spector, Ronnie, 170, 171, 173–77, 184, 352n72. *See also* "Be My Baby"

Spectrum, 191, 224

statusphere, 149–50, 156, 159, 183

Stax Records, 35, 241, 246–47, 257, 259, 265, 274. *See also* Bell, Al; Hayes, Isaac; *Shaft*

St. Clair, Kristian, 164, 351n45

Stevens, Sufjan, 210, 326, 330

Stills, Stephen, 191, 193*fig.* See also Crosby, Stills, Nash (and Young)

stock arrangements, 62–64

Stoller, Mike, 24–26, 28–29, 148–49, 159–60, 169, 171, 286

Stone Poneys, 221

Stone, Sly, 243, 244, 245, 252, 255, 259, 260, 264, 287

Stordahl, Axel, 94, 96–98, 98*ex.*, 131, 135, 136

Strange, Billy, 168, 169, 192*fig.*

"Strawberry Fields Forever," 321

Street Scene, 81, 248

Summer, Donna, 294, 321

sunshine pop, 8, 188–89, 193*fig.*, 196, 210–13

Super Fly, 242

surf pop idioms, 151–52, 162–67, 179, 201, 204

Sweet Baby James, 194, 227

Swing Easy!, 128, 130, 132, 142, 142*fig.*

symphonic jazz, 5–6, 22–23, 46–83, 85, 87, 89, 328. *See also* Grofé, Ferde; Lange, Arthur; Whiteman, Paul

symphonic soul, 12, 29, 33, 159, 237–80 (chapter 7), 281–318 (chapter 8); Jay-Z and, 13, 16, 18, 37–38. *See also* "Can I Live"; disco; Hayes, Isaac; Philadelphia soul; sophistisoul; White, Barry

symphonic swing, 7, 91–96

Szwed, John, 85, 86

Tagg, Philip, 13, 39–40, 257, 284

Taylor, Diana, 42–43, 49–50

Taylor, James, 190–97, 193*fig.*, 221, 234

teenage symphonies, 152–54, 162, 174, 176, 181–83, 186. *See also* Spector, Phil; Wall of Sound

Temptations, 29, 240–46, 252–56, 254*ex.*, 259, 265

Tender Trap, The, 142, 144

"Thank You (Falettinme Be Mice Elf Agin)," 249, 253

"Theme from *Shaft*" (track), 242, 245–53, 250*ex.*, 251*ex.*, 256, 257–59

"Then He Kissed Me," 151, 153, 162–63, 168, 172–73, 350nn26, 39

"There Goes My Baby," 24–26, 286

"This Guy's in Love with You," 201–3, 203*ex.*

Tijuana Brass, 51, 163, 202, 204, 274–77

To Be Continued . . ., 35, 237, 242

topics (musical style, tone, timbre), 2–3,
12–13, 21, 39–42, 185, 255, 284; characteristic scoring effects, 49, 55, 65–66;
cinematic, 251, 257; citational topics,
272; classical topics (a.k.a. classical
register), 29–30, 39–43, 215, 220;
Indian scoring topics, 69–70; jazz-luxe,
232, 237; recombinant style topics, 12,
21, 42, 217, 223–24, 234, 284–85, 330;
style modes, 76–77; topic theory,
334n5, 335n29, 339n4
Troubadour, 191, 193, 193*fig.*, 221
"TSOP (The Sound of Philadelphia),"
265–70, 268–69*ex.*, 311
Turtles, 193*fig.*, 209, 211, 220, 225

"Unforgettable," 124–25, 125*ex.*
Unplugged television series, 324
Untouchables, The, 145–46, 145*ex.*
"Uptown," 159–60, 176

Vallee, Rudy, 87, 118, 134–35, 136
vaudeville aesthetic, 48, 52–54, 56
vinyl vixen album covers, 111–12, 138,
334n43

Wagner, Richard, 152–53, 154, 163,
165–67, 176, 182–83
Wald, Elijah, 47
"Walk Away Renee," 210, 214, 215
Walker, Scott, and Walker Brothers, 35,
216, 223
Wall of Sound: aesthetics and production
25, 148, 151, 159–73; reception, 154,
178, 184–86. *See also* Spector, Phil;
teenage symphonies
Webb, Jimmy, 192*ex.*, 205, 206
Weisbard, Eric, 195
West, Kanye, 14–16, 23*fig.*, 39, 42–43
Weston, Paul, 98–99, 111, 112, 127, 128,
136–38
"We've Only Just Begun," 190, 197
What's Going On? (album and song), 33,
243, 256, 296
"Whispering," 59, 62, 340n45
White, Barry, 281–318 (chapter 8); Black
respectability and excellence politics

and, 315–18; disco and, 267, 281, 285,
289–91, 296–302, 309; formula and,
240, 256, 266–67, 279, 286, 288,
291–302, 309; image and, 283–84,
310–15; Isaac Hayes and, 22, 240,
265–66, 270, 279–80, 284–300, 304,
309–15; Love Unlimited (trio) and,
282, 310–11, 313; Love Unlimited
Orchestra and, 264, 266, 282–83,
289–92, 304, 306–7, 312–14; Muzak/
easy listening accusations and, 41, 266,
279, 285–89, 298, 305; Philadelphia
soul and, 264–65, 285, 293, 298, 317;
production practice and, 292–309;
sophistisoul and, 240, 264–67, 284–
88, 304–5. *See also* "Love's Theme";
"You're the First, My Last, My
Everything"
Whiteman, Paul, 22, 23*fig.*, 46–83 (chapter
2), 87, 88*tab.*, 90–91; jazz historiography and, 47, 56–58, 66, 74–75, 103;
Whitemanesque entertainment aesthetics of, 47–48, 50, 53–57, 59, 61–63, 76,
80, 82, 102. *See also* "By the Waters of
the Minnetonka"; Experiment in Modern Music concert(s); *King of Jazz*;
symphonic jazz; vaudeville aesthetic
"Whiter Shade of Pale," 211
Whitesell, Lloyd, 76–77, 121
Whitfield, Norman, 31–35, 32*ex.*, 34*ex.*,
38, 244–45, 255–56
Whitfield, Pete, 297–302
Wilson, Brian, 152, 193*fig.*, 211, 216–20,
219*ex.*, 223. *See also* Beach Boys; "God
Only Knows"; *Pet Sounds*
Wired Strings (a.k.a. Hustler's Symphony
Orchestra), 6, 13–14, 16, 19, 22,
23*fig.*, 34
Wolfe, Thomas, 149–50, 156–59, 180. *See
also* statusphere
Wrecking Crew, 148–236 (chapters 5 and
6), 192*fig. See also associated artists,
musicians, and producers*
Wriggle, John, 81

"Yesterday," 200, 206, 223
Young, Neil, 193*fig.*, 221, 222

Founded in 1893,
UNIVERSITY OF CALIFORNIA PRESS
publishes bold, progressive books and journals
on topics in the arts, humanities, social sciences,
and natural sciences—with a focus on social
justice issues—that inspire thought and action
among readers worldwide.

The UC PRESS FOUNDATION
raises funds to uphold the press's vital role
as an independent, nonprofit publisher, and
receives philanthropic support from a wide
range of individuals and institutions—and from
committed readers like you. To learn more, visit
ucpress.edu/supportus.